CASS SERIES ON SOVIET (RUSSIAN) MILITARY EXPERIENCE

SOVIET OPERATIONAL AND TACTICAL COMBAT IN MANCHURIA, 1945

CASS SERIES ON SOVIET (RUSSIAN) MILITARY EXPERIENCE
Series Editor: David M. Glantz
ISSN: 1462-0944

This series focuses on Soviet military experiences in specific campaigns or operations.

1. David M. Glantz, *From the Don to the Dnepr, Soviet Offensive Operations, December 1942 to August 1943* (ISBN 0 7146 3401 8 cloth, 0 7146 4064 6 paper)
2. David M. Glantz, *The Initial Period of War on the Eastern Front: 22 June–August 1941* (ISBN 0 7146 3375 5 cloth, 0 7146 4298 3 paper)
3. Carl van Dyke, *The Soviet Invasion of Finland, 1939–40* (ISBN 0 7146 4653 5 cloth, 0 7146 4314 9 paper)
4. Leonid Grenkevich, *The Soviet Partisan Movement 1941–1944*, edited and with a Foreword by David M. Glantz (ISBN 0 7146 4874 4 cloth, 0 7146 4428 5 paper)
5. Tony Le Tissier, *Race for the Reichstag: The 1945 Battle for Berlin* (ISBN 0 7146 4929 5 cloth, 0 7146 4489 7 paper)
6. Robert Seely, *Russo-Chechen Conflict, 1800–2000: A Deadly Embrace* (ISBN 0 7146 4992 6 cloth, 0 7146 8060 5 paper)

CASS SERIES ON THE SOVIET (RUSSIAN) STUDY OF WAR
Series Editor: David M. Glantz
ISSN: 1462-0960

This series examines what Soviet military theorists and commanders learned from the study of their own military operations.

1. Harold S. Orenstein, translator and editor, *Soviet Documents on the Use of War Experience*, Volume I, *The Initial Period of War 1941*, with an Introduction by David M. Glantz (ISBN 0 7146 3392 5 cloth)
2. Harold S. Orenstein, translator and editor, *Soviet Documents on the Use of War Experience*, Volume II, *The Winter Campaign 1941–1942*, with an Introduction by David M. Glantz (ISBN 0 7146 3393 3 cloth)
3. Joseph G. Welsh, translator, *Red Armor Combat Orders: Combat Regulations for Tank and Mechanized Forces 1944*, edited and with an Introduction by Richard N. Armstrong (ISBN 0 7146 3401 8 cloth)
4. Harold S. Orenstein, translator and editor, *Soviet Documents on the Use of War Experience*, Volume III, *Military Operations 1941 and 1942*, with an Introduction by David M. Glantz (ISBN 0 7146 3402 6 cloth)
5. William A. Burhans, translator, *The Nature of the Operations of Modern Armies* by V.K. Triandafillov, edited by Jacob W. Kipp, with an Introduction by James J. Schneider (ISBN 0 7146 4501 X cloth, 0 7146 4118 9 paper)
6. Harold S. Orenstein, translator, *The Evolution of Soviet Operational Art, 1927–1991: The Documentary Basis*, Volume I, *Operational Art, 1927–1964*, with an Introduction by David M. Glantz (ISBN 0 7146 4547 8 cloth, 0 7146 4228 2 paper)
7. Harold S. Orenstein, translator, *The Evolution of Soviet Operational Art, 1927–1991: The Documentary Basis*, Volume II, *Operational Art, 1965–1991*, with an Introduction by David M. Glantz (ISBN 0 7146 4548 6 cloth, 0 7146 4229 0 paper)
8. Richard N. Armstrong and Joseph G. Welsh, *Winter Warfare: Red Army Orders and Experiences* (ISBN 0 7146 4699 7 cloth, 0 7146 4237 1 paper)
9. Lester W. Grau, *The Bear Went Over the Mountain: Soviet Combat Tactics in Afghanistan* (ISBN 0 7146 4874 4 cloth, 0 7146 4413 7 paper)
10. David M. Glantz and Harold S. Orenstein, editor and translator, *The Battle for Kursk 1943: The Soviet General Staff Study* (ISBN 0 7146 4933 3 cloth, 0 7146 4493 5 paper)
11. Niklas Zetterling and Anders Frankson, *Kursk 1943: A Statistical Analysis* (ISBN 0 7146 5052 8 cloth, 0 7146 8103 2 paper)
12. David M. Glantz and Harold S. Orenstein, editor and translator, *Belorussia 1944: The Soviet General Staff Study* (ISBN 0 7146 5102 8 cloth)
13. David M. Glantz and Harold S. Orenstein, editor and translator, *The Battle for L'vov, July 1944: The Soviet General Staff Study* (ISBN 0 7146 5201 6 cloth)
14. Alexander O. Chubaryan and Harold Shukman, editors, *Stalin and the Soviet–Finnish War, 1939–40* (ISBN 0 7146 5203 2 cloth)

SOVIET OPERATIONAL AND TACTICAL COMBAT IN MANCHURIA, 1945:

'AUGUST STORM'

DAVID M. GLANTZ

FRANK CASS
LONDON • PORTLAND, OR

First published in 2003 in Great Britain by
FRANK CASS PUBLISHERS
Crown House, 47 Chase Side, Southgate
London N14 5BP

and in the United States of America by
FRANK CASS PUBLISHERS
c/o ISBS, 5824 N.E. Hassalo Street
Portland, Oregon, 97213-3644

Website: www.frankcass.com

British Library Cataloguing in Publication Data

Glantz, David M.
Soviet operational and tactical combat in Manchuria, 1945:
'August Storm'. – (Cass series on Soviet (Russian) military experience)
1. Union of Soviet Socialist Republics. Armiia – Drills and
tactics 2. World War, 1939–1945 – Campaigns – China –
Manchuria 3. World War, 1939–1945 – Russia (Federation)
I. Title
940.5'425

ISBN 0-7146-5300-4 (cloth)
ISSN 1462-0944

Library of Congress Cataloging-in-Publication Data

Glantz, David M.
Soviet operational and tactical combat in Manchuria, 1945: August storm / David
M. Glantz.
p. cm. – (Cass series on Soviet (Russian) military experience; 8)
Includes bibliographical references and index.
ISBN 0-7146-5300-4 (cloth)
1. World War, 1939–1945 – Campaigns – China – Manchuria. 2. World War,
1939–1945 – Soviet Union. 3. Manchuria (China) – History – 1931–1945. 4. Soviet
Union – History, Military. I. Title: August storm. II. Title. III. Series.

D767.3.G57 2003
940.54'25–dc21

2002074079

Typeset in 10.5/12 Ehrhardt MT by Cambridge Photosetting Services
Printed in Great Britain by MPG Books Ltd, Victoria Square, Bodmin, Cornwall

Contents

APPENDICES:

Illustrations

22. Captured Japanese heavy artillery piece at Hutou.
23. Marshal Meretskov examines a Japanese strong point at Hutou.

39th Army
24. Lieutenant General N. N. Oleshev, Commander, 113th Guards Rifle Corps (39th Army).
25. 39th Army troops move forward into jumping-off positions.
26. 39th Army forces cross the Manchurian border.
27. 39th Army tanks crossing the Grand Khingan Mountains.
28. Troops attacking the Halung–Arshaan Fortified Region.
29. 39th Army troops entering Wangyemiao.

36th Army
30. 36th Army artillery shelling Hailar.

15th Army
31. Rear Admiral N. V. Antonov, Commander, Amur River Flotilla.
32. Japanese strong point at Fuchin.
33. American-made amphibious vehicles with the 15th Army.

Southern Sakhalin and Kuril Islands
34. Vice Admiral V. A. Andreev, Commander, Northern Pacific Flotilla.
35. Major General A. R. Gnechko, Commander, Kamchatka Defensive Region.
36. Captain 1st Rank D. G. Ponomarev, Commander, Petropavlovsk Naval Base.
37. Naval infantry loading for the landing at Odomari.
38. Japanese civilians returning to Odomari.
39. The amphibious assault on Shumshir Island (artist's rendition).

Maps

Figures and Tables

FIGURES

TABLES

Abbreviations

SOVIET FORCES

A	army
AEB	assault engineer-sapper brigade
BGBn	border guards battalion
Cav–Mech GP	cavalry-mechanized group
CD	cavalry division
FD	forward detachment
FFR	field fortified region
FR	fortified region
Gds	guards
GKO	*Gosudarstvennoi komitet oborony* (State Defense Committee)
GRU	*Glavnoe razvedyvatel'noe upravlenie* (Main Intelligence Directorate)
HSPR	heavy self-propelled artillery regiment
MB	mechanized brigade
MC	mechanized corps
MNRA	Mongolian People's Red Army
MnRR	mountain rifle regiment
MRD	motorized rifle division
NKO	*Narodnyi komissariat oborony* (People's Commissariat of Defense)
NKPS	*Narodnyi komissariat put'soobshchenii* (People's Commissariat of Communication Routes)
NKVD	*Nordnyi Komissariat Vnutrennykh Del* (People's Commissariat of Internal Affairs)
PGB	*Primorskaia gruppa voisk* (Coastal Group of Forces)
RBA	Red Banner Army
RBn	rifle battalion
RC	rifle corps
RD	rifle division

RAG   regimental artillery group
TA   tank army
TB   tank brigade
TC   tank corps
TD   tank division
TO&Es   tables of organization and equipment or establishments
TVD   *teatr voennykh deistvii* (theaters of military operations)
UR   *ukreplennyi raion* (fortified regions)

JAPANESE FORCES

BGU   border guards unit
IB   independent mixed brigade
ID   infantry division
IR   infantry regiment
IBn   infantry battalion

Symbols

SOVIET

⌐▬▬▬▬⌐   Front boundary

⌐▬▬▬▬⌐   Army boundary

⌐- - - - - -⌐   Corps boundary

⌐▬▬▬⌐   Division/brigade boundary

⬭   Infantry unit assembly area

⬭ ⬭   Tank/mechanized unit assembly area

⬭   Cavalry unit assembly area

⌣↓⌣   Infantry unit deployed or moving

⌣◇◇⌣   Tank/mechanized unit deployed or moving

⌣↧⌣   Cavalry unit deployed or moving

⌣◈◈⌣   Self-propelled artillery unit deployed or moving

◇▬▬◇   Tanks in firing positions

◈▬▬◈   Self-propelled guns in firing position

JAPANESE

	Field fortifications, defensive positions
	Fortified region, permanent
	Section position
	Squad position
	Platoon position
	Company position
	Battalion position
	Regiment position
	Brigade position
	Division position
— xx —	Division boundary
— xxxx —	Army boundary
— xxxxx —	Area army boundary
— xxxxxx —	Kwantung Army boundary

Introduction

The Soviet Far East Command's strategic offensive of August 1945 against the Kwantung Army shattered Japanese defenses around the periphery of Manchuria in seven days and achieved total victory in less than two weeks, ending Japanese domination of northeastern Asia (see Map 1). The command commenced its strategic envelopment operation, a self-styled 'Cannae', by attacking shortly after midnight on 9 August 1945 with three separate *fronts* with a total of ten armies, one cavalry-mechanized group, and more than one million men.

Advancing in the dark along multiple converging axes on a broad front, often across seemingly impassable terrain and in drenching August rains, the advancing Soviet forces exerted unbearable pressure on the surprised Japanese defenders. By tailoring their forces to advance rapidly in all types of terrain and by leading the advance wherever possible with armored forward detachments, the Soviets generated requisite speed and offensive momentum to overwhelm Japanese defenses and preempt Japanese defenses in the depths of Manchuria.

The surprise Soviet offensive achieved immediate spectacular success. The three attacking *fronts* penetrated western, eastern, and northern Manchuria, overcame or bypassed the formidable Japanese defenses and covering forces along the border, paralyzed Japanese command and control, and entered central Manchuria with astonishing ease, while the Kwantung Army struggled in vain to survive. The massive scale of the Soviet attack was matched by the audaciousness, skill, and relentlessness with which it was conducted.

The three combined-arms armies, one tank army, and single cavalry-mechanized group of Marshal of the Soviet Union R. Ia. Malinovsky's Trans-Baikal Front swept into Manchuria from the desert wastes of Mongolia, bypassed Japanese border defenses, thrust across the undefended, yet formidable, terrain of the Grand Khingan Mountains, and erupted deep in the Japanese rear. Five days later, Malinovsky's forces threatened the major population centers in Manchuria and rendered the Japanese High Command incapable of effective resistance.

Simultaneously, four combined-arms armies of Marshal of the Soviet Union K. A. Meretskov's 1st Far Eastern Front smashed Japanese defenses

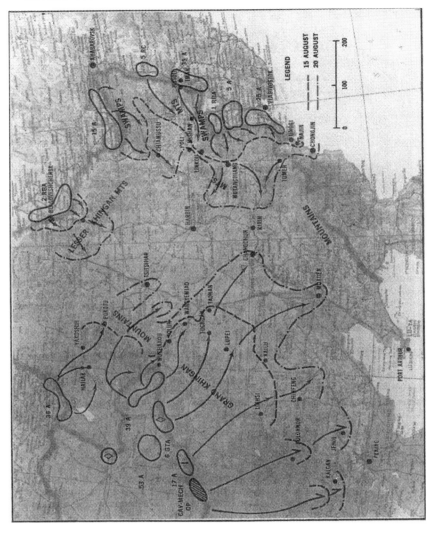

Map 1. The Manchurian Campaign

2

in eastern Manchuria and, by 16 August, had captured the key cities of Mutanchiang and Wangching, collapsing Japanese defenses anchored on the formidable terrain in that region. Supplementing the violent slashing Soviet attacks from east and west, two combined-arms armies of Army General M. A. Purkaev's 2d Far Eastern Front struck and overcame Japanese defenses in northern Manchuria, completing the ring of fire around the beleaguered Kwantung Army.

Before the campaign was over, Soviet forces had expanded their ambitious offensive beyond the confines of Manchuria to encompass vital Japanese-occupied territory in Korea, the Japanese Empire's important island outposts to the north, and, almost, the Japanese Home Islands themselves. Soviet forces advanced through northern Korea to the famed 38th Parallel, conquered the southern half of Sakhalin Island and the entire Kurile Island chain, and postured menacingly against the northernmost Japanese Home Island of Hokkaido. By 1 September 1945, the Soviet Union had emerged as a significant power in northeast Asia and the Pacific basin.

Throughout the Manchurian offensive, each of the 11 Soviet armies that made up the Far East Command's three operating *fronts* advanced along its own distinct axis, often through terrain the Japanese considered unsuitable for the conduct of large-scale military operations. Coupled with the Soviet Army's ability to achieve strategic surprise and employ imaginative operational and tactical techniques, the failure of the Japanese to defend this impassable terrain conditioned the rapid and utter defeat of the Kwantung Army. Although the Japanese did not formally surrender until 20 August, by 16 August Soviet forces had secured all the objectives necessary for complete victory.

The case studies that make up this book examine in detail the tactical combat that occurred in ten specific sectors during the Manchurian offensive. I have selected these cases because, collectively, they vividly depict the diverse sorts of military operations the terrain of Manchuria required the Soviet Army to conduct (see Map 2).

The initial case study describes the penetration operation the 1st Far Eastern Front's 5th Army conducted against Japanese fortified defenses in the heavily wooded and hilly highlands in eastern Manchuria. It details the intricate and painstaking planning required to penetrate the extensive Japanese defenses, emphasizing in particular the operational and tactical techniques the 5th Army employed to overcome, bypass, and isolate Japanese fortified defensive positions and impart momentum to its subsequent offensive. By doing so, it offers an excellent example of maneuver at the lowest tactical level, across impassable terrain, and against strong fortifications.

The case study that details the advance to Pamientung by the 1st Far Eastern Front's 1st Red Banner Army focuses on an attack by a single Soviet rifle division across a roadless, hilly, and forested region that the Japanese only lightly defended. To accomplish its mission, the advancing rifle division

Map 2. Index to Case Study Locations

literally had to construct roads as it advanced, all the while advancing quickly enough to reach the Japanese rear area before the Japanese could regroup and erect a viable defense. The 1st Red Banner Army succeeded in this venture only by carefully tailoring its forces to match terrain conditions and providing significant engineer support at the lowest tactical level.

The third case study, the 35th Army's Advance to Mishan, shows how this 1st Far Eastern Front's army conducted successful military operations in a swampy and boggy region the Japanese considered unsuited for the conduct of large-scale military operations. During the operation, two rifle divisions with armor support conducted a major river crossing and a four-day operation through swamplands to envelop Japanese defenses and isolate the important Japanese fortified region at Hutou in eastern Manchuria. This case study highlights the techniques the Soviets used to task-organize forces to overcome seemingly insurmountable terrain obstacles.

The case study on the Battle for Mutanchiang provides complete details on the only set-piece battle of major proportions to occur during the Manchurian offensive. During the intense fighting, the 1st Far Eastern Front's 5th Army and 1st Red Banner Army, which were advancing along parallel and converging axes, struck imposing Japanese defensive positions east of the city of Mutanchiang. By employing armor-heavy forward detachments that imparted momentum to the advance, the advancing Soviet forces were able to preempt Japanese defenses east of the city, destroy defending Japanese forces piecemeal, and drive Japanese forces from Mutanchiang more than ten days ahead of schedule. Although successful, this rapid Soviet thrust also illustrates some of the drawbacks of conducting deep operations along separate axes in difficult terrain.

The case study entitled the 35th Army's Reduction of Hutou Fortress, written by Dr Edward Drea, focuses on the destruction of Japanese forces in the Hutou Fortified Region by Soviet forces after the 1st Far Eastern Front's 35th Army had bypassed and isolated the Japanese fortress. Based on detailed Japanese as well as Soviet sources, the case study demonstrates how Soviet forces reduced a major fortified complex by relying on massed air and artillery fire and small tailored assault groups, rather than on costly massed infantry assaults, to systematically reduce each strongpoint.

In terms of difficult terrain, the most remarkable Soviet operations in Manchuria took place in the west, where the Soviets massed large forces in remote areas and committed these forces to operations across seemingly impassable ground. Although the 6th Guards Tank Army carried out the most dramatic advances in this region, it did so against negligible opposition. However, such was not the case in the sector of the Trans-Baikal Front's 39th Army. The case study covering the 39th Army's envelopment of the Halung-Arshaan Fortified Region examines in detail the techniques this army employed to engage and destroy Japanese forces entrenched in strong

5

fortified regions in western Manchuria, which were flanked by the Grand Khingan Mountains.

The 39th Army adopted an indirect approach by attacking along two separate axes through territory the Japanese believed to be unsuited for the conduct of military operations. This audacious advance, led by maneuverable, armor-heavy forward detachments at every level of command, caught the Japanese utterly by surprise, rendered their fortifications superfluous, and quickly brushed aside resisting Japanese units.

Of all the operational and tactical techniques the Soviet Army employed in Manchuria, the creation and employment of forward detachments proved most valuable. The bold and deep operations conducted by carefully tailored forward detachments represented the most innovative aspect of the campaign, one that both created and preserved the momentum of the Soviet advance. The case study on the 36th Army's advance to Hailar investigates the successful employment of the army's 205th Tank Brigade as it served as a forward detachment spearheading the army's dramatic advance.

The extensive river system of northeastern Manchuria, with its associated numerous swamps and marshes, formed a major obstacle to offensive operations and forced the Soviet Army to conduct extensive joint amphibious operations. The case study on the 15th Army's advance to Chiamussu, which describes the army's ground and riverine operations which it conducted jointly with the Amur River Military Flotilla, focuses on how the army coordinated and conducted successful amphibious operations that produced relatively high rates of advance in a region that was almost totally impenetrable by ground forces operating in isolation.

As the Far East Command punished the Kwantung Army in Manchuria proper, the *Stavka* [Soviet High Command] expanded the scope of the offensive to encompass strategically vital Sakhalin Island and the Kuril Island chain. Two case studies cover these operations in unprecedented detail. The first details the 16th Army's operations in conjunction with the Pacific Fleet to conquer the southern portion of Sakhalin Island. This varied operation began with the penetration of the heavily fortified Japanese Koton Fortified Region, which dominated the only feasible axis of advance southward along the island's spine and concluded with amphibious operations to seize key ports on the island's west coast. The 5th Rifle Corps' penetration operation is an ideal case of combat against dense fortifications in hilly, heavily wooded, and marshy terrain. The second case study, the Kamchatka Defensive Region's assault on the Kuril Islands, offers a detailed examination of the complex amphibious operations that produced some of the bitterest fighting in the campaign and the heaviest Soviet Army losses.

As microcosms of the strategic struggle that occurred throughout Manchuria, these ten case studies illuminate the tactical details that conditioned overall Soviet Army victory. While doing so, they also provide glimpses of the often missing human dimension of combat. Ultimately, the performance of division, brigade, regiment, battalion, company, and platoon commanders, and, above all, their subordinate individual soldiers, determined the outcome of battle. While the human factor is often lost when studying the strategic and operational levels of war, it dominates at the tactical level. It is to those soldiers, most of whom remain nameless, that this volume is dedicated.

1

The 5th Army's Penetration of the Border Fortified Zone: The Penetration of a Prepared Defense

To fulfill the missions the *Stavka* assigned to it, Vasilevsky's Far East Command faced a myriad of challenging offensive tasks. The most difficult of these was to penetrate the imposing array of prepared Japanese defensive positions that blocked all feasible routes of advance into eastern Manchuria (see Map 3). Even in the best terrain and weather conditions, a penetration operation can be a costly process. However, the task is doubly difficult to fulfill successfully in the waning days of a Manchurian summer, when the monsoon rains arrive to refresh the verdant landscape of eastern Manchuria. In these circumstances, only intensive, detailed, and meticulous planning and preparations and skillfully conducted offensive operations can produce positive results. Such was the challenge facing the 1st Far Eastern Front's combat-experienced 5th Army.

TERRAIN CONSIDERATIONS IN EASTERN MANCHURIA

The most direct axis of advance from the Soviet Far Eastern provinces into central Manchuria ran directly from the Soviet Far Eastern border near Suifenho across the hills of eastern Manchuria through Mutanchiang to Harbin in the central valley of Manchuria. To the south a secondary axis extended from the Soviet Far Eastern border east of Tungning toward Wangching and Yenchi, and to the north a lesser axis ran cross the Ussuri River north of Lake Khanka toward Linkou and Harbin from the northeast. The Suifenho–Mutanchiang–Harbin axis paralleled the Eastern Manchurian Railroad, and along it, as if attesting to its strategic importance, the Japanese

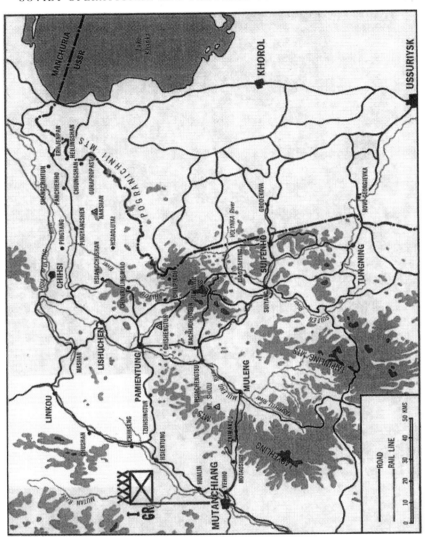

Map 3. Soviet 5th Army's and 1st Red Banner Army's Area of Operations

had erected some of their most formidable defensive positions in Manchuria. Anchored on the Suifenho Fortified Region, these Japanese defensive fortifications dominated the principal approach into eastern Manchuria in much the same fashion as the Maginot Line had canalized the main approaches into eastern France in June 1940 (see Maps 4a,b).

The Japanese fortified zone in eastern Manchuria was flanked on the north and south by dense forests and rugged rolling mountains, which the Japanese considered utterly impenetrable by modern mobile armies and even difficult for experienced and well-equipped infantry to traverse. However, few Japanese military commanders appreciated how the Germans had overcome the Maginot Line in 1940. More astute and certainly more experienced than their Japanese counterparts, Soviet commanders consciously planned to replicate the German Army's feat of 1940 by traversing the seemingly impassable terrain in eastern Manchuria by conducting extensive operational envelopments of Japanese forces in the border region. Furthermore, since even operational envelopments aimed at achieving deep objectives would leave large concentrations of Japanese forces isolated but still astride their communication and supply routes to the rear, the 1st Far Eastern Front's attacking armies planned to conduct simultaneous and numerous shallow tactical envelopments against the fortified regions themselves to isolate and destroy them at minimum cost.

MISSIONS AND TASKS

Vasilevsky's Far Eastern Command entrusted Meretskov's 1st Far Eastern Front with the task of penetrating Japanese border defenses in eastern Manchuria. The *Stavka's* 28 June 1945 directive, which assigned Meretskov's *front* its offensive mission, required Meretskov to

> Deliver the main attack with a force of two combined-arms armies (the 1st Red Banner Army with 6 rifle divisions and the 5th Army with 12 rifle divisions), one mechanized corps, and one cavalry division to penetrate Japanese defenses on a 7.5 mile (12 kilometer) front north of Grodekovo and attack in the general direction of Muleng and Mutanchiang with the immediate mission of reaching the Poli, Ninguta [Ningan], Tuntsinchen [Shihhuachen], and Sanchohou Station front by the 23d day of the operation.
>
> Subsequently, operate in the direction of Harbin and Changchun to reach the Harbin, Changchun, Antu, and Ranan [Nanam] front.[1]

After capturing Mutanchiang and consolidating its forces on the western bank of the Mutan River, as well as at Wangching and Yenchi, Meretskov's *front* was to continue its offensive toward Kirin, Changchun, and Harbin. Separate armies on each flank would support the 5th Army's main attack.

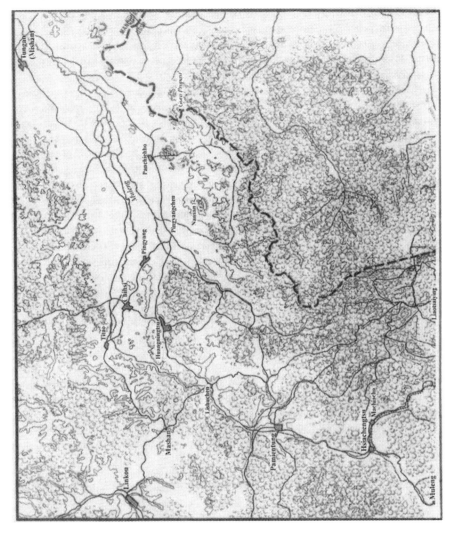

Map 4a. 1st Red Banner Army's Operational Sector

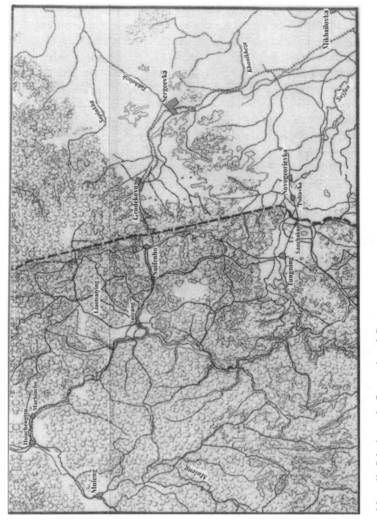

Map 4b. 5th Army's Operational Sector

Meretskov planned to deploy his *front* in a single echelon of armies. He ordered Colonel General N. I. Krylov's 5th Army to make the main attack in coordination with Colonel General A. P. Beloborodov's 1st Red Banner Army, which was to attack on Krylov's right flank. Krylov was to launch his main attack in the direction of Mutanchiang, penetrate Japanese border defenses in a 7.5-mile (12-kilometer) sector north of Grodekovo, destroy the Japanese Volynsk (Kuanyuentai) Center of Resistance in the Border Fortified Region, and advance 25 miles (40 kilometers) to capture the Taipingling Pass and Suifenho by the fourth day of the operation.

In formulating this mission, Meretskov expected his 5th Army to advance 37–50 miles (60–80 kilometers) deep and to secure crossings over the Muleng River in the vicinity of Muleng by the eighth day of the operation. By the eighteenth day, the army was to have secured Mutanchiang on the Mutan River in conjunction with the 1st Red Banner Army, which was to advance on Mutanchiang from the northeast. Once Mutanchiang had been captured, Meretskov planned to commit his mobile group, the 10th Mechanized Corps, in the 5th Army's sector, so that it could exploit the offensive to Kirin, where it would link up with the Trans-Baikal Front's forces, which were advancing across the Grand Khingan Mountains toward Kirin from the west.[2]

THE JAPANESE DEFENSES

The mission Meretskov assigned to Krylov's 5th Army was as ambitious as it was extensive. The success of Krylov's plan depended on the ability of his forces to overcome difficult terrain, strong fortifications deployed in depth, and a determined although under-strength and unsuspecting enemy. The Japanese Border Fortified Region extended across a front of 25 miles (40 kilometers) north and south of the main highway and railroad line running through the village of Suifenho.[3] Though in most areas the fortified region was 6.2–12.4 miles (10–15 kilometers) deep, along the highway and railroad line its depth stretched from 18.6 to 21.8 miles (30 to 35 kilometers).

The Border Fortified Region consisted of four distinct centers of resistance, each covering a frontage of 1.6–8.1 miles (2.5–13 kilometers) to a depth of 1.6–5.6 miles (2.5–9 kilometers). The Northeastern and Eastern Centers of Resistance (which the Japanese collectively called the Suifenho Fortified Region) protected the approach to Suifenho village from the east along a 6.2–7.5-mile (10–12-kilometer) front north and south of the main Eastern Manchurian rail line. Just under 6.5 miles (20 kilometers) to the north, the Volynsk Center of Resistance (Kuanyuentai) occupied the wooded, brush-covered hills north and south of the Volynka River. Just over 6 miles (10 kilometers) south of Suifenho, the Southern Center of Resistance (Lumintai) sat on dominant hills overlooking the Soviet Far Eastern Province.

These four centers of resistance protected 15.5 miles (25 kilometers) of the 5th Army's overall frontage of 25 miles (40 kilometers), and the Japanese had interspersed numerous smaller field works in between them. A fifth center of resistance, which consisted of lighter field trenches, dominated the road junction of Suiyang, 18.6 miles (30 kilometers) west of the village of Suifenho. Grassy, brush-covered hills surrounded the Border Fortified Region and extended 6.2 miles (10 kilometers) to the rear, finally merging into the higher wooded mountains extending to the Muleng River.

The northern flank of the Border Fortified Region blended into the heavily wooded, brush-covered, and presumably impassable eastern Manchurian mountains north of the Volynka River. This lightly defended sector extended 37 miles (60 kilometers) from the northern edge of the Border Fortified Region to the Mishan Fortified Region northwest of Lake Khanka. The southern flank of the fortified region tied in loosely with the northern flank of the Tungning (called by the Soviets the Pogranichnaia) Fortified Region, which was located 15.5–18.6 miles (25–30 kilometers) to the south.[4]

The Japanese centers of resistance consisted of underground reinforced concrete fortifications, gun emplacements, power stations, and warehouses. Many of the reinforced concrete pillboxes had walls up to 3.3–4.9 feet (1–1.5 meters) thick, with armor plating or armored gun turrets. Some even came equipped with elevators for transporting the gun and its ammunition. In August 1945, the four main centers of resistance contained 295 concrete pillboxes, 145 earth and timber pillboxes, 58 concrete shelters, 69 armored turrets, 29 observation posts and command posts, and 55 artillery positions.

Each center of resistance consisted of from three to six major strong points, each encompassing 299,000 square yards (250,000 square meters), situated up to 1.2 miles (2 kilometers) apart. The strong points themselves were usually located on dominant heights and consisted of reinforced concrete positions or several timber and earth bunkers, as well as antitank, machine gun, and artillery firing positions. Machine gun bunkers were positioned every 820–1,148 feet (250–350 meters), and artillery positions with underground entrances 1,640–2,296 feet (500–700 meters) or less apart.[5] The centers of resistance usually contained military settlements, complete with warehouses and a water supply. Communications trenches tied the entire complex of strong points together. The outer defenses of each strong point and the defenses of the center as a whole included multiple barbed wire obstacles, antipersonnel and antitank mines, antitank ditches, and anti-infantry obstacles, usually covered by interlocking fields of machine gun fire.

Although the Japanese planned for a regiment to defend each center of resistance, a battalion could offer a credible defense because of the strength of the fortifications. Therefore, Soviet planners considered each center of resistance equivalent to the strength of a full infantry division. Infantry companies usually defended strong points, and sections, squads, and platoons

15

manned the strong points' outposts and satellite bunkers. So organized, these Fortified Border Regions formed the first important Japanese line of defense in Manchuria.

Field works located 50 miles (80 kilometers) to the west in the heavily wooded mountains west of the Muleng River formed the Japanese second line of defense. A third line of defense anchored at Mutanchiang, 93–112 miles (150–180 kilometers) to the west, completed the defensive zone across which the Japanese hoped to delay and wear down advancing Soviet forces. For the Japanese defensive plan to function properly, the Border Fortified Region had to take its toll of Soviet strength and time.

General Shimizu whose Japanese 5th Army was responsible for defending much of eastern Manchuria, positioned General Shiina's 124th Infantry Division to defend the critical Suifenho sector (see Table 1). Shiina assigned one infantry battalion from each of his three infantry regiments to defend the border region proper. The 1st Battalion of the 273d Infantry Regiment defended the Volynk (Kuanyuentai) Center of Resistance, the 1st Battalion of the 271st Infantry Regiment the Northeastern and Eastern Center of Resistance (Suifenho), and one company of the 1st Battalion, 272d Regiment, defended the Southern Center of Resistance (Lumintai).[6] Additional Japanese security, construction, and reserve units in the border region were available to reinforce the regular border garrison, which numbered in excess of 3,000 men.[7]

TABLE 1: ORDER OF BATTLE OF THE JAPANESE 124TH INFANTRY DIVISION, 9 AUGUST 1945

124th Infantry Division – General Shiina Masataka

271st Infantry Regiment	1 battalion at Suifenho
272d Infantry Regiment	1 battalion at Lumintai
273d Infantry Regiment	1 company at Kuanyuentai
124th Artillery Regiment	
124th Engineer Battalion	
Raiding Battalion, at Hsiachengtzu	

Attached units

31st Independent Antitank Battalion (minus 1 battery)
20th Heavy Field Artillery Regiment (minus 2 batteries)
1st Independent Heavy Artillery Battery (150 mm guns)
Tungning Heavy Artillery Regiment, 1 battalion (minus 1 battery)
Mutanchiang Heavy Artillery Regiment (8 × 240 mm howitzers)
13th Mortar Battalion
Two independent engineer battalions

Source: 'Record of Operations Against Soviet Army on Eastern Front (August 1945)', *Japanese Monograph No. 154* (Tokyo: Military History Section, US Army Forces Far East, 1954), 225–32.

The bulk of Shiina's 124th Infantry Division was garrisoned at Muleng, Suiyang, and Hsiachengtzu, 25–50 miles (40–80 kilometers) west of the border. On 8 August 1945, some of these units were building fortifications in the mountains west of Muleng in anticipation of a future conflict with the Soviet Union.[8]

The 126th Infantry Division of Shimizu's 5th Army, whose headquarters were situated at Pamientung, defended on the 124th Infantry Division's left flank, while the 3d Army's 128th Infantry Division, headquartered at Lotzokou, defended its right flank. However, since both units defended broad sectors, neither was able to provide any support to the 124th Infantry Division. Likewise, the 5th Army and First Area Army, whose headquarters were at Mutanchiang, could provide only minimal reinforcements to Shiina's division from army and area army support troops and military school units.

FORCE STRUCTURE, DEPLOYMENT, AND TRAINING

Meretskov structured his 1st Far Eastern Front's forces so as to insure rapid reduction of this Japanese Fortified Region. He reinforced Krylov's 5th Army massively so that it could maneuver through the fortified region and, if need be, crush the Japanese defenses by sheer weight of tank and artillery firepower. With reinforcements, Krylov's army counted four rifle corps with 12 rifle divisions, one fortified region, five tank brigades, six heavy self-propelled artillery regiments, 22 artillery brigades, four engineer brigades, one antiaircraft artillery division, and numerous supporting units and subunits totaling 692 tanks and self-propelled guns, 2,945 guns and mortars, and 432 multiple rocket launchers [*Katiushas*] (see Table 2).[9]

Meretskov ordered Colonel General of Aviation I. M. Sokolov's 9th Air Army to provide air support for Krylov's army. Sokolov responded by ordering his air army's 252d Assault and 250th Fighter Aviation Divisions to support both the 5th Army and the 1st Red Banner Army during the penetration operation and the ensuing pursuit. Throughout the offensive, the 9th Air Army's 34th Bomber Aviation Division and 19th Bomber Aviation Corps were to provide on-call support for Krylov's forces as required, however, under strict air army control.[10] These bomber units would provide invaluable assistance in the reduction of the heavily fortified Japanese fortified regions.

By July 1945 the 5th Army forces had completed their long rail movement from the Konigsberg area in East Prussia and had occupied concentration areas in the Ussurysk, Spassk-Dal'nii, and Khorol regions, 62–75 miles (100–120 kilometers) east of the Soviet–Manchurian border. After about two weeks spent reorganizing and training, on 22 July Krylov's forces began moving into assembly areas 9.3–15.5 miles (15–25 kilometers) from the border.

TABLE 2: COMPOSITION OF SOVIET 5TH ARMY, 9 AUGUST 1945

5th Army – Colonel General N. I. Krylov

17th Rifle Corps: Lieutenant General N. A. Nikitin
  187th Rifle Division: Major General I. M. Savin
  366th Rifle Division: Colonel I. A. Manuilov
45th Rifle Corps: Major General N. I. Ivanov
  157th Rifle Division: Colonel N. F. Kusakin
  159th Rifle Division: Colonel N. I. Fedotov
  184th Rifle Division: Major General B. B. Gorodovikov
65th Rifle Corps: Major General G. H. Perekrestov
  97th Rifle Division: Major General A. K. Makar'ev
  144th Rifle Division: Colonel N. T. Zorin
  190th Rifle Division: Colonel N. G. Stavtsev
  371st Rifle Division: Colonel A. S. Loginov
72d Rifle Corps: Major General A. I. Kazartsev
  63d Rifle Division: Colonel A. I. Gordienko
  215th Rifle Division: Major General A. A. Kazarian
  277th Rifle Division: Major General S. T. Gliadyshev
105th Fortified Region
72d Tank Brigade: Colonel N. S. Grishin
76th Tank Brigade: Lieutenant Colonel V. P. Chaplygin
208th Tank Brigade: Colonel M. I. Nikitin
210th Tank Brigade: Colonel L. P. Krasnoshtin
218th Tank Brigade: Colonel A. P. Velichko
333d Guards Self-propelled Artillery Regiment
378th Guards Self-propelled Artillery Regiment
395th Guards Self-propelled Artillery Regiment
478th Guards Self-propelled Artillery Regiment
479th Guards Self-propelled Artillery Regiment
480th Guards Self-propelled Artillery Regiment
78th Separate Armored Train
15th Guards Gun Artillery Brigade
225th Gun Artillery Brigade
226th Gun Artillery Brigade
227th Gun Artillery Brigade
236th Gun Artillery Brigade
107th High-power Howitzer Artillery Brigade
119th High-power Howitzer Artillery Brigade
223d High-power Howitzer Artillery Brigade
218th Corps Artillery Brigade
219th Corps Artillery Brigade
220th Corps Artillery Brigade
222d Corps Artillery Brigade
237th Howitzer Artillery Brigade
238th Howitzer Artillery Brigade
61st Antitank (Tank Destroyer) Artillery Brigade
20th Special-power Gun Artillery Regiment
32d Separate Special-power Artillery Battalion
34th Separate Special-power Artillery Battalion
696th Antitank (Tank Destroyer) Artillery Regiment

53d Mortar Brigade
55th Mortar Brigade
56th Mortar Brigade
57th Mortar Brigade
283d Mortar Regiment
17th Guards-Mortar Brigade
20th Guards-Mortar Brigade
26th Guards-Mortar Brigade
2d Guards-Mortar Regiment
26th Guards-Mortar Regiment
42d Guards-Mortar Regiment
72d Guards-Mortar Regiment
74th Guards-Mortar Regiment
307th Guards-Mortar Regiment
48th Antiaircraft Artillery Division
   231st Guards Antiaircraft Artillery Regiment
   1277th Antiaircraft Artillery Regiment
   1278th Antiaircraft Artillery Regiment
   2011th Antiaircraft Artillery Regiment
726th Antiaircraft Artillery Regiment
129th Separate Antiaircraft Artillery Battalion
300th Separate Antiaircraft Artillery Battalion
461st Separate Antiaircraft Artillery Battalion
20th Motorized Assault Engineer Sapper Brigade
23d Engineer-Sapper Brigade
63d Engineer-Sapper Brigade
46th Motorized Engineer Brigade
55th Separate Pontoon-Bridge Battalion
Weapons
   692 tanks and self-propelled guns
   2,945 guns and mortars
   432 rocket launchers

Source: M. V. Zakharov, ed., *Final: istoriko-memuarny ocherk o razgrome imperialisticheskoi iapony v 1945 godu* [Finale: A historical memoir-survey about the rout of imperialistic Japan in 1945] (Moscow: 'Nauka', 1969), 401.

Because of the difficult heavily wooded terrain, the assembly areas for the 1st Far Eastern Front's forces were closer to the border than the assembly areas of other forces assigned to the Far East Command. The movement into assembly areas, which was conducted primarily at night under stringent control to maintain complete secrecy, was completed by 25 July. Once in their assembly areas, the 5th Army's formations and units continued preparatory training for their specific combat missions. Krylov's forces moved forward to their jumping-off positions for the assault adjacent to the border during the nights of 1–6 August.[11]

All rifle troops moved forward into their assigned jumping-off positions in accordance with detailed, strict, and carefully orchestrated unit movement plans, and army and corps engineers and sappers prepared each position units were to occupy well in advance. The army's artillery units also deployed into prepared positions during a single 4–5-hour period under the cover of darkness. All the while, army engineers and sappers carefully camouflaged all of this movement into the 5th Army's 40-mile (65-kilometer) sector along the border to maintain operational secrecy and ensure that the ensuing assault surprised the defending Japanese.

The 1st Far Eastern Front's operational deception [*maskirovka*] plan, which regulations required be included in the *front's* overall offensive plan, required engineer forces to camouflage the forward deployment of all troops and supporting equipment. To do so, the engineers erected vertical masking walls and camouflaged overhead covers along all roads and tracks into the forward area, often under Japanese observation. The 5th Army's sector alone contained 11 miles (18 kilometers) of vertical walls and 1,515 overhead covers, all designed to block enemy observation of forward deploying forces.[12]

To carry out the army's complex movement plans effectively, special groups of officers, detailed from the Commandant's Service at *front* and army headquarters, manned an extensive array of movement control points to guide 5th Army units forward. Except for those associated with the signals traffic of normal border units, all radio communications networks maintained strict silence. While all of these preparations were under way, the fortified regions stationed along the border carried on normal defensive duties and even harvested crops as usual. Soviet troops, who themselves did not know about the impending offensive, performed routine garrison and field duties and were even permitted their normal leaves and passes.

During both the movement phase and the temporary pauses in concentration and assembly areas, all force commanders and their staffs carried out intensive and focused training for the impending offensive. Training plans prepared by every regiment and battalion in the 5th Army included such subjects as combat operations in wooded and mountainous terrain, assaults on fortified defensive positions, and overcoming water obstacles during marches and assaults, and the units and subunits conducted actual field training on these subjects while on the move forward.

Tank and self-propelled artillery units designated to support the offensive also trained on the difficult terrain over which they would have to operate, while artillery units conducted practice firing throughout July while in their concentration areas. At every level of command, commanders and their staff conducted war games and command post exercises to improve coordination within their forces and mutual cooperation between themselves and adjacent units and to practice the precise operational tasks required by their assigned mission.

During this training, groups of officers within the *front* who had experience in operating against German fortified regions in the European theater shared their knowledge in classes with less experienced officers in the 5th Army and other 1st Far Eastern Front armies. In addition, Krylov's staff formed similar teams of officers who had extensive experience in the Far East to educate regiment, battalion, and company commanders on Japanese equipment, tactics, and fortifications and familiarize them with the terrain over which they were to operate.[13] The 5th Army completed its movement forward to jumping-off positions along the border on 6 August.

ARMY AND CORPS PLANS

To fulfill his assigned mission, Krylov deployed the 5th Army in two echelons of rifle corps, concentrating the bulk of his forces in a 7.5-mile (12-kilometer) sector of his overall army sector of 40 miles (65 kilometers) to achieve overwhelming superiority over the opposing Japanese forces. The army's first echelon consisted of the 65th, 72d, and 17th Rifle Corps and the 105th Fortified Region deployed from north to south (right to left) across the army sector. The 45th Rifle Corps, which formed Krylov's second echelon, deployed into positions 25–30 kilometers to the rear. All of the attacking rifle corps and divisions also formed in two–echelon combat formations except the 65th Rifle Corps' 190th Rifle Division, which deployed in single echelon formation to protect the heavily wooded and hilly region on the 5th Army's right flank.

By concentrating the bulk of the army's forces in the northern half of his army's sector, Krylov created relatively narrow main attack sectors for all of his subordinate formations and units. For example, while the army conducted its main attack in a 7.5-mile (12-kilometer) sector, the rifle corps did so in 3.1–3.8-mile (5–5.6-kilometer) sectors, rifle divisions in 1.6–1.7-mile (2.5–2.8-kilometer) sectors, and rifle regiments in 0.6–1.1-mile (1.0–1.8-kilometer) sectors.

This careful concentration of forces permitted the creation of sufficient operational and tactical densities of men and weapons in the designated penetration sectors to facilitate rapid penetration of the Japanese fortified region. For example, once deployment was complete, the 5th Army deployed one rifle division per 0.7 mile (1.1 kilometer) of front and 402 (250) guns and mortars and 48 (30) tanks and self-propelled guns per mile (kilometer) of front along its main attack axis. The army's two-echelons army configuration placed 39 rifle battalions in the first echelon of its forward rifle divisions and 69 rifle battalions in the second echelons of rifle divisions, rifle corps, and army, thus providing sustaining strength for the offensive.[14]

Krylov ordered Major General A. I. Kazartsev's 72d Rifle Corps to conduct his army's main attack in a 3.1-mile (5-kilometer) sector south of the Volynka River, penetrate the Volynsk Center of Resistance, destroy the defending enemy, and capture strong points Sharp [Ostraia] and Pear [Grusha], 1.6–3.1 miles (2.5–5 kilometers) deep into the fortified region by the end of the first day of the operation. By the end of the second day, Krylov required Kazartsev's forces to penetrate 5 miles (8 kilometers) deep and threaten Japanese communications routes into Suifenho from the west. Subsequently, Kazartsev's corps was to develop the offensive northwestward along the road and railroad through the villages of Liaotsaiying and Suiyang to capture Machiacho Station and passes through the Taipingling Mountains, at a depth of 25 miles (40 kilometers) into the Japanese rear area.

To sustain 72d Rifle Corps' assault, General Krylov attached a vast array of supporting forces to Kazartsev's rifle corps, including eight artillery brigades (two of which were high-power), four artillery regiments, three artillery battalions (of which two were special-power), two mortar brigades, two brigades and two regiments of guards-mortars, two tank brigades, two self-propelled artillery brigades, and one engineer-sapper brigade. In addition, during the artillery preparation, Krylov also ordered the 45th Rifle Corps, which was in second echelon, to reinforce Kazartsev's preparatory fire with fire from three of its artillery regiments. With this support, Kazartsev massed 14,380 troops, 1,092 guns and mortars, 198 tanks and self-propelled guns, and 824 light and heavy machine guns in his corps' 3.1-mile (5-kilometer) wide main attack sector. This created operational and tactical densities of 4,628 (2,876) men, 8.7 (5.4) rifle battalions, 351 (218) guns and mortars, and 64 (40) tanks and self-propelled guns per mile (kilometer) of front.[15]

Kazartsev deployed his 72d Rifle Corps with Kazarian's 215th and Gordienko's 63d Rifle Divisions in first echelon and Gladyshev's 277th Rifle Division in second echelon. Gordienko's 63d Rifle Division, which was deployed on the rifle corps's left flank and was supported by Velichko's 218th Tank Brigade and the 479th Heavy Self-propelled Artillery Regiment, was to conduct the main attack to secure strong point Pear. On the rifle corps' right flank, Kazarian's 215th Rifle Division, supported by Krasnoshtin's 210th Tank Brigade and the 333d Heavy Self-propelled Artillery Regiment, was to attack to seize strong point Sharp. By day's end, each rifle division was supposed to have captured a lodgment up to 3.1 miles (5 kilometers) deep into the enemy defenses.[16]

Gladyshev's 277th Rifle Division, in the 72d Rifle Corps' second echelon, was to follow the 63d Rifle Division in the assault. On the morning of the third day, Gladyshev's division was to lead the rifle corps' pursuit from the Liaotsaiying area (11.2 miles (18 kilometers) deep) to capture the road junction at Suiyang. All rifle divisions of the 72d Rifle Corps formed in two echelons of regiments, while rifle regiments formed in single echelon (except the 215th Rifle Division's 711th Rifle Regiment, which formed in two echelons in order to attack the northern flank of strong point Sharp).

Both of the 72d Rifle Corps' first echelon rifle divisions formed assault groups, which they specifically tailored to attack individual Japanese fortified points. The 215th Rifle Division employed assault groups of up to platoon

22

size, formed from the rifle companies of first echelon regiments. In the 63d Rifle Division, reinforced rifle companies of first echelon regiments formed larger assault detachments. In addition, both first echelon rifle divisions used advanced battalions organized on the basis of one per rifle division to initiate the night attack in the wake of the reconnaissance detachments and assault groups.[17]

On the right flank of Kazartsev's 72d Rifle Corps, Major General G. H. Perekrestov's 65th Rifle Corps was to conduct a supporting attack with four rifle divisions. Perekrestov's mission was to penetrate the Volynsk Center of Resistance north of the Volynka River, seize the so-called Camel [*Verblud*] strong point, and to advance to a depth of 5–6.2 miles (8–10 kilometers) by the end of the first day of the operation. Thereafter, the 65th Rifle Corps was to develop the offensive and capture Machiacho Station by the end of the third day of the operation.

Perekrestov deployed his rifle corps with Stavtsev's 190th, Makar'ev's 97th, and Zorin's 144th Rifle Divisions in first echelon and Loginov's 371st Rifle Division in second echelon. Concentrated on the corps' left flank, the 144th Rifle Division was to conduct the assault against strong point Camel. Meanwhile, the 97th and 190th Rifle Divisions were to sweep across the virtually undefended, but heavily wooded, sector north of Camel to envelop that strong point and maintain loose contact with the forces of Beloborodov's 1st Red Banner Army, which were advancing on the 5th Army's right flank. Perekrestov's first echelon rifle divisions formed assault groups and designated advanced battalions similar to those formed by the 72d Rifle Corps.

Nikitin's 17th Rifle Corps, which was deployed on the left flank of Perekrestov's 72d Rifle Corps, was to attack to isolate the Northeastern and Eastern (Suifenho) Centers of Resistance in cooperation with the 105th Fortified Region and several border guard battalions. Approximately two regiments of Savin's 187th Rifle Division, backed up by Manuilov's 366th Rifle Division in the corps' second echelon, were to attack into the gap between the Volynsk and Northeast Centers of Resistance and then swing southwestward around the rear of the Japanese defenses, ultimately to cut the rail line and highway running from Suifenho to Suiyang. One regiment of Savin's 187th Rifle Division was to cooperate with the 105th Fortified Region and 20th Assault Engineer-Sapper Brigade and capture the critical railroad tunnels and highway leading across the border into Suifenho village from the east.

Finally, Major General N. I. Ivanov's 45th Rifle Corps, which was in the 5th Army's second echelon, was to exploit the successes achieved by the 5th Army's two first echelon rifle corps. Krylov planned to commit Ivanov's rifle corps into combat early on the fifth day of the offensive so that it could lead the offensive westward across the Muleng River.

The 1st Far Eastern Front's initial directive assigning Krylov's army its offensive missions required the 5th Army to organize a massive artillery offensive in support of its attack and assigned the army considerable reinforcing artillery. Accordingly, Krylov organized his artillery offensive in five distinct phases.[18] One day prior to the ground assault, special artillery groups were to engage and destroy permanent Japanese fortifications along the border. Then, artillery would fire in support of the advanced battalions for a period of one and one-half hours to two hours on the night of the actual assault. Prior to the main forces' advance, the artillery was to fire a four-hour artillery preparation against successive concentrations and then, during the main forces' attack, a single powerful barrage and fire on additional consecutive concentrations. Finally, artillery was to provide fire support to accompany the advancing tank and infantry forces into the depth of the Japanese defenses.

To perform the varied missions required by the elaborate artillery offensive, Krylov formed heavy artillery groups at every level of command, including heavy gun and mortar groups in rifle regiments, rifle divisions, and rifle corps. In addition, each rifle corps formed an artillery destruction group and long-range artillery group, the former to engage and destroy fortified point targets and the latter to deliver interdiction fire and destructive fire on deep targets. The high density of artillery in support of Krylov's 5th Army marked the first time in the Second World War that Soviet forces massed such extensive artillery concentrations in such hilly and brush-covered terrain.

To insure adequate artillery support throughout the duration of the offensive, the 5th Army's fire plan incorporated measures to deploy artillery forward so as to guarantee the advancing forces constant fire support from at least 50 per cent of all of the army's artillery weapons at all times. After the penetration operation was complete, Meretskov planned to re-subordinate part of the artillery reinforcing Krylov's army to the adjacent 25th and 1st Red Banner Armies.

The 1st Far Eastern Front's aviation support plan included a two-phased air operation in support of the 5th Army and 1st Red Banner Army. During the period of preparatory fires, echeloned short-range and long-range bombers and assault aircraft were to conduct 1,578 air sorties to destroy enemy targets. During the assault phase of the offensive, the plan called for 1,330 air sorties to support the ground attack. To better support the forces deployed forward, between 4 and 9 August, Meretskov relocated fighter and ground assault aircraft from peacetime airfields deep in the rear to bases 15.5–18.5 miles (25–30 kilometers) from the state border. During the same period, bomber aircraft from the 34th Bomber Aviation Division redeployed to new bases 37–43 miles (60–70 kilometers) from the border and aircraft from the 19th Bomber Aviation Division to bases 106–124 miles (170–200 kilometers) from the border.[19]

Despite these extensive and careful preparations, on the eve of the attack Krylov cancelled the first three periods of the artillery offensive and the air destruction missions. Explanations as to why he did so vary.[20] Ultimately, it was the *front* commander who decided whether or not to fire the preparation. In his memoirs, Krylov claims that insufficient intelligence concerning the precise location of Japanese positions negated the value of the advanced destructive fires and the requirement to achieve surprise negated the value of only partial destruction of enemy fortifications. Consequently, Krylov noted, he decided to destroy enemy firing positions with a surprise night attack by advanced battalions rather than by artillery fire. Further, he claimed that he planned to fire a four-hour artillery preparation only if the attack by the advanced battalions failed. In any case, heavy rains deluged the region for six hours on the evening prior to the attack, lessening the potential effectiveness of any artillery preparation and, hence, reinforcing the argument for abandoning it. The same situation materialized in all of the 1st Far Eastern Front's sectors except at Hutou, where artillery strikes went as planned.

One of the most difficult problems confronting the 1st Far Eastern Front's military planners was how to employ tanks and heavy self-propelled guns in the difficult terrain of eastern Manchuria. It was abundantly clear that the *front's* forces could overcome or destroy the heavy Japanese fortified defensive positions and achieve the high rate of advance the operational plan required only if it employed armor effectively. Consequently, commanders tailored their tank and self-propelled gun units so that they could operate effectively in the difficult terrain and adjusted the tactical missions they assigned to these forces to guarantee maximum effectiveness.

Meretskov reinforced Krylov's 5th Army with five tank brigades and six heavy self-propelled gun artillery regiments to provide requisite fire support for the infantry formations and increase their offensive punch and mobility. In general, he reinforced each rifle division operating along a main attack axis with one tank brigade and one heavy self-propelled gun regiment totaling 86 tanks and self-propelled guns, thereby establishing armor densities of 48 (30) tanks and self-propelled guns per mile (kilometer) of front. After the 5th Army's lead rifle divisions penetrated the enemy's tactical defense zone, the reinforced tank brigades were to form forward detachments at rifle corps and rifle division level and begin to exploit into the operational depths at high speed. In addition, Meretskov planned to employ the 249 tanks and self-propelled guns of Vasil'ev's 10th Mechanized Corps as a *front* mobile group to exploit the 5th Army's success.[21]

Meretskov's *front* headquarters also lavished extensive engineer support on the 5th Army to help it overcome the formidable terrain, conduct combat at night, and destroy or bypass the imposing Japanese fortified positions. The army's engineer forces conducted engineer reconnaissance to detect enemy engineering measures, terrain obstacles, and the condition of enemy engineer forces; installed camouflage; and repaired and constructed roads and bridges, defensive positions, and lines of departure. When the attack commenced, engineer-sapper forces assigned to the more than 100 assault groups formed in the 5th Army participated actively in the reduction of Japanese fortified positions.

To supplement the routine work of assault units during the offensive, the 5th Army formed two obstacle-clearing detachments in each first echelon rifle company. In addition, special road and bridge detachments consisting of one rifle battalion and one to three sapper platoons formed in the rear of each rifle regiment to repair movement routes and facilitate the forward deployment of artillery.[22]

With all of their attack preparations complete, the combat echelons of the 5th Army rested in their jumping-off positions on the evening of 8 August, surrounded by the anonymity of darkness and soaked by August rains, and waited for the order to advance. Across the border, 1.2–1.9 miles (2–3 kilometers) distant, the Japanese rested easily, manning only selected firing positions in their fortified zone, lulled perhaps as much by the security of the rain and the darkness and the hopes of deferred battle as by faulty intelligence. The intelligence picture painted by Shiina's 124th Japanese Infantry Division explains the complacency:

> During July and August, the division received information from subordinate and lateral units indicating the gravity of the situation with regard to the USSR. This information was utterly inconsistent with the optimistic information received from higher commands. The division was at a loss for the truth, and consequently was often apt to take an optimistic view.[23]

The stunning developments that would transpire during the first few hours of 9 August would take stark and immediate advantage of that Japanese complacency.

Nor were Japanese commands in the deeper rear area any less complacent. So confident were Japanese commanders that peace would prevail that General Shimizu, the commander of the Japanese 5th Army, was hosting a five-day conference and tabletop war game with his division commanders and chiefs of staff at his headquarters at Yehho on the night of 8–9 August. The attendees included Shiina of the 124th Infantry Division and his chief of staff.

THE 5TH ARMY'S ATTACK

At 0100 on 9 August, the advanced battalions with supporting tanks and self-propelled guns of Krylov's 5th Army crossed the state border and, in darkness and heavy rain, slowly made their way toward the Japanese forward security outposts and advanced positions (see Maps 5a, b). The forces advanced without an artillery preparation, in near silence, as the driving rain muffled the sounds of their movements. During the first hours of their advance, only scattered machine gun fire and exploding grenades punctuated that silence as the Soviet assault units overran many Japanese positions caught totally unaware.

The advanced battalions then spread out in assault group configuration to destroy individual Japanese positions, whenever possible infiltrating through gaps in the Japanese defenses to threaten the vulnerable flanks of individual defensive positions and to gain the rear of the defenses. The advanced battalions captured many of these positions before the stunned Japanese could occupy them and seized others by surprise after short, intense fights. However, in a few instances, Japanese forces were able to react more quickly, and occupied all defensive positions in major strong points, and offered credible resistance.

In the sector of Perekrestov's 65th Rifle Corps on the right flank of Krylov's 5th Army, the advanced battalions of Stavtsev's 190th and Makar'ev's 97th Rifle Divisions advanced steadily over heavily wooded and hilly terrain to envelop strong point Camel from the north. By 0400 hours the troops from the two rifle divisions had penetrated 2.5–3.7 miles (4–6 kilometers) into the forests, crossed the Shunlienchuan River, and occupied positions to the rear of strong point Camel. Simultaneously, an advanced battalion from the 785th Rifle Regiment of Zorin's 144th Rifle Division, commanded by Major G. I. Glazunov, struck strong point Camel frontally. With tremendous exertions, the Japanese defenders were able to man their defensive positions within Camel and successfully repulsed Glazunov's initial attack.

By 0700 hours, however, Glazunov's advanced battalion, now reinforced by tanks and 152 mm self-propelled guns, was ready to resume the attack. After an intense 10 minute artillery barrage, Glazunov ordered his 4th and 5th Companies to assault the front slopes of strong point Camel under the cover of direct fire from his tanks and self-propelled guns. At the same time, Glazunov's 6th Company attacked Camel from the south. The simultaneous assault captured four pillboxes, killed 100 Japanese troops defending the strong point, and paved the way for the 144th Rifle Division's main force to join the attack.[24]

While Perekrestov's rifle corps was initiating its assault, the advanced battalions of Kazarian's 215th and Gordienko's 63d Rifle Divisions of Kazartsev's 72d Rifle Corps advanced to assault Japanese strong points Sharp, Officer [*Ofitserskaia*], and Pear, which were located south of the Volynka River. Captain I. Shcherbakov's company of Captain D. E. Moskalev's 3d Battalion of the 707th Rifle Regiment, which was serving as the advanced battalion of Kazarian's 215th Rifle Division, moved forward to assault Japanese strong point Sharp at 0100 hours. Shcherbakov's company was to attack and capture the main Japanese defensive position in strong point Sharp.

In preparation for the assault, Shcherbakov and his officers and non-commissioned officers had spent all day on 8 August studying the terrain and

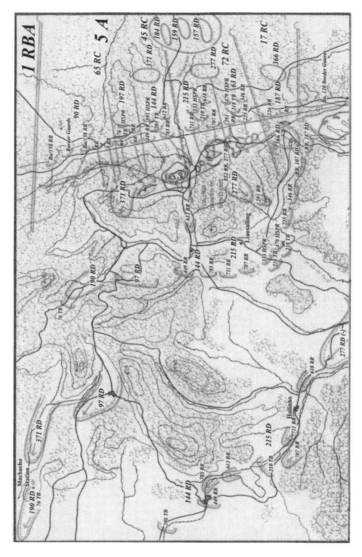

Map 5a. Soviet 5th Army Operations, 9–10 August 1945

28

Map 5b. Soviet 5th Army Operations, 9–10 August 1945

29

Japanese defenses and had worked out a plan for approaching and reducing the strong point. They determined that it would require two hours of painstaking movement to reach the strong point. Therefore, at 0100 hours on 9 August the company began its advance with a reconnaissance team advancing through the darkness, using a compass azimuth to guide its movement forward. As the reconnaissance team advanced, it laid telephone cable to guide the rifle platoon that followed in its wake, and the remaining platoons followed in column. Each soldier carried an automatic weapon with 300 rounds of ammunition, a knife, and 6–8 hand grenades, and the riflemen advanced linked hand-in-hand to avoid becoming lost in the darkness and rain.

At about 0300 hours, while sappers cut and marked lanes through the barbed wire and minefields protecting the approaches along its front slope, Shcherbakov's rifle company approached strong point Sharp and maneuvered to attack. By 0315 hours the rifle platoons of Shcherbakov's rifle company had surrounded the strong point, and the other companies of Moskalev's battalion were in position to assault Sharp. The coordinated assault began shortly after 0315 hours but without support from the self-propelled guns or tanks, whose movement forward had been delayed by the swampy terrain. Employing explosives, backpack flamethrowers, gasoline bottles, and hand grenades, the advanced battalion captured about half of the pillboxes and firing positions within strong point Sharp by 0500 hours.[25] At the same time, the advanced battalion of Gordienko's 63d Rifle Division had occupied strong point Officer, just south of strong point Sharp and was preparing the way for the division's main force to advance through the gap between strong points Sharp and Pear.[26]

Farther south, in the sector of Nikitin's 17th Rifle Corps, heavy fighting raged for control of the railroad tunnels east of Suifenho. An advanced battalion from Savin's 187th Rifle Division moved forward to seize the concrete blockhouses and defensive positions covering the tunnels. While the advanced battalion was conducting its assault, a battalion from the 20th Assault Engineer-Sapper Brigade cut lanes through minefields and, supported by tanks, attacked Japanese defensive positions at the end of the tunnel from the flank and rear. The 20th Assault Engineer-Sapper Brigade destroyed five pillboxes and enabled the advanced battalion to secure the rail tunnels by 0600 hours on 9 August.[27]

The initial attacks by the 5th Army's advanced battalions achieved their goal. By employing surprise, maneuver, and well-coordinated assaults, the battalions captured many of the most important Japanese strong points and gained footholds in those remaining intact. Their successful actions permitted the main forces of Krylov's army to advance as planned at 0830 hours on 9 August and advance on schedule through and beyond the Japanese fortified region. The advanced battalions' success also negated any further need for an extensive artillery preparation. Thereafter, direct fire from accompanying tanks and self-propelled guns and on-call artillery and aviation strikes supported the advance of the army's main force.

Krylov's sudden and violent night assault caught the Japanese totally by surprise. The attack's timing (at night), the appalling weather conditions (rain), and the rapid infiltration of Japanese defenses by Soviet assault groups utterly paralyzed the defenders and quickly severed vital enemy communications to and between most defensive sectors. Consequently, at best, Japanese commanders at all levels had only a fragmented and wholly inaccurate idea of the situation that they confronted.

The Japanese never recovered from this initial shock, and their paralysis and inability to respond effectively to Soviet attacks persisted throughout the remainder of the campaign. Underscoring the confusion that prevailed in Japanese ranks, the chief of staff of the Japanese 3d Army later reported to his captors that the Soviet offensive was such a surprise that, during the night of 8–9 August and up to 1200 hours on 9 August, the army staff did not know, and could not obtain, any news about what was happening along the border and where its units were located.[28]

General Shimizu, the Japanese 5th Army commander, received notification of the attack by phone shortly after 0100 hours on 9 August. The initial reports from the border sectors mentioned Soviet over-flights of the border region and some Soviet shelling of Japanese defensive positions at Hutou. Shimizu immediately reported these incidents to General Kita at the First Area Army and summoned his division commanders and their chiefs of staff to a meeting at 0300 hours in the Yehho Officers Club. Once assembled, Shimizu told his assembled officers that artillery shelling was under way and that 'an element of their Soviet infantry seems to have broken through the border'.[29] He then issued the following initial orders:

> The plan of the army for meeting the situation is that border elements will delay the advance of the attacking enemy by taking advantage of terrain and established border positions, while the main force will destroy the enemy's fighting power by putting up stubborn resistance in depth in our main defensive positions ...
>
> Elements of the 124th Infantry Division will occupy the established border positions at Lumintai, Suifenho, and Kuanyuehtai in an effort to stem the hostile advance, while the division's main force will immediately take up MLR [main line of resistance] positions west of Muleng and will destroy the enemy fighting power by opposing him in our defensive positions disposed in depth.[30]

Each division commander passed orders received from Shimizu telephonically to his staff and then departed Yehho for his headquarters. Shiina of the 124th Infantry Division traveled by car to Muleng, where he arrived near dawn shortly after a Soviet air attack on the city. Shiina went to his headquarters and issued initial orders to his divisional units. The division's main forces' regiments were to occupy their designated positions in the main line of resistance (MLR) and intercept and destroy advancing Soviet forces, and the garrisons in Suifenho and Kuanyuehtai were to delay the Soviet advance.

Shiina then sent Colonel Asu, the commander of the 271st Infantry Regiment, to Suiyang to supervise the evacuation of military stores, military personnel, and Japanese residents. Other orders issued by Shiina authorized the use of support personnel to augment tactical units on the Muleng defense line, mandated shipment of supplies forward from Mutanchiang depot, and instituted a demolition plan for bridges, roads, barracks, and government buildings.

After notifying the civil government of the attack and his intentions, Shiina ordered his headquarters to prepare defensive positions on Mount Ikkoko, west of the Muleng River.[31] Wherever possible, Shiina's orders were carried out, albeit in an uncoordinated and piecemeal fashion. For example, within the constraints of Shiina's demolition plan, several key bridges were destroyed prematurely, severely hindering the withdrawal of Japanese forces and equipment from the forward defensive area.

While the Japanese higher commands desperately attempted to cope with the frightening developments of 9 August, Meretskov and Krylov accelerated the Soviet offensive. While Krylov's advanced battalions completed the process of cutting corridors through the Japanese fortified defenses, his main forces began moving forward. The second echelon rifle divisions of his forward rifle corps began to detach forces to complete the reduction of isolated, but as yet unconquered, Japanese strong points. At 0930 hours, the advanced battalions of Stavtsev's 190th and Makar'ev's 97th Rifle Divisions in Perekrestov's 65th Rifle Corps attacked and destroyed the military settlements on the west slope of strong point Camel. An hour before, the main forces of Makar'ev's rifle division and Zorin's 144th Rifle Division had attacked past Camel into the operational depths of the Japanese defenses.

Immediately, Makar'ev and Zorin formed forward detachments, each consisting of a tank brigade, a heavy self-propelled artillery regiment, and a battalion or regiment of motorized infantry, and ordered them to spearhead their divisions' subsequent advance. By nightfall on 9 August, the forward detachment of Makar'ev's rifle division had advanced 12.4 miles (20 kilometers) via Jumonji Pass toward Machiacho Station and Zorin's forward detachment had raced forward 10 miles (16 kilometers) and reached Liaotsaiying. The second echelon forces of Perekrestov's 65th Rifle Corps continued to contain and destroy the remaining Japanese positions on strong point Camel.

South of the Volynka River, the advanced battalions of Kazartsev's 72d Rifle Corps continued to reduce Japanese strong points Sharp and Pear. By 1200 hours on 9 August, the forces of Kazarian's 215th Rifle Division had secured control of the Japanese military settlement on the western slopes of strong point Sharp and cut the vital military road running north and south 3.1 miles (5 kilometers) inside the Manchurian border. The advanced battalion of Gordienko's 63d Rifle Division also continued its assault against strong point Pear.

Meanwhile, the forward detachment of Kazarian's rifle division, which consisted of Krasnoshtin's 210th Tank Brigade and the 333d Heavy Self-propelled Artillery Regiment with infantry support, exploited the advanced battalions' success by advancing westward toward Suiyang at 1500 hours on 9 August. Another forward detachment, formed around the nucleus of Velichko's 218th Tank Brigade and the 479th Heavy Self-propelled Artillery Regiment, led the advance of Gordienko's rifle division on a route parallel to but south of Kazarian's forward detachment.

By day's end on 9 August, the forward detachments of Perekrestov's rifle corps had pushed 9.3–11 miles (15–18 kilometers) deep into the Japanese rear area. While the forward detachments began the exploitation, Perekrestov tasked the 862d Rifle Regiment of Gladyshev's 277th Rifle Division in his corps' second echelon with reducing the remaining Japanese positions in strong point Sharp.[32]

Thus, by nightfall on 9 August, the lead elements of Krylov's 5th Army had thrust 10–13.7 miles (16–22 kilometers) into the Japanese rear area on a front of 22 miles (35 kilometers). By doing so, his forces had accomplished in a single day missions that his forces were supposed to achieve by the second and third days of the attack. By thoroughly disrupting the timing of Japanese contingency plans, the speed of his advance had the effect of totally pre-empting all effective Japanese resistance. Worse still for the Japanese, Krylov's forward detachments maintained the momentum of his advance. Meanwhile, to the rear, his second echelon forces undertook the arduous and sometimes gruesome task of reducing remaining Japanese strong points, which often held out to the last man. Supported by the direct fire of heavy self-propelled guns (152 mm), infantry companies and sappers used high explosives and flamethrowers to reduce each Japanese position, a three-day process.

Meretskov announced Krylov's success in an operational report he sent to Vasilevsky at 0300 hours on 10 August:

The 5th Army reached the line of the eastern slopes and main passes of the Huanvotshilin (Hsinhoilin) mountain range, Fantsi (former Kitai Bazar), Laoitsin (inclusive), and Huanfyntai (border post) with its first echelon (two rifle regiments from the first echelon rifle divisions). The army captured the strongly fortified Volynsk center of resistance in the Pogranichnaia Fortified Region and seized trophies (guns, ammunition, warehouses, and prisoners).

In the Pogranichnaia region, the 5th Army's 105th Fortified Region captured three railroad tunnels and penetrated into Pogranichnaia from the east and southeast, capturing Pogranichnaia Station and fighting in the center of Pogranichnaia.[33]

The Japanese higher commands tried frantically but with little effect to restore their defensive positions and establish new defenses on 9 August. That afternoon Japanese Imperial General Headquarters issued an emergency order to commanders in all theaters that read, 'The Soviet Union declared war on Japan and launched attacks at several places along the Soviet–Japanese and Soviet–Manchukuoan border at 0000 hours 9 August. However, the scale of these attacks is not large.'[34]

The initial Kwantung Army estimate of the deteriorating situation, which it issued that evening, echoed the totally unrealistic tone of the Imperial General Headquarters order: 'The main force of the enemy on the eastern border [is] attacking between Pingyangchen and Tungning ... [The estimated force is] three infantry divisions and between two and three armored brigades.'[35] In reality, at that precise time, 15 Soviet rifle divisions and eight tank brigades were assaulting the already shattered Japanese defensive positions in that sector. Soon after, the Japanese First Area Army command finally acknowledged that Soviet forces had broken through the border defenses at Suifenho and Kuanyuehtai in the 124th Infantry Division's sector and at Jumonji Pass near the divisional boundary of the 124th and 126th Infantry Divisions.[36] Soviet armor, said the report, also threatened the Suifenho–Mutanchiang railroad and highway. In turn, Shimizu's 5th Army ordered its units to take up planned defensive positions and, on the afternoon of 9 August, reinforced Shiina's 124th Infantry Division with two battalions from Hitomi's 135th Infantry Division (see Map 6).

In the 124th Infantry Division's sector, Colonel Asu, the commander of the division's 271st Regiment, arrived in Suiyang at 1200 hours and proceeded to evacuate supplies and personnel. He organized a convoy of trucks that left that evening and arrived the next day at the Muleng River. His convoy, however, was unable to cross the river because the bridge had been destroyed in accordance with General Shiina's demolition plan. The Japanese appeared to be working at cross-purposes. A subsequent attempt by Asu to move the vehicles across the river by fording and ferrying failed. Hard pressed by advancing Soviet units, Asu's troops escaped down the river, leaving most of the irreplaceable equipment behind. The abandoned equipment included several new Model 90 75 mm howitzers sorely needed by the division for fire support.[37]

A similar instance of rapidly decaying Japanese command and control occurred elsewhere in the 124th Infantry Division sector. At about midday on 9 August, Shimizu at the 5th Army assigned the Mutanchiang Heavy Artillery Regiment to the control of Shiina's 124th Infantry Division. However, the artillery unit, which was situated at Hsiachengtzu, had no tractors with

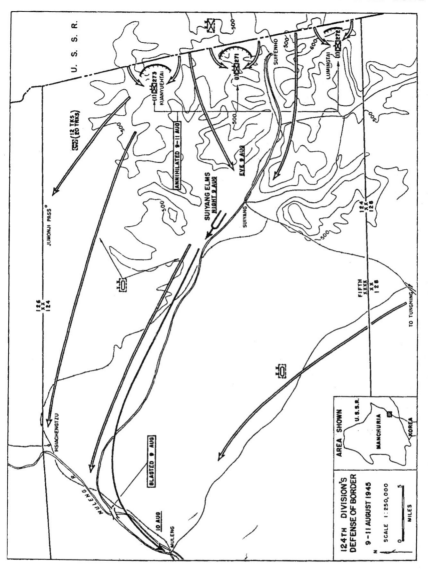

Map 6. Japanese 124th Infantry Division Defense of the Border, 9–11 August 1945

which to move its guns. Therefore, to prevent them from falling into Soviet hands, the Japanese had to destroy all six of the valuable howitzers. While the chaotic evacuation of Japanese rear service soldiers and civilians from the forward area continued at 1400 hours on 9 August, Shiina and a portion of his staff moved to new defensive positions west of the Muleng River. Reports to his headquarters on the evening of 9 August indicated that heavy fighting was taking place along the border but that Japanese morale was still high.[38]

Soviet forces capitalized on the confusion in Japanese ranks early on 10 August by beginning a rapid exploitation into the depths of the Japanese defense. Perekrestov's 65th Rifle Corps advanced across the Taipingling Mountains along two axes, through the Jumonji Pass in the north and along the main rail line in the south, to converge on Machiacho Station. At the same time, Kazartsev's 72d Rifle Corps marched through Suiyang, ordering Gordienko's 63d Rifle Division to make a wide sweep south and west toward Muleng and sending Kazarian's and Gladyshev's 215th and 277th Rifle Divisions along the rail line toward Machiacho in the wake of the 65th Rifle Corps' 144th Rifle Division.

Meanwhile, Nikitin's 17th Rifle Corps advanced southward into the rear of the Suifenho Fortified Region where it was to link up with elements of Chistiakov's 25th Army and complete the encirclement of the Tungning Fortified Region. Forward detachments, operating 6.2–9.3 miles (10–15 kilometers) ahead of their parent main forces, led the advance of all of Krylov's rifle corps along virtually every trafficable axis of advance.

This rapid Soviet advance preempted any and all Japanese efforts to establish new intermediate defense lines or withdraw in good order to planned defensive positions in the rear. In the wake of Krylov's advancing forward detachments, the lead rifle regiments of his three rifle corps' rifle divisions followed and systematically liquidated isolated or encircled Japanese defenders. By the evening of 10 August, Krylov's 5th Army had utterly shattered Japanese border defenses across a front of 47 miles (75 kilometers) and had advanced 11–19 miles (18–30 kilometers) into the interior of Manchuria. By the morning of the next day, Krylov's dogged forward detachments were 50 miles (80 kilometers) deep and across the Muleng River, forcing the Japanese to fall back into defenses in the mountains west of Muleng. On the evening of the same day, the Far East Command announced that Soviet forces had snuffed out the last remnants of Japanese resistance in the Border Fortified Region.

CONCLUSIONS

In the initial period of its offensive, Krylov's 5th Army crushed Japanese resistance in the Border Fortified Region and lunged 50 miles (80 kilometers) into eastern Manchuria during an astonishingly brief period of only of two and one-half days. Thorough Soviet planning, precise coordination, and near total surprise stunned the Japanese defenders and left them paralyzed and unable to react effectively to the sudden blow. Within about 60 hours, Krylov's forces bypassed, neutralized, isolated, or destroyed fortified defenses along the border upon which the coherence of the Kwantung Army's defense plans depended and did so at a minimum cost in Soviet Army manpower.

Led by strong and audacious forward detachments, the rapid Soviet advance through and beyond the fortified region generated sufficient offensive momentum to carry Soviet forces to the banks of the Muleng River virtually unimpeded before the Japanese were fully aware of the gravity of the situation. Japanese commanders failed to react to the Soviet assault in timely fashion. Only on 11 August was the 5th Army able to establish a new defensive line in the mountains west of Muleng. The new defenses, however, were manned by troops who were severely shaken, disorganized, and demoralized by the catastrophes that had befallen them during the previous two days. For example, Shiina's 124th Infantry Division lost three maneuver battalions and a major portion of its equipment during the fighting along the border and its hasty retreat to new defensive positions.

The performance of Krylov's 5th Army clearly exceeded even Vasilevsky's expectation. In 60 hours Krylov's forces had fulfilled missions that Vasilevsky's offensive timetable had expected the army to take eight days to achieve. The army accomplished this feat by meticulous and secret operational planning, well-coordinated and time-phased application of combat power, effective organization for combat, and imaginative exploitation of difficult terrain.

The Far East Command and 5th Army's meticulous planning within a suffocating cloak of secrecy guaranteed the offensive caught the Japanese totally by surprise. The timed application of combat power through the sequential employment of assault groups, advanced battalions, echeloned rifle regiments, rifle divisions, and rifle corps and forward detachments imparted an initial momentum to the attack that the army was able to sustain all the way to Mutanchiang. The employment of forces carefully tailored to suit their combat mission contributed to the rapid Soviet success with only minimal casualties and material losses. The assault groups relied on maneuver, the firepower of tanks and self-propelled guns, and the engineer skills of sappers to avoid costly frontal assaults. The specially tailored advanced battalions and forward detachments overcame 'inhibiting' terrain and confounded the Japanese, who, until disaster stared them directly in the face, remained convinced that no army could penetrate such 'impassable' terrain.

In short, Krylov's forces surprised the Japanese regarding the timing, location, manner, and strength of their attacks. The success his army achieved on 9 and 10 August was a measure of that surprise. With this success in hand, on 11 August Krylov's army continued its rapid advance westward toward Mutanchiang.

NOTES

1. V. A. Zolotarev, ed., *Russkii arkhiv: Sovetsko–iaponskaia voina 1945 goda: Istoriia voenno-politicheskogo protivoborstva dvukh derzhav v 30-40-e gody: Dokumenty i materially v 2 t.*, T. 18 (7-1) [The Russian archives: The Soviet–Japanese War of 1945: A military-political history of the struggle between two powers in the 30s and 40s: Documents and materials in two volumes, Vol. 18 (7-1)] (Moscow: 'Terra', 1997), 333. See also, *Istoriia vtoroi mirovoi voiny 1939–1945* [A history of the Second World War 1939–1945], 2 vols (Moscow: Voenizdat, 1980), 2:199–200 (hereafter cited as *IVMV*).

2. L. N. Vnotchenko, *Pobeda na dal'nem vostoke: Voenno-istoricheskii ocherk o boevykh deistviiakh Sovetskikh v avguste–sentiabre 1945 g.* [Victory in the Far East: A military-historical survey about the operations of Soviet forces in August–September 1945] (Moscow: Voenizdat, 1971), 96–8. The 1st Far Eastern Front commander explains his mission in K. A. Meretskov, *Serving the People* (Moscow: Progress Publishers, 1971), 344–6.

3. N. I. Krylov, N. I. Alekseev, and I. G. Dragan, *Navstrechu pobede: Boevoi put 5-i armii, oktiabr 1941g–avgust 1945g.* [Toward victory: The combat path of the 5th Army, October 1941–August 1945] (Moscow: 'Nauka', 1970), 423. For details on the Japanese defenses, see also 'Proryv Volynskogo ukreplennogo raiona 72-m strelkovym korpusom (po materialam 1-go Dal'nevostochnogo fronta)' [The penetration of the Volynsk fortified region by the 72d Rifle Corps (based on materials from the 1st Far Eastern Front)] in *Sbornik takticheskikh primereov po opytu Otechestvennoi voiny*, No. 21 (iiul'–avgust 1946 g.) [Collection of tactical examples based on the experiences of the Patriotic War, No. 21 (July–August 1946)] (Moscow: Voenizdat, 1947), 61–3. Prepared by the Directorate for the Study of War Experience of the General Staff and classified secret. Hereafter cited as 'Proryv'.

4. Japanese border fortifications are described in 'Small Wars and Border Problems', *Japanese Studies on Manchuria*, Vol. 11, Pt. 2 (Tokyo: Military History Section, US Army Forces, Far East, 1956).

5. Vnotchenko, *Pobeda*, 52–4, and 'Proryv', 62–3.

6. 'Record of Operations Against Soviet Army on Eastern Front (August 1945)', *Japanese Monograph No. 154* (Tokyo: Military History Section, US Army Forces Far East, 1954), 225–32. Hereafter cited as *JM 154*.

7. 'Proryv', 63.

8. *JM 154*, 181–3 and 226–8.

9. For further details, see, P. Tsygankov, 'Nekotorye osobennosti boevykh deistvii 5-i armii v Kharbino–Girinskoi operatsii' [Some characteristics of the 5th Army's combat operations during the Harbin–Kirin operation], *Voenno-istoricheskii zhurnal* [Military-historical journal], No. 8 (August 1975), 83. Hereafter cited as *VIZh* with appropriate number and page. Originally, the 5th Army had five tank brigades, six self-propelled artillery regiments, and 12 separate self-propelled artillery battalions, for a total of 692 tanks and self-propelled guns. See V. Ezhakov, 'Boevoe primenenie tankov v gorno-taezhnoi mestnosti po opytu 1-go Dal'nevostochnogo fronta' [The combat employment of tanks in mountainous-taiga regions based on the experience of the 1st Far Eastern Front], *VIZh*, No. 1 (January 1974), 78. Before the operation began, the 1st Far Eastern Front transferred one of these brigades (the 72d Tank Brigade) to the 25th Army, thus reducing the 5th Army's tank and self-propelled gun strength to 607. See also I. E. Krupchenko, ed., *Sovetskie tankovie voiska 1941–45* [Soviet tank forces, 1941–45] (Moscow: Voenizdat, 1973), 323, and Krylov, *Navstrechu*, 427.

10. Vnotchenko, *Pobeda*, 116–17.
11. Krylov, *Navstrechu*, 425, and Vnotchenko, *Pobeda*, 79–80.
12. Krylov, *Navstrechu*, 429–30. Details on engineer support of 5th Army forward deployment are covered in A. F. Khrenov, 'Wartime Operations: Engineer Operations in the Far East', *USSR Report: Military Affairs No. 1545* (21 November 1980): 81–97, JPRS 76847, translated by the Foreign Broadcast Information Services from the Russian article in *Znamia* [Banner], August 1980.
13. Krylov, *Navstrechu*, 430–2, and Meretskov, *Serving the People*, 334.
14. Tsygankov, 'Nekotorye', 84; Krylov, *Navstrechu*, 428–30; and Vnotchenko, *Pobeda*, 101–2. All three sources relate the combat missions of all 5th Army rifle corps.
15. See 'Proryv', 64; Vnotchenko, *Pobeda*, 102; and Krylov, *Navstrechu*, 436–7.
16. 'Proryv', 65.
17. Vnotchenko, *Pobeda*, 103, and 'Proryv', 65.
18. The original 5th Army artillery fire plans are found in Vnotchenko, *Pobeda*, 106; Tsygankov, 'Nekotorye', 84; and Krylov, *Navstrechu*, 433–4. The full scope of artillery support of 5th Army is described in M. Sidorov, 'Boevoe primenenie artillerii' [The combat use of artillery], *VIZh*, No. 9 (September 1975), 15–17.
19. Vnotchenko, *Pobeda*, 115–17.
20. For the varying explanations as to why an artillery preparation was not fired, see Krylov, *Navstrechu*, 433–5; Vnotchenko, *Pobeda*, 108; and Meretskov, *Serving the People*, 350.
21. Ezhakov, 'Boevoe primenenie', 78, credits the 10th Mechanized Corps with 371 tanks and self-propelled guns. Vnotchenko, *Pobeda*, 95, gives the corps' strength as 249 tanks and self-propelled guns. The difference reflects reassignment of one tank brigade and one self-propelled artillery battalion from the 5th Army to the 25th Army and the 10th Mechanized Corps.
22. Tsygankov, 'Nekotorye', 86.
23. See *JM 154*, 230.
24. V. Pavlov, 'In the Hills of Manchuria', *Voennyi vestnik* [Military herald], No. 9 (August 1975), 30–2, translated into English by the Office of the Assistant Chief of Staff, Intelligence, US Department of the Army; Krylov, *Navstrechu*, 436; and Vnotchenko, *Pobeda*, 208.
25. Krylov, *Navstrechu*, 437–8, and Vnotchenko, *Pobeda*, 200–2.
26. For additional details on the 72d Rifle Corps assault, see 'Proryv', 68–9.
27. For additional details on the tunnel fight, see Khrenov, 'Wartime Operations', 89; Krylov, *Navstrechu*, 438; and Vnotchenko, *Pobeda*, 209.
28. Vnotchenko, *Pobeda*, 199.
29. *JM 154*, 59, 181.
30. Ibid., 181–2.
31. Ibid., 233–4.
32. Krylov, *Navstrechu*, 440–1; Tsygankov, 'Nekotorye', 86–8; Vnotchenko, *Pobeda*, 208–11.
33. Zolotarev, *Russkii arkhiv*, 18 (7-1), 333.
34. *JM 154*, 6.
35. Ibid., 8–9.
36. Ibid., 60–1.
37. Ibid., 185–6.
38. Ibid., 234.

2

The 1st Red Banner Army's Advance to Pamientung: Operations in Heavily Wooded Mountains

TERRAIN

The most rugged terrain sector that the 1st Far Eastern Front's forces had to negotiate when they launched their offensive into eastern Manchuria was the mountainous and heavily forested region along and west of the Soviet–Manchurian border extending northward from Suifenho to the northwestern shore of Lake Khanka (see Maps 3 and 4a and b). The only portion of this region where the terrain was suitable for conducting military operations was in the extreme north, where a 25-mile (40-kilometer) sector of open and rolling hills cut by occasional gulleys and streams extended from the northwestern shore of Lake Khanka southwestward to the eastern end of the Pogranichnaia [Border] Mountains. Although this sector contained several dirt roads, they ran northward from the town of Khorol in the Far East Province past the western shore of Lake Khanka to Mishan and not into central Manchuria. Therefore, from a military standpoint this axis was suitable only for a secondary attack.

West of this narrow corridor adjacent to the western shore of Lake Khanka, a chain of low mountains called the Pogranichnaia Mountains rises sharply from the plain. Anchored in the east on heights named Gora Propast' [Mount Precipice], these mountains, which are covered by dense forest and brush and rise in places to heights of almost 3,280 feet (1,000 meters), extend 50 miles (80 kilometers) southwestward along the border to a point 22 miles (35 kilometers) east of the town of Pamientung. The mountains then turn southward toward the region west of Suifenho and Tungning, where they merge into another series of broad mountain ranges, including the Taipingling Mountains, that extend southward east of Mutanchiang to the Wangching region, where they connect to the even higher craggy peaks of mountain ranges along the northern Korean border.

The only axis of advance suitable for military forces to conduct operations through this mountain barrier was the narrow north–south corridor west of Lake Khanka and the narrow corridors extending from east to west through Suifenho to Mutanchiang and through Tungning southwestward through Lotzukou to Wangching. Therefore, when Meretskov began formulating the 1st Far Eastern Front's plan for the invasion of eastern Manchuria, his most daunting task was determining how he could employ three of his four armies most effectively in the operational sector south of Lake Khanka that contained only two feasible axes of advance. His imaginative decision was to employ two of these armies, Krylov's 5th and Chistiakov's 25th on the more suitable Suifenho and Tungning axes, and his third army, Beloborodov's 1st Red Banner, to conduct a supporting attack along an axis that Japanese planners considered utterly unsuitable for the conduct of military operations, namely, directly across the mountainous salient where the Pogranichnaia Mountains made their southward turn.

MISSIONS AND OBJECTIVES

After formulating his operational plan, Meretskov ordered Colonel General A. P. Beloborodov, the commander of the 1st Red Banner Army, to deploy his army in the gap between Krylov's 5th Army, which was to conduct the *front's* main attack south of Lake Khanka, and Zakhvataev's 35th Army, which was to attack north of the lake. Krylov's mission was to attack westward along the Suifenho axis to overcome the Japanese fortified region along the border, and Zakhvataev's 35th Army was to attack westward in the sector north of Lake Khanka against the Japanese fortified regions at Hutou and Mishan. In between, Beloborodov's army was to launch a secondary attack to surprise the Japanese, penetrate through the mountain barrier along and west of the border and, ultimately, support Krylov's advance to Mutanchiang and Zakhvataev's operations against Mishan. This was no mean task.

From the very start of planning, it was clear to Beloborodov that the chief obstacle his forces faced was the forbidding terrain to his front rather than any prospective Japanese armed resistance. In his own words:

As former Far Easterners, the particular features of the terrain over which we were to advance were generally known to us, since the taiga [brushy forests] was the same on both sides of the frontier. Mountain ranges with elevations of up to 1000 meters separated the Soviet Maritime provinces from the central Manchurian plain like a barrier. The mountains were solidly covered with virgin forests of large oaks, cedar, pine, linden and birch, all overgrown with liana and wild grape alternating with creeping brush and underbrush. Thickets filled the spaces between trees, covering the ground like carpets with spines as long as one's finger and strong and sharp as a sewing needle. For an inexperienced person, in a literal sense, these naturally created obstacles could strip a person within several minutes, cutting into your flesh and piercing the thick soles of your footwear. Here it would have been difficult even for experienced infantry. Along the foothills, narrow and also overgrown valleys, which were called ravines or creek valleys, stretched for many kilometers. Through them flowed streams and creeks that were so swampy that even tanks as powerful and maneuverable as the T-34s became stuck. These swamps were not only located in the low-lying areas but also on the hills. If you fought your way to the top of a hill you would become stuck in weak crumbling and wet dirt. These were the particular features of the mountain taiga in his region.[1]

On 8 July 1945, Meretskov ordered Beloborodov's 1st Red Banner Army to conduct the *front's* main attack due west from the border across the mountainous terrain of the southern sector of the Pogranichnaia Mountains toward Pamientung in close concert with Krylov's 5th Army, which was to attack westward in the more favorable terrain sector to the south. Beloborodov's forces were to penetrate to a depth of 19 miles (30 kilometers) by the end of the third day of operations, and while doing so, to clear Japanese forces from the mountainous taiga region west of the border. Once through the formidable terrain barrier along the border, the 1st Red Banner Army was to employ strong mobile forces to capture Pamientung and the city of Linkou by the eighth day of the operation. Subsequently, Beloborodov was to wheel the bulk of his forces southwestward and reach the Mutan River north of Mutanchiang by the end of the eighteenth day of the operation, where his forces were to cooperate with Krylov's 5th Army in the capture of Mutanchiang.

Simultaneously, smaller forces on the 1st Red Banner Army's right wing were to attack northward along the western shore of Lake Khanka against the southern flank of the Japanese Mishan Fortified Region and assist the 35th Army in overcoming that major Japanese defensive region.[2]

Indicative of the difficult terrain he was being ordered to traverse, Meretskov ordered the 1st Red Banner Army to advance to a total depth of 93–112 miles (150–180 kilometers) in a period of 18 days, for an average rate of advance of 5–6 miles (8–10 kilometers) per day, while Soviet regulations expected rates of advance of up to 62 miles (100 kilometers) per day in favorable terrain. In a terrain sense, the most difficult period for Beloborodov's forces would be during their initial advance through the 11–12.4 miles (18–20 kilometers) of heavily forested mountains located immediately west of the border. Although this region was sparsely populated and had only a few mountain huts scattered along forest tracks, the Japanese had constructed a few border outposts in the area, which were connected to one another by 'mountain paths through which it would be difficult for even two persons to pass'.

As Beloborodov recalled, 'We were to move through this region ... with six rifle and antiaircraft artillery divisions, more than 400 tanks and self-propelled guns, a heavy artillery brigade, two combat engineer brigades and thousands of motor vehicles with cargo.'[3] As for the Japanese, they had left this sector lightly defended, scarcely suspecting that any force beyond light infantry could traverse it.

JAPANESE DEFENSES

Lieutenant General Nomizo Kazuhiko's 126th Infantry Division, whose headquarters was at Pamientung, was responsible for defending the border sector along the Pogranichnaia Mountains (see Map 7). Nomizo's division, which was subordinate to Shimizu's 5th Army, anchored the left flank of 5th Army's defenses between Suifenho and Lake Khanka. The 126th Infantry Division's defensive posture mirrored that of Shiina's 124th Infantry Division in that its defense consisted of a series of defensive positions and lines extending from the immediate border region westward to a depth of 50–62 miles (80–100 kilometers). The division's forward defenses were located along a 75-mile (120-kilometer) long line extending north and south of Pamientung, 19–22 (30–35 kilometers) west of the border, although the division maintained a few smaller defensive outposts and observation posts along the border proper.

The 126th Infantry Division's forward defenses formed two distinct sectors, the first protecting the approaches to the town of Pingyang, which was situated 50 miles (80 kilometers) northeast of Pamientung, and the second at Pamientung proper. Even heavier defenses, extending 43 miles (70 kilometers) from the village of Shangchihtun, north of Gora Propast', to the village of Hsiaolutai, protected the sector the Japanese considered the most likely secondary avenue of operations along which Soviet forces could invade Manchuria. This line tied in with the southernmost defenses of the 135th Infantry Division at Mishan. Farther to the southwest was a second defensive line covering the approaches to Pamientung. This defensive line ran 25 miles (40 kilometers) from the village of Chingkulingmiao to the Jumonji Pass, across a sector the Japanese considered too rough and heavily wooded for major operations and, consequently, in need of only light defenses.

The Pingyang defense sector contained important field fortifications around or near the villages of Shangchihtun, Panchiehho, Nanshan, and Hsiaolutai, together with smaller forward outposts. Although the 126th Infantry Division's defense plan called for one to two battalions of infantry to defend each of

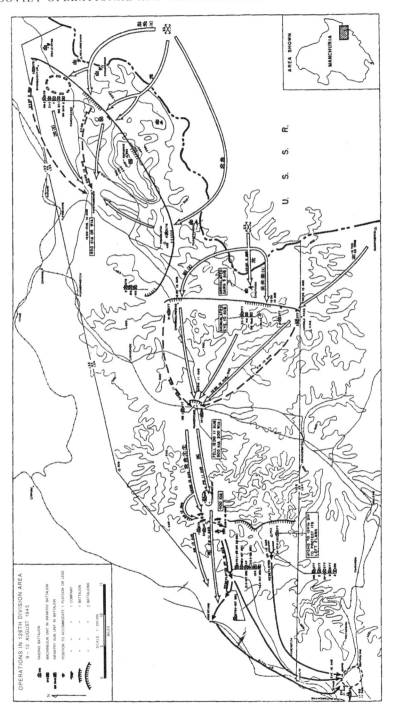

Map 7. Operations in the Japanese 126th Infantry Division Area, 9–12 August 1945

these fortified positions, on 9 August only platoon- or company-size units garrisoned each one. To the south, the Pamientung defensive line consisted of fortified positions at Chingkulingmiao, Lishan, and Jumonji Pass, each of which was manned by a platoon to company-size force, with advanced outposts on the border.[4]

The mission of Japanese forces manning the Pingyang defensive sector was to delay the enemy for as long as possible in front of their forward defensive positions and then conduct a fighting withdrawal through Pingyang and Lishuchen to other defensive positions to the rear. The garrison unit stationed at Hsiaolutai, together with separate outposts along the border, had the unrealistic mission of defending that position 'to the last man'.[5] The Japanese forces manning the Pamientung defensive sector were to defend their positions and, if the positions fell, were expected to conduct guerrilla warfare in the enemy's rear. Any withdrawing Japanese forces were to destroy all roads, tracks, bridges, and barracks so as to slow the enemy advance.

An intermediate Japanese defensive line located just east of the cities of Pamientung and Lishuchen covered the approaches to the vital bridges across the Muleng River. A third defensive line, located near Tzuhsingtun, west of Pamientung, extended from north to south through the hills between Mutanchiang and Pamientung. Here the 126th, 135th, and 124th Infantry Divisions were to occupy prepared field positions to present a solid defensive front against any enemy forces advancing against Mutanchiang from the northeast or east in the event the border defenses failed.

On 9 August the 126th Infantry Division consisted of the following units and subunits deployed in the following locations (see Tables 3 and 4):

TABLE 3: JAPANESE 126TH INFANTRY DIVISION COMPOSITION, 9 AUGUST 1945

277th Infantry Regiment
278th Infantry Regiment
279th Infantry Regiment
126th Field Artillery Regiment
126th Engineer Battalion
126th Transport Regiment
126th Signal Unit
Raiding battalion
20th Heavy Field Artillery Regiment (1 battery)
31st Independent Antitank Battalion (1 battery)

Source: 'Record of Operations Against Soviet Army on Eastern Front (August 1945)', *Japanese Monograph No. 154* (Tokyo: Military History Section, US Army Forces Far East, 1954), 246–7.

TABLE 4: JAPANESE 126TH INFANTRY DIVISION DEFENSIVE
DISPOSITIONS, 9 AUGUST 1945

Location	*Strength*
Pingyang Sector	
Shangchihtun	1 platoon
Erhjenpan	1 squad
Panchiehho	1 battalion (–) (2d Battalion, 278th Infantry Regiment)
Nanshan	1 platoon
Hsiaolutai	1 company
Hsiangchushan	1 company (reinforced by two machine gun platoons)
Pamientung Sector	
Chingkulingmiao	1 company
Lishan	1 company (reinforced by one machine-gun platoon and a regimental gun)
Chiupikou	1 squad
Jumonji Pass	1 platoon
Pamientung	2 companies, 1 company of the raiding battalion (1st Battalion, 277th Infantry Regiment)

Source: 'Record of Operations Against Soviet Army on Eastern Front (August 1945)', *Japanese Monograph No. 154* (Tokyo: Military History Section, US Army Forces Far East, 1954), 247, 250–3.

Of this overall force, approximately two infantry battalions defended the positions along the border, an infantry battalion and company from the 278th Infantry Regiment occupied defenses at Pingyang, and a battalion (minus one company) from the 277th Infantry Regiment defended the Pamientung sector.

On the eve of the Soviet attack, the division commander, Nomizo, was attending the 5th Army's commanders' conference at Yehho, and while much of the division's staff was at Pamientung, many of its troops were well to the rear working to construct field fortifications in the Tzuhsingtun region. Thus, the division trusted the small forces it had deployed forward to take maximum advantage of the difficult terrain to buy time necessary for the division to deploy into more credible defensive positions to the rear. The main question that remained unanswered was whether or not Soviet forces would permit these small forces to accomplish their ambitious mission.

1ST RED BANNER ARMY OPERATIONAL PLANNING

After receiving his orders from Meretskov on 8 July, Beloborodov began planning his army's offensive. The most formidable problem Beloborodov faced was that of conducting deep operations at a relatively high rate of advance with so large a force over very restrictive terrain. On 9 August, Beloborodov's army consisted of two rifle corps of three rifle divisions each, three tank brigades, two fortified regions, and a sizeable array of supporting forces (see Table 5).

TABLE 5: SOVIET 1ST RED BANNER ARMY COMPOSITION, 9 AUGUST 1945

1st Red Banner Army – Colonel General A. P. Beloborodov
26th Rifle Corps: Major General A. V. Skvortsov
22d Rifle Division: Major General N. K. Svirs
59th Rifle Division: Major General M. S. Batrakov
300th Rifle Division: Major General K. G. Cherepanov
59th Rifle Corps: Major General V. A. Semenov
39th Rifle Division: Colonel D. V. Makarov
231st Rifle Division: Major General Ia. E. Timoshenko
365th Rifle Division: Colonel M. K. Gvozdikov
6th Fortified Region
112th Fortified Region
75th Tank Brigade: Lieutenant Colonel L. D. Krupetskoi
77th Tank Brigade: Colonel I. F. Morozov
257th Tank Brigade: Colonel G. S. Anishchik
48th Separate Tank Regiment
335th Guards Self-propelled Artillery Regiment
338th Guards Self-propelled Artillery Regiment
339th Guards Self-propelled Artillery Regiment
213th Gun Artillery Brigade
216th Corps Artillery Brigade
217th Corps Artillery Brigade
60th Antitank (Tank Destroyer) Artillery Brigade
52d Mortar Brigade
33d Guards–Mortar Regiment
54th Guards–Mortar Regiment
33d Antiaircraft Artillery Division
1378th Antiaircraft Artillery Regiment
1710th Antiaircraft Artillery Regiment
1715th Antiaircraft Artillery Regiment
1718th Antiaircraft Artillery Regiment
115th Separate Antiaircraft Artillery Battalion
455th Separate Antiaircraft Artillery Battalion
721st Separate Antiaircraft Artillery Battalion
12th Engineer-Sapper Brigade
27th Engineer-Sapper Brigade
Weapons:
402 tanks and self-propelled guns

Source: M. V. Zakharov, ed., *Final: istoriko-memuarny ocherk o razgrome imperialisticheskoi iapony v 1945 godu* [Finale: A historical memoir-survey about the rout of imperialistic Japan in 1945] (Moscow: 'Nauka', 1969), 401.

The total absence of roads in the sector of Beloborodov's army meant that his forces would have to build and maintain their own roads if they were to make their way across the almost 20 miles (32 kilometers) of forested wasteland between the border and the relatively open country east of Pamientung. Yet even makeshift roads constructed by engineers and sappers could transport only a limited force before the very weight of traffic and follow-on heavy weaponry rendered them impassable for necessary supply columns.

Therefore, instead of deeply echeloning his forces to attack over a limited number of axes of advance, Beloborodov decided to form his army in a single echelon attack formation spread out to encompass many axes of advance. By doing so, however, the army commander consciously ran the risk of small and scattered Japanese forces using the difficult terrain to slow or stop his multiple, but dispersed and therefore weakened, advancing columns. To address and reduce that danger, Beloborodov carefully task organized his forces, particularly his tank and attached engineer forces, so that he generate and sustain a steady advance.

On 12 July Beloborodov visited the Maritime Group of Forces, which was headquartered at Voroshilov-Ussuriisk, to try to convince Meretskov of the correctness and feasibility of his offensive plan. Meretskov's previous instructions to the 1st Red Banner Army commander had specifically directed him to deploy his forces in two echelons with three rifle divisions forward to lead the advance. Beloborodov, however, argued for a single echelon attack configuration with four rifle divisions leading the attack; apparently convincingly, since Meretskov eventually approved his plan.[5]

Two days after the 1st Red Banner Army's forces had completed their movement into their assembly areas, on 24 July Beloborodov issued combat orders to his subordinate forces.[7] He ordered the 112th Fortified Region and the 6th Field Fortified Region, each of which consisted of five machine gun and machine gun-artillery battalions, to deploy on his army's extreme right flank between the western shore of Lake Khanka and the eastern end of the Pogranichnaia Mountains opposite the Japanese Mishan Fortified Region.[8] The two fortified regions, which had operated in this sector for some time and were familiar with the terrain, were to protect the army's right flank, prevent a Japanese counterattack southward from Mishan along the west shore of Lake Khanka, and, if the occasion arose, conduct limited offensive operations in support of the army's main thrust.

To the west, in the mountain mass facing the Japanese Pingyang defenses, Beloborodov deployed the 397th Rifle Regiment of the 59th Rifle Corps' 231st Rifle Division and assigned to it a defensive mission similar to those he gave to the two fortified regions. Lieutenant General A. M. Maksimov, Beloborodov's deputy, was responsible for controlling operations along the broad 75-mile (120-kilometer) front on the 1st Red Banner Army's right wing. Beloborodov reinforced Maksimov's force with two heavy self-propelled artillery regiments to form an antitank reserve and the 60th Antitank (Tank Destroyer) Artillery Brigade.

Beloborodov planned to launch the 1st Red Banner Army's main attack in a narrow 10-mile (16-kilometer) sector on the army's left flank with the concentrated forces of Skvortsov's 26th and Semenov's 59th Rifle Corps, each with two rifle divisions abreast in the first echelon. The two rifle corps were to penetrate Japanese defenses along the border, overcome the heavily forested and mountainous zone west of the border, and advance simultaneously along two axes toward Pamientung and Lishuchen to capture these important rail and dirt road junctions on the Muleng River. Thereafter, the two rifle corps were to advance along widely divergent axes to capture Linkou and the northern approach to Mutanchiang in three distinct phases:

- Phase 1 – four to five days to capture Muleng, Lishuchen, and Linkou,
- Phase 2 – six to eight days to reach the northern outskirts of Mutanchiang, and
- Phase 3 – four to six days to defeat and destroy Japanese forces at Mishan and Mutanchiang in cooperation with the 35th and 5th Armies.

After completing his initial planning, Beloborodov then considered the vital matter of providing requisite fire, engineer, and logistical support for the offensive. Organizing continuous artillery support throughout the entire duration of the attack was particularly vexing because of the impenetrable terrain and the lack of roads and tracks on the Soviet side of the border along which artillery could deploy forward. Just bringing the artillery into its initial firing positions across the rugged terrain was a tremendously daunting challenge. This factor, plus the thin Japanese defenses in the region, led Beloborodov to plan no preparatory artillery fire.[9] Nevertheless, by late evening on the night prior to his assault, 50 per cent of the army's artillery was in position to provide supporting fires if they proved necessary. Finally, elements of the 1st Far Eastern Front's 9th Air Army were to support the attack by conducting numerous sorties against Japanese headquarters, communications facilities, and fortified positions to the rear.

The second problem Beloborodov faced was providing sufficient mobile fire support by tanks and self-propelled artillery to produce a rate of advance high enough to overcome the terrain impediments, secure his designated initial objectives, and sustain the advance along numerous separate axes of advance to his army's final objectives. He planned to do so with reinforcements provided by the 1st Far Eastern Front. These amounted to three tank brigades, three heavy self-propelled artillery regiments, and a heavy tank regiment. When added to the 1st Red Banner Army's six self-propelled artillery battalions organic to its rifle divisions, this raised the army's armor strength to a total of 410 tanks and self-propelled guns.[10] Beloborodov attached two tank brigades and a single heavy self-propelled artillery regiment to each of his subordinate rifle corps. After the two corps completed their passage through the mountainous wooded terrain zone along the border, the tank brigades were to be employed as the nuclei of forward detachments to lead the army's subsequent advance.

Meretskov also provided the 1st Red Banner Army with extensive heavy engineer support both to prepare army jumping-off positions and to help build and maintain roads through the forests along which the army could deploy. Prior to the army's final forward deployment, the attached engineer and sapper forces carved trails 66 feet (20 meters) wide, crisscrossing the area between the army's assembly areas and jumping-off positions east of and along the border. They also constructed infantry firing points, artillery firing positions, many observation posts, and two major radial roads leading to the border, over which the army's forces could deploy forward. The engineers also established survey markers and directional aids on the hills along the front so that the army's forces could orient themselves properly as they moved forward through the forests.[11]

CORPS AND DIVISIONAL PLANNING

In response to Beloborodov's orders, Skvortsov and Semenov deployed their rifle corps in two-echelon formation, each with two rifle divisions in first echelon and one in second (see Figure 1). Both rifle corps commanders concentrated their tank and self-propelled artillery units close behind their first echelon rifle divisions so that the tank brigades could move forward quickly and exploit the initial attack's success by serving as forward detachments. Each of the rifle corps' first echelon rifle divisions was to advance along two or three separate axes on roads constructed by the engineers as they advanced.

FIGURE 1: SOVIET 1ST RED BANNER ARMY COMBAT FORMATION,
9 AUGUST 1945

Army	1st echelon	26th Rifle Corps		59th Rifle Corps	
	2d echelon				
	Reserve				
Rifle Corps	1st echelon	300th Rifle Division	22d Rifle Division	39th Rifle Division	231st Rifle Division
	2d echelon	59th Rifle Division		365th Rifle Division	
	Reserve				

The experiences of the 26th Rifle Corps' 300th Rifle Division, which led the rifle corps' advance toward Pamientung, illustrates in microcosm the detailed planning and careful task organization of forces required to conduct the offensive successfully (see Table 6). Commanded by Major General K. G. Cherepanov, the division deployed along a narrow front of 1.6 miles (2.5 kilometers) in the 26th Rifle Corps' first echelon with Svirs' 22d Rifle Division on its right flank.[12] Cherepanov's rifle division was reinforced by the 45th Howitzer Artillery Regiment, one tank company from Colonel Anishchik's 257th Tank Brigade, and the 156th Sapper Battalion.

The 300th Rifle Division's mission was to attack westward along the Mount Tiershiyihao, Chishengshan, and Pamientung axis initially, cut its way through the heavily wooded region west of the border, capture the western slope of Mount Tiershiyihao, and seize crossing sites over the Shitou Ho (river) by day's end on 9 August. Subsequently, the division was to advance on and capture the town of Pamientung. The depth of the division's immediate mission was 1.9 miles (3 kilometers), and its mission of the day was 3.1 miles (5 kilometers) deep. The extremely limited depth of these missions resulted directly from the difficult terrain and the requirement to build roads as the division advanced.

TABLE 6: COMPOSITION OF THE SOVIET 300TH RIFLE DIVISION, 9 AUGUST 1945

1049th Rifle Regiment
1051st Rifle Regiment
1053d Rifle Regiment
822d Artillery Regiment
336th Separate Antitank (Tank Destroyer) Battalion
459th Separate Self-propelled Artillery Battalion
756th Separate Signal Battalion
591st Separate Sapper Battalion
Training battalion

Source: V. Timofeev, '300-ia strelkovaia divisiia v boiakh na Mudan'tszianskom napravlenii' [The 300th Rifle Division in combat along the Mutanchiang axis], *Voenno-istoricheskii zhurnal* [Military-historical journal], No. 8 (August 1978), 50.

To cross the 19 miles (30 kilometers) of mountainous taiga terrain, Cherepanov formed his rifle division into two march-columns of two echelons each, marching along two narrow axes of advance with the division's main body on the left flank. Lieutenant Colonel K. V. Panin's 1049th Rifle Regiment was to march on the right axis, and Lieutenant Colonel M. F. Buzhak's 1051st Rifle Regiment on the left, both painstakingly advancing through the dense forests and brush to the Shitou Ho (River). After crossing the river, both regiments were to deploy in combat formation and continue the advance toward Pamientung. Lieutenant Colonel K. A. Malkov's 1053d Rifle Regiment was in second echelon, and the division's training battalion was in reserve.

The division's forward detachment, which consisted of two machine gun companies, a squad of sappers from the 1053d Rifle Regiment, and two SU-76 self-propelled guns, supported by the fire of the 45th Howitzer

Artillery Regiment, were to advance in column formation behind the 1051st Rifle Regiment's 1st Rifle Battalion. The forward detachment's mission was to capture Hill 748.8 and to support the seizure of bridgeheads over the Shitou Ho by elements of the division's main body. The divisional artillery was to support the forward detachment's assault against Hill 748.8. After reaching the Shitou Ho, a tank company from Anishchik's 257th Tank Brigade was to first reinforce the forward detachment and then become the corps' forward detachment with the mission of pushing rapidly westward toward Pamientung.

To overcome the small but scattered Japanese forces manning defensive positions on the 300th Rifle Division's axis of advance, Cherepanov organized small assault groups in each of the first echelon rifle regiment's forward rifle companies. Each assault group consisted of a rifle platoon, one or two sapper squads, one or two tanks or self-propelled guns, a squad of antitank rifles, and one or two teams of backpacked flamethrowers. For several weeks before the operation commenced, the 300th Rifle Division's troops, staff, and assault groups conducted exercises and training over similar terrain, specifically learning how to prepare roads and to conduct operations over such ground against typical Japanese strong points.

THE 1ST RED BANNER ARMY'S ATTACK

At 1800 hours on 8 August, troops of Cherepanov's 300th Rifle Division and other 1st Red Banner Army forces deployed forward through the darkness and occupied their jumping-off positions for the next morning's assault through the dense forest. As nightfall cloaked the furtive movements of thousands of soldiers, so did torrential rains, increasing the apprehension of commanders all across the front. General Beloborodov recalled the vivid scene:

> Lightning flashed unexpectedly. Dazzling streaks split the darkening sky in half. Thunder sounded, becoming ever louder. The taiga sounded still more menacing. The downpours approached. Already the first drops resounded on the leaves. We entered the dugouts – and glanced at our watches. Sixty minutes remained until the attack. Should we delay the attack? No, under no circumstances! Indeed the rain will hinder not only us but also the enemy.
>
> How slowly the time passes. But now the long-awaited moment approaches. The forward detachments start forward without an artillery preparation. It was at 0100 hours Far Eastern time on 9 August 1945. The army's forces were crossing state boundary.[13]

Marshal Meretskov, who was also anxiously awaiting the beginning of the attack with Beloborodov at the 1st Red Banner Army's command post, recorded more practical thoughts:

The assault group of the 1st Far Eastern Front, consisting of the 1st Red Banner and 5th Armies, was to assault the Japanese after a powerful artillery barrage. But a sudden tropical rainstorm overturned our plans. Torrents of water lashed the troops waiting for the signal to attack. Our artillery was silent. As in the Berlin Operation, we intended to begin the attack in the middle of the night in the blinding light of searchlights. And now the driving rain had spoilt everything, and a way out had to be found.

It was already 0100 hours. We could wait no longer. At the time I was at General Beloborodov's Command Post. A word of command and the mass of men and equipment would go into action. Should I order the gunners to open fire? It was too late to ask for weather forecasts or to gather any other additional information. I had to decide and decide immediately, taking into account the objective data at my disposal. That meant that not a second was to be lost in deliberations. I gave the command, and troops lunged forward without an artillery barrage. Advance units gained control of road centres and broke into villages sowing panic among the Japanese. The surprise factor played its part. Taking advantage of the downpour and the pitch-dark night, our troops broke into the fortified areas catching the Japanese unawares. Nothing could stop our men now.[14]

In pitch darkness and in column formation, at 0100 hours on 9 August, the forces of the 1st Red Banner Army's first echelon rifle divisions attacked westward into the forests, each column led by the task-organized regimental forward detachment (see Map 8). In the sector of Cherepanov's 300th Rifle Division, each of the two regimental columns was led by a rifle battalion with five T-34 tanks, two automatic weapons companies to provide security, and a platoon of sappers to prepare the march route. The tanks, placed at the head of each column, knocked down trees and saplings as they advanced. In turn, the infantry that followed gathered up the cord wood trees, and the sappers worked them into a crude, though serviceable, corduroy track 16.4 feet (5 meters) wide. Follow-on units systematically widened the crude route to 23 feet (7 meters) and ultimately improved it enough to carry two-way traffic. The four engineer battalions of the attached army road detachments improved the road, built bridges as necessary in each division's sector, regulated traffic, and directed the forward movement of the army's second echelon.

The first segment of the regiments' main columns, consisting of rifle, engineer, artillery, and specialized units all task-organized for mutual support, marched 1.9–3.1 miles (3–5 kilometers) behind the regimental forward detachments. Other serials of the division march-column followed at intervals of 2.5–3.4 miles (4–5.5 kilometers). Each succeeding serial further improved the road and evacuated vehicles that had bogged down in the mud and undergrowth. Altogether, the 300th Rifle Division's teams of tanks, infantry, and sappers constructed more than 6.8 miles (11 kilometers) of tree, brush,

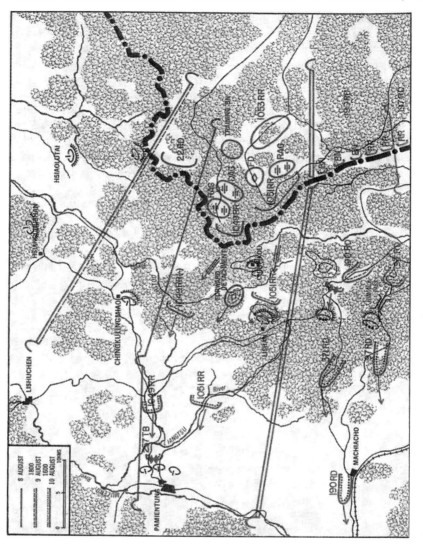

Map 8. Soviet 1st Red Banner Army Operations, 9–10 August 1945

and twig corduroy road as they marched slowly westward through the forest.[15] The other first echelon divisions of Beloborodov's army accomplished similar engineering feats over slightly shorter distances.

During the impenetrable darkness of the early morning, the forward detachments leading the two regimental columns of Cherepanov's rifle division slowly edged their way through the heavy forest virtually undetected by the sole Japanese outpost at Chiupikou, 3.1 miles (5 kilometers) west of the border. As dawn broke over the rain-soaked forest, the regiments' main forces followed under gray, rain-laden skies. Shortly after dawn, the lead battalion of Buzhak's 1051st Rifle Regiment surprised and overpowered the small Japanese outpost at Chiupikou. The remainder of the column moved westward, literally chopping its way toward the Shitou Ho.

By day's end, Buzhak's rifle regiment had captured crossings over the Shitou Ho just southwest of Hill 748.8, and Panin's 1049th Rifle Regiment had advanced across the slope of Mount Tiershiyihao and had put two rifle battalions across the Shitou Ho River. On Panin's order, the 3d Battalion of the 1049th Rifle Regiment remained in the rear to help construct a road over which the regimental artillery and rear services would advance. Both regiments thus advanced 2.5–3.1 miles (4–5 kilometers) on the first day of the offensive, liquidating the token Japanese force along the immediate border.

But if Japanese resistance was nil, the taiga was another matter altogether. Despite the elaborately planned road construction efforts, the rich black soil, heavy vegetation, and persistent rain combined to plague the 300th Rifle Division as it advanced. Cherepanov's division artillery, supply trains, and heavy attached artillery and bridging units stuck fast in the mud and lagged significantly behind his main force on the first day of the advance. To solve this potentially serious problem, Cherepanov ordered Malkov's 1053d Rifle Regiment, the division's training battalion, the 3d Battalion of Panin's rifle regiment, and two sapper battalions to improve the road so that it could be used for transporting artillery and vital supplies forward. These efforts paid off immediately. By the morning of 10 August, the division's forward detachment, Anishchik's 257th Tank Brigade, moved into bridgeheads on the west bank of the Shitou Ho, which had been captured hours before by the regimental forward detachments, where they awaited Skvortsov's order to begin the exploitation toward Pamientung. The other units of Cherepanov's division prepared to follow in Anishchik's wake.

For the Japanese, the developments on 9 August were as dreary as the weather (see Map 7). Colonel Masashi Tanaka, the chief of staff of Nomizo's 126th Infantry Division, described the action on 9 August from the vantage point of the fortified position at Panchiehho:

The night of 8–9 August, moonless and drizzling without a letup, was filled with an air of ghostliness at Panchiehho, when all of a sudden at

55

midnight, a strange light was seen and the drone of aircraft heard to the south. Soon thereafter, enemy aircraft were sighted crossing the Soviet–Manchurian border. At about the same time, several shots were heard from the direction of our border lookout positions; telephone communication with them was completely disrupted.[16]

The Japanese garrison commander at Panchiehho reported the incidents to the division intelligence liaison officer at Pingyang, who informed him of other Soviet attacks along the 126th Infantry Division's entire front. At division headquarters in Pamientung, the division intelligence officer awoke at midnight to the sound of enemy aircraft. Shortly thereafter, both the Pingyang and Pamientung sectors reported attacks by an 'overwhelmingly superior enemy'.[17] The intelligence officer immediately transmitted this news to the 5th Army headquarters and to his division commander, who was attending Shimizu's commanders' conference at Yehho.

In the Pamientung sector, the commander of the 1st Battalion, 277th Infantry Regiment, sighted Russian aircraft flying westward shortly before dawn and immediately ordered his forces to prepare their defenses, destroy bridges, and barricade the roads. At 1000 hours on 9 August, the small Japanese garrison at Lishan notified the battalion commander that the enemy had annihilated the 20 men of the Chiupikou unit just before daybreak. The enemy, however, had not yet reached Lishan.[18]

Already acutely aware that an attack was in progress, at 0300 hours on 9 August, Shimizu at the 5th Army issued new orders to his subordinate divisions. The order to the 126th Infantry Division required it to:

Occupy established positions extending from Jumonji Pass to Shangchihtun (through Lishan and Panchiehho) in an effort to delay the enemy advance and to facilitate the movement of the 135th Division toward Linkou. The main force will hold established positions in the vicinity of Tzuhsingtun, west of Pamientung, and will destroy the enemy fighting power by resisting in our defensive positions disposed in depth.[19]

At the same time, Shimizu attached one battery of the 31st Independent Antitank Battalion and one battery of the 20th Heavy Field Artillery Regiment to the 126th Infantry Division to beef up its antitank and artillery support.[20] Immediately after receiving orders for his 126th Division, Nomizo left Yehho by motor car for Pamientung.

By the evening of 9 August, combat and intelligence reports received by the 126th Infantry Division's staff were painting a fragmented, but distinctly gloomy picture. In the Pingyang sector, the Chiungshan observation unit's 15 men had been annihilated in the early morning hours, as were the forces manning a similar small outpost to the north at Heilungshan. By nightfall Russian troops were reported to be massing east of Panchiehho in estimated division strength. In view of the threat looming over his defenses, the garrison commander at Panchiehho evacuated his forces at midnight and withdrew them westward to Pingyangchen, arriving there at 0900 on 10 August. Instead of finding relief and time to regroup at Pingyangchen, the Japanese commander unexpectedly encountered two Russian columns, one following him from Panchiehho and the other approaching Pingyangchen from Hsiaolutai to the south.[21]

In the Pamientung sector on the evening of 9 August, the Japanese garrisons at Chingkulingmiao and Lishan reported no Soviet activity, although they could hear men and machines approaching their positions from the east and southeast. What the Japanese heard were the advancing forces of Cherepanov's 300th Rifle Division, which was completing its advance through the forests adjacent to the Shitou Ho River. At the same time, Anishchik's forward detachment was passing through the lighter woods in between the two Japanese outposts.

Beloborodov's two rifle corps continued their relentless advance on 10 August. On the right flank of Skvortsov's 26th Rifle Corps, Svirs' 22d Rifle Division pushed steadily forward toward Chingkulingmiao, while on its right flank, Makarov's and Timoshenko's 39th and 231st Rifle Divisions of Semenov's 59th Rifle Corps advanced into the heart of the Pingyang defense zone, overrunning Japanese defenses at Hsiaolutai and Pingyangchen. At 0500 hours the same day, the lead elements of Panin's 1049th and Buzhak's 1051st Rifle Regiments from Cherepanov's 300th Rifle Division emerged suddenly from their bridgeheads on the western bank of the Shitou Ho River and lunged forward through the final 5–6 miles (8–10 kilometers) of forest separating them from the more open country east of Pamientung.

Since Japanese resistance was still negligible, Skvortsov ordered Anishchik's 257th Tank Brigade to begin performing its duties as the 26th Rifle Corps' forward detachment to accelerate the corps' advance. Anishchik immediately formed his brigade and supporting forces in combat march-column and advanced westward, hoping to bypass the remaining Japanese strong points east of Pamientung. To help Anishchik perform his mission, Beloborodov reinforced the brigade's 25 tanks with a battery of self-propelled guns, an automatic weapons company, and a sapper platoon.[22]

Anishchik's reinforced tank brigade advanced westward north of Hill 748.8 into the valley of the Liangtsu Ho (River) early in the morning and then wheeled northwest along the river toward Pamientung. Buzhak's 1051st Rifle Regiment followed in its wake, quickly annihilating the Japanese strong point at Lishan at 0800 hours. To the north, Panin's 1049th Rifle Regiment moved westward out of the Shitou Ho Valley, bypassing the Japanese defensive positions at Chingkulingmiao, positions which were already under assault by Svirs' 22d Rifle Division, advancing westward parallel to Cherepanov's 300th Rifle Division.

To the south, on Cherepanov's left flank, Colonel N. G. Stavtsev's 190th Rifle Division of Krylov's 5th Army, which was advancing westward toward Machiacho Station, encountered the defenses and encampment of a platoon of the Japanese 126th Infantry Division's 277th Infantry Regiment at Jumonji Pass. The attacking Soviet troops set fire to the Japanese barracks at 1000 hours, but the fire quickly spread into the adjacent brush, temporarily halting the Soviet advance. Eventually, Soviet riflemen outflanked and assaulted the Japanese positions under the cover of tank fire. After suffering heavy losses, the Japanese commander, Second Lieutenant Kawakami, withdrew his platoon northwest through the forests toward Pamientung.[23]

At the same time, Buzhak's 1051st Rifle Regiment began carefully reducing the defenses of the reinforced Japanese infantry company at Lishan. Buzhak's forces first infiltrated through the Japanese defenses to surround the garrison and then poured heavy observed artillery fire on the remaining defensive positions. Then, in mid-afternoon, Buzhak's troops stormed and captured the defenses, by evening killing the Japanese commander and almost all of his men.[24]

Despite the fact that Japanese defenses were crumbling to its left and right, the Japanese company dug in around the strong point at Chingkulingmiao defended its position successfully against repeated attacks by Svirs' 22d Rifle Division throughout all of 10 August, primarily because it occupied good defensive terrain. Late in the day, however, reinforcements from Panin's 1049th Rifle Regiment of the 300th Rifle Division threatened Japanese withdrawal routes from the south, and Svirs' forces began to infiltrate the Japanese position successfully. Faced with certain encirclement and destruction, the Japanese garrison commander withdrew his infantry company along a mountain path back to positions east of Pamientung, where it arrived on 11 August and rejoined the rest of the battalion.[25]

Meanwhile, Anishchik's reinforced 257th Tank Brigade drove rapidly westward toward Pamientung, leaving Soviet riflemen and artillery to deal with bypassed Japanese defensive positions. At 1600 hours on 10 August, Anishchik's force encountered two companies of the 1st Battalion, 277th Infantry Regiment, and one company of the 126th Infantry Division's Raiding Battalion manning well-prepared defensive positions 2.5 miles (4 kilometers) northeast of Pamientung. Lacking any antitank weapons, the Japanese desperately resorted to suicide tactics; the troops of the raiding company threw themselves bodily at the Soviet tanks. 'Each individual in the main body of the 1st Company of the Raiding Battalion armed himself with explosives, and rushed the enemy tanks. Although minor damage was inflicted on a majority of them [the tanks], the explosives were not of sufficient strength (3–7 kilograms) [6.6–15.4 pounds] to halt the tanks.'[26]

During the assault on Pamientung, 'Shturmovik' aircraft of the 78th Assault Aviation Regiment supported Anishchik's tank brigade by relentlessly pounding Japanese troop and artillery positions, while Anishchik's tanks and self-propelled artillery punished the Japanese with direct fire. At 2000 hours on 10 August, the lead elements of Cherepanov's and Svirs' 300th and 22d Rifle Divisions reached the battlefield and deployed to add their weight to the assaults by Anishchik's forward detachment. Reinforced first by the 300th Rifle Division's 1051st Rifle Regiment, Anishchik's tank brigade attacked Japanese defenses on the town's northern outskirts at 2100 hours, broke through the defenses, and entered the town's north section.

Soon after, the combined forces of Anishchik's forward detachment and the two rifle divisions of Skvortsov's 26th Rifle Corps assaulted Japanese defenses in the town from three sides and captured the railroad station and the bridge over the Muleng River in the northern half of the town, forcing the Japanese survivors to withdraw westward across the Muleng River toward the 126th Infantry Division's main defensive line at Tzuhsingtun. The concerted Soviet assault surrounded the remainder of the Japanese garrison, about 500 men, in the southern and eastern portions of the town.

Early on 11 August, Skvortsov's forces simultaneously assaulted and crushed the last Japanese defenses in eastern and southern Pamientung and, by noon, occupied the entire town. The Japanese 126th Infantry Division lost 700 men in the defense of Pamientung, including 500 dead, 100 of which were '*kamikazes*' from the division's Raiding Battalion. Although the intense and lengthy fight undoubtedly produced significant Soviet casualties as well, the Japanese reported destroying only two Soviet tanks and disabling seven others, vividly illustrating the difficulties the Japanese experienced when trying to halt Soviet tank attacks with only suicide tactics.[27] On the morning of 11 August, while the final struggle for Pamientung was in progress, Beloborodov dispatched Anishchik's forward detachment westward toward Tzuhsingtun in pursuit of the retreating Japanese forces.

The success of Skvortsov's 26th Rifle Corps in general and Cherepanov's 300th Rifle Division and Anishchik's forward detachment in particular was accompanied by similar successes in other sectors of Beloborodov's 1st Red Banner Army. For example, while the 257th Tank Brigade was spearheading the 26th Rifle Corps' dramatic and successful advance to Pamientung, Krupetskoi's 75th Tank Brigade, also operating as a forward detachment, achieved similar success leading the advance of Semenov's 59th Rifle Corps. Krupetskoi's tank brigade, followed by Makarov's 39th Rifle Division, captured Lishuchen late on 11 August and then Linkou on 13 August.

During the same period, Gvozdikov's 365th and Timoshenko's 231st Rifle Divisions swept northwestward to capture Pingyangchen and Pingyang, severing the rail and road communications of the Japanese 135th Infantry Division based at Linkou with its forward elements around Hutou and the Mishan Fortified Region north of Lake Khanka. On Beloborodov's extreme right flank, Maksimov's operational group, which consisted of the 112th

Fortified Region, the 6th Field Fortified Region, and a regiment of the 231st Rifle Division, struck Japanese defenses in the lowlands west of Lake Khanka. In two days of light fighting, Maksimov's forces liquidated Japanese border defenses, captured Panchiehho, and were threatening the Japanese Mishan Fortified Region from the south.

CONCLUSIONS

The operations by Beloborodov's 1st Red Banner Army and Skvortsov's 26th Rifle Corps in general and by Cherepanov's and Svirs' 300th and 22d Rifle Divisions in particular were notable as much for their mastery of operations in difficult terrain as they were for the armed resistance they overcame. In fact, the Japanese offered only weak and disorganized resistance to Beloborodov's forces as they advanced on Pamientung and Linkou. In large measure, most of Beloborodov's spectacular success was a product of erroneous Japanese intelligence assessments which argued that a major Soviet attack in such impassable terrain was unlikely. Therefore, Shimizu's 5th Army and Nomizo's 126th Infantry Division concentrated the bulk of their defending forces to block conventional avenues of approach, specifically to the south at Suifenho and in the more trafficable region north and west of Lake Khanka. Elsewhere in the sector, they deployed only pathetically small outposts to detect and block the light Soviet forces they expected to meet.

What distinguished Beloborodov's operation most were his successful introduction of so massive a force into and through the seemingly impassable region and his skillful employment of forward detachments to lead his advance and preempt Japanese defenses along his army's axes of advance. Beloborodov's army fulfilled its assigned mission by virtue of meticulous preliminary operational planning, by carefully tailoring its forces to cope with the difficult terrain, and by performing prodigious engineering feats. As a result, the weak and immobile Japanese security outpost defenses were powerless to prevent his army's advance.

Beloborodov's decision to launch his offensive in a single echelon combat formation brought maximum pressure to bear on Japanese defenses along the entire front. His army initiated its attack along every feasible axis of advance, and where axes did not exist, they simply constructed new ones across the virgin forests. Lacking any depth whatsoever, the Japanese defenses quickly fell victim to the single echelon Soviet attack. Attacked everywhere simultaneously, nowhere were the Japanese able to defend successfully, and once Soviet forces had pierced the thin Japanese defensive crust, total victory was assured. Thereafter, Beloborodov's mobile forward detachments began an active pursuit, which Japanese forces were unable to halt until they reached the outskirts of Mutanchiang.

Other major factors in the 1st Red Banner Army's victory were the close coordination [*vzaimodeistvie*] of infantry, artillery, armor, and engineer-sapper forces down to the lowest tactical level and the careful task organization and tailoring of tactical units to suit their specific combat mission. Close cooperation between tanks, infantry, and sappers down to company level proved essential to the construction of vital advance routes stretching through the forests along the border. Similar close cooperation between tanks, infantry, and artillery within the forward detachments permitted them to begin their exploitation early and sustain their exploitation to greater depths than usual. Detailed planning and implementation of communications procedures and movement control insured that each march serial in the advancing army maintained a proper mix of infantry, tanks, artillery, and engineers.

As was the case in other regions of Manchuria, congenital Japanese underestimation of Soviet military capabilities played into the Soviets' hands and was a major factor in the Soviets' offensive success. As a result, the 1st Red Banner Army's forces overcame the heavily forested zone west of the border and captured Pamientung and crossings over the Muleng River within the astonishingly brief period of 50 hours. The Japanese, who had expected to be able to defend this sector for far longer, had no other choice but to withdraw to hasty defenses to the west. This set the stage for Beloborodov's army to begin a concerted advance toward the main Japanese defensive positions north and east of the vital city of Mutanchiang.

NOTES

1. A. Beloborodov, 'Na sopkakh Man'chzhurii' [In the hills of Manchuria], *VIZh*, No. 12 (December 1980), 30.
2. *IVMV*, 2:203.
3. Beloborodov, 'Na sopkakh Man'chzhurii', 30.
4. *JM 164*, 250–3, describes Japanese defenses in the 126th Infantry Division's sector.
5. Ibid., 251.
6. Beloborodov, 'Na sopkakh Man'chzhurii', 31–3, and Beloborodov, *Skvoz ogon i taigu* [Through the fire and taiga] (Moscow: Voenizdat, 1969), 14–16.
7. Beloborodov, 'Na sopkakh Man'chzhurii', 34–5.
8. A field fortified region was more mobile than a regularly configured fortified region; hence, it was more capable of conducting offensive combat.
9. *IVMV*, 2:205. Vnotchenko in *Pobeda*, 107, states that the 1st Red Banner Army planned no artillery preparation. However, in his memoirs, *Serving the People*, Meretskov implies that Beloborodov's army was going to employ searchlights to supplement an artillery preparation (as in the Berlin operation). No other accounts, however, support this claim.
10. Vnotchenko, *Pobeda*, 92, states that the 1st Red Banner Army's armor strength was 410 tanks and self-propelled guns. However, V. Ezhakov, 'Boevoe primenenie', 78, claims that the army had 402 tanks and self-propelled guns. This difference probably reflects the actual number of armored vehicles that were operable on 9 August.

11. Vnotchenko, *Pobeda*, 129.
12. Details on the 300th Rifle Division's operations are found in V. Timofeev, '300-ia strelkovaia diviziia v boiakh na Mudan'tsianskom napravlenii' [The 300th Rifle Division in combat along the Mutanchiang axis], *VIZh*, No. 8 (August 1978), 50–5.
13. Beloborodov, *Skvoz*, 21.
14. Meretskov, *Serving the People*, 15–16.
15. Khrenov, 'Wartime Operations', 87–8; *IVMV*, 2:227–8; and Vnotchenko, *Pobeda*, 206–7, all describe the road-building feat.
16. *JM 154*, 253–64.
17. Ibid.
18. Ibid., 267.
19. Ibid., 182.
20. Ibid., 183.
21. Ibid., 266–7. The Japanese battalion commander and most of his officers were killed in the heavy fighting at Pingyangchen on 10 August with elements of the 231st Rifle Division of the 1st Red Banner Army's 59th Rifle Corps. After dark the remnants of the Japanese force broke through Soviet lines and scattered westward and northward into the hills. Of the 850 Japanese soldiers engaged at Pingyangchen, 650 were killed or wounded.
22. Vnotchenko, *Pobeda*, 216.
23. *JM 154*, 257–68.
24. Ibid., 186, 268 and Vnotchenko, *Pobeda*, 216.
25. *JM 154*, 258–9.
26. Ibid., 259; Timofeev, '300-ia strelkovaia', 63; Beloborodov, 'Na sopkakh Man'chzhurii', *VIZh*, No. 1 (January 1981), 45; and Vnotchenko, *Pobeda*, 216–17.
27. Japanese and Soviet sources offer conflicting Japanese casualty tolls at Pamientung. *JM 154*, 259, reports that Japanese losses were 700 men, of which 600 were killed, while Vnotchenko, *Pobeda*, 217, states that 400 Japanese died in the action.

3

The 35th Army's Advance to Mishan: Operations in Swampy Lowlands

TERRAIN

Among the most vexing realities that the 1st Far Eastern Front's military planners faced while orchestrating their portion of the Manchurian strategic offensive were the imposing terrain barriers in eastern Manchuria that blocked access into the vital central Manchurian valley. These barriers, which primarily take the form of vast mountainous and forested regions and expansive swamps and bogs, severely limit the number of suitable axes of advance along which military forces can advance into Manchuria's central valley. Indeed, it seemed to Soviet planners as if all of the solid ground in eastern Manchuria rose and fell precipitously, while the little flat ground that did exist was inundated by water and swampy marshes which threatened to consume within its depths any men or equipment attempting to cross it.

Such was certainly the case in the sector immediately north of Lake Khanka, where Meretskov's 1st Far Eastern Front ordered Lieutenant General N. D. Zakhvataev's 35th Army to conduct its offensive. The sector of Zakhvataev's army extended about 124 miles (200 kilometers) north from the eastern shore of Lake Khanka. Meretskov's directive ordered Zakhvataev's army to advance westward north of Lake Khanka, capture the Japanese fortified region at Mishan, isolate and destroy the fortified region at Hutou, and, ultimately, advance along the Poli and Harbin axes to protect the right flank of the 1st Far Eastern Front's main shock group, which was operating to the south. The problem was that, while executing these missions, Zakhvataev's army had to overcome the extremely adverse geographical conditions in his army's operational sector.

Geographically, the region through which Zakhvataev's army was to operate consisted (and still consists) primarily of primordial swampland and marshy lowlands, punctuated in numerous places by low hills that protrude like monuments from the swamps and marshes. This region is bounded on the south by Lake Khanka, on the east by the Sungacha and Ussuri Rivers, and on the north and west by the Wanta Shan (mountains), which extended diagonally from northeast to southwest across the depths of the army's operational sector west of the Sungacha and Ussuri Rivers. While the northeastern extremity of the Wanta Shan almost touches the Ussuri River near Bikin, the central and southwestern end extends north of the towns of Hulin, Feite, and Mishan (Tungan).

Just west of the Sungacha and Ussuri Rivers, a spongy and swampy belt 6.2–12.4 miles (10–20 kilometers) wide stretches from the village of Taiyangkang, east of Lake Khanka, northward past the Muleng River to north of Hutou fortress. A few sparsely wooded hills rise 164–262 feet (50–80 meters) above the swamps, while, to the west, similar hills proliferate in number and reach heights of 1,312 feet (400 meters). The Japanese Paishihshen Fortified Region and the Mishan Fortified Region 18 miles (30 kilometers) to the west rested on these hills.

The Muleng River, which flows from the Mishan area in the southwest northeastward past Feite and Hulin to enter the Ussuri River south of Hutou, drains the entire basin region between Lake Khanka and the Wanta Shan. In the western portion of the region, a force can exit from the lowlands region and travel up the valley of the Muleng River through Chihsi and Linkou into the eastern Manchurian hills or northwestward across the Wanta Shan from Mishan to the lower ground around Poli. However, occasional swamps also hindered movement in places along both of these exit routes.

JAPANESE DEFENSES

The Japanese 5th Army had constructed two large and several smaller fortified regions to defend the Hutou–Mishan axis and to prevent the passage of Soviet forces through it. The most important of these, the Hutou Fortified Region, was anchored around the town of Hutou and the hills scattered north of the confluence of the Muleng and Ussuri Rivers. The reinforced concrete fortifications within this fortified region at and north of Hutou formed a formidable obstacle to any force advancing westward along the Sungacha River by blocking the road from the Ussuri River through Hulin to Mishan. The Hutou Fortress's heavy artillery pieces also threatened rail traffic on the Soviet Trans-Siberian railroad, whose main line ran along and parallel to the Ussuri River at Iman.

The second major fortified region, the Mishan Fortified Region, extended south and east from Mishan on the low rolling hills north of Lake Khanka. This fortified region also blocked any westward movement along the Hulin and Mishan road. To the east, the smaller Paishihshen Fortified Region blocked any advance by hostile forces westward between the Muleng River and Lake Khanka. The combination of natural and man-made obstacles west of the Sungacha and Ussuri Rivers made Zakhvataev's task all the more challenging. As Meretskov later noted in his memoirs, 'It is hard to say what was more difficult for 35th Army: to assault fortified areas or to negotiate places where there was more water than land and where the men waded waist-deep for tens of kilometers at a stretch.'[1]

The Japanese 5th Army assigned responsibility for the defense of the region between Lake Khanka and the Wanta Shan to General Hitomi's 135th Infantry Division, whose headquarters were at Tungan, and to the 15th Border Guard Unit, based at the Hutou Fortified Region. In theory at least, the 1st Manchukuoan Infantry Division stationed in the Poli region to the west backed up Hitomi's force. Because the region it defended was so extensive, the 135th Infantry Division's subordinate units were widely scattered (see Tables 7 and 8).

TABLE 7: COMPOSITION OF THE JAPANESE 135TH INFANTRY DIVISION, 9 AUGUST 1945

368th Infantry Regiment
369th Infantry Regiment
370th Infantry Regiment
135th Artillery Regiment
135th Engineer Battalion
Raiding battalion
20th Heavy Field Artillery Regiment (1 battery)

Source: 'Record of Operations Against Soviet Army on Eastern Front (August 1945)', *Japanese Monograph No. 154* (Tokyo: Military History Section, US Army Forces Far East, 1954).

The 135th Infantry Division's 368th Infantry Regiment, whose headquarters was at Hulin, had two battalions at and east of the town and two others working on fortifications in the Chihsing main line of resistance, north of Mutanchiang. The division's 369th Infantry Regiment had its headquarters at Tungan, three battalions in the Mishan and Paishihshen Fortified Regions, one battalion at Chihsing, two companies at Paoching and Jaoho on the Ussuri River north of the Wanta Shan, and a platoon at Tangpichen, west of Lake Khanka. The main body of the 370th Infantry Regiment and its headquarters were at Linkou, while one battalion was at Chihsing. The division's support units were at Tungan, except for the engineer battalion and two batteries of the artillery regiment, which were preparing field works at Chihsing, and the raiding battalion located near Linkou with one company at Feite.[2]

Hitomi's infantry division manned scattered outposts along the border in the extended sector north and south of Hutou and adjacent to the north-western shores of Lake Khanka. North of Hutou, a company-size element

TABLE 8: JAPANESE 135TH INFANTRY DIVISION DEFENSIVE
DISPOSITIONS, 9 AUGUST 1945

Location	Strength
Hutou sector	
Jaoho	1 company, 369th Infantry Regiment
Tumuho	1 company, 368th Infantry Regiment
Hutou	15th Border Guard Unit
Paoching	1 company, 369th Infantry Regiment
Hulin	Headquarters, 368th Infantry Regiment
	2 battalions, 368th Infantry Regiment
Sungacha River outposts	1 platoon, 368th Infantry Regiment
(south of Hutou)	
Tachiao	1 company, 368th Infantry Regiment
Mishan and Paishihshen Fortified Regions	3 battalions, 369th Infantry Regiment
Tangpichen outpost	1 platoon, 369th Infantry Regiment
(west of Lake Khanka)	
Feite	1 raiding company and 1 battery of the
	20th Heavy Field Artillery Regiment
Tungan	Headquarters, 135th Infantry Division
	Headquarters, 369th Infantry Regiment
	1 battalion, 135th Artillery Regiment
Linkou	Headquarters, 370th Infantry Regiment
	3 battalions, 370th Infantry Regiment
	Raiding Battalion (1 company)
Chihsing (north of Mutanchiang)	1 battalion, 370th Infantry Regiment
	1 battalion, 369th Infantry Regiment
	2 battalions, 368th Infantry Regiment
	2 battalions, 135th Artillery Regiment
	135th Engineer Battalion

Source: 'Record of Operations Against Soviet Army on Eastern Front (August 1945)', Japanese Monograph No. 154 (Tokyo: Military History Section, US Army Forces Far East, 1954).

of the 369th Infantry Regiment manned fortified positions at Jaoho on the Ussuri River, and a platoon-size force from the 368th Infantry Regiment occupied Tumuho, 25 miles (40 kilometers) up river from Jaoho; south of Hutou, a platoon of the 368th Infantry Regiment manned security outposts in a 43-mile (70-kilometer) sector along the western banks of the Ussuri and Sungacha Rivers. East of Lake Khanka, a company from the 368th Infantry Regiment garrisoned a series of four small, fortified outposts at and south of the small village of Tachiao. Each of these outposts consisted of five to ten log emplacements, firing trenches, and communication trenches.

    Farther to the rear, the division had constructed a forward defensive line in the narrow pass through the Wanta Shan at Mashan, 12.4 miles (20 kilometers) east of Linkou. This defensive line protected the railroad line running westward from Mishan and Tungan to Linkou. The division's main defensive position, at Chihsing north of Mutanchiang, formed the northern sector of the 5th Army main line of resistance.[3]

According to the 5th Army's defensive plan, the 15th Border Guard Unit, which numbered four infantry companies, two artillery companies, and one engineer platoon, totaling about 1,500 men, was to defend the Hutou Fortified Region, one of the strongest Japanese fortified regions in Manchuria. Just over 4 miles (7 kilometers) long and 6.2 miles (10 kilometers) deep, the region consisted of 19 reinforced concrete fortifications and eight log forts, numerous armored firing positions, minefields, barbed wire entanglements, and an imposing network of obstacles. Armament of the region consisted of one 410 mm howitzer, several 100 mm guns, and many automatic weapons.[4]

Other permanent fortified regions in the 135th Infantry Division's sector were located at Hulin and Mishan. The smaller Hulin Fortified Region comprised 23 permanent fortified positions defending the Hutou–Mishan road, 31.1 miles (50 kilometers) from the border. The larger Mishan Fortified Region surrounded the town of Mishan and had outer works, including the small Paishihshen Fortified Region, which extended southward and southeastward to the northern shore of Lake Khanka.

In the event of war with the Soviet Union, Hitomi's operational plan was only one segment of the Japanese 5th Army's overall defense plan. According to Shimizu's plan, Hitomi's infantry division was to establish forward defensive positions at Mashan and a main defensive line at Chihsing and emphasize a defense in depth along the Linkou and Chihsing road. One infantry battalion, an artillery battery, and an engineer element were to man the Mashan position with orders to inflict as much damage as possible on advancing enemy forces without becoming decisively engaged. The eight infantry battalions, with artillery and engineer support, manning the Chihsing line constituted the division's main body, which was to halt the enemy advance short of Mutanchiang. Three battalions of Manchurian troops stationed at Mashan constituted Hitomi's reserve.

As becomes clear from the 135th Infantry Division's missions, the forces manning defenses along the border were to play a distinctly secondary role in the division's defense. Specifically, if possible, the border garrisons were to hold their positions to exact as high a toll as they could on advancing Soviet forces. If forced to withdraw, they were to exhaust the enemy by conducting guerrilla warfare.[5]

Thus, the approximately 20,000 men assigned to the 135th Infantry Division and 15th Border Guard Unit defended the border to a considerable depth, with their forces concentrated in a narrow strip along the Hutou, Mishan, and Linkou railroad line and road, which was the only trafficable artery and high speed avenue of approach through the division's sector north of Lake Khanka. Although in theory the 1st Manchukuoan Infantry Division, which was garrisoned at Poli, could provide Hitomi with additional reinforcements, as developments would soon indicate, the political and military reliability of Manchukuoan troops was at best questionable.

In fact, the 135th Infantry Division itself was far from a crack force:

> The combat effectiveness of the 135th Division was estimated to be one of the lowest of the divisions in Manchuria. Equipment was extremely inferior. Infantry units used the old Model 31 mountain guns (75 mm) instead of the new infantry regimental guns (75 mm), and had no battalion guns (37 mm). It possessed only one-half its authorized number of light and heavy machineguns. Two of the three artillery battalions were equipped with three field pieces per battery, the other with four trench mortars per battery. The division's water supply and purification unit consisted of personnel but no equipment. The division had its full quota of horses.
>
> Most company commanders were second lieutenants; some were warrant officers. The quality of the noncommissioned officers was generally poor, as was the quality of the men. Both in training and in the condition of their equipment they were at a disadvantage.[6]

THE 35TH ARMY'S MISSIONS AND OPERATIONAL PLANNING

The task Meretskov assigned to Zakhvataev's 35th Army was to defeat and destroy Japanese forces occupying the prepared defensive positions at Hutou and Mishan and to prevent the Japanese 135th Infantry Division from interfering with the advance of 1st Red Banner Army on the 35th Army's left flank. Zakhvataev's precise mission was:

> To protect the railroad and highway in the Guberovo and Spassk-Dal'nii sector with a portion of your forces and launch your main thrust with the main force from the region southwest of Lesozavodsk into the flank and rear of the Hutou Fortified Region and capture it. Subsequently, exploit the attack in the direction of Poli and, in cooperation with the 1st Red Banner Army, destroy the enemy's defensive groupings and protect the operations of the *front's* main shock group from the north.[7]

In short, Zakhvataev's forces were to envelop Hutou from the south, completely isolate the fortress, and continue their operations to the west without concern for the bypassed fortress.

Originally, Zakhvataev's army consisted of the 264th, 66th, and 363d Rifle Divisions, the 109th Fortified and 8th Field Fortified Regions, and a limited number of supporting units. In addition, on the eve of the offensive, Meretskov provided the 35th Army with necessary artillery, tank, and engineer support to enable its forces to carry out their missions in the difficult terrain over which they had to advance (see Table 9).

TABLE 9: SOVIET 35TH ARMY COMPOSITION, 9 AUGUST 1945

35th Army – Lieutenant General N. D. Zakhvataev

264th Rifle Division: Major General B. L. Vinogradov
66th Rifle Division: Colonel F. K. Nesterov
363d Rifle Division: Colonel S. D. Pechenenko
109th Fortified Region
8th Field Fortified Region
125th Tank Brigade: Lieutenant Colonel A. V. Kuz'min
209th Tank Brigade: Lieutenant Colonel S. M. Iakovlev
215th Army Gun Artillery Brigade
224th High-power Howitzer Artillery Brigade (4 battalions of 24 203 mm)
62d Antitank (Tank Destroyer) Artillery Brigade, 3 regiments (6 batteries)
54th Mortar Brigade
67th Guards–Mortar Regiment
13th Separate Armored Train Regiment (2 trains)
9th Separate Armored Train Regiment (2 trains)
1647th Antiaircraft Artillery Regiment
43d Separate Antiaircraft Artillery Battalion
110th Separate Antiaircraft Artillery Battalion
355th Separate Antiaircraft Artillery Battalion
280th Separate Engineer Battalion

Weapons:
205 tanks and self-propelled gun
955 guns and mortars

Source: M. V. Zakharov, ed., *Final: istoriko-memuarny ocherk o razgrome imperialisticheskoi iapony v 1945 godu* [Finale: A historical memoir-survey about the rout of imperialistic Japan in 1945] (Moscow: 'Nauka', 1969), 401.

Because much of the terrain was not well suited for employing armor, Meretskov attached only two tank brigades to Zakhvataev's army, just enough tanks to provide a minimum of infantry support. However, since the 35th Army had to reduce several heavily fortified regions and other prepared defenses, the 1st Far Eastern Front reinforced the army with ten artillery battalions, which enabled Zakhvataev to form an army artillery group for use in the reduction of Hutou fortress.

In addition, Zakhvataev employed three tank destroyer battalions dispatched to his army from the 1st Far Eastern Front's reserve to form an army tank destroyer artillery group and two guards-mortar battalions to create a special rocket artillery group.[8] Finally, the *front* reinforced the 35th Army with an engineer battalion to augment its own divisional engineer units and help them cope with the problem of operating through the swampy and marshy regions, and provided other smaller sapper units to assist in reducing the fortified regions.

Zakhvataev's final operational plan fully addressed the missions Meretskov assigned to him.[9] He deployed his army in single echelon formation designed to take advantage of the weakest portion of the Japanese defenses, the region directly across the Sungacha River from Pavlo-Federovka. Zakhvataev's plan required Colonel S. D. Pechenenko's 363d Rifle Division and Colonel F. K. Nesterov's 66th Rifle Division supported, respectively, by Lieutenant Colonel A. V. Kuz'min's 125th Tank Brigade and Lieutenant Colonel S. M. Iakovlev's 209th Tank Brigades, to conduct the army's main attack in the sector opposite Pavlo-Federovka. The 215th Army Gun Artillery Brigade, the 54th Mortar Brigade, and the 62d Antitank (Tank Destroyer) Artillery Brigade were to provide fire support for the assault across the Sungacha River, the latter by delivering direct fire into Japanese outposts on the far bank.

Each of the attacking rifle divisions planned to assault across the river in a sector from 5 to 6.2 miles (8 to 10 kilometers) wide by employing a two echelon combat formation, and each division would advance along two regimental axes, each of which was 1.9 miles (3 kilometers) wide. Reconnaissance groups from the two divisions' reconnaissance battalions were to reconnoiter crossing sites, and border guard detachments and advanced battalions formed by each of the first echelon rifle regiment were to seize bridgeheads across the river at the crossing sites.

To support the actual amphibious crossing across the Sungacha River, which was 121–197 feet (40–60 meters) wide and 23–26 feet (7–8 meters) deep, the army provided each attacking division with 25 A-3 assault boats to supplement the handmade rafts each group of soldiers was supposed to construct. After the lead forces of both divisions had crossed the river, the army's 31st Pontoon-Bridge Battalion was to construct 12 and 30 ton bridges, across which the army's heavy equipment was to pass.

Adjacent to the winding and unfordable Sungacha River were extensive swampy regions and marshlands that stretched 7.5–9.3 miles (12–15 kilometers) inland from both banks of the river. Dense vines and impenetrable patches of marsh grass and reeds covered the river's banks and the many inlets and channels that crisscrossed the approaches to the river. Therefore, prior to the attack, the engineers had to prepare an extensive network of approach routes to the crossing sites by laying down fascine matting made from locally procured wood and sheet metal and by building gravel roads over the swampy terrain throughout the army's entire southern sector.[10]

Zakhvataev's artillery, organized into regimental and divisional artillery groups, was to support the ground attack by firing a three-stage artillery operation. Before the river assault crossing began, an intense preparation consisting of 15 minutes of intense barrage fire would soften up Japanese defenses on the far bank. After the infantry began the assault crossing, artillery would fire a one-hour artillery preparation against consecutive concentrations. For 6–9 hours after the crossing was complete, artillery would fire in support of the infantry as it penetrated deeper into the Japanese defenses. All the while, the army's long-range artillery and guards-mortar (*Katiusha* – rocket artillery) groups would reinforce the preparation as required.[11]

After securing bridgeheads on the western bank of the Sungacha River, Pechenenko's and Nesterov's two rifle divisions were to clear Japanese units from the western bank of the river, advance westward along the Tachiao, Peilingtsi, and Paishihshen axis, and ultimately cut the railroad and rail line between Hulin and Mishan. The divisions would then link up with Vinogradov's 264th Rifle Division advancing westward from Hutou and together assault and capture the Japanese Fortified Region at Mishan.

While the division's main attack force was striking across the Sungacha River toward Mishan, Vinogradov's 264th Rifle Division and the 109th Fortified Region were to conduct an assault across the Ussuri River in a 1.2 mile (2 kilometer) sector west of Iman, isolate and, in so far as possible, reduce the Hutou Fortified Region, and subsequently advance westward along the Hutou, Hulin, and Feite road to link up with the army's main attack group. An army artillery group, including subgroups specifically organized to conduct destruction missions and counter-battery fire, was to support the 264th Rifle Division's attack. The artillery destruction group consisted of the 224th High-power Howitzer Artillery Brigade equipped with 24 203 mm howitzers.[12]

As in the case of the main attack group, advanced battalions would initiate Vinogradov's assault by forcing the Ussuri River to seize bridgeheads on the river's western bank. To ensure maximum surprise, the advanced battalions leading both the main and supporting attack groups were to begin their operations during the early morning darkness.

Pursuant to Meretskov's instructions, Zakhvataev's forces prepared for the offensive with the utmost secrecy. Engineers and sappers constructed and improved unit jumping-off positions only during the hours of darkness, often severely hindered by the incessant late summer showers and high water in the river and adjacent streams. Nevertheless, by the end of July, the army's engineers had managed to construct more than 29 miles (46 kilometers) of trench lines and separate trenches, nine command and observation posts for the army and subordinate divisions, and about 100 artillery-firing emplacements. Two corduroy roads, along which the troops were to deploy forward, were laid for 12.4 miles (20 kilometers) across the swamp. To conceal this intense work from prying Japanese eyes, the engineers built and erected elaborate screening fences and overhead camouflage nets to conceal open areas.[13]

Throughout the preparatory period before the offensive, army and divisional reconnaissance organs carried out intensive observation of Japanese forward positions only from specially equipped hidden observation points. To help ensure surprise, all army forces except border guard units and the fortified regions maintained total radio silence, except for deceptive transmission under the control of army intelligence. During the last three days preceding the

71

attack, all of the regimental, battalion, and company commanders assigned to the assault rifle divisions personally reconnoitered the terrain and Japanese positions in the forward area.

With his army's offensive preparations complete, in the early evening of 8 August, Zakhvataev and his personal representatives in other sectors of the front issued oral instructions directing the army's forces to march forward through the pouring rain, occupy their jumping-off positions, and prepare to conduct the river crossing the next morning. After several hours of painstaking movement in the darkness, shortly after midnight the troops of the 35th Army's three attacking rifle divisions settled into their jumping-off positions and waited for the order to advance.

DIVISION PLANNING

On the 35th Army's left flank, Pechenenko's 363d Rifle Division deployed along a 3.7-mile (6-kilometer) front, with Major G. N. Golub's 404th Rifle Regiment on the right and Lieutenant Colonel N. A. Martynov's 395th Rifle Regiment on the left and Major M. L. Grudinin's 488th Rifle Regiment in second echelon.[14] Pechenenko's rifle division had Kuz'min's 125th Tank Brigade (less one battalion), the 54th Mortar Brigade, the 39th Artillery Regiment, and the 1635th Antitank Artillery Regiment attached and was supported by fires from the army's two artillery groups and *Katiushas* from the 67th Guards–Mortar Regiment (less one battalion).

Across the river in the impenetrable darkness lay the 363d Rifle Division's initial objectives, the four fortified villages of Tachiao, Maly Huankang, Maly Nangan, and Taiyangkang. The first three villages were situated from north to south across the 363d Rifle Division's front at a depth of about 5–6 miles (8–9.6 kilometers) west of the Sungacha River. The fourth, Taiyangkang, was located between Maly Nangan and the eastern shore of Lake Khanka. Each village contained 5–10 log bunkers and numerous machine gun positions protected by barbed wire entanglements. In addition, Maly Huankang had a 118-foot-(36-meter) high observation tower topped with an armored cupola. The infantry company of the Japanese 368th Infantry Regiment stationed at Tachiao had squad- and platoon-size elements defending each of the fortified villages.

According to Pechenenko's attack plan, Golub's 404th Rifle Regiment was to assault across the Sungacha River with its 1st and 3d Rifle Battalions in first echelon, advance through the swamps to capture, first, the hamlet of Maly Huankang, and, next, the village of Tachiao, both by the end of the first day of operation. Golub's 2d Rifle Battalion, which was to advance in the wake of the two first echelon battalions, was to be prepared to outflank the two Japanese strongholds, if necessary.

Martynov's 395th Rifle Regiment was to assault across the river on the 404th Rifle Regiment's left flank, capture Maly Nangan, and seize Taiyangkang by the end of the first day. Grudinin's 488th Rifle Regiment was to follow behind the 404th Rifle Regiment and prepare to join combat on the right flank of Golub's regiment and begin the exploitation northwest from Tachiao toward Paishihshen.

Nesterov deployed his 66th Rifle Division in a 3.7-mile (6-kilometer) sector on the right flank of Pechenenko's 363d Rifle Division, with Lieutenant Colonel Pavlenko's 341st Rifle Regiment on the left flank, Major Tsarev's 33d Rifle Regiment on the right, and its third regiment (the 108th) in second echelon.[15] Nesterov's division was to assault across the Sungacha River, liquidate Japanese border outposts, and advance on Tachiao from the east in coordination with Golub's 404th Rifle Regiment of the 363d Rifle Division. After capturing Tachiao, Nesterov's entire division was to advance northward toward Peilingtsi and exploit the attack to sever the Hulin–Mishan railroad and road. Finally, Kuz'min's 125th and Iakovlev's 209th Tank Brigades were to concentrate in assembly areas on the east bank of the Sungacha until sufficient crossing equipment was available to move them across the river.

THE 35TH ARMY'S ATTACK

Midnight arrived and passed as Zakhvataev's troops rested expectantly in the darkness of their jumping-off positions in the Pavlo-Federovka sector while heavy rain soaked them to the skin (see Map 9). At 0100 hours on 9 August, small assault groups from the NKVD's 57th Border Guards Detachment forced the Sungacha and Ussuri Rivers on boats and cutters equipped with muffled motors. As the artillery preparation began, the detachments attacked and seized the small Japanese security outposts along the river's western bank, liquidating the last outpost by 0200 hours.[16]

Reconnaissance groups from two first echelon rifle divisions splashed or ferried across the rivers hard on the heels of the border troops. Two such groups from Captain F. T. Cherednichok's 118th Separate Reconnaissance Company of Pechenenko's 363d Rifle Division pushed inland to reconnoiter the Japanese defensive positions at Maly Huankang. At 0215 hours, after the preparatory artillery fire had lifted, the four advanced battalions of the 363d and 66th Rifle Divisions seized bridgeheads on the river's western bank. There was no Japanese resistance.

Army engineers then quickly assembled pontoon bridges across the Sungacha River and, between 0700 and 0800 hours, the men and equipment of the division's first echelon rifle regiments completed concentrating their troops on the western bank and prepared to move across the swamps toward the four

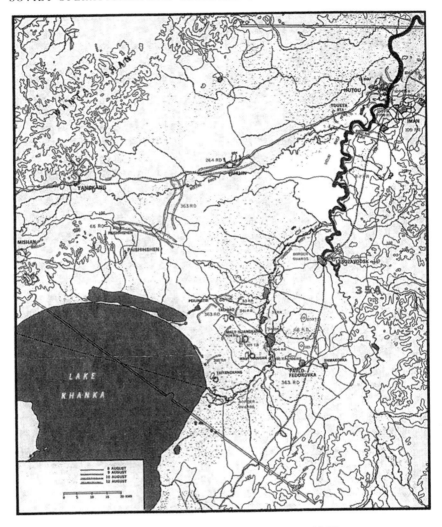

Map 9. Soviet 35th Army's Operations, 8–12 August 1945

Japanese strong points. However, the steady heavy rain made movement through the swamps agonizingly slow if not almost impossible. Therefore, Zakhvataev formed special engineer-sapper detachments to build trails and column routes along which the regiments could advance. Three engineer battalions and three rifle battalions prepared the trails and routes in the 363d Rifle Division's sector and one engineer battalion and two rifle battalions did the same in the 66th Rifle Division's sector.[17]

Exploiting the tedious labors of these trail detachments, Pavlenko's and Tsarev's 341st Rifle and 33d Rifle Regiments of Nesterov's 66th Rifle Division recorded excellent progress despite the terrible terrain. Encountering no enemy resistance, the advancing riflemen sloshed over 4 miles (7 kilometers) through the swamps, reaching positions 1.2 miles (2 kilometers) northeast of Tachiao by 2000 hours on 9 August. After digging in to await the arrival of the 363d Rifle Division's lead elements, they dispatched reconnaissance teams toward Peilingtsi.

Unlike Nesterov's rifle division, which advanced unhindered by Japanese resistance, Pechenenko's 363d Rifle Division ran into heavy opposition. Throughout the morning, the troops in the forward battalions of Pechenenko's first echelon rifle regiments pushed westward through waist-deep swamps, laboriously carrying machine guns and mortars on their backs in order to keep them dry, while artillery pounded Japanese positions to their front. The sun finally burned through the morning gloom at about 1100 hours, and the weather became hot and humid, adding to the troops' discomfort.

At about 1200 hours, Captain N. I. Vodolazkin's 1st Rifle Battalion of Golub's 404th Rifle Regiment finally emerged from the swamps, reaching the solid higher ground just east of Maly Huankang, and deployed to attack the small village strong point. Captain I. G. Lialiakin's 2d Rifle Battalion, which had been in second echelon, moved forward to support the assault. The chief obstacles to their assault were five pillboxes connected by trenches and covered by barbed wire, which defended the approaches to Maly Huankang, and the objective of their attack was the armored tower, which dominated the low-lying landscape.[18]

At 1300 hours, just as the supporting artillery lifted its fire to avoid hitting its own troops, Vodolazkin's battalion began its assault with two rifle companies deployed on line. No sooner had the attack begun when heavy Japanese small arms and machine gun fire pinned down the advancing infantry, and additional machine gun fire from the elevated armored cupola and pillboxes drove Vodolazkin's troops back to their starting positions.

It was abundantly clear to Vodolazkin that only heavier artillery fire could reduce the Japanese strong point. However, as the Soviet riflemen neared the fortified village and the regimental and divisional artillery tried to deploy forward to keep within supporting range, the guns and vehicles became mired in the swamps. It took two hours for the artillerymen, with infantry assistance, to free the guns from the gooey muck and bring them forward to support the attack.

After tremendous exertions, by 1500 hours on 9 August, the artillerymen and infantry managed to haul four 76 mm guns from the 501st Artillery Regiment and a battery of guns from the 187th Antitank Artillery Battalion into a position from which they could deliver requisite fire against the Japanese strong points. Golub also brought the 404th Rifle Regiment's flamethrower company forward to support the 1st and 3d Rifle Battalions when they resumed their attacks.

After the supporting artillery poured 15 minutes of indirect fire into the Japanese strong points from concealed positions, Vodolazkin's and Lialiakin's riflemen resumed their assault. However, once again, the artillery fire had caused little damage to the steel and concrete Japanese emplacements, and renewed infantry assault also failed. Golub then repositioned his artillery so that it could take the pesky Japanese emplacements under direct fire over open sites. After bombarding the Japanese positions for three more hours, at 1800 hours a gun crew from the 501st Artillery Regiment finally destroyed the tower and armored cupola with an armor-piercing shell.

With the menacing tower eliminated, the artillery fire slackened, and the two rifle battalions jointly destroyed the other Japanese defensive positions one by one. Late in the afternoon, the two battalions inched forward under cover of artillery fire and, when the fire lifted, rushed the last Japanese defenses from three sides. By 1900 hours Golub's regiment had finally cleared the last Japanese troops from Maly Huankang and soon after resumed its advance to the northwest. Meanwhile, to the south, Martynov's 395th Rifle Regiment captured Maly Nangan and advanced westward toward Taiyangkang against lighter resistance.

By dusk on 9 August, Golub's 404th Rifle Regiment, with the 468th Separate Self-propelled Artillery Battalion and the 501st Artillery Regiment in support, had advanced to positions 1.2–1.9 miles (2–3 kilometers) south and southwest of Tachiao. By this time Martynov's 395th Rifle Regiment, with the 472d Mortar Regiment and 187th Antitank Artillery Battalion in support, had cleared Taiyangkang of Japanese and had reached positions 1.9 miles (3 kilometers) northwest of that village. Ten tanks from Kuz'min's 125th Tank Brigade had finally crossed the Sungacha River and reached Maly Huankang, but the rest of Kuz'min's tanks were still struggling to cross the river.[19]

By the evening of 9 August, Nesterov's and Pechenenko's rifle divisions had mastered both the swamps and the Japanese resistance and had captured all of their assigned objectives save Tachiao, although their troops were nearing the southern and northeastern approaches to that last Japanese strong point.

Farther north in the Hutou sector, Vinogradov's 264th Rifle Division, the 109th Fortified Region, and 8th Field Fortified Region began their assault on Hutou at 0100 hours on 9 August. Vinogradov softened up Japanese defenses prior to the infantry assault by conducting a 15-minute artillery strike on Hutou, followed by a longer period of methodical fire against the fortified positions in the Hutou Fortified Region. The Japanese responded with what Soviet accounts describe as 'a hurricane of fire' against Soviet positions east of the Ussuri River, in particular against the town of Iman and an important Trans-Siberian Railroad bridge over a tributary of the Ussuri, just northeast of Iman. Zakhvataev answered by sending 49 Il-4 bombers, escorted by 50 fighters, to conduct two hours of air strikes against Japanese positions at Hutou.[20]

Protected by the artillery fire and air strikes, the 1056th and 1060th Rifle Regiments of the 264th Rifle Division, which were to assault across the Ussuri River north of Iman directly into the eastern and northern face of the Hutou Fortress, led their attack with advanced battalions. By 1100 hours on 9 August, the 1060th Rifle Regiment's advanced battalion succeeded in gaining a small lodgment on the river's western bank north of Hutou, and the 1056th Rifle Regiment's advanced battalion did likewise just south of Hutou.

Having completed their crossing operations by nightfall, the two regiments' main forces then advanced to capture the Japanese defensive strong point at Krepost' (fortress), just south of Hutou. South of Iman, the 1058th Rifle Regiment's 5th Company, supported by two companies from the 109th Fortified Region and one company from the 8th Field Fortified Region, crossed the Ussuri and advanced to the Yuehya Station southwest of Hutou, where the small force severed the Hutou–Hulin railroad line.[21]

The forces of Zakhvataev's 35th Army continued their advance in both sectors on 10 August. In the army's northern sector, Vinogradov's 264th Rifle Division continued its difficult fight for possession of the numerous fortified positions in and around Hutou. While his 1058th Rifle Regiment struggled along the southern approaches to the town of Hutou, his 1056th Rifle Regiment, together with units from the 109th Fortified Region, battled for possession of the wharf and river facilities in the town's eastern outskirts. After repelling several Japanese counterattacks, the two rifle regiments finally launched a coordinated assault on the town from three sides, capturing the wharf area and the town proper by evening on 10 August.

Despite losing the town of Hutou, Japanese forces continued their stubborn defense of the Hutou Fortified Region north and northwest of the town and in several strong points south of the town and north of the Sungacha River. Therefore, Zakhvataev ordered his 1056th Rifle Regiment and 109th Fortified Region to isolate and reduce the fortified positions and assigned them heavy artillery support to do so, while he ordered the remainder of his army's forces to commence an advance westward toward Hulin (see Chapter 5 for details on the reduction of Hutou Fortified Region).

While Vinogradov's task forces were battling for possession of Hutou on 10 August, Zakhvataev's southern shock group, the 66th and 363d Rifle Divisions, set about developing its attack westward through Tachiao and Peilingtsi toward its ultimate objectives, the Japanese fortified regions at Paishihshen and Mishan. To do so, the shock group formed an army-level forward detachment to lead its advance. The detachment consisted of the 3d Tank Battalion, 125th Tank Brigade, with machine gunners riding on the tanks, the 473d Separate Self-propelled Artillery Battalion, and a rifle battalion from the 66th Rifle Division's 33d Rifle Regiment. The detachment's mission was to cut the Hulin–Mishan railroad line and road by day's end on 11 August. The remainder of Kuz'min's 125th Tank Brigade, reinforced by the 468th Separate Self-propelled Artillery Battalion, was supposed to accompany the 363d Rifle Division's advance.[22]

Even though the Japanese offered little resistance and retreated rapidly along what few roads there were in the face of the 35th Army's advance, the swampy terrain in the region created tremendous problems for advancing Soviet units, in particular because the trails and roads could not support the heavy weaponry and equipment. Consequently, Zakhvataev undertook a series of extreme measures to maintain the momentum of his offensive.

First, he ordered each advancing rifle regiment to form a road and bridge construction detachment to build and improve the routes of advance. Each of these detachments consisted of a single rifle battalion and one to three engineer or sapper battalions. Second, Zakhvataev reinforced the 66th Rifle Division's lead rifle regiment with the 11th Pontoon Bridge Brigade and an engineer battalion and assigned the 50th Separate Engineer Battalion to work with the 488th Rifle Regiment, which was leading the 363d Rifle Division's advance. Finally, he ordered the personnel of the 209th and 125th Tank Brigades (minus the 3d Battalion, 125th Tank Brigade) to lend their support to the road building effort.

In addition to delaying the advance, this intensive roadwork and the poor trafficability in the region also produced an acute army-wide fuel shortage. So serous was this problem that, on 9 August, the army had to resort to using jerry cans to transport necessary fuel 6.2 miles (10 kilometers) forward from the Sungacha River's western bank. The next day, the army had to employ tractors to tow fuel-laden pontoon sections across the swamp.[23] This lamentable combination of fuel shortages and terrain difficulties ultimately forced the 35th Army to curtail the use of tanks in the 66th and 363d Rifle Divisions' sectors. However, even without the tanks, the forward elements of the two rifle divisions approached Peilingtsi by the evening of 10 August, only slightly behind schedule.

The Soviet attack on 9 August had clearly caught the Japanese by surprise. General Hitomi, the commander of the 135th Infantry Division, and Colonel Takeshi Nishiwaki, the commander of the 15th Border Guard Unit, received word of the attack at 0300 hours, while they were attending the commanders' conference at 5th Army headquarters in Yehho. Initially, Hitomi ordered his troops to delay the Soviets along the border to buy time to establish new defenses at Mashan on the road to Linkou and at Chihsing, along the 5th Army's main line of resistance. By successfully occupying these defensive positions, Hitomi expected to be able to protect the withdrawal of his division's forces from the forward area. After telephoning these orders to the division headquarters at Tungan, the two commanders departed Yehho at 0600 hours by rail to rejoin their forces.[24]

After he had reached his headquarters at Tungan 12 hours later, Hitomi reviewed the deteriorating tactical situation and learned that all of the division's border outposts along the Sungacha and Ussuri Rivers were under attack and that the division had lost communications with most of its forward units. Because the Soviet attack had also isolated Hutou, Colonel Nishiwaki was unable to rejoin his command. Hitomi then issued new orders calling for all units in the division that could do so to withdraw to the Mashan and Chihsing defenses. In accordance with the 5th Army's orders, the 15th Border Guard Unit was to hold on to its defensive positions around Hutou, presumably to the death.

At midnight, Hitomi and his headquarters staff departed Tungan by vehicle and drove to Poli, where they arrived 14 hours later.[25] From this point on, Hitomi concerned himself only with his division's withdrawal to Chihsing and, ultimately, to Mutanchiang, and he left all of his forces still fighting along the border to their own devices. Elements of the 368th Infantry Regiment withdrew from Hulin at midnight on 9 August and traveled on foot across the Wanta Shan, ultimately to Linkou. The division's forces at Tungan and Feite retreated to Poli on 9 August, and units along the immediate border that had not already been annihilated in the fighting on 9 August continued to resist the Soviet advance.[26] Actually, only these forces and the remnants of the Japanese force at Hulin and Tungan offered any further resistance to the Soviet 35th Army's subsequent advance.

On 11 August the forces of Zakhvataev's 35th Army continued their advance westward against slackened Japanese resistance. Now the terrain posed the paramount difficulty for the advancing units. At 1100 hours that day, the army forward detachment captured Peilingtsi, at which point the fuel shortage brought its advance to an abrupt halt. The acute fuel shortage and impassable terrain forced Zakhvataev to withdraw the bulk of his tank forces from combat. Timoshenko's 209th Tank Brigade, which had already withdrawn, reverted to *front* reserve at 2000 hours on 11 August, while Kuz'min's 125th Tank Brigade (less the battalion with the army's forward detachment) returned to Pavlo-Federovka, where it soon loaded on rail cars at Shmakovka Station for transport to Mishchurin Rog. By circuitous railroad and road route south of Lake Khanka, the brigade ultimately rejoined the 363d Rifle Division at Mishan.[27]

Meanwhile, after capturing Paishihshen the previous day, on the morning of 12 August, Pechenenko's 363d Rifle Division wheeled northward toward Hulin to link up with Vinogradov's 264th Rifle Division, which was advancing westward from Hutou. At 1300 hours on 12 August, the lead elements of the 35th Army's forward detachment, spearheaded by four tanks and six self-propelled guns, captured the town of Mishan, even though the main force of Pechenenko's rifle division stretched 18.6–21.7 miles (30–35 kilometers) through the swamps and lowlands to the rear.

Late on 13 August, the lead elements of Nesterov's 66th Rifle Division captured Tungan and the next day, in coordination with the 363d Rifle Division, occupied the Mishan Fortified Region, which Japanese forces had largely abandoned. Thus, by 13 August, Zakhvataev's 35th Army had accomplished its primary mission. To the east, the 264th Rifle Division's 1058th Rifle Regiment and the 109th Fortified Region continued operations to reduce Japanese defenses in the Hutou Fortified Region, while the 66th and 363d Rifle Divisions continued their pursuit of Japanese forces to Poli and Linkou.

CONCLUSIONS

Since Japanese forces in the 35th Army's operational sector offered little resistance after Soviet forces liquidated their small border outpost, other than the Hutou Fortified Region, the chief impediment to Zakhvataev's advance were the daunting terrain obstacles his forces had to overcome, in particular the swamps, marshes, and extensive flooded ground west of the Sungacha River. The subsequent performance of the 35th Army clearly demonstrated that forces with limited artillery and armor support could operate in such a region, but only if they were properly trained and task organized to do so and if they had adequate engineer and logistical support.

In this instance, the 35th Army attached requisite engineer support to each of its subordinate rifle divisions and required each division to devote a considerable proportion of its energy to road building and maintenance and the provision of logistical support. Zakhvataev's subordinate commanders, in particular those in the 66th and 363d Rifle Divisions, imaginatively employed a variety of field expedients to help overcome the fuel shortage and terrain problems.

Yet, in the final analysis, even their careful planning and skillful execution of the advance did not forestall the army commander's decision to abandon employing armor in such terrain. Ultimately, the geographical barriers so impeded Soviet operations that the army's main force cut the road from Hulin to Mishan a day late, even though it encountered no significant Japanese resistance. However, even this brief delay was simply academic, since the Japanese had already ordered their troops to abandon the region and because, by 10 August, the 264th Rifle Division had already isolated and encircled Hutou.

Zakhvataev's 35th Army succeeded in accomplishing its assigned mission, and, while doing so, left a valuable operational legacy in terms of lessons learned about how to conduct successful military operations in swampy, marshy, and flooded terrain.

NOTES

1. Meretskov, *Serving the People*, 344.
2. *JM 154*, 183, 275–6, and 'Record of Operations Against Soviet Russia on Northern and Western Fronts of Manchuria and in Northern Korea (August 1945)', *Japanese Monograph No. 155* (Tokyo: Military History Section, US Army Forces Far East, 1954), 266. Hereafter cited as *JM 155*. The 135th Infantry Division's strength on 9 August was 14,228 men.
3. *JM 154*, 276, 281.
4. S. Pechenenko, 'Armeiskaia nastupatel'naia operatsiia v usloviiakh dal'nevostochnogo teatra voennykh deistvii' [An army offensive operation in the conditions of the Far Eastern theater of military operations], *VIZh*, No. 8 (August 1978), 44; *JM 155*, 266; and Zenkoku Kotokai [National Hutou Society], ed., *SoMan kokkyo Koto: yosai no senki* [The Soviet–Manchurian border: The battle record of the Hutou Fortress] (Tokyo: Zenkoku Kotokai jimukyo-ku, 1977). Hereafter cited as *SoMan kokkyo*.
5. *JM 154*, 276–7.
6. Ibid., 282.
7. Vnotchenko, *Pobeda*, 94.
8. M. V. Zakharov, ed., *Final: istoriko-memuarny ocherk o razrome imperialisticheskoi iapony u 1945 godu* [Finale: A historical memoir-survey about the rout of imperialistic Japan in 1945] (Moscow: 'Nauka', 1969), 401. Vnotchenko, *Pobeda*, 94, places the 35th Army's tank and self-propelled gun strength at 166 combat vehicles, while Ezhakov, 'Boevoe primenenie', 79, places it at 205. Vnotchenko's figure, however, does not include the 209th Tank Brigade, which was transferred to *front* control during the operation.
9. Pechenenko, 'Armeiskaia', 44–5, and S. Pechenenko, '363-ia strelkovaia diviziia v boiakh na Mishan'skom napravlenii' [The 363d Rifle Division in combat along the Mishan axis], *VIZh*, No. 7 (July 1975), 41.
10. Pechenenko, 'Armeiskaia', 45.
11. Sidorov, 'Boevoe', 16; Pechenenko, 'Armeiskaia', 45; and Vnotchenko, *Pobeda*, 107.
12. Sidorov, 'Boevoe', 20.
13. Pechenenko, '363-ia', 41.
14. Details of 363d Rifle Division deployment and combat operations are found in Pechenenko, '363-ia', 39–46.
15. Pechenenko, 'Armeiskaia', 45.
16. Vnotchenko, *Pobeda*, 203.
17. Ibid.
18. Ibid., 204; Pechenenko, '363-ia', 43–4.
19. Pechenenko, '363-ia', 44.
20. Vnotchenko, *Pobeda*, 204.

21. Pechenenko, 'Armeiskaia', 46.
22. Ibid., 47.
23. Vnotchenko, *Pobeda*, 213–14.
24. *JM 154*, 181–2, 285.
25. Ibid., 284–9.
26. Ibid., 301.
27. Krupchenko, *Sovetskie*, 321, and Pechenenko, 'Armeiskaia', 47.

4

The Battle for Mutanchiang:
Set-Piece Battle

CONTEXT AND TERRAIN

The 1st Far Eastern Front's rapid and successful penetration of the Japanese defenses in eastern Manchuria did not necessarily seal the fate of the defending Kwantung Army. What ultimately decided the issue in this region was the Battle of Mutanchiang, one of the few set-piece struggles fought between the two sides during the Soviet Manchurian offensive. In essence, the Battle of Mutanchiang took the form of a series of successive engagements, which took place from 12 through 16 August along two major axes converging on the city of Mutanchiang and culminated with the Soviet capture of the city and the collapse of significant Japanese resistance in the region.

It was only natural that Mutanchiang was the 1st Far Eastern Front's preeminent military target. Not only was the city situated astride the main railroad and road leading into central Manchuria from the east, but it also served as the headquarters venue for the Japanese First Area Army. Further, the 5th Army also had its headquarters in nearby Yehho, just across the Mutan River from Mutanchiang.

The city of Mutanchiang itself occupied a strategic location on the west bank of the Mutan River at the junction of major roads leading westward from Suifenho and Muleng, southwestward from Pamientung, and southward from Linkou (see Map 10). Any Japanese forces wishing to withdraw from Jaoho, Hutou, Mishan, Pamientung, Suifenho, or any other location near the eastern Manchurian border north of Suifenho had to do so by passing through the city.

East of Mutanchiang, the heavily wooded Laoyeh Ling Mountains rose to form a formidable barrier for any enemy forces intent upon advancing toward Mutanchiang from Pamientung to the northwest or Muleng to the east. The mountain range extended from west of Pamientung in the north and southward to east of Mutanchiang to Lake Chingpo and Tunhua in the south, and its peaks rose to heights of from 2,296 feet (700 meters) to almost 3,608 feet (1,100

Map 10. The Approaches to Mutanchiang

meters). This rugged mountain range, which any prospective enemy force would have to cross, provided the city with a thoroughly credible protective barrier.

THE JAPANESE 5TH ARMY'S INITIAL DEFENSE PLAN

As Kwantung Army defensive planning indicated, the Japanese First Area Army and its subordinate 5th Army completely understood Mutanchiang's strategic significance. Accordingly, their initial defensive plans anchored Japanese defenses in eastern Manchuria on a series of defensive lines east of and along the Laoyeh Ling Mountains. The first two defensive lines extended along the eastern border itself and behind the Muleng River, 43 miles (70 kilometers) west of the border. Behind these first two lines, the Japanese 5th Army erected a third line, in reality a main line of resistance, along the crest of the Laoyeh Ling Mountains. All three of the infantry divisions subordinate to General Shimizu's 5th Army, the 135th, 126th, and 124th Infantry Divisions, had already constructed prepared field fortifications along the Laoyeh Ling Defensive Line and were continuing to improve those defensive positions when war began. Furthermore, a sizeable portion of the forces assigned to all three divisions actually garrisoned the defensive line.

The Laoyeh Ling Defensive Line itself was subdivided into three separate sectors, each of which was defended by one of the 5th Army's subordinate infantry divisions. General Hitomi's 135th Infantry Division, headquartered to the north in Tungan, was responsible for defending the northernmost sector of the line, which extended southeastward from the Mutan River just north of Chihsing halfway to Tzuhsingtun. On 8 August Hitomi's force in or near the Chihsing sector consisted of two infantry battalions from the 369th Infantry Regiment, one battalion each from the 368th and 370th Infantry Regiments, most of the division's training battalion, and the bulk of the 135th Engineer Battalion.

To the south, General Nomizo's 126th Infantry Division manned the sector from west of Tzuhsingtun southward along the crest of the mountains to just north of Mount Shozu. His force included the 279th Infantry Regiment, three infantry battalions from the 277th Infantry Regiment, slightly less than three battalions of the 278th Infantry Regiment, two batteries of the 126th Artillery Regiment, and the entire 126th Engineer Battalion. General Shiina's 124th Infantry Division manned the southern sector of the mountain defense line, which extended from north of Mount Shozu southward to a point 9.3 miles (15 kilometers) south of the Muleng–Mutanchiang road. Shiina had at his disposal the 272d Infantry Regiment (less one company), three battalions of the 273d Infantry Regiment, the 124th Artillery Regiment, the 124th Engineer Battalion, and supporting artillery from the 5th Army.[1]

Throughout June and July, all three of the 5th Army's infantry divisions had worked hard to improve the viability of the Laoyeh Ling defensive line. However, in early August that work was still far from complete.

After the Soviet invasion began early on 9 August, Shimizu ordered his 5th Army's three infantry divisions to occupy the partially completed Laoyeh Ling Defensive Line and defend it in accordance with the army's most recent plan.[2] In part, Shimizu's order read:

> The border elements will delay the advance of the attacking enemy by taking advantage of the terrain and established border position, while the main force will destroy the enemy's fighting power by putting up stubborn resistance in depth in our main defensive positions extending from the western side of Muleng through the west side on Pamientung to the area south of Linkou.
>
> Elements of the 124th Division will occupy the established border positions at Lumingtai, Suifenho, and Kuanyuehtai in an effort to stem the hostile advance, while the division's main force will immediately take up MLR [main line of resistance] positions west of Muleng and will destroy the enemy's fighting power by opposing him in our defensive positions disposed in depth.
>
> Elements of the 126th Division will occupy established positions extending from Jumonji Pass to Shangchihtun (through Lishan and Panchiehho) in an effort to delay the enemy advance and to facilitate the movement of the 135th Division toward Linkou. The main force will hold established positions in the vicinity of Tzuhsingtun, west of Pamientung, and will destroy the enemy fighting power by resisting in our defensive positions disposed in depth.
>
> Elements of the 135th Division will occupy the established border positions extending from Miaoling to the vicinity of Jaoho to delay the hostile advance; the main force will take positions in the established positions of the Chihsing sector (south of Linkou) and destroy the enemy fighting power by opposing him in our defensive positions disposed in depth. In addition, some divisional units will hold the advance position at Mashan to prevent a rapid hostile advance to the Linkou area.
>
> Operational boundaries between the zone assigned to divisions are as follows: (The division listed first will be responsible for the defense of the line.)
>
> *The 128th and 124th Divisions* – The line linking Hsinglung (about 10 kilometers south of Mutanchiang), Hill 1,115 (about 40 kilometers south of Motaoshih), and the southern end of the established position at Lumingtai (about 10 kilometers south of Suifenho).
>
> *The 124th and 126th Divisions* – The line linking Hualin, Hsiachengtzu and Jumonji Pass.

The 126th and 135th Divisions – The line linking Malanho [Mulenho], Hill 800, Huangnihotzu, and Manjenchuankou.

The 135th and 134th Divisions – The line linking Poli and Aerhchinshan.

The 15th Border Garrison Unit will defend existing border positions firmly and will cut off the enemy line of communications in the Iman sector to facilitate the Army's operations.

Annex (Showing Attachment of Units)

124th Division
   31st Independent Antitank Battalion (minus one battery)
   20th Heavy Field Artillery Regiment (minus two batteries)
   1st Independent Heavy Artillery Battery (150 mm cannons)
   One battalion (minus one battery) of the Tungning Heavy Artillery Regiment
   Mutanchiang Heavy Artillery Regiment
   13th Mortar Battalion
   Two provisionally organized independent engineer battalions

126th Division
   One battery of the 31st Independent Antitank Battalion
   One battery of the 20th Heavy Field Artillery Regiment

135th Division
   One battery of the 20th Heavy Field Artillery Regiment

15th Border Guard Garrison
   Hutou Army Hospital.[3]

Thus, Shimizu's defense plan assumed that any Soviet advance would occur primarily along axes of advance the Japanese assessed as trafficable and, hence, most likely to be used by any invader. If their hypothesis proved correct, the 5th Army expected its forward units to delay the Soviets long enough for it to erect a formidable defensive line east of Mutanchiang. The Japanese hypothesis, however, proved false.

Contrary to Shimizu's expectation, the Soviets launched their offensive in considerable strength along virtually every possible axis of advance without regard to trafficability. The expanding torrent of Soviet forces quickly overwhelmed the Japanese border garrisons, forcing Japanese forces in the forward area to withdraw in haste and considerable chaos. As a result, the three divisions of the Japanese 5th Army occupied their main defensive line along the Laoyeh Ling Mountains literally in the presence of advancing Soviet forces and never had the opportunity to reorganize or regroup. Meretskov's advancing forces compelled Japanese forces to conduct a continuous fighting withdrawal from the border, along the distant and close approaches to Mutanchiang, and in the immediate vicinity of the city itself.

THE INITIAL SITUATION

The Battle of Mutanchiang occurred in two distinct phases. During the first phase, which lasted from 12 through 14 August, the 1st Far Eastern Front's 5th Army and 1st Red Banner Army engaged the main forces of the Japanese 126th and 124th Infantry Divisions in two separate sectors along the distant approaches to Mutanchiang, 31–50 miles (50–80 kilometers) northeast and east of the city. Then, after eliminating the defending 124th Infantry Division from the defense effort, from 14 to 16 August, the two Soviet armies converged on the city and attacked the defending Japanese 126th and 135th Infantry Divisions. The speed and coherence of the Soviet advance forced the Japanese to defend Mutanchiang in disjointed fashion and prevented them from consolidating and concentrating their forces for a coordinated defense of the city.

By nightfall on 11 August, the forces of Beloborodov's 1st Red Banner Army and Krylov's 5th Army had overwhelmed Japanese border defenses across the entire Japanese 5th Army's operational front and had advanced more than 50 miles (80 kilometers) deep into eastern Manchuria. The towns of Pamientung, Lishuchen, and Muleng on the Muleng River were in Soviet hands, and, to the northeast, Zakhvataev's 35th Army was fast closing in on Mishan from the south and east. Japanese forces that escaped annihilation along the border streamed westward in utter disorder.

The three infantry divisions of Shimizu's 5th Army attempted to carry out their commander's orders to occupy the main line of resistance east of Mutanchiang but were hard pressed to do so in organized fashion (see Map 11). Late on 9 August, Hitomi, the commander of the 135th Infantry Division, whose forces manned forward positions in the Jaoho, Hutou, and Mishan sectors, ordered his main force units in the Linkou, Tungan, and Hulin region to withdraw as quickly as possible and man their defensive sectors north of Chihsing, where four of the division's nine battalions were already in position.[4] Hitomi left an infantry battalion from the 370th Infantry Regiment and a Manchurian battalion at Mashan to defend the high-speed approach route into Linkou from the east and an infantry battalion from the 369th Infantry Regiment at Tungan to cover the withdrawal of any surviving forces from the border region.

Many of the division's forces originally located at Tungan, Feite, and Hulin were unable to withdraw, since Soviet forces quickly cut the railroad line to the west. Most of these either traveled to Poli and were subsequently

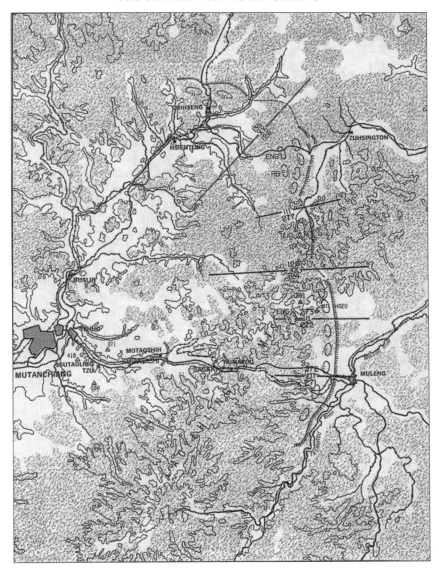

Map 11. Japanese Defenses East of Mutanchiang (the Laoyeh Ling Defensive Line), 9 August 1945

transported to Yehho by rail or simply faded away into the mountains to be disarmed by Soviet forces in September and October.

Late on 9 August, Shimizu tried to contact Hitomi to order him to send two of his infantry battalions at Chihsing to reinforce the 124th Infantry Division's defense east of Mutanchiang, where Shimizu now estimated that the Soviets were making their main effort. After failing to reach Hitomi on the 9th, on 10 August Shimizu directly intervened, ordering the two battalions to move to Yehho.[5] At 1200 hours the next day, the two battalions (one from the 368th Infantry Regiment and the other from the 370th Infantry Regiment) arrived at Taimakou, east of Mutanchiang, together with one raiding battalion, and were formed into the Sazaki Detachment. However, the unexpectedly rapid Soviet advance forced Shimizu to order this force to the rear to defend the Yehho perimeter. The arrival of additional withdrawing 135th Infantry Division units was expected on 12 August. In short, because of Soviet pressure, the 5th Army had abandoned any idea of defending in the Chihsing main line of resistance.

Also on the night of 10 August, Shimizu ordered Nomizo's 126th Infantry Division to withdraw its main forces from the Pamientung region area to Yehho but to leave sufficient forces along the main line of resistance near Tzuhsingtun to cover the withdrawal of both the 126th and the 135th Infantry Divisions.[6] At noon the next day, Shimizu sent Nomizo additional orders, which captured the army commander's ambitious but utterly unrealistic intent:

> At present the enemy mechanized force is desperately engaging the 124th Infantry Division in the vicinity of Muleng.
>
> The army intends to crush the attack of the enemy mechanized force in the area east of the Mutanchiang River.
>
> The 126th Division will occupy a position extending from the vicinity of Yingchitun to Hill 371 via the Freight Depot Hill and Ssutaoling and will crush the attack of the enemy mechanized force. One heavy field artillery battery, the raiding battalion of the 135th Division, the 2d and 3d Companies of the 15th Independent Engineer Regiment, and four tanks will be attached to the division.[7]

Nomizo responded to Shimizu's 10 August directive by ordering the 2d Battalion of the 279th Infantry Regiment, commanded by Lieutenant Yamagishi, to defend the sector from Tzuhsingtun to Hill 792 together with the 3d Battalion of the 277th Infantry Regiment, one company of the 31st Antitank Battalion and one-third of the Raiding Battalion's 1st Company.

Yamagishi deployed his battalion, the antitank company, and the company of the raiding battalion west of Tzuhsingtun to protect the division's withdrawal and the 3d Battalion of the 277th Infantry Regiment on Hill 792 to protect the 124th Infantry Division's left flank.[8] Meanwhile, the main force of the 126th Infantry Division and its commander, Nomizo, reached Yehho late on 11 August, where they deployed in accordance with new orders from the 5th Army.

While the 126th Infantry Division was deploying into the Laoyeh Ling Defensive Line and the Yehho region, on the morning of 11 August, Shiina's 124th Infantry Division had already occupied its main line of resistance (MLR) positions west of Muleng (see Map 12). Even while the survivors of the original Soviet onslaught straggled into the division's defensive line, Soviet forward patrols were already probing their main defensive positions.

By this time, the Japanese 135th, 126th, and 124th Infantry Divisions manned defensive positions extending from the Mutan River north of Chihsing eastward into the mountains to just west of Tzuhsingtun and then arching southward through the mountains parallel to the west bank of the Muleng River to a point about 9 miles (15 kilometers) south of the Muleng–Mutanchiang road. The 135th and 126th Infantry Divisions' covering forces north of Chihsing and west of Tzuhsingtun and the 124th Infantry Division's forces west of Muleng were the first to resist the Soviet advance. Intense fighting broke out just as soon as each Japanese unit deployed into position.

1ST RED BANNER ARMY'S ADVANCE, 11–13 AUGUST

Early in the morning on 11 August, Beloborodov ordered his forces that had just captured Pamientung to exploit their success by advancing northwest toward Linkou and southwest toward Mutanchiang. To insure that his pursuit was rapid enough to preempt any Japanese attempts to regroup and establish new defensive positions, Beloborodov ordered that forward detachments be formed around the nucleus of his army's tank brigades to lead the advance of each of his rifle corps. Accordingly, Lieutenant Colonel Krupetskoi's 75th Tank Brigade was to spearhead the advance of General Semenov's 59th Rifle Corps, and Colonel Anishchik's 257th Tank Brigade the advance of Skvortsov's 26th Rifle Corps. By mid-afternoon on 11 August, the two forward detachments had crossed the Muleng River and lunged deep into the Japanese rear areas.

The lead rifle divisions of the two rifle corps, now reorganized into march-column formation, prepared to follow in their wake. The remaining forces of Beloborodov's army, many of which were still scattered along the makeshift and now thoroughly ground-up corduroy roads and tracks stretching miles to the rear, were to follow once they had completed their passage through the Pogranichnaia Mountains.

Krupetskoi's 75th Tank Brigade, reinforced by an automatic weapons company from the 39th Rifle Division's 254th Rifle Regiment mounted on

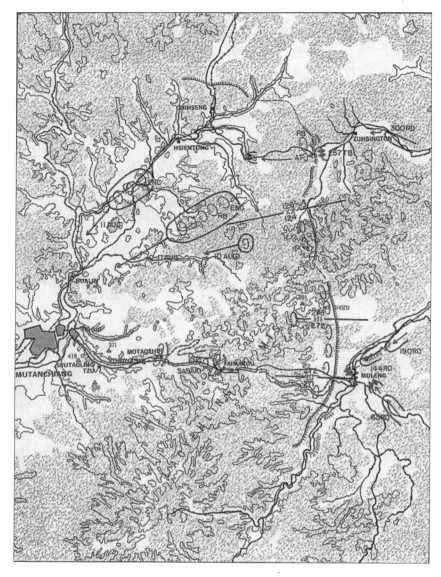

Map 12. The Battle for Mutanchiang, the Situation on 11 August 1945

the tanks and self-propelled guns, marched from the Lishuchen region through Mashan Pass toward Linkou. Colonel Makarov's 39th Rifle Division trailed behind in the vanguard of Semenov's rifle corps. Beloborodov specifically ordered Krupetskoi's tank brigade to cut the railroad line at Linkou in order to isolate remaining elements of the Japanese 135th Infantry Division, which were then attempting to withdraw by rail from the Mishan area.[9]

At 0600 hours on 12 August, while approaching Mashan, Krupetskoi's tank brigade ran into an infantry battalion of the 370th Infantry Regiment and a Manchurian infantry battalion occupying defensive positions behind the Hsia Muleng Ho (River). Although heavy rains had swollen the river and flooded its banks, the bridge across the river seemed to be intact. However, as the brigade's lead tank attempted to cross the bridge, both bridge and tank exploded, victims of Japanese mines. The tank brigade then laid down heavy suppressive fire on the Japanese positions, while sappers worked frantically to repair the bridge. By this time, Semenov, the 59th Rifle Corps commander, arrived at Mashan to supervise operations against the Japanese force.[10]

To avoid being outflanked, the Japanese forces defending Mashan had occupied positions on the north bank of the river overlooking the bridge. Dug in on the southern slope of a series of hills 0.6 miles (1 kilometer) northeast of Mashan Station, other Japanese troops were able to protect the main defensive position's left flank. At 1100 hours on 12 August, under cover of artillery fire, Krupetskoi's tank brigade regrouped into new positions to attack the Japanese left flank. Two hours later, the 1st Rifle Battalion of the 39th Rifle Division's 50th Rifle Regiment, supported by the tank brigade, routed the Japanese in the hills east of Mashan. By 1800 hours this force had completed its passage through the hills around the Japanese left flank and then intercepted, surrounded, and destroyed a Japanese battalion withdrawing westward along the railroad to Mashan.

The sharp fight for possession of Mashan and the key pass through the mountains continued well into the evening of 12 August, when Japanese forces counterattacked, only to be driven off in the direction of Tutao. Meanwhile, having finished repairing the bridge across the Hsia Muleng Ho, the 39th Rifle Division's 254th Rifle Regiment crossed the river and drove off the remaining Japanese defenders. With the road to Linkou now clear of Japanese forces, Krupetskoi's forward detachment moved on toward Linkou, with Makarov's 39th Rifle Division bringing up the rear. At 0700 hours on 13 August, the lead elements of the 75th Tank Brigade entered Linkou, and the remainder of the brigade and the 39th Rifle Division followed several hours later.

Before their departure from Linkou, the Japanese defenders had burned most of the important buildings in the city and left behind small suicide squads [*smertniks*] to harass the Soviet troops. Most of the Japanese defenders, however, withdrew southward toward Mutanchiang and northward into the mountains.[11] According to Beloborodov, the Japanese left small covering forces and *kamikaze* troops along possible Soviet routes of advance from the Linkou region: 'Along the routes of withdrawal – day and night groups of *smertniks* fired on the columns of our forces, perpetrated diversionary acts, and fell upon our rear and transport units.'[12]

While heavy rains continued to hinder Beloborodov's forces as they advanced on Linkou, the weather situation became even more critical when Beloborodov's forces turned southward along the muddy and rapidly deteriorating road to Mutanchiang. This road, which offered the only access into Mutanchiang from the north, crossed forested and mountainous regions and was severely broken up and washed away by the continuous rains. The movement of auto transport was so difficult that engineers and sappers had to build bypasses and corduroy the road in many sectors.[13] The absence of multiple trafficable routes southward from Linkou meant that Beloborodov's force could not pursue the Japanese along parallel routes. Hence, on 13 August, Semenov's 59th Rifle Corps forces marched southward toward Mutanchiang in a single, long column led by Krupetskoi's forward detachment.

While Semenov's 59th Rifle Corps was capturing Mashan and Linkou, Anishchik's 257th Tank Brigade, which formed the nucleus of the forward detachment leading the advance of Skvortsov's 26th Rifle Corps, moved westward from Pamientung toward the railroad station at Hsientung. The forward detachment's mission was to crush Japanese resistance, preempt the Japanese from establishing new defenses, and reach the Mutanchiang area by day's end on 12 August (see Map 13).

West of Tzuhsingtun, however, Anishchik's task force encountered Yamagishi's battalion of the 279th Infantry Regiment, reinforced by a company of antitank guns, which was posted on a hill overlooking the road. Japanese accounts of the ensuing fight claim that Yamagishi's small force failed to damage Anishchik's force and that the Soviet tank brigade bypassed the Japanese defenses and headed westward after a short one-hour skirmish.[14] In fact, the Japanese infantry in their antitank defense did exact a toll on Anishchik's tank brigade. According to a Soviet account:

Having crossed a ravine, the tanks neared Koutsykho [Tzuhsingtun]. The road widened somewhat, but nevertheless only two machines could pass through side by side, almost joined together. We could clearly see wooden peasant huts when explosions began to resound. The Japanese antitank guns opened fire from the heights. The column stopped to return the fire. Finding detours, the tankers penetrated into the depth of the strong point, and battle boiled over. Tank motors bellowed on the heights; among the tangle of trenches, pillboxes, dugouts, and artillery positions; over the precipices; and in front of the inaccessible grades. The Japanese guns often struck home, and the grass huts and grass blazed. The battle lasted

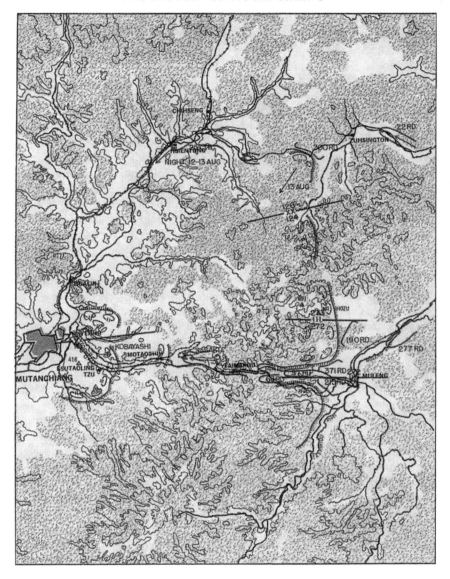

Map 13. The Battle for Mutanchiang, the Situation on 12 August 1945

for more than an hour, perhaps the bloodiest since the beginning of combat. Finally the enemy faltered, hundreds of his retreating soldiers littered the slopes of the hills and valley of marshy streams. The tanks ... pursued the fugitives. The victory was achieved at a dear price. Senior Lieutenant Dmitriev and Lieutenant Bezrukov, reconnaissance platoon leader Demin and Sergeant Zotov of the automatic weapons company died heroes' deaths. Many received serious wounds.[15]

This heavy fighting, combined with the arduous road march, seriously reduced the tank strength of Anishchik's brigade from its original authorized strength of 65 tanks. Nevertheless, his brigade continued its march toward Hsientung.

Meanwhile, after Anishchik's forward detachment bypassed his defensive position, Yamagishi regrouped his forces on the heights to await the arrival of the main Soviet infantry force. Just as he expected, the advanced elements of General Cherepanov's 300th Rifle Division approached Yamagishi's defenses at 1000 hours on 12 August, and the division's lead regiment deployed for combat under the protective cover of artillery fire. By noon, heavy artillery fire was pummeling Yamagishi's hilltop defenses north of the road. Shortly thereafter, Cherepanov's troops tried to outflank the Japanese defenses from the north, but Yamagishi countered this maneuver by moving the bulk of his forces from the hills south of the road to the hilltop positions on his right flank north of the road. Cherepanov immediately shifted his artillery fire to this sector and forced Yamagishi to withdraw his forces to the western slopes of the hills for protection.

By nightfall, Cherepanov's riflemen controlled the left rear of the Japanese positions and both hills north of the road. Although Yamagishi launched repeated counterattacks to regain the hills during the evening of 12 August, all of his efforts failed. Outflanked and in danger of complete encirclement, Yamagishi had no choice but to withdraw his forces into the forests south of the road before daybreak on 13 August. By this time, his force had lost 400 of its original 650 men, four antitank guns, two battalion guns, and three machine guns.[16]

On 13 August, Yamagishi's small force retreated southwestward across the mountains toward Mutanchiang. After dodging advancing Soviet forces it finally arrived in the region northeast of Yehho two days later, only to find that Soviet forces had already invested Mutanchiang. Thereafter, the frustrated detachment headed northwest to Tungchingcheng, where it finally surrendered to Soviet forces on 20 August. As for the pursuing forces of Skvortsov's 26th Rifle Corps, after smashing Japanese positions at Tzuhsingtun, Cherepanov's 300th Rifle Division pushed on toward Hsientung to reinforce Anishchik's forward detachment, while Svirs' 22d Rifle Division stretched out behind it on the road from Pamientung.

While Cherepanov's 300th Rifle Division was battling with Yamagishi's covering detachment at Tzuhsingtun on 12 August, Anishchik's forward detachment raced forward to gain a foothold at Mutanchiang. At 0900 hours on 12 August, his 257th Tank Brigade approached Hsientung from the east, routed a Japanese outpost posted on the eastern approaches to the town in a one-hour engagement, and, by 1900 hours, had captured the railroad station and Japanese logistics depot at Hsientung that supported the Chihsing defensive line. At Hsientung, Anishchik's forward detachment also destroyed 40 warehouses and seized enough fuel to refill its almost dry fuel tanks. It also destroyed a troop train full of Japanese soldiers from the 135th Infantry Division, who were *en route* south from Linkou to Mutanchiang.

The previous sharp engagement west of Tzuhsingtun and the march along the marshy road, however, had taken their toll on the brigade, reducing its strength to a total of only 19 tanks.[17] Nonetheless, Anishchik continued his march south along the railroad toward the vital railroad bridge across the Mutan River at Hualin. At 0500 hours on 13 August, Anishchik's tank brigade roared into Hualin and, without a pause to be reinforced, captured the town's railroad station (see Map 14). The bridge lay only 1.4 miles (2 kilometers) beyond.

The Japanese force defending the bridge and the approaches to Mutanchiang consisted of one battalion of the 370th Infantry Regiment, supported by a section of regimental guns, under the command of Major Takikawa, which was dug in just south of Hualin Station.[18] Ten tanks of Anishchik's 257th Tank Brigade attacked the defending Japanese in column formation, with its self-propelled guns firing in support. Beloborodov later recounted the action:

> The tanks rushed towards the bridge, and, when they neared it, a large explosion resounded, and the railroad bridge fell into the river. Japanese artillery struck from the heights, tens of machine guns rattled from roadside culverts, and soldiers in greenish tunics, who were stooping under the heavy loads of mines and explosives, rose up from camouflaged foxholes, running toward the tanks. The Soviet troops struck them with pointblank fire from automatic weapons and flung hand grenades. Bursts of fire from the tanks' machine guns mowed down the *smertniks* [*kamikazes*]. They did not retreat until virtually all of them were slaughtered.
>
> The tanks repeated the attack two hours later. The enemy, however, brought up a new detachment of *smertniks* supported by artillery. Attempts by sappers to clear new paths through the minefields were unsuccessful; one could simply not approach them because of the brutal fire.[19]

A Japanese account of the fighting captured the frustration of the Japanese soldiers over their inability to destroy the Soviet T-34, an incident reminiscent

Map 14. The Battle for Mutanchiang, the Situation on 13 August 1945

of the sad fate of US Task Force Smith in the opening phases of the Korean War:

> Our artillery laid fire on the enemy tanks in the rear in order to obstruct the repair of tanks (while our close quarter teams attacked the tanks from the roadside). However, even though the enemy tanks were hit, since the projectiles were not armor piercing, the actual damage was practically nil ... The enemy calmly repaired his tanks on a spot exposed to us. His behavior was arrogant and insolent in the face of our impotence. His tanks remained along the road in column and avoided the swampy ground nearby. Some of the tank crews were observed to consist of female as well as male soldiers.[20]

At 1800 hours on 13 August, Anishchik once again ordered his tanks to advance into Hualin, where they occupied a defensive line in a small settlement near the railroad station. By mid-evening, however, the Japanese counterattacks had become so fierce that the tank brigade could no longer hold on to the station. Therefore, Anishchik ordered his small forces to withdraw northward under withering fire to a hill 0.6 miles (1 kilometer) north of Hualin, where it established all-round defensive positions along the steep banks of a stream leading to the Mutan River. The sharp fight in Hualin reduced the tank brigade's strength to only seven tanks.[21]

Although the Japanese 135th Infantry Division's forces managed to halt the impetuous dash by Anishchik's forward detachment to the vital bridge at Hualin, the Japanese force suffered a significant reverse in the process. On the morning of 13 August, General Hitomi, the 135th Infantry Division commander, entrained at Linkou for Mutanchiang with elements of his 370th Infantry Regiment and a battalion of the 20th Heavy Field Artillery Regiment. Although he was aware that Soviet troops were in the region, if necessary the general planned to fight his way through them.

At 2010 hours the trains carrying Hitomi arrived in Hualin only to learn that the railroad bridge had already been blown up in accordance with the First Area Army's orders. Within minutes, Anishchik's tank brigade attacked the trains, destroying them and many of the Japanese troops aboard. A Japanese account later described the incident:

> When the train was nearing Hualin on the evening of the 13th, headquarters personnel observed that the railroad bridge as well as its vehicular bridge across the Mutanchiang River had been destroyed (apparently by First Area Army units which had withdrawn earlier). Our troops quickly got off the train and endeavored to engage the tanks but were thrown into great confusion. Some were killed by tank shells, some sought cover in the forest, and others jumped into the Mutanchiang River and attempted to swim across it. General Hitomi, accompanied by some of his officers and

men, narrowly escaped danger and took shelter in a mountainside along the right bank of the river.[22]

Despite his close encounter with death, Hitomi and the remnants of his entourage later made their way to Mutanchiang, where he assumed command of the shattered remnants of his division. As a result of the attack on the trains, the Soviets claimed to have killed 900 Japanese soldiers and destroyed six locomotives, 24 field guns, 30 trucks and other vehicles, 30 railroad cars filled with ammunition, 800 rifles, and 100 machine guns.[23]

After midnight, Anishchik and his brigade's remaining seven tanks remained in their defensive position north of Hualin, waiting for reinforcements necessary to permit his depleted forces to resume the attack toward Mutanchiang. The vital reinforcements began arriving the next morning. Cherepanov's 300th and Svirs' 22d Rifle Divisions, which were strung out along the muddy road from Pamientung, immediately dispatched two self-propelled artillery battalions with 25 guns to strengthen Anishchik's defenses and drove their infantry mercilessly forward to link up with the hard-pressed forward detachment.[24]

To the north, Semenov's 59th Rifle Corps dispatched Krupetskoi's 75th Tank Brigade southward along the railroad from Linkou to Hualin. After Krupetskoi's brigade dispersed small Japanese units defending the road at Chushan and Santoa-hetsi, 22 miles (35 kilometers) north of Hualin, only the deteriorating rain-soaked roads hindered the brigade's forward progress. Beloborodov was convinced he would have sufficient forces concentrated at Hualin by the morning of 14 August to begin a major assault on the Japanese defensive lines covering the northern approaches to Mutanchiang proper.

THE 5TH ARMY'S ADVANCE, 11–13 AUGUST

While the forces of Beloborodov's 1st Red Banner Army were sweeping forward from Pamientung and Lishuchen through Linkou and Tzuhsingtun to Hualin, Krylov's 5th Army pummeled the defenses of the Japanese 124th Infantry Division east of Mutanchiang. The defensive positions of Shiina's infantry division extended along a 15.5-mile (25-kilometer) front stretching from north to south in the mountains west of the Muleng River.

The 124th Infantry Division's 273d Infantry Regiment, less one infantry battalion, and the 272d Infantry Regiment, less one infantry company, defended the 10-mile (16-kilometer) sector north of the Muleng–Mutanchiang road, which Shiina designated the northern and central defensive sectors, respectively. The division's 271st Infantry Regiment, less one battalion, defended the remaining 5-mile (8-kilometer) sector south of the road, which was termed the southern defensive sector. A battalion of divisional artillery supported each of the infantry regiments, while a battery of the 1st Independent Heavy Artillery and 20th Heavy Field Artillery Regiments, minus two batteries, provided fire support from positions in the rear of the central sector (see Map 15).[25]

The 5th Army's most important and dangerous operational sector was situated along the Muleng–Mutanchiang railroad and road, where Nomizo's 124th Infantry Division was dug in. To provide adequate reinforcements to ensure that Nomizo's infantry division could defend its sector effectively, Shimizu formed a special detachment under Colonel Sasaki, the commander of the 1st Engineer Command, and attached it to Nomizo's division. The so-called Sasaki detachment, which consisted of the 1st Battalion of the 368th Infantry Regiment and the 1st Battalion of the 370th Infantry Regiment, had just arrived from the 135th Infantry Division's defense line north of Chihsing. Shimizu ordered the detachment to deploy along the Muleng–Mutanchiang road east of Taimakou with orders to intercept and halt any Soviet mechanized units that managed to penetrate the 124th Infantry Division's defenses.[26]

Convinced that his defenses were now secure, late in the evening of 11 August, Shiina moved the headquarters of his 124th Infantry Division to Mount Shozu, behind the division's central sector, so that he could personally coordinate the impending action. Intelligence reports received from the 5th Army that evening estimated the opposing Soviet force at two divisions, composed chiefly of mechanized units, with more reinforcements approaching from Suifenho.

The Japanese 5th Army's assessment was indeed accurate, even though it neglected to mention the host of Soviet forces following the two lead Soviet divisions. At the same time as the 5th Army's intelligence officers were formulating their assessment on the night of 11–12 August, the forward elements of Makarov's and Zorin's 97th and 144th Rifle Divisions of Perekrestov's 65th Rifle Corps, each led by tank brigades, crossed the Muleng River and captured the town of Muleng. Kazarian's 215th, Stavtsev's 190th, and Loginov's 371st Rifle Divisions followed behind them, stretched out in extended column formations along the winding road from Hsiachengtsu to Muleng. To the south, Gordienko's 63d Rifle Division was approaching Muleng from the southwest along yet another road. The remainder of Krylov's 5th Army was deploying forward in a seemingly endless march column of infantry, tanks, artillery, and engineers extending from Machiacho Station to Suiyang.

Eager to speed the movement of Krylov's army forward to Mutanchiang, Meretskov ordered the 5th Army commander to form a 'strong' army forward detachment and dispatch it directly along the road from Muleng to Mutanchiang to rupture the Japanese defenses in a single lightning blow. Krylov designated Chaplygin's 76th Tank Brigade as the nucleus of the

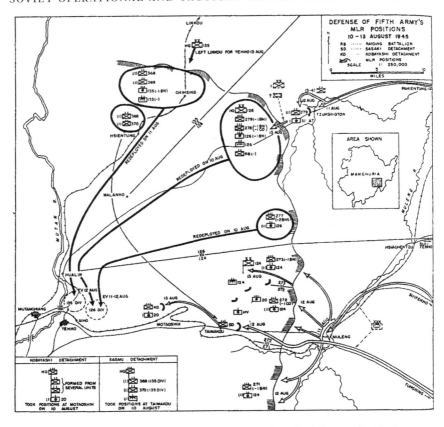

Map 15. Defense of 5th Japanese Army's MLR Positions, 10–13 August 1945

forward detachment and reinforced it with the 478th Heavy Self-propelled Artillery Regiment and two rifle battalions with automatic weapons.[27]

At dawn on 12 August, while Krylov's artillery pounded Japanese defensive positions north and south of the Mutanchiang road, Chaplygin's forward detachment launched a concerted attack against the right flank of the Japanese 272d Infantry Regiment manning Nomizo's central defensive sector (see Map 12). Within minutes of the assault beginning, heavy fire from Japanese heavy and medium artillery had halted the riflemen accompanying Chaplygin's tank brigade. The brigade itself also ran into very heavy resistance near Plivuchi Station, where the Japanese 272d Infantry Regiment conducted battalion-size counterattacks, supported by artillery, mortars, and artillery fire from two armored trains, against it. Even though Chaplygin's tanks and riflemen were able to fend off the counterattack, they were unable to advance any further.

With his initial thrust thwarted, Krylov personally reinforced the forward detachment with the 785th Rifle Regiment from Zorin's 144th Rifle Division and two battalions from the 233d Rifle Regiment of Makar'ev's 97th Rifle Division, as well as with additional tanks and self-propelled guns in an attempt to restore momentum to the attack. Following a powerful 30-minute artillery preparation, Chaplygin's reinforced forward detachment finally broke through the Japanese defenses in a narrow 2.5-mile (4-kilometer) sector and exploited its success by advancing to the eastern outskirts of Taimakou.[28] The fighting raged on all day as Japanese artillery pounded the narrow Soviet penetration corridor, and Japanese infantry launched repeated counterattacks in an attempt to seal the Soviet penetration. Nevertheless, Chaplygin's assault had carved a huge breech between the 124th Infantry Division's 271st Infantry Regiment south of the Mutanchiang road and the 272d Regiment north of the road.

At 0900 hours the next morning, Nomizo received a full report concerning what had transpired in his central sector:

At about 0900 hours on 13 August, a tragic report was brought to the command post by a mounted noncommissioned officer from the Central Sector Unit commander. It stated: 'Because of the difficulty of holding our positions, the regiment will launch a counterattack with the regimental colors in the lead. This is perhaps the last report from our regiment to the division.'

The division commander was astonished at the Central Sector Unit commander's desire to launch a suicide attack in full strength instead of continuing organized resistance and was rather suspicious of the lack of tenacity on the part of the Central Sector Unit. Its front was the most vital to the entire Army, and the engagement had only recently been initiated. General Shiina therefore ordered the Central Sector Unit commander to put up stubborn resistance by holding his positions.[29]

With his central defensive sector smashed and Soviet forces approaching Taimakou, the Japanese 5th Army commander, Shimizu, formed yet another stopgap force to halt the furious Soviet advance. This time he formed a 1,000-man battalion, composed of students from the Reserve Officers Candidate Training Unit at Shitou, a 600-man detachment from the Intendance Reserve Officers Candidate Training Unit, and one battery of the 20th Heavy Field Artillery Regiment (150 mm), and placed it under the command of Colonel Kobayashi, the commander of the 3d Field Fortification Unit. Shimizu ordered Kobayashi to position his small task force at Motaoshih, midway between Taimakou and Mutanchiang, with orders to block the road to Mutanchiang at all costs.[30] By the evening of 12–13 August, Chaplygin's reinforced forward detachment, which was still in the vanguard of Krylov's army, had overcome the Sasaki detachment's defenses at Taimakou and had reached Motaoshih, where it promptly engaged Kobayashi's ersatz detachment.

The Japanese 5th Army postwar accounts downplay the effectiveness of all Japanese resistance in the Laoyeh Ling Defensive Line and regard the 124th Infantry Division's defensive positions as having been irrevocably split asunder by the evening of 12 August. The 124th Infantry Division's accounts of the action, however, credit the division with far greater success, particularly in its defense along the main road to Mutanchiang. While they confirm the overall success of Chaplygin's thrust along the road, Soviet versions of the fighting also attest to the 124th Infantry Division's strenuous resistance and desperate counterattacks.[31]

The heavy fighting along the Muleng–Mutanchiang road continued throughout 13 August (see Map 14). Gordienko's 63d and Zorin's 144th Rifle Divisions, led by Chaplygin's tanks and self-propelled guns, widened the initial breakthrough corridor along the road to 3.1–4.3 miles (5–7 kilometers) and penetrated down the road to a depth of 18.6 miles (30 kilometers) despite constant Japanese counterattacks in from platoon to battalion strength and constant shellfire from Japanese artillery and mortar batteries positioned on their flanks. Colonel Kobayashi and many of his men perished during the fighting, and, by 1200 hours on 13 August, his detachment had been essentially annihilated.

A Japanese account recorded the devastation:

On the evening of the 12th, [the Kobayashi detachment] was engaged by an enemy unit equipped with 20 to 30 tanks which after penetrating the Muleng sector had advanced westward. The rapidly advancing mechanized unit came suddenly under the gunfire of the Kobayashi Detachment, especially its attached artillery (one battery of the 150 mm howitzer unit), and when two or three leading tanks were either destroyed or rendered unserviceable, the enemy units hastily fell back and subsequently became more cautious. At night the detachment launched a daring close–quarter counterattack on the camping area of the Soviet mechanized unit and struck terror into the enemy's heart. The detachment had no antitank defenses other than one heavy field artillery battery and some explosives. When the battle was resumed on the morning of the 13th, the detachment suffered many casualties (including Colonel Kobayashi and several key officers) despite the brave fighting of all officers and men. By noon of that day, the vicinity of Motaoshih at last was penetrated. Thereafter, remnants of the detachment remained in the area and harassed the enemy rear while others either withdrew to the vicinity of Yehho and joined the main forces of the army or fell back to the Tungchingcheng and Ningan areas where they were disarmed late in August.[32]

Thus, by nightfall on 13 August, the forward elements of Krylov's 5th Army had captured the key passage through the Laoyeh Ling Mountains and now confronted the main Japanese defenses east of Yehho and Mutanchiang proper. To the rear, Soviet forces were pressing the right flank of the 272d Infantry Regiment northward away from the road and the 271st Regiment's left flank southward away from the road. The remainder of Krylov's army was now pouring into the breech.

As Krylov's forces penetrated through the central defense sector of the Japanese 124th Infantry Division's defense line, the remainder of Nomizo's division struggled to hold on. Although his central sector had already been pierced, Nomizo's other defensive sectors were still intact (see Map 15). Therefore, he utterly rejected any idea of withdrawal. Consequently, while the division's 272d Infantry Regiment fought for its very life all day long, trying to prevent Soviet forces (the 63d and 144th Rifle Divisions) from reaching the outskirts of Yehho, his other regiments came under increasing pressure from newly arrived Soviet forces that immediately attacked both north and south of the Mutanchiang road.

North of the Mutanchiang road, on 13 August, Makar'ev's 97th and Loginov's 371st Rifle Divisions of Perekrestov's 65th Rifle Corps struck the southern flank of the Japanese 272d Infantry Regiment, while south of the road, Kazarian's 215th and Gladyshev's 277th Rifle Divisions of Kazartsev's 72d Rifle Corps attacked the left flank of the 271st Infantry Regiment. Simultaneously, Stavtsev's 190th Rifle Division of Perekrestov's rifle corps and Colonel N. F. Kusakin's 157th Rifle Division of Ivanov's 45th Rifle Corps assaulted the 272d Infantry Regiment's positions frontally with concentrated artillery support. Early the next day, Stavtsev's rifle division attacked the left flank of the Japanese 273d Infantry Regiment and Makar'ev's 97th and Loginov's 371st Rifle Divisions launched a concerted assault against 272d Regiment's central sector from the south, forcing the regiment to withdraw in disorder to the southern foothills of Mount Shozu.

At 0900 hours on 14 August, Shiina once again relocated his division command post, this time to a site located 6.2 miles (10 kilometers) west of Mount Shozu. Only a few minutes later, Soviet rocket and artillery fire almost obliterated the top of Mount Shozu. According to Japanese accounts, 'So intense was the concentration that Shozusan [Mt. Shozu] instantly became a bald mountain.'[33] A coordinated Soviet assault on the summit, supported by continuing intense artillery fire, finally overwhelmed the stubborn Japanese defenders. The commanders of the 20th Heavy Field Artillery Regiment and the Mutanchiang Heavy Artillery Regiment and most of their men were killed by the onslaught, and their guns destroyed.[34] Thereafter, Shiina lost all communications with his remaining subordinate units. His last formal order read:

> All personnel of the division, with firm determination to die in honor, shall repeatedly carry out raiding tactics under cover of darkness and will smash the enemy's combat strength bit by bit. To this end all units will carry out tenacious attacks according to the following procedures.
>
> The main target of attack will be the enemy located along the Mutanchiang road.
>
> Units north of the road will charge and break through the enemy line to the south; those south of the road will charge and break through to the north. Each will advance to the hilly zone of the opposite side. In the daytime they will endeavor to seek cover and conceal their movements and intentions as much as possible. During the ensuing night they will return and repeat the same action.
>
> In attacking, adjoining units will maintain close contact and exercise utmost care to avoid engagements among themselves.
>
> Movement towards the sector west of Taimakou will be prohibited.
>
> The raiding tactics stipulated in these instructions will be carried out beginning on the night of 15 August.[35]

All organized resistance by the Japanese 124th Infantry Division gradually sputtered out after the night of 14 August (see Map 16). Thereafter, the division's shattered remnants were capable only of harassing Soviet columns marching westward toward Mutanchiang, forcing Soviet forces to secure their flanks and conduct clearing operations north and south of the road.

As described by a Japanese veteran:

> After dark the entire combat area became somewhat quiet, although rifle shots could be heard intermittently, both far and near. At the division headquarters, all personnel, including the division commander, discarded unnecessary items of equipment and clothing. Lightly clad, they spent the night at ease.

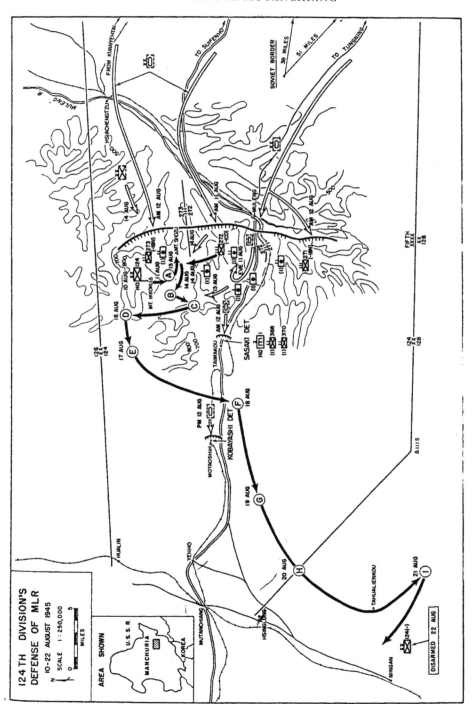

Map 16. Japanese 124th Infantry Division's Defense of the MLR, 10–22 August 1945

With the morning of 15 August, rifle shots and the roaring of heavy guns were heard continuously and with renewed intensity all over the battlefield. We gradually became familiar with the sound of rocket launchers. Meanwhile Headquarters was busy making preparations for the first night raiding attack.[36]

After receiving word of the Imperial cease-fire by radio late on 15 August and confirming its validity, Shiina's division ceased raiding operations and tried to withdraw to the southwest. After a lengthy assembly period, at 0300 on 18 August, the division broke through the endless columns of Soviet troops, trucks, and tanks on the road between Taimakou and Motaoshih. Separate groups of Japanese continued to cross the road during the next evening as well. Then the division moved through the mountains toward the Ningan area, where, after the Kwantung Army's surrender, it, too, surrendered to Soviet forces on 22 August.

After the 124th Infantry Division's resistance collapsed, the forces of Krylov's 5th Army cleared the remnants of Japanese forces from his army's lines of communication, while Krylov and his staff planned the final assault on Mutanchiang and assembled forces necessary to crush Japanese resistance once and for all on the eastern outskirts of the city (see Map 17).

Thus, by the evening of 13–14 August, the forces of Krylov's 5th Army had crossed the Laoyeh Ling Mountains and virtually obliterated the Japanese 124th Infantry Division, denying the Japanese any opportunity to conduct an orderly fighting withdrawal westward to Yehho and Mutanchiang. However, the combined effects of distance, terrain, and Japanese resistance had exacted a toll on Krylov's forces and their offensive timetable.

While the army's advance was indeed spectacular, these three factors prevented Krylov, as well as Beloborodov to the north, from bringing overwhelming power to bear on the Japanese defenses at Mutanchiang. Both Beloborodov's 1st Red Banner and Krylov's 5th Armies were stretched out over 60 miles (100 kilometers) along the roads from the Manchurian border across the Muleng River to the approaches to Mutanchiang. Worse still, many of Krylov's rifle divisions were deployed on the flanks of the penetration north and south of the Mutanchiang road, trying to clear the remnants of Japanese forces from their flanks.

Although the forward elements of both 1st Red Banner Army and 5th Army had crossed the Laoyeh Ling Mountains well ahead of schedule, the fragmented but often bitter Japanese resistance and the long advance had forced both armies to disperse their forces. Both Beloborodov and Krylov still had to concentrate sufficient force to overcome Japanese defenses at Mutanchiang, which by this time was defended by a sizeable Japanese force.

Because of these problems, Meretskov ordered Vasil'ev's 10th Mechanized Corps, the *front's* designated mobile group, which he originally intended to

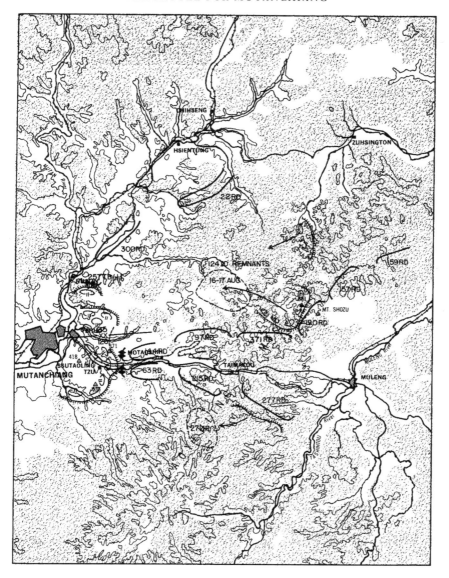

Map 17. The Battle for Mutanchiang, the Situation on 14 August 1945

commit to combat in the 5th Army's sector to instead relocate southward and go into action in the 25th Army's sector, where prospects for a successful operational exploitation seemed more favorable.[37] Having reached this decision, Meretskov ordered Krylov's 5th Army to assault and defeat Japanese forces at Mutanchiang in conjunction with Beloborodov's 1st Red Banner Army.

THE BATTLE FOR MUTANCHIANG, 14–16 AUGUST

The Situation Late on 13 August

According to the 1st Far Eastern Front's original offensive plan, Krylov's 5th Army was to attack Japanese defenses east of Mutanchiang while Beloborodov's 1st Red Banner Army advanced on Mutanchiang from the north. However, the only forces Krylov could bring to bear on Japanese defenses east of Mutanchiang on the evening of 13 August were the two division groups from Perekrestov's and Kazartsev's 65th and 72d Rifle Corps that had already been struggling for days along that axis. The remainder of both rifle corps and his third rifle corps were either still engaged in liquidating the remnants of the Japanese 124th Infantry Division, securing his lines of communications, or marching forward from the rear.

Krylov's forces fighting along the Mutanchiang road included Zorin's 144th Rifle Division of Perekrestov's rifle corps, reinforced by Velichko's 218th Tank Brigade and the 395th Heavy Self-propelled Artillery Regiment, and Gordienko's 63d Rifle Division of Kazartsev's rifle corps, reinforced by Krasnoshtin's 210th Tank Brigade and the 479th Heavy Self-propelled Artillery Regiment.

Echeloned to the right, Makar'ev's 97th, Loginov's 371st, and Stavtsev's 190th Rifle Divisions of Perekrestov's 65th Rifle Corps were still battling with remnants of the 124th Infantry Division north of the Muleng–Mutanchiang road. Echeloned to the left, Kazarian's 215th and Gladyshev's 277th Rifle Divisions of Kazartsev's 72d Rifle Corps were advancing against remnants of the Japanese 124th Infantry Division's 271st Infantry Regiment, which was fighting in isolation south of the Mutanchiang road. Kazarian's division was situated 6.2 miles (10 kilometers) southwest of Motaoshih Station, and Gladyshev's, 15.5 miles (25 kilometers) southwest of Muleng.

Far to the north, Colonel N. I. Fedotov's 159th Rifle Division of Ivanov's 45th Rifle Corps was protecting the right flank of Krylov's army in the wide sector from Machiacho to Hsiachengtsu, while to the rear Colonel N. F. Kusakin's 157th and Major General B. B. Gorodovikov's 184th Rifle Divisions were still marching forward along the road from Suiyang. Krylov's only other major maneuver force, Major General T. V. Dedeogly's 84th Separate

Cavalry Division, was in the *front* reserve at Muleng, where it would remain until early 15 August when Krylov ordered it to conduct a long raid around the Japanese right flank.[38]

By the evening of 13–14 August, the Japanese 5th Army's defenses north and south of Mutanchiang had coalesced to the extent that Shimizu's forces manned relatively continuous defense lines in a semi-circle north and east of the city. Forward of the northern sector, Major Takikawa's *ad hoc* battalion from the 135th Infantry Division had managed to stabilize the situation at Hualin by halting the forward elements of Beloborodov's 1st Red Banner Army, while the remainder of the 135th Infantry Division (three battalions) manned defense lines just north of Mutanchiang (see Map 17). East of Mutanchiang, although they had lost the village of Motaoshih to the advancing Soviet forces, the *ad hoc* detachments and the 126th Infantry Division's forward elements had at least slowed up the Soviet advance sufficiently for defenses to jell to the rear.

The Japanese 126th and 135th Infantry Divisions deployed into their defensive positions around Mutanchiang in accordance with a directive the 5th Army headquarters had issued at 1200 hours on 11 August. In the directive, Shimizu ordered Nomizo's 126th Infantry Division to occupy defenses east and southeast of the city, with three regiments on line, and Hitomi's 135th Infantry Division to occupy defenses northeast of Mutanchiang and protect all approaches to Yehho from Hualin.[39]

Nomizo deployed his 126th Infantry Division with the 277th Infantry Regiment (two battalions) dug in facing south, south of Yingchitun, the 278th Regiment (three battalions) facing southeast on a hill south of the freight depot, and the 279th Regiment (three battalions) from the village of Ssutaoling to Hill 371 facing eastward north of the Muleng road. The division's artillery regiment, with one heavy field artillery battery, deployed west of Ssutaoling with orders to provide supporting fire on the approaches to Ssutaoling and Hill 371. The troops assigned to the raiding battalions of the 126th and 135th Infantry Divisions jointly deployed in foxholes along the road from Ssutaoling to Yehho with the mission of interdicting all Soviet traffic along the road. The 126th Infantry Division's troops had managed to dig in thoroughly by the evening of 13 August.

After his harrowing scrape with death only hours before, Hitomi ordered his 135th Infantry Division to occupy two defensive sectors northeast of Mutanchiang and to protect the approaches to Yehho from Hualin. Supported by a battalion of divisional artillery, the 370th Infantry Regiment (two battalions) defended the left sector along the Hualin road. A single battalion of the 369th Infantry Regiment, backed by one battalion of the 368th Infantry Regiment and a company of engineers, occupied the right sector, which extended to the foothills of the mountains northeast of Mutanchiang. As before, Major Takikawa's battalion of the 370th Infantry Regiment protected the division's front from its positions at Hualin, while its parent division dug in to its rear.

By the evening of 13 August, Hitomi's division had completed establishing its firing and communications trenches; however, the defensive positions were not yet totally interconnected. Furthermore, both defending Japanese divisions lacked barbed wire entanglements and proper antitank obstacles and had only negligible artillery support. The 126th Infantry Division, for example, had only 20 guns, and the 135th Infantry Division, only ten. Worse still, considering what they were about to face, the divisions had only a handful of light tanks in support.

The 1st Red Banner Army's Assault

Early on 14 August, Beloborodov acted decisively to break the stalemate at Hualin and restore momentum to his army's advance on Mutanchiang. Early in the morning, he ordered Skvortsov's 26th Rifle Corps to reinforce Anishchik's forward detachment, which was still occupying all-round defenses on a hill north of the town with forces from the rifle corps' two lead rifle divisions, which were still *en route* from Tzuhsingtun (see Map 17). Skvortsov complied by ordering Cherepanov's 300th and Svirs' 22d Rifle Divisions to dispatch forward detachments, each of which consisted of the division's self-propelled artillery battalions, to reinforce Anishchik's force. The two divisional forward detachments raced forward and joined the depleted 257th Tank Brigade, enabling Anishchik to resume his assault on Hualin Station.

The previous day's fighting had seriously sapped the strength and morale of the Takikawa Battalion, which was defending Hualin. Especially debilitating to Japanese morale was the Soviets' ability, even during the night, to evacuate successfully tanks that had been damaged the previous day.[40] A Japanese after-action report described the vexing problem:

> Our artillery laid fire on the enemy tanks in the rear in order to obstruct the repair of tanks. However, even though the enemy tanks were hit, since the projectiles were not armor piercing, the actual damage was virtually nil. (In close quarter fighting a minimum of one kilogram of explosive charge is required to render a T34 tank inoperative. Any less amount is totally ineffective.) The enemy calmly repaired his tanks on a spot exposed to us. His behavior was arrogant and insolent in the face of our impotence. His tanks remained along the road in column, and avoided the swampy ground nearby. Some of the tank crew members were observed to consist of female as well as male soldiers.[41]

On the afternoon of 14 August, Anishchik's reinforced forward detachment resumed its assault on Takikawa's battalion and drove the Japanese southward

1. Major General G. N. Perekrestov, Commander, 65th Rifle Corps (5th Army).

2. 5th Army assault group advances.

3. Soviet artillery conducting direct fire against a Japanese strong point.

4. 5th Army infantry assault a Japanese position near Grodekovo.

5. 5th Army's force advance toward Suiyang.

6. 5th Army tanks and infantry advance toward Muleng.

7. Japanese fortified positions destroyed by heavy Soviet artillery.

8. 5th Army assault troops await the order to advance.

9. 5th Army troops entering Muleng.

10. In the Ussuri taiga before the attack.

11. Major General G. G. Cherepanov, Commander, 300th Rifle Division (26th Rifle Corps, 1st Red Banner Army).

12. Tanks advancing with mounted infantry.

25. 39th Army troops move forward into jumping-off positions.

26. 39th Army forces cross the Manchurian border.

27. 39th Army tanks crossing the Grand Khingan Mountains.

28. Troops attacking the Halung–
Arshaan Fortified Region.

29. 39th Army troops entering Wangyemiao.

30. 36th Army artillery shelling Hailar.

31. Rear Admiral N. V. Antonov, Commander, Amur River Flotilla.

32. Japanese strong point at Fuchin.

33. American-made amphibious vehicles with the 15th Army.

34. Vice Admiral V. A. Andreev, Commander, Northern Pacific Flotilla.

35. Major General A. R. Gnechko, Commander, Kamchatka Defensive Region.

36. Captain 1st Rank D. G. Ponomarev, Commander, Petropavlovsk Naval Base.

37. Naval infantry loading for the landing at Odomari.

38. Japanese civilians returning to Odomari.

39. The amphibious assault on Shumshir Island (artist's rendition).

from Hualin Station after losing three tanks to Japanese fire. Takikawa's battalion, however, still clung to advanced positions on a ridge 1.6 miles (2.5 kilometers) north of the 135th Infantry Division's main defensive line south of Tzumeiholo. The situation in the 1st Red Banner Army's sector then stabilized for the remainder of the day, since Beloborodov lacked requisite forces with which to overwhelm the Japanese defenses. Until such time as he did, Anishchik's forces could only nibble away at the Japanese defenses.

By late evening on 14 August, Anishchik's forward detachment still consisted only of his 257th Tank Brigade and the two self-propelled artillery battalions of the 22d and 300th Rifle Divisions. The rifle regiments of Cherepanov's 300th and Svirs' 22d Rifle Divisions remained strung out over the 25 miles (40 kilometers) of road stretching northeast to Tzuhsingtun, while the other forces of Skvortsov's 26th Rifle Corps were busily improving and repairing the roads even farther to the rear. It was a similar tale for Semenov's 59th Rifle Corps, whose lead elements were approaching Chihsing but whose rifle divisions were also strung out far to the rear along the road from Linkou.

Furthermore, because Beloborodov had such a limited force facing Japanese defenses south of Hualin and the terrain was so rough, Beloborodov's ability to maneuver his forces was severely restricted. The make-up of Anishchik's force, which consisted primarily of tanks and self-propelled guns, prevented any maneuver off the roads through the adjacent marshy and boggy woods and fields. Since the Japanese had destroyed the bridge spanning the Mutan River at Hualin, Beloborodov's forces could not cross the river until sufficient reinforcements were available to conduct an assault crossing. The only remaining bridge was at Yehho, which was still well behind the Japanese main defense line.

Therefore, Beloborodov ordered Anishchik's force to fix the defending Japanese while his remaining forces closed in on Hualin. Meanwhile, he formulated a new plan to envelop the Japanese defenses once reinforcements arrived by assaulting across the river south of Hualin and then attacking along both sides of the Mutan River.

On the morning of 15 August, while Anishchik's 257th Tank Brigade engaged the Japanese forward positions north of Tzumeiholo, the main body of Cherepanov's 300th and Svirs' 22d Rifle Divisions, accompanied by Morozov's 77th Tank Brigade and Skvortsov's 26th Rifle Corps headquarters, finally reached Hualin (see Maps 18a and b). Skvortsov immediately prepared a two-pronged offensive to commence on the afternoon of 15 August.[42]

According to Skvortsov's plan, Svirs' 22d Rifle Division was to force the Mutan River using makeshift means at Huashulintsin, 6.2 miles (10 kilometers) north of Mutanchiang, and attack the city of Mutanchiang from the northwest. Because of a lack of bridging equipment, however, no armor could accompany Svirs' rifle division. Meanwhile, Cherepanov's 300th Rifle Division and

Anishchik's reinforced 257th Tank Brigade were to attack due south against Japanese defenses along the Hualin–Yehho road shortly after noon.

Attacking as ordered, the 1049th Rifle Regiment and training battalion of Cherepanov's rifle division, supported by an SU-76 self-propelled gun battalion from Svirs' rifle division, launched Skvortsov's main attack on the right flank with the mission of capturing Tzumeiholo, attacking across the Mutan River near Yehho, and then advancing into the eastern part of Mutanchiang. Cherepanov's 1051st Rifle Regiment, with a self-propelled battalion and Anishchik's tank brigade in support, delivered a supporting attack on the left flank toward Yehho Station with the mission of crossing the Mutan River near the recently destroyed bridge and then advancing into the southeastern portion of the city. The 52d Mortar Brigade and 54th Guards-Mortar Regiment provided necessary fire support. Initially, these combined assaults overwhelmed the Takikawa battalion's defensive position and drove the Japanese force back to a stream north of Tzumeiholo, although Takikawa's headquarters also escaped.

A Japanese account described what transpired:

On the 15th, the enemy repeated the pattern of the attacks of the preceding day. In the morning he launched an attack using tanks as the spearhead, coordinated with infantry, artillery, and air. By noon most of the positions of the front line battalion had been seized, although battalion headquarters itself continued to hold out. Enemy tanks then advanced to a small stream between the first and second line battalions and, with close support from his infantry and artillery, attempted such a determined penetration of the division's position that a major battle began.[43]

The 'major battle' the Japanese report referred to was Skvortsov's general assault on the Japanese 135th Infantry Division's main line of defense, which began just after noon on 15 August, when Morozov's 77th Tank Brigade joined battle in support of Cherepanov's 300th Rifle Division.[44] From his army command post, however, Beloborodov did not like the slow progress he observed:

The report of General Skvortsov was not pleasing. On the main axis, the division of Cherepanov [the 300th Rifle Division] advanced slowly. The road from Hualin Station to Yehho Station was mined, and tanks advanced with difficulty. All was not going well with the crossing of General Svirs' Division [the 22d Rifle Division] in the vicinity of the destroyed bridge. Thus, we decided Konstantin Petrovich Kazakov [the chief of Army Artillery] would remain here and assist with the corps artillery, Maksim Nikolaevich Safonov [the Chief of Engineer Forces] would go to the river crossing, and I would go to the 300th Rifle Division – to Cherepanov.

Fornilii Georgievich Cherepanov was in a difficult position. His division was striking the main blow, but his forces were small. The order said, 'The 300th Rifle Division ...' and so on. But in reality? One regiment was still on the march. The second regiment – of Mikhail Frolovich Buzhak – was deployed facing east to cover the division's left flank. It turns out that only the 1049th Rifle Regiment of Lieutenant Colonel Konstantin Vasil'evich Panin, with supporting tanks, was attacking southward towards Yehho.[45]

Thus, the piecemeal nature of Skvortsov's assault failed to achieve the overall objective. Beloborodov's army had yet to establish contact with the 65th Rifle Corps of Krylov's 5th Army, which was advancing on Yehho from the east, and until such contact was made, the advance by Cherepanov's 300th Rifle Division would continue to experience severe difficulty. Therefore Beloborodov decided to personally supervise the ensuing action. Under heavy enemy fire, Beloborodov made his way to Cherepanov's forward observation point, where he learned that the general had just been seriously wounded. Beloborodov immediately ordered Colonel Lubiagin, Skvortsov's deputy corps commander, to take command of the assault and then joined Lieutenant Colonel Panin at his regimental command post just north of Tzumeiholo. Beloborodov later described the price his army paid for the advance toward Yehho Station:

The mountain road from Nan'chatsi south was literally crammed with smertniki [kamikazes]. There were groups of them even midst the mine-fields. The rifle battalions of Captains E. N. Baibus, D. I. Sindiashkin, and I. P. Artemenko advanced together with tanks; and our sappers fearlessly advanced forward creating paths through the mine fields under heavy artillery and machine gun fire of the enemy, simultaneously destroying smertniki in hand-to-hand combat.[46]

Japanese accounts testify to the ferocity of the day's fighting:

Meanwhile, the battle in the 135th Division positions continued, with the enemy's attacks mounting in fury. Several of his tanks got as far as the vicinity of the division headquarters. Our close-quarters combat teams [the raiding battalions] continued their suicidal attacks and amid the bursting shells and shouts of both sides the twilight engagement took on a ghastly appearance. Night fell before the battle reached the decisive stage. The enemy's front line troops retired to the line of the small stream, and the battlefield gradually became quiet.[47]

By nightfall on 15 August, the forward elements of Cherepanov's rifle division and Anishchik's and Morozov's tank brigades consolidated along the stream just north of Tzumeiholo, 3.1 miles (5 kilometers) short of their

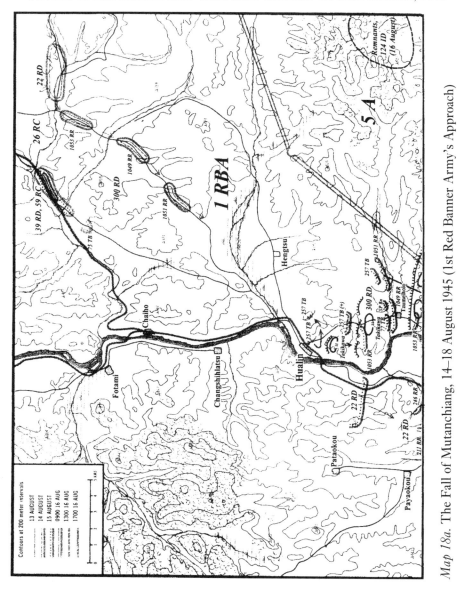

Map 18a. The Fall of Mutanchiang, 14–18 August 1945 (1st Red Banner Army's Approach)

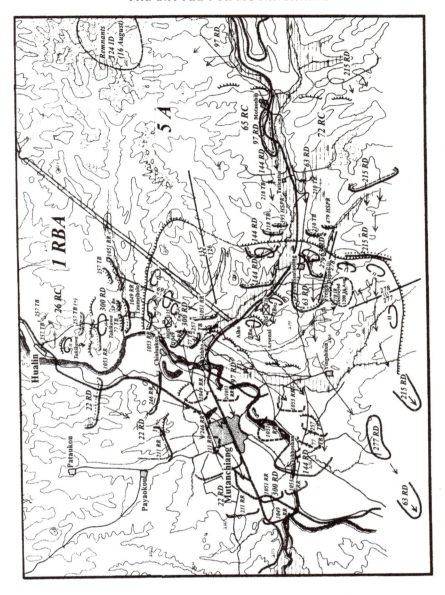

Map 18b. The Fall of Mutanchiang, 14–18 August 1945 (Final Assault)

assigned objective. Beloborodov returned to his headquarters to learn that Svirs' 22d Rifle Division, less its artillery and heavy equipment, had finally managed to cross the Mutan River. By evening, Svirs' lead rifle regiments, the 211th and 246th, were only 2.5–3.1 miles (4–5 kilometers) north of Mutanchiang, and Svirs' reconnaissance teams had already penetrated into the outskirts of the city, where Japanese defenses were very weak. However, the 22d Rifle Division lacked the artillery and tanks with which to exploit its momentary advantage.

With Svirs' division safely across the Mutan River, Beloborodov decided to launch a coordinated attack against Japanese defenses on both sides of the river on the morning of 16 August. After a short artillery preparation, the full 300th and 22d Rifle Divisions would attack, supported by additional armor and artillery units just arrived on the battlefield.

The 5th Army's Assault

While Beloborodov's forces were striking southward from Hualin on 14 and 15 August, the forces of Krylov's 5th Army continued their assaults on Japanese defenses on the eastern approaches to Mutanchiang (see Map 17). By the evening of 13 August, Zorin's 144th Rifle Division of Perekrestov's 65th Rifle Corps, supported by Velichko's 218th Tank Brigade and 395th Heavy Self-propelled Artillery Regiment, was concentrated north of the Mutanchiang road only 1.8 miles (3 kilometers) southeast of Ssutaoling. At the same time, Gordienko's 63d Rifle Division of Kazartsev's 72d Rifle Corps, supported by Krasnoshtin's 210th Tank Brigade and the 479th Heavy Self-propelled Artillery Regiment, were deployed just 2 kilometers east of Hill 371, which was located just north of Ssutaoling.

Krylov ordered the two reinforced rifle divisions to assault Japanese defenses east of Mutanchiang before midday on 14 August. Just over one infantry battalion of the Japanese 126th Infantry Division's 279th Infantry Regiment defended the approaches to Hill 371, and three battalions of the division's 278th Infantry Regiment manned defenses facing east and south toward Ssutaoling and the hills to the south.

At 1100 hours on 14 August, Krylov's artillery opened fire on Japanese artillery positions on low hills north of Ssutaoling in an attempt to neutralize the Japanese batteries. Two hours later the Soviets shifted their concentrated fire to the hill near Ssutaoling itself. Elements of Velichko's 218th Tank Brigade, reinforced by infantry, then assaulted the defenses of the 3d Battalion, 279th Infantry Regiment, which consisted of field fortifications forming a sharp salient southeast of Hill 371. By 1500 hours Velichko's force had annihilated the Japanese defenders. Shortly thereafter, troops of the 144th Rifle Division occupied Hill 371, although during the night they had to repulse several desperate Japanese counterattacks.

A veteran of the 126th Division's fight describes the action early on 14 August:

> At about 1000 hours on the 14th enemy artillery took positions on both sides of the road approaching Ssutaoling. An hour later it opened fire, initially selecting our artillery positions north of Ssutaoling Hill as targets. While continuing this fire, the enemy at 1300 began laying a concentration of fire on Ssutaoling Hill itself.
>
> On the division's [the 126th Infantry Division] left flank, meanwhile, another enemy force, consisting of about seven tanks, attacked positions in a salient southeast of Hill 371, held by the 3d Battalion of the 279th Regiment. Outposts troops, concealing themselves in trenches, made desperate efforts to hold their positions, but by 1500 hours all of them, about thirty in number, had been annihilated by enemy tank fire. Immediately thereafter, enemy infantry advanced and occupied the Hill 371 positions, and hence gained a favorable observation post. That night our troops launched night attacks in an attempt to recapture it, but failed mainly because the enemy was able to reinforce his positions repeatedly.[48]

Meanwhile, tanks from Krasnoshtin's 210th Tank Brigade and riflemen from Gordienko's 63d Rifle Division assaulted the defenses of the 279th Infantry Regiment's main forces in an attempt to capture Ssutaoling and adjacent Ssutaoling Hill. After the initial assault failed, Krylov organized a four-hour artillery barrage, which destroyed or damaged Japanese defensive works and disorganized the Japanese defenders. When the artillery fire ended, the 63d Rifle Division's 226th Rifle Regiment finally seized the crest.[49]

A veteran of the Japanese 126th Infantry Division later recalled the fight:

> Meanwhile, the regiment's main body was locked in an infantry-tank-artillery struggle in the Ssutaoling Hill position. Enemy tanks were unable to move to the upper part of this hill. The enemy thereafter began a four-hour concentration of fire on the summit and finally destroyed our positions there completely. With the summit positions out, about thirty enemy tanks then attacked the road at the slopes and at the same time fired on the northern slope of the Hill. Infantry troops near the road concealed themselves in firing trenches and let the enemy tanks pass over them. When the enemy infantry following the tanks came close our men opened fire. The enemy was put in great confusion.
>
> Immediately afterwards enemy tanks in reserve to the rear moved up and fired upon our troops one by one. By sunset the Ssutaoling positions, but not the village of Ssutaoling, were in enemy hands. In an attempt to recapture them, heroic close-quarter combat teams organized by the Engineer unit repeatedly engaged the enemy, and succeeded in destroy-

ing eight tanks. Artillery units concentrated their fire on the enemy tanks without giving thought to the counter-battery fire being placed on their positions; sixteen enemy tanks were destroyed by our battery of the 20th Heavy Field Artillery Regiment and ten by the 126th Artillery Regiment.

After sunset the division continued its attempt to recapture Ssutaoling Hill. Taking advantage of the brief lull at night in the enemy's use of tanks and artillery, the division sent out close-quarter units of the raiding battalion. The enemy's security measures around his newly won positions were very effective, however, and prevented our elements from gaining measurable success. The division also directed the 279th Infantry Regiment to launch a night assault. This assault also failed for the same reason. The enemy suspended his attacks during the night and concentrated on strengthening the security of his position.[50]

Another account, written by a veteran of the 126th Division, presented another perspective on the fierce fighting:

About fifty or sixty enemy guns were deployed east of Ssutaoling, near the main road, on the morning of the 14th preparing to assault the Ssutaoling Heights and Hill 371 simultaneously. Beginning at about 1100 hours the enemy tanks directed their main firepower on our division artillery positions arrayed south and north of the old tank unit barracks. At about 1300 hours the enemy began to place neutralization fire on our artillery while placing concentrated fire on the Ssutaoling Heights. At about the same time, seven enemy tanks came rushing into the southeastern salient of the 371 Meter Hill and, in spite of the brave fighting of the defending soldiers, the enemy captured the hill at about 1500 hours, and thus the Japanese lost this advantageous observation point. The enemy shelling of the Ssutaoling Heights, meanwhile, continued for four hours with the result that our position was thoroughly destroyed. At about 1500 hours in the midst of this shelling, about thirty enemy tanks, supported by infantry, rushed the Ssutaoling Heights. The defending soldiers allowed the tanks to pass through and then fired on the infantrymen following. The enemy foot troops fled in great confusion. Following this the enemy tank reserves in the rear rained gunfire on our defending engineers, who staged a vigorous close-quarters counterattack. Finally, however, most of the Ssutaoling positions were captured by the enemy. The division conducted night attacks on Ssutaoling and the 371 Meter Hill to recapture them, but unfortunately these were not successful.[51]

After the day's brutal fighting, Krylov's forces consolidated their newly won positions on the heights and prepared to launch new attacks against the stubborn Japanese defenses at Ssutaoling village the next morning (see Maps 18a and b). From 0800 to 1600 hours on 15 August, the 5th Army's artillery and tanks blasted Japanese artillery positions, knocking out all but one of the

24 Japanese artillery pieces, as well as destroying all four Japanese tanks and antitank guns.[52]

During the fierce bombardment, Gordienko's 63d Rifle Division, with Krasnoshtin's tanks and self-propelled guns in support, renewed its attack, this time striking the 278th Infantry Regiment south of Ssutaoling. Gordienko's troops forced the Japanese regiment to withdraw and severed its communications with division headquarters. Soviet tanks also reached 126th Infantry Division headquarters, where it encountered desperate and fanatical Japanese resistance, later described by a participant in the battle:

> As soon as our antitank guns had been silenced, approximately 30 enemy tanks appeared in front of the main positions of the 278th Regiment. They opened fire immediately and inflicted heavy damage, picking off the defenders one by one and disabling our heavy weapons. As a result of this enemy tank attack, the regiment moved its headquarters to a kaoliang farm. At about 1600 hours its telephone communications with division headquarters was completely disrupted. During this engagement, the 278th Regiment destroyed four enemy tanks and disabled five.
>
> Shortly afterwards, fifteen enemy tanks appeared in front of the division command post. One squad of fire men of the Transport Unit, each armed with a 15 kilogram explosive, attacked the leading five tanks in a suicide charge, one tank per man, and successfully demolished all five tanks. The succeeding tanks, after witnessing this scene, retreated hurriedly toward Ssutaoling. Enemy infantry following the tanks on foot were also put to route [sic].[53]

Severely shaken by the reverse, Krasnoshtin's tanks withdrew to Ssutaoling to regroup. With Soviet tanks attacking the division's headquarters and with all divisional artillery destroyed, Nomizo, 126th Infantry Division commander, contemplated desperate measures to restore the situation:

> On receipt of the first report concerning the advance of enemy tanks in the immediate front of the command post, division headquarters concluded that the fighting had entered its final stages. When the chief of staff asked the division commander 'What shall we do?', the commander answered calmly: 'Since I entrust you with everything, you can do as you see fit.' The chief of staff said: 'Then, I will order the final charge.' He immediately announced this to all personnel of the headquarters and directed that preparations be made. The time was 1800 hours.
>
> Meanwhile, however, the destruction of the five leading enemy tanks and the route [sic] of the others had taken place, and upon learning of this heroic act, the chief of staff decided that the headquarters did not have to resort to the final charge. The enemy artillery discontinued firing and the battlefield became rather quiet.[54]

The unexpectedly strong resistance by the Japanese 126th Division's forces east of Mutanchiang prompted Meretskov at 1st Far Eastern Front headquarters to amend the 5th Army's mission. Rather than battering itself to pieces against Japanese defenses east of Mutanchiang, instead, early on 15 August, Meretskov ordered his army to sidestep the city to the south, leaving only a portion of its force to cooperate with Beloborodov's 1st Red Banner Army in the reduction of the fanatical Japanese resistance.

The orders, which Meretskov issued at 1645 hours on 15 August, directed Krylov to wheel his 5th Army's forces to the south in an attempt to turn the Japanese right flank south of Mutanchiang by advancing through Ningan to Kirin and Changchun.[55] Krylov ordered strong forward detachments formed around the nucleus of Krasnoshtin's and Velichko's 210th and 218th Tank Brigades to lead the turning movement.

At the same time, Meretskov ordered Dedeogly's 84th Cavalry Division, which was still in *front* reserve at Muleng, to advance into the mountains southwest of Muleng, then along the Tashihtou valley and through the Laoyeh Ling Mountains toward Ningan. A separate detachment of the cavalry division, with a small number of tanks attached, was to advance south from Muleng to establish contact with Chistiakov's 25th Army at Tachienchang.[56]

Over night on 15–16 August, Perekrestov's 65th Rifle Corps prepared to resume its attacks against Japanese defenses east and southeast of Mutanchiang the next morning, while, to the north, Beloborodov made final preparations for Skvortsov's 26th Rifle Corps to attack the city from the northwest and northeast. Skvortsov's mission was to capture Yehho and insert his infantry across the Mutan River into Mutanchiang proper. After capturing Yehho, Anishchik's and Morozov's 257th and 77th Tank Brigades, still attached to Skvortsov's corps, were to continue the advance southwestward to provide armor support for the 5th Army's 65th Rifle Corps.

Beloborodov completed deploying his forces to deliver what he hoped would be the final assault on the Japanese 135th Infantry Division's defensive positions at 0700 hours on 16 August.[57] East of the Mutan River, Cherepanov's 300th Rifle Division, supported by Anishchik's and Morozov's tank brigades, were to advance directly on Yehho with the 1049th Rifle Regiment on the right flank and the 1051st Rifle Regiment on the left. The 1053d Rifle Regiment, deployed in the division's second echelon, was to try to force its way across the Mutan River north of Yehho. On the west bank of the Mutan River, after regrouping its forces over night, Svirs' 22d Rifle Division was to attack Japanese defenses at Mutanchiang from the north and northwest, with its 246th and 211th Rifle Regiments in first echelon.

Facing inevitable destruction, however, the Japanese higher commands had already decided to abandon Mutanchiang to the Soviets. The day before, General Kita, the First Area Army commander, granted Shimizu permission to withdraw his shattered forces to Tunhua or Hengtaohotzu if its position at Mutanchiang became untenable.

> The invading Soviet Army has broken through the Manchurian border at various points. The Kwantung Army plans to organize a structure for a protracted war of resistance with the Manchurian–Korean border zone running along Mount Paektu (Changpaishan) as the final defense line.
>
> [The First Area Army plans a long resistance, using the area around Tunhua as the last redoubt.]
>
> The Fifth Army will try to hold the positions east of the Mutanchiang River as long as possible and then retreat to the locality of Tunhua or Hengtaohotzu.[58]

With the situation rapidly deteriorating, at 1200 hours on 15 August, Shimizu, the 5th Army commander, ordered his forces to begin general withdrawal to Hengtaohotzu after midnight (see Map 19).

> Under cover of night, the Army plans today to cross the Mutanchiang River to withdraw to the vicinity of Hengtaohotzu, where it will map out its further course.
>
> At 2400 hours tonight the 126th Infantry Division will withdraw toward the west side of the Mutanchiang City by way of the Hsinglung Bridge. The road on the south side of Yehho village will be used by the 126th Division.
>
> The 135th Division will withdraw from its positions at the same time and cross the bridge on the west side of Yehho by way of the road on the north side of Yehho, and will withdraw first toward the northwestern side of the Mutanchiang City.
>
> To cover the Army's withdrawal the Shihtou Reserve Officers' Candidate Unit will secure its present position (the line from the eastern end of Yehho to the southern heights), and after the main force of the Army is completely across the river, will withdraw toward the west side of the Mutanchiang City.
>
> All units will send a liaison officer to the former office building of the First Area Army Headquarters at about 0800 on the 16th to receive further orders.[59]

Although the withdrawal orders that the 5th Army's divisions subsequently prepared for their subordinate units echoed the substance of Shimizu's withdrawal order, many of those units were still in heavy contact with Soviet forces and never received the orders. As a result, the 126th Infantry Division's 278th Infantry Regiment and the 135th Infantry Division's Takikawa Battalion had no choice but to fend for themselves when the Soviet forces resumed their assaults the next morning.[60] A Japanese survivor described the failed effort to notify the 278th Infantry Regiment of its commander's intentions:

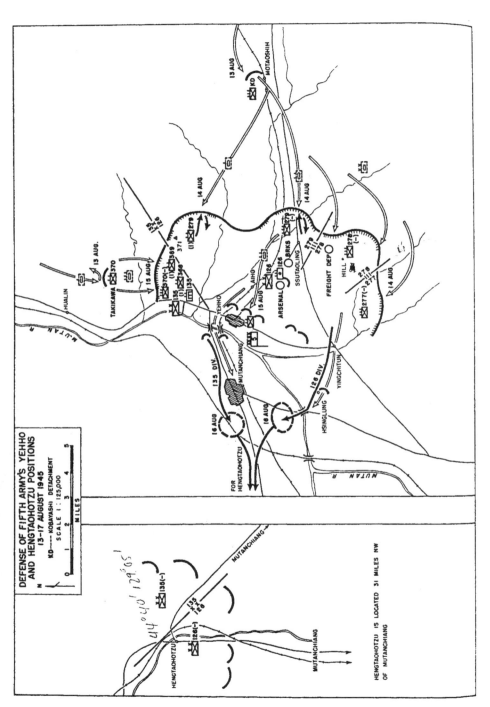

Map 19. Defense of the Japanese 5th Army's Yehho and Hengtaohotzu Positions, 13–17 August 1945

The regimental liaison officer who had received the withdrawal order at division headquarters directed a noncommissioned officer and private to carry the order to the 278th Regiment. At that time, the regimental head-quarters was located in a kaoliang farm, about 1 kilometer from the position it had occupied during daytime. The two enlisted couriers failed to locate the new site of regimental headquarters in spite of the fact that they searched until dawn. They concluded that the order must have been trans-mitted to regimental headquarters by other means, and returned to the west bank of the Mutanchiang River without conveying the order.[61]

Nomizo's 126th Infantry Division began its withdrawal at 2300 hours on 15 August, and, by 0800 hours, all of its subordinate units except the isolated 278th Infantry Regiment had crossed the Hsinglung bridge. Hitomi's 135th Infantry Division also completed much of its withdrawal by dawn, leaving only Takikawa's battalion to resist the Soviet advance.

At 0700 hours on 16 August, Beloborodov's and Krylov's forces began their final assault on Mutanchiang from the north and east (see Maps 18a and b, 19, and 20).[62] Crushing the Takikawa Battalion's defenses, Lubiagin's 300th Rifle Division, supported by Anishchik's and Morozov's armor, advanced due south toward Yehho Station as volleys of rocket artillery struck the Japanese rear areas and ignited ammunition warehouses. The few men of the Takikawa Battalion who survived the assault filtered away from the battlefield in groups of twos and threes. By 0900 hours, Panin's 1049th Rifle Regiment had captured Yehho Station, while tanks of Morozov's 77th Tank Brigade raced toward the Mutan River, only to find the bridge in ruins. Because the Japanese had destroyed all three bridges, Beloborodov then ordered his two tank brigades to attack southward along the eastern bank of the river, while his infantry prepared to cross it on makeshift rafts, logs, small boats, and by other impro-vised means. However, heavy Japanese artillery and small arms fire from the far bank thwarted the 1051st Rifle Regiment's attempts to cross the river.

West of the river, at 0900 hours, troops from Svirs' 22d Rifle Division drove into Mutanchiang from the northwest. After completing its concen-tration in final jumping-off positions at 0600 hours, Svirs' 211th Rifle Regiment began its assault at 0900 hours, entered the northwestern suburbs of Mutanchiang, and reached the railroad station. This attack surprised Japanese rear guards defending the Mutan River and forced them to with-draw. At 0920 hours Svirs' 246th Rifle Regiment entered the northern side of the city along the rail line.

Within several hours, all three of Lubiagin's regiments had also entered the city. His 1049th Rifle Regiment crossed the Mutan River on fishing boats at 1100 hours, while farther north his 1053d Rifle Regiment, in his second echelon, crossed south of Tzumeiholo on improvised rafts. Shortly there-after, the 1051st Rifle Regiment crossed the river south of the 1049th Rifle

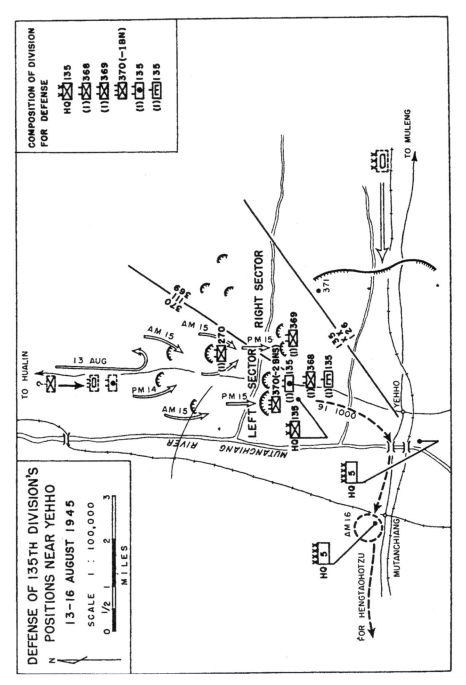

Map 20. Defense of the Japanese 135th Infantry Division's Positions near Yehho, 13–16 August 1945

Regiment. The combined assault by the 300th Rifle Division's three rifle regiments from all sides forced the Japanese rear guard to abandon the city completely by 1300 hours. Thereafter, isolated groups of diehard Japanese soldiers fought to the end in the cellars and basements of demolished buildings. Lubiagin's troops managed to clear the southwestern part of the city of Japanese troops by late afternoon, while Svirs' forces took all day to reach the western side of the city.

While the 300th Rifle Division was crossing the Mutan River into the city, Anishchik's and Morozov's 257th and 77th Tank Brigades advanced southward east of Yehho and linked up with Zorin's 144th Rifle Division of 5th Army's 65th Rifle Corps. Together, these units captured Yehhoshan, a village on the Mutan River 1.9 miles (3 kilometers) south of Mutanchiang, seizing an undestroyed bridge across the river that provided unhindered passage into the southeastern sector of Mutanchiang. At 1000 hours on 16 August, Perekrestov's 65th Rifle Corps of Krylov's 5th Army completed destroying Japanese forces east and southeast of Yehho when his units enveloped and destroyed the Japanese 278th Infantry Regiment.

A Japanese survivor described the regiment's gruesome demise:

> Meanwhile, the commander of the 3d Battalion, Major Ueda, visited regimental headquarters before dawn on the 16th and told the regimental commander that the division's main body had withdrawn. The regimental commander, however, declared, 'I am ready to die here. I will not withdraw until I receive a definite order to do so.'
>
> At about 1000 hours, while still in position near the kaoliang farm, the 278th Regiment was completely enveloped by a powerful enemy force consisting of infantry, tank, and artillery units. The regimental commander fought bravely and in the face of rapidly mounting casualties. At 1200 hours the officers and men of the regiment assembled the regimental colors. Being determined to die at the position, the regimental commander, Colonel Hajima Yamanaka, respectfully bowed to the east, burned the regimental colors, rallied the assembled men, and led a last charge toward the south. Then together with Major Ueda, the 3rd Battalion Commander, he committed *hara-kiri* in the presence of the enemy.[63]

With the ceremonial destruction of the 278th Infantry Regiment, the bloody battle for Mutanchiang had ended. At 2400 hours the same day, Meretskov dispatched a report on the battle to Vasilevsky, cryptically recounting his *front's* accomplishments:

Periodic Report by the 1st Far Eastern Front Headquarters to the Supreme High Commander of Soviet Forces in the Far East Concerning the Capture of the City of Mutanchiang

2400 hours 16 August 1945

1. After fierce combat during 15 and 16 August 1945, the 1st Far Eastern Front's 1st Red Banner Army and 5th Army crushed the enemy grouping in the Mutanchiang region by a combined blow from the northeast and east and again captured the city of Mutanchiang, the large road and railroad center and defensive center protecting the approaches to Harbin and Kirin. While doing so, the heavily fortified suburban enemy position covering the approaches to the city of Mutanchiang was penetrated from the east and northeast.

2. Having forced the Mutanchiang River, at 2000 hours on 16 August 1945, the 1st Red Banner and 5th Armies are developing the offensive; the 1st Red Banner Army in the direction of Harbin, and the 5th Army through Ningan (Ninguta) to Emy, Kirin, and Changchun.

The commander of the 1st Far Eastern Front
Marshal of the Soviet Union Meretskov
Member of the 1st Far Eastern Front's Military Council
Colonel General Shtykov
Chief of Staff of the 1st Far Eastern Front
Lieutenant General Krutikov.[64]

CONCLUSIONS

The Battle for Mutanchiang ended when the remnants of Shimizu's 5th Army withdrew northwest to Hengtaohotzu and ultimate Soviet captivity in Siberia. After capturing Mutanchiang, Beloborodov's 1st Red Banner Army consolidated its forces to strike westward toward Harbin, while Krylov's 5th Army marched southwest toward Ningan and Kirin.

During four days of the most intense combat that Soviet forces experienced during the Manchurian campaign, Beloborodov's and Krylov's armies drove the Japanese 5th Army's three infantry divisions westward from 93 to 112 miles (150 to 180 kilometers), in the process inflicting heavy casualties on them. The initial rapidity of the Soviet advance, in particular, the 1st Red Banner Army's, disrupted the original Japanese plans to defend a main line of resistance in the Laoyeh Ling Mountains east of Mutanchiang. It also forced the Japanese to fragment their forces by leaving behind detachments to protect the border, delay the Soviet advance, and protect the withdrawal of their own main forces. By doing so, the Japanese had up to one-third of their forces isolated and destroyed in the border region. Ultimately, the two advancing Soviet armies compelled the surviving Japanese divisions to defend at Mutanchiang in considerably reduced strength, without adequate supporting artillery and armor, and along truncated, woefully incomplete defensive lines.

The only division in the Japanese 5th Army that was able to occupy fully its assigned defensive sector in the Laoyeh Ling Defensive Line was the 124th Infantry Division. However, the division's defense proved too weak to withstand a determined thrust by several Soviet tank brigades, which split it asunder. Once penetrated by sizeable Soviet forces, the defense protected virtually nothing but empty mountainous terrain and became utterly irrelevent to the ultimate Japanese defense of Mutanchiang. The Japanese 126th and 135th Infantry Divisions could not redeploy rapidly enough to even mildly hinder the Soviet advance through the Laoyeh Ling Defensive Line. As a result, they had no choice but to defend against the concentrated forces of two powerful Soviet armies at Mutanchiang. By that time it was a defense that could not succeed.

Although Beloborodov and Krylov skillfully maneuvered their forces to preempt Japanese defense of the Laoyeh Ling Line, the token Japanese resistance and difficult terrain they encountered combined to thwart their efforts to seize Mutanchiang from the march. The pesky and effective forward detachments the 1st Red Banner and 5th Armies employed to generate the spectacularly high initial rates of advance proved incapable of sustaining their advance to the armies' final objectives. Falling victim to their initial dramatic successes, their long and exhausting marches and occasional fights eroded their combat strength to the point where they were unable to sustain the momentum of their advance. This reality, combined with the overextension of their parent armies across the rugged terrain of eastern Manchuria, prevented either from bringing sufficient power to bear on Japanese defenses at Mutanchiang without a time-consuming effort to concentrate the forces of the two armies.

For example, Beloborodov himself lamented the lack of sufficient forces at Hualin to overcome token Japanese resistance on 13 and 14 August, at a time when his army was able to concentrate only a reinforced tank brigade to battle the Japanese defenders. Nor did the addition of several more rifle regiments to his force at Hualin the next day materially effect the situation. Only two days later, on 16 August, was Beloborodov able to concentrate enough force to record any offensive progress, and, by that time, the Japanese defenders were already withdrawing from the battlefield.

Krylov experienced the same phenomenon in his 5th Army. Although the lead forward detachments of his army reached the distant approaches to Mutanchiang on the evening of 13 August, the bulk of his army's strength remained on the flanks of the penetration or strung out to the rear, desperately trying to catch up with his army's vanguard. Only by the evening of 15 August

129

did Krylov have sufficient strength to smash the Japanese defenses and, even then, his forward forces encountered fierce enough resistance to force both him and his *front* commander to alter his army's offensive plan and commit the *front's* mobile group along another operational axis.

Despite these problems, Beloborodov's and Krylov's armies utterly disrupted Japanese defensive plans, in the process inflicting heavy casualties on all of the Japanese 5th Army's infantry divisions. Shimizu's 5th Army reported 20,000 combat casualties out of its overall effective strength of about 60,000 men, including 9,391 killed. Hitomi's 135th Infantry Division lost an estimated 3,000 men killed in action, and probably another 6,000 wounded out of its overall line strength of just over 14,000 men, including 1,500 killed in the border region and another 1,000 in the fighting for Yehho.

Nomizo's 126th Infantry Division lost a reported 2,050 men killed and perhaps as many as 4,500 wounded during the eight days of battle out of its initial strength of just over 16,000 men. Finally, Shiina's 124th Infantry Division lost in excess of 2,300 killed in action and another 4,500 wounded out of its initial strength of just over 14,800 men.[65] The First Area Army acknowledged another 5,000 battlefield casualties suffered by its forces during the fighting. While gruesome enough in their own right, these figures appear far more realistic than the Soviet claims that 40,000 Japanese fell in the defense of Mutanchiang.[66]

On the other hand, the after-action accounts by veterans of the Japanese 5th Army and First Area Army claim that Japanese forces inflicted 7,000–10,000 casualties on Soviet forces and destroyed more than 300 Soviet tanks during the Battle of Mutanchiang.[67] This estimate may not be far from the truth. Recent official Soviet calculations of its army's losses indicate that the 1st Far Eastern Front suffered 21,069 casualties in the Manchurian campaign, including 6,324 killed, captured, or missing and 14,745 wounded and sick. At least half of these probably occurred during the fighting at and around Mutanchiang.[68]

Despite the tenacious Japanese defense and the difficult terrain in eastern Manchuria, the 1st Far Eastern Front's 1st Red Banner and 5th Armies accomplished their objectives well ahead of schedule. They preempted Japanese attempts to create a strong contiguous defensive line east of and at Mutanchiang and captured Mutanchiang on the eighth day of the offensive, ten days ahead of schedule. The two armies' success was due primarily to the employment of audacious and rapid advance over terrain the Japanese thought impassable for military forces. The ensuing advance carried Soviet forces to the gates of Mutanchiang and virtually paralyzed the Japanese command and control structure. Throughout the battle, the Japanese soldiers and their officers displayed absolute discipline and unmatched if not suicidal determination as they carried out their orders unhesitatingly and sacrificed themselves for what was already clearly a lost cause.

130

NOTES

1. The 20th Heavy Artillery Regiment (less one battalion), the Tungning Heavy Artillery Regiment, the 31st Antitank Battalion, and the 13th Mortar Battalion reinforced the 124th Infantry Division. See *JM 154*, 183.
2. The complete Japanese 5th Army defense plan appears in *JM 154*, 181–3.
3. *JM 154*, 182–93.
4. Ibid., 288–9.
5. Ibid., 190, 200.
6. Ibid., 199.
7. Ibid., 263–4.
8. Ibid., 260, 263.
9. Beloborodov, *Skvoz*, 42.
10. Ibid., 43, and *JM 154*, 286.
11. Beloborodov, *Skvoz*, 43–4, 49–50.
12. Ibid., 50.
13. Ibid.
14. *JM 154*, 260, 199.
15. Beloborodov, 'Na sopkakh Man'chzhurii', 46.
16. *JM 154*, 199, 260–1.
17. Beloborodov, 'Na sopkakh Man'chzhurii', 46.
18. *JM 154*, 207, 292–4.
19. Beloborodov, 'Na sopkakh Man'chzhurii', 46.
20. *JM 154*, 293.
21. Vnotchenko, *Pobeda*, 218, and Krupchenko, *Sovetskie*, 322, claim that the 257th Tank Brigade lost six tanks destroyed and 35 men killed on 13 August. More detailed accounts of the day's action at Hualin are found in Beloborodov, *Skvoz*, 45–8, and Beloborodov, 'Na sopkakh Man'chzhurii', 46–7.
22. *JM 154*, 200–1, 278, 297–9.
23. Beloborodov, *Skvoz*, 46, and Vnotchenko, *Pobeda*, 218.
24. Beloborodov, 'Na sopkakh Man'chzhurii', 46.
25. *JM 154*, 235, map 2, and map 4.
26. Ibid., 190, 195, map 4.
27. Ezhakov, 'Boevoe primenenie', 80, and Vnotchenko, *Pobeda*, 220.
28. Krylov, *Navstrechu*, 443–4, and *JM 154*, 236–8.
29. *JM 154*, 236.
30. Ibid., 196–7, map 4.
31. For Soviet perspectives on the fighting, see Vnotchenko, *Pobeda*, 220–1. The 124th Infantry Division's vivid description is in *JM 154*, 195–7, 236–8.
32. *JM 154*, 204–5.
33. Ibid., 239.
34. Ibid., 238–9; Krylov, *Navstrechu*, 446; and Vnotchenko, *Pobeda*, 256–7.
35. *JM 154*, 240.
36. Ibid., 240–1.
37. Vnotchenko, *Pobeda*, 221–2.
38. The 5th Army dispositions as of 14 August are from Vnotchenko, *Pobeda*, 256–7, and Krylov, *Navstrechu*, 446.
39. *JM 154*, 202–4, 263–6, map 1.
40. Beloborodov, 'Na sopkakh Man'chzhurii', 46–7, and *JM 154*, 293–6, map 1.
41. *JM 154*, 293.

42. Beloborodov, 'Na sopkakh Man'chzhurii', 48; Vnotchenko, *Pobeda*, 253; and Timofeev, '300-ia', 53–4.
43. *JM 154*, 296.
44. For details on this engagement from the 135th Infantry Division and 5th Army's perspective, see *JM 154*, 208, 286–97.
45. Beloborodov, 'Na sopkakh Man'chzhurii', 48.
46. Ibid., 48–9.
47. *JM 154*, 297.
48. Ibid., 266–7.
49. Vnotchenko, *Pobeda*, 224–54, and Krylov, *Navstrechu*, 446.
50. *JM 154*, 205–6, 266–8.
51. Ibid., 205–5.
52. Ibid., 269.
53. Ibid.
54. Ibid. 270.
55. Vnotchenko, *Pobeda*, 255.
56. Ibid., 256–7.
57. Additional details on the 1st Red Banner Army's plan are found in Beloborodov, *Skvoz*, 68–9, and Vnotchenko, *Pobeda*, 256; and the 300th Rifle Division plan is in Timofeev, '300-ia', 53–4.
58. *JM 154*, 67, 210. The portion of the order in brackets is in the First Area Army's version of the order, but not the 5th Army's.
59. Ibid., 211.
60. Ibid., 212.
61. Ibid., 272.
62. Beloborodov, *Skvoz*, 69–72; Beloborodov, 'Na sopkakh Man'chzhurii', 48–61; Timofeev, '300ia', 54–65; Vnotchenko, *Pobeda*, 258–9; and Krylov, *Navstrechu*, 447.
63. *JM 154*, 272–3.
64. Zolotarev, ed., *Russkii arkhiv'*, T. 18 (7-1), 353.
65. *JM 154*, 69, 215, 273, 302, and *JM 155*, 266. In places, the figure in these two sources conflict.
66. *IVMV*, 2:244.
67. *JM 154*, 69, 216.
68. G. F. Krivosheev, ed., *Rossiia i SSSR v voinakh XX veka: Statisticheskoe issledovanie* [Russia and the USSR in Twentieth Century Wars: A statistical survey] (Moscow: 'Olma-press', 2001), 309.

5

The 35th Army's Capture of the Hutou Fortress: Reduction of a Fortified Region

HUTOU: STRATEGIC SIGNIFICANCE

Hutou was an isolated, but strategically important, link in Japanese defenses in eastern Manchuria. Its high ground on the western bank of the Ussuri River north of its confluence with the Sungacha River provided good observation points from which to watch rail traffic on the Soviet Far Eastern Railroad. Because this rail line was the only one between Khabarovsk and Vladivostok, it would assume critical strategic importance in the event hostilities should erupt in the Far East. Moreover, the high ground just north of Hutou City controlled access to the only east–west railroad and road capable of handling heavy vehicle and rail traffic on the northern approaches to Mishan. Whoever controlled these heights controlled the avenues of approach in eastern Manchuria because the surrounding terrain was mainly swamp and bog.

JAPANESE FORCES

The Japanese had begun construction of fortified positions at Hutou in 1933, in part because the Soviets had erected fortifications of their own at Iman, across the Ussuri River from Hutou (see Map 21). To man the fortifications, the Japanese assigned the 4th Border Guard Unit (BGU), which had about 7,000 personnel organized into four infantry battalions of three rifle companies each, one artillery regiment consisting of two batteries of 24 guns, and one engineer battalion.

In accordance with the Kwantung Army's fortification policy for border defense, construction units and conscripted native labor built the permanent ferro–concrete emplacements along the high ground dominating the strategic avenues of approach.[1] The Kwantung Army's strategic assessment of terrain

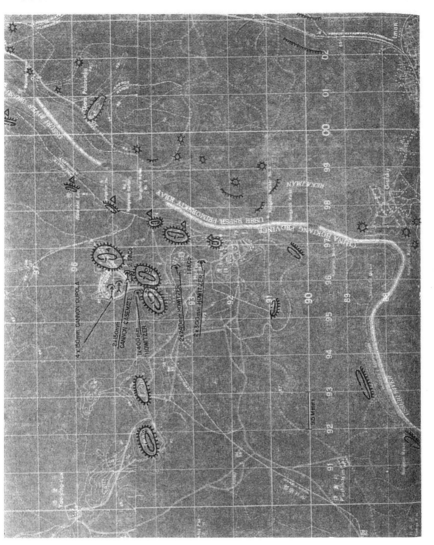

Map 21. Japanese and Soviet Positions on Eve of the Attack

dictated the Hutou fortress's isolated and exposed position, so army planners tried to insure that the fortress itself would be almost impregnable. They designated Hutou a 'special' category of fortress.[2] This meant that it had concrete walls and roofs up to 9 feet (3 meters) thick, was impervious to artillery fire, and was able to withstand a direct hit by a one-ton bomb. The only other Japanese fortifications to enjoy a 'special' designation were sections of the Hailar positions of western Manchuria.

The Japanese constructed the Hutou complex without dead space. They designed the fire pattern to blanket the 984 feet (300 meters) ahead of defensive obstacles and relied on oblique and flanking fire from adjacent units rather than on frontal fire to cover the dead spaces. One battalion or, in special cases, one company manned individual fortified positions. A company's frontage and depth was 643–1,093 yards (600–1,000 meters). Battalion sectors were generally 1,312–2,187 yards (1,200–2,000 meters) in width and depth.[3]

The completed Hutou forts had above-ground entrances, exits, observation posts, artillery and machine gun apertures, sally ports for local counterattacks, and weather observation posts. Underground were the communications system, living quarters, baths, water and supplies, generators, a communications room, and provisions. As mentioned, 9-feet (3-meter) thick concrete protected the key sections.

This fortress and the extensive Japanese fortification system in eastern Manchuria resembled a Manchurian Maginot Line. Like the Maginot Line planners, the Japanese did not expect the forts to hold back an enemy attack. Instead, the defenders would hold their positions and subsequently threaten the rear of the hostile invader, while friendly mobile forces prepared to counterattack. Also like the Maginot Line concept, the Japanese Manchurian defense designers assumed that certain types of terrain were impassable by large numbers of troops and equipment. Such thinking characterized Japanese defensive concepts.

The Hutou fortifications were on an approximately 5-mile (8-kilometer) frontage and a 3.7-mile (6-kilometer) depth. The 4th BGU Table of Organization and Equipment (TO&E) meshed perfectly with the assigned defensive frontages. Although the unit had only one engineer company, it compensated for this deficiency with two additional artillery companies, which were assigned directly to the garrison. The Japanese had a total of 59 artillery pieces at Hutou in addition to their eight medium mortars, 18 antiaircraft guns, and ten antiaircraft machine guns. They divided the fortress into three districts for defensive responsibilities, each garrisoned by four infantry companies and an artillery unit, respectively.

Although the Hutou garrison enjoyed a surplus of men and equipment in relation to its mission, garrison life there was especially hard. The physical isolation and severe climatic conditions made life bleak. High humidity in the underground forts rusted weapons, spoiled food, and proved unhealthy for the troops stationed there. The forts lacked soundproofing, so every noise reverberated throughout the fortress. There was no air circulation equipment, although vents and exhausts for gases and human waste did exist. The Kwantung Army declared the fortress a restricted area, and identification was required to enter the zone, which began just north of Hutou City. When local trains neared Hutou, conductors or guards pulled curtains over the windows so the passengers could not see the fortifications. From 1941 on, local authorities censored all mail and photographs. Hutou was a bleak tour of duty.

The Japanese were unable to maintain the high personnel and equipment standards of the 4th BGU because of vast personnel transfers as units in Manchuria were transferred to the Pacific fighting fronts. In February 1945, 4th BGU personnel served as cadre and fillers for the newly organized 122d Infantry Division. Their equipment was also shifted, in particular antiaircraft artillery and antiaircraft machine guns. In order to maintain this strategically important fortification system (not to mention justifying the huge sum of money expended in constructing the forts), the Kwantung Army, on 20 July 1945, used the remaining members of the disbanded 4th BGU as a nucleus for the new 15th BGU, supplemented by 600 additional troops who had been called up during the July 1945 general mobilization. The 15th BGU had approximately 1,400 officers and men (see Table 10).

TABLE 10: JAPANESE 15TH BORDER GUARD UNIT STRENGTH

Authorized TO&E	Actual TO&E	Frontage/Depth
12 infantry companies	4 infantry companies	8,000/6,000 meters
3 artillery batteries	2 artillery companies	
4 artillery companies	1 engineer platoon (4)	
1 engineer company		

Even these units were not up to authorized TO&E strength. One infantry support company was equipped with obsolete 37 mm antitank guns, and there were 13 artillery pieces in the artillery companies. Also attached to the fortress were non-combatants like the Hutou Army Hospital, commanded by a major with a staff of 40–50 attached military personnel, 500 Japanese civilians and dependents, and 200 Koreans. In short, the 15th BGU was hopelessly understrength and had only 20 days to prepare itself before the Soviet forces struck it.

Like the other fortified areas along the eastern Manchurian border, the Hutou garrison, as an advanced unit, would use its defenses to check the Soviet advance and thus allow the 135th Infantry Division time to conduct its retrograde movement to the redoubt area. Volunteers would also raid enemy rear areas to disrupt the Soviet advance.[4] A second mission assigned to the garrison units was the destruction of the key railway bridges of the Soviet Far Eastern Railway, which spanned tributaries of the Ussuri River just north of Iman.

The original Soviet bridge, about 4.7 miles (7.5 kilometers) from Hutou, fell easily within the 7.9-mile (12.75-kilometer) range of the Japanese Type 30 cm howitzer. Aware of the Japanese construction efforts around Hutou in the late 1930s, the Soviets, in turn, built a detour rail line and a new steel bridge some 10.6 miles (17 kilometers) from Hutou. In January 1942, to foil the Soviet attempt to prevent artillery interdiction of the key rail artery, the Japanese secretly deployed a monstrous Type 40 cm howitzer capable of hurling a 2,200 pound (1,000 kilogram) shell more than 13 miles (21,000 meters). The gun was never test-fired because the Japanese did not want to reveal its presence to the Soviets. Its mission was simple: to destroy the Soviet new steel bridge with the first few rounds it fired. This doctrine was consistent with Japanese field artillery practices. In 1943 a 24 cm locomotive gun with a range of more than 31 miles (50 kilometers) also arrived at Hutou. In summary, the Hutou fortress had the twin missions of delaying and interdicting the enemy.

SOVIET FORCES

Lieutenant General N. D. Zakhvataev, commander of the Soviet 35th Army, controlled Soviet forces opposite Hutou. The 35th Army's mission was to use a portion of its forces to cover the lateral railroad and highway in the area of Guberovo and Spassk-Dal'nii and to make the main thrust from the region of Pavlo-Federovka on the army's left flank in order to isolate, bypass, and reduce Hutou, while covering the right flank of the 1st Far Eastern Front's main attack farther south (see Maps 22a and b).

The Soviets regarded Hutou as a considerable strong point, and they correctly estimated that the Japanese had positioned themselves in a narrow section of the most vulnerable Iman sector and had echeloned their units in great depth along the railroad and highway running from Hutou to Mishan and thence into the interior of Manchuria.[5] The entire Soviet strategy for the Manchurian campaign depended on speed to prevent the Japanese from regrouping or consolidating their forces. For that reason, the Soviets could not afford to get bogged down in a contest for Hutou. Instead, Soviet mobile units would bypass the main Japanese defenses, and specially tasked units would stay behind to reduce the fortress. The Soviets calculated the garrison at Hutou at 3,000 effectives, about double what the Japanese actually had available.

Zakhvataev concluded that an attack across swampy terrain west of Pavlo-Federovka would find the point of weakest Japanese resistance. His

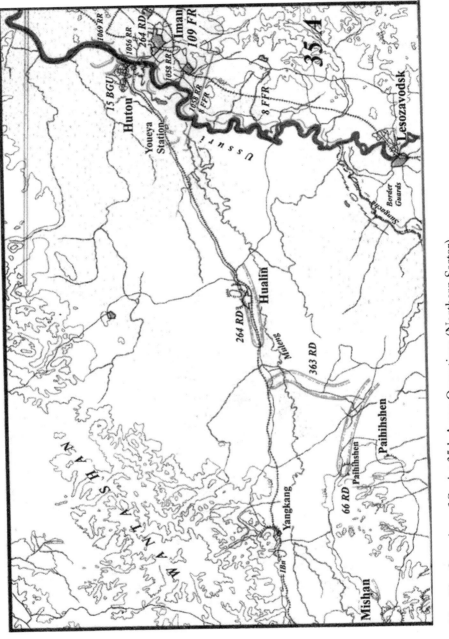

Map 22a. Overview of Soviet 35th Army Operations (Northern Sector)

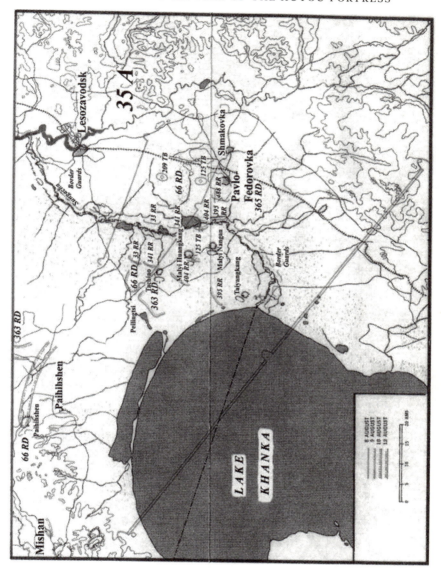

Map 22b. Overview of Soviet 35th Army Operations (Southern Sector)

main forces would strike from there toward Hulin to cut the railroad between Hulin and Mishan. Subsequently, Major General B. L. Vinogradov's 264th Rifle Division and the 109th Fortified Region opposite Hutou would make an auxiliary thrust to the south of Hutou to destroy the Hutou–Hulin grouping, and then, in cooperation with other units of the 1st Red Banner Army, they would attempt to rout enemy forces at Mishan.[6]

Soviet fortified region units and border guards detachments complemented Soviet 35th Army forces. Opposite Hutou was the 109th Fortified Region, approximately a regiment-size grouping. This fortified region was one of 14 such entities in the 1st Far Eastern Front's area of operations.[7] The unit had the mission of defending about 31 miles (50 kilometers) along the Ussuri River, from about 16 miles (25 kilometers) south of Hutou to approximately 9.3 miles (15 kilometers) north of the Japanese strong point. A comprehensive defensive network of Soviet barbed wire obstacles, antitank ditches, field emplacements, pillboxes, and observation posts dotted the otherwise drab terrain east of the Ussuri. Broken terrain, cut by numerous sloughs and pockets of marshy ground, characterized the area near both banks of the Ussuri.

Iman City, 3.4 miles (7 kilometers) southeast of Hutou City, was the headquarters of the 57th Border Guards Detachment. According to Japanese records, the 57th had about 2,300 personnel and six gunboats, which their river patrol guards used.

Members of the fortified regions and the border guards detachments had remained in the Soviet Far East throughout the Soviet–German War (22 June 1941–7 May 1945). They had the detailed knowledge of the region that comes only with years of personal observation and experience. Their expertise would greatly benefit the Soviet forces when they crossed the Soviet–Manchurian border because border guards units would make the initial crossing of the Ussuri and destroy the Japanese outposts that they had watched for so many years. Fortified region and border guards troops would also serve as guides to help the regular Soviet units through otherwise unfamiliar terrain.

THE SOVIET 35TH ARMY'S ATTACK

On the evening of the Soviet attack, members of the 15th BGU were conducting routine patrol and observation duties. The unit commander, Colonel Nishiwaki Takeshi, was at Yehho, about 200 miles (320 kilometers) southeast of Hutou, attending a 5th Army Headquarters briefing for division, brigade, and associated unit commanders.[8] There had been local indicators of Soviet activity, but higher headquarters dismissed such warnings, apparently because they did not coincide with the Kwantung Army's estimate that a Soviet attack before September was unlikely.

On 5 and 6 August, for example, small Soviet patrols crossed the border about 25 miles (40 kilometers) south of Hutou,[9] and on 6 August the BGU headquarters intelligence unit at Hutou reported intercepting a Soviet signal to the effect that the Soviets would soon attack Manchuria.[10] On the afternoon of 8 August, troops patrolling around Hutou's northernmost outpost, about 19 miles (30 kilometers) north of the main defenses, discovered pontoon rafts in the Ussuri River. They assumed that the rafts were debris from a Soviet summer military exercise.

Even after Soviet artillery began to rain down upon the Japanese on 9 August, no one at headquarters believed that they were under attack. They could, of course, hear the artillery barrage, but the Japanese thought that it was associated with the night exercises the Soviets occasionally conducted. Indeed, during June and July 1945, battalions, regiments, and divisions assigned to 35th Army had conducted such exercises on terrain similar to the area of their forthcoming operations.[11]

Exactly when the Soviets opened artillery fire on the Japanese remains uncertain. The Japanese claim that the barrage began shortly after midnight on 9 August, while Soviet accounts set the time at 0100 hours that day.[12] Thunderstorms had erupted throughout the Maritime Provinces during the evening of 8 August, so the *front* commander decided to break through the Japanese fortified positions without a prolonged artillery preparation, relying instead on the cover of darkness and the heavy downpour to gain offensive surprise. Artillery preparation was conducted only in the sector of the 35th Army.[13]

Japanese casualties from the shelling were negligible, but the bombardment cut the road, railroad, and communications networks around Hutou in several places. Outposts were unable to contact their headquarters to report Soviet crossings of the Ussuri. At 0100 hours, under the cover of a short artillery preparation, Soviet border guards troops of the 57th Border Detachment in platoon to company strength crossed the Ussuri on cutters with muffled motors or other types of boats throughout the 35th Army sector. In the Hutou area, one such detachment landed north of Hutou and overran and scattered the 18 Japanese defenders there. At 0200 hours, again under cover of Soviet artillery, the lead elements of the 1058th Rifle Regiment's advanced battalion crossed the Ussuri and, south of Hutou City, annihilated a Japanese outpost that had been covering the southern approaches to the main road and railway to Mishan.[14]

At 0500 hours the Soviet artillery fire lifted. Expecting an immediate Soviet ground assault, the Japanese took advantage of the lull to issue an emergency assembly order and to gather up several hundred dependents near Hutou and take them into the fortress for shelter. One hour later the Soviet artillery bombardment resumed; the temporary respite was a Soviet tactic to confuse the defenders into thinking an attack was imminent, thus

141

forcing them into the open to repulse it. This time small-caliber guns firing from positions on the Ussuri's east bank joined the barrage. Fire was accurate enough to keep Japanese heads down, but casualties were slight. Damage to open field fortifications, unreinforced positions, and roads, however, was extensive.

About 0800 hours approximately two battalions of Soviet riflemen from the 1056th Rifle Regiment started to cross the Ussuri south of Hutou City, while smaller, diversionary crossings occurred east of the city. By 1100 hours the Soviets had succeeded in establishing a firm bridgehead north and south of the city, despite suffering heavy casualties from two Japanese mortar crews.[15] Nevertheless, the Soviets had avoided a costly frontal attack on Hutou by moving to outflank the main fortress and to envelop the position.

During this entire time, the Japanese artillery had remained silent and had not returned Soviet fire. The Japanese had heavy artillery available, but a lack of trained artillerymen hampered getting the guns into action. Moreover, the artillery commander, Captain Oki Masao, had to do double duty as fortress commander. The guns consequently were not used to best effect during the early stage of the battle. Because the railway gun had not fired a single shot in anger against the Soviets, 5th Army Headquarters ordered it pulled back to Mishan shortly after dawn.

Captain Oki did not know whether this was a localized Soviet attack or the vanguard of a Soviet invasion because communications with other friendly units had been disrupted, and the fortress commander was absent and unable to provide any guidance. Oki was not alone in his confusion; Kwantung Army Headquarters waited until 0600 hours on 9 August (5–6 hours after the commencement of the Soviet invasion) before issuing orders to its subordinate units to destroy the invaders in accordance with respective operational plans.[16]

Not until 1100 hours did the acting commander of the 15th BGU authorize his artillery to return Soviet fire. At that time he ordered BGU forces to counterattack Soviet troops on the Ussuri's west bank and his artillery to suppress Soviet positions and artillery batteries.[17] The 40 cm howitzer then fired at the Iman railway bridge, while the 15 cm guns hit at Soviet artillery batteries opposite Hutou Station (see Map 23). These specific targets had long been plotted on firing tables and had their meteorological data computed, so the initial rounds were very accurate. The one-ton projectiles hit the Iman bridge and, according to Japanese sources, temporarily closed it to rail traffic.[18]

The Soviets retaliated with a renewed artillery barrage directed against the now revealed Japanese artillery positions. An aviation force consisting of 49 IL-14 bombers, provided cover by 50 fighters, mounted a two-hour bombing raid on the defensive works, particularly the Japanese artillery batteries. Russian artillery fire was especially violent because there were ten

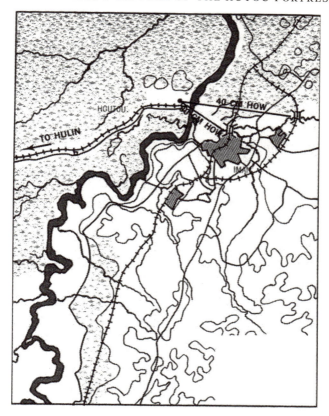

Map 23. Japanese Artillery Coverage at Hutou

battalions of a Soviet army artillery group in place in order to destroy the permanent emplacements at Hutou.[19] Soviet artillery concentrated on the Japanese 40 cm howitzer and scored a direct hit on the concrete embrasure protecting the gun. Altogether, the 40 cm howitzer would fire 74 rounds before a direct hit and explosion inside the cupola destroyed the gun and its crew on 12 August.

Under the artillery and air cover, Soviet troops continued to cross the Ussuri during the day and expand the Soviet bridgehead (see Map 24). Troops from the 1056th Rifle Regiment continued crossing east and south of Hutou and overran two small Japanese outposts just south of Hutou (called by the Soviets *Krepost'* [fortress]). Two composite companies of the 109th Fortified Region, one company of the 1058th Rifle Regiment, and one company of the 8th Field Fortified Area were also across the river.[20] The 1056th Rifle Regiment slowly began moving northward toward Hutou City and the Japanese observation post at Rinkodai. The 1058th Rifle Regiment and 109th Fortified Region advanced toward the Yuehya Railroad Station southwest of the city, while other elements of the regiment approached Hutou City from the west.

Thus, the 1058th and 1056th Rifle Regiments of Vinogradov's 264th Rifle Division enveloped Hutou to the south and cut the Hutou–Mishan road. As the two regiments advanced to secure the city, the 1060th Rifle Regiment prepared to move westward toward Hulin. The 264th Rifle Division had carried out its first essential mission by bypassing and isolating the Hutou complex, thereby securing the right flank of the *front's* battle group.

At Hutou, Vinogradov's rifle division, again under the cover of its artillery, tanks, and aircraft, isolated the fortress and moved against the city.[21] The Japanese defenders slowly withdrew from their outposts toward the fortified region, while using the cover of darkness to launch local counterattacks. Japanese troops assigned to the 2d Artillery Company exited the fortress near the central entrance and tried to dislodge the Soviet attackers on the riverbank. These soldiers seem to have had some success because they returned carrying artillery ammunition, weapons, and food. Another raiding party of infantrymen was less fortunate and was never heard of again.

The weather cleared on 10 August, but smoke and debris soon concealed the Hutou fortress from view. At 0630 hours Soviet and Japanese gunners began exchanging artillery fire. That duel lasted until about 1100 hours, when Soviet light bombers flew at low level to bomb and strafe Japanese gun positions. Soviet bombers did inflict heavy casualties and destroyed one Japanese artillery piece. The aircraft were able to bomb with impunity because the Japanese had no antiaircraft artillery or machine guns to defend themselves against air attack.

The Soviets launched the main attack against Hutou City from the south, with diversionary attacks to the north and center of the fortress. The intent

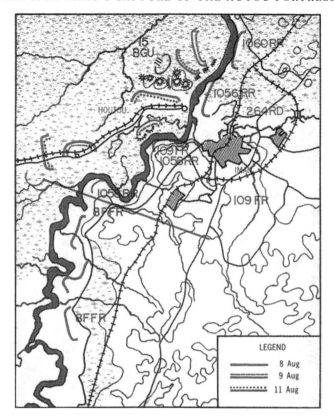

Map 24. Soviet 35th Army's Attack on Hutou

was to secure the city and thrust into the Japanese fortified zone north of Hutou. The 1056th Rifle Regiment and machine gun battalions of the 109th Fortified Region engaged in heavy fighting to capture the Hutou piers just east of the town.[22] The 1058th Rifle Regiment attacked the southern suburbs in an attempt to sweep through the city to the north and split the defenders in two. Soviet troops managed to reach the defenses of 1st Company, 15th BGU before a Japanese counterattack and hand-to-hand fighting drove them back south. By nightfall, the Soviets, in spite of two Japanese counterattacks, had been able to seize the town of Hutou. They had less success against the fortifications adjacent to the city.[23] Indicative of the hard fighting, a captured Soviet lieutenant told the Japanese that he had had almost no sleep for three days and nights.[24]

To reduce the Japanese fortifications, the Soviets formed assault groups from the attached combat engineer battalion and the forward rifle companies of the division's first echelon battalions (see Map 25). These assault groups would infiltrate and reduce the Japanese positions. The division assault groups consisted of a rifle platoon with a field engineer and an antitank squad, one or two tanks or self-propelled artillery mounts, two machine gun squads, and two man-pack flamethrower crews.[25] Obstacle clearing groups included three or four machine gunners and three or four combat engineers equipped with mine detectors, prodders, two bangalore torpedoes, clippers, and compasses. Each first echelon rifle company had two such groups.[26] One Japanese account refers to 'infiltration attacks', which were probably the Soviet assault and obstacle clearing groups working themselves into position for night attacks.

That evening, after the Soviet capture of Hutou City, a fierce Soviet artillery barrage raked the Japanese defenders in the fortified areas. The Soviets followed up the bombardment with a three-pronged attack by units from the 1056th Rifle Regiment, 1058th Rifle Regiment, and 109th Fortified Region. In this situation the Soviets relied on the forward battalions to penetrate the fortified areas. Taking advantage of darkness to conceal their movements and to attain surprise, they tried to seal off or destroy key strong points within the fortified areas by dawn.[27] The direct assaults on the night of 10 August failed.

After their failure to cut the fortress in half with a single offensive thrust, the Soviets became more cautious. The 35th Army commander ordered the 1056th Rifle Regiment and 109th Fortified Region to destroy 'methodically individual fortifications'.[28] The 1058th Rifle Regiment joined the 1060th in the army advance toward Hulin and Mishan. Soviet artillery and bombers pulverized the Japanese positions. This bombardment was so terrifying that the Japanese could not leave their underground positions to fight back. On the morning of this saturation fire, Soviet rifle units, accompanied by tanks (probably assault guns), again infiltrated Japanese defenses.

146

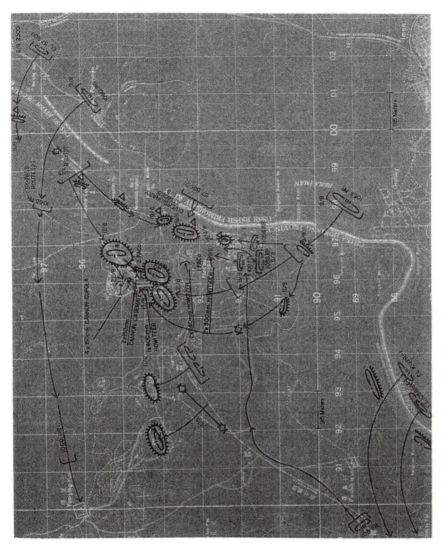

Map 25. Soviet Reduction of the Hutou Fortress

Assault groups overran the observation post for the central Japanese defenses. After destroying that pocket of resistance, they attempted to identify and bypass the strongest centers of Japanese defenses, leaving those for the rifle regiments to reduce.[29] Meanwhile, other Soviet units swung northwest around the fortifications.

At mid-morning two Soviet rifle companies working their way from the south to the north stormed Hill 119 and annihilated a platoon-size Japanese force defending that high ground. About the same time, a Japanese outpost manned by 18 soldiers and flanking the southern approaches to Hutou from Hill 90 was overrun, and the defenders listed as missing in action.

These small unit actions were characteristic of the Soviets' systematic isolation and reduction of the fortress. They were not spectacular operations, but they achieved their purpose of dividing the fortress and blinding its eyes.

That afternoon the 2d Artillery Company's 30 cm gun position, located just south of Hill 103, came under attack by approximately three rifle companies. The Japanese managed to destroy their own guns before they had to withdraw. Matters got worse for the Japanese. Following up the capture of Hill 119, the Soviets surrounded the heights and cut off all contact between 2d Company, 15th BGU, and the main fortress. The 2d Infantry Company existed in isolation and would fight on until 26 August before succumbing to the Soviet onslaught.

The Soviets spent 12 August consolidating their gains and using their newly won high ground to spot for their artillery. Soviet forward observers atop Hills 90 and 119 called down accurate artillery fire on the Japanese defenders. Japanese artillery was unable to return the fire because the Soviet spotters were adjacent to them in dead spaces. As their artillery pummeled the Japanese, the Soviets made preparations for their next major assault on the fortress.

On 13 August Soviet artillery, tanks, and infantry launched a concentrated assault on the very center of the Hutou fortress and on the only Japanese observation post (Rinkodai) remaining on the high ground overlooking the Ussuri. With assault groups leading the way, Soviet riflemen and tanks struck the fortress from the west, or rear, approach. First, they overran a Japanese outpost on the northeast side of the fortress and then sent infantry and tanks to drive a wedge from the west. Simultaneously, to the east, Soviet troops took the summits in the 3d Infantry Company, 15th BGU, defensive sector, despite Japanese counterattacks and hand grenade battles. From this high ground, the Soviets dispatched assault groups to infiltrate the Japanese fortifications. After locating the exhaust vents of the fortress, Soviet combat engineers poured gasoline into the vents and ignited the fuel. Garrison members sheltering underground were asphyxiated. This practice became a standard Soviet tactic to drive the Japanese to the surface.

During this fighting, one of the Soviet tanks supporting the infantry apparently scored a direct hit on a 15 cm gun belonging to the nearby 2d Battery of the 2d Artillery Company. Assault teams and heavy artillery destroyed 30 Japanese weapons emplacements in a single day, probably 13 August.[30] The 109th Fortified Region units conducted many of these combined arms attacks.

The Japanese platoon occupying the summit at Rinkodai, the high ground just above the fortress observation post, had been waging a bitter four-day struggle. The 50 men had been fighting since the evening of 9 August. Finally, on 13 August, the Soviets dislodged the defenders, but the Japanese regrouped and attacked up the slope. Their counterattack surprised the Soviets and swept them from the heights. The Soviets, in turn, drove the Japanese from the high ground, and the positions changed hands several times as nearby Japanese observers with binoculars witnessed grenade exchanges and hand-to-hand combat. Soviet numbers spelled victory, and, waving a huge red flag, Soviet infantrymen stormed the heights and drove away the Japanese. That night, however, a 22-year-old probational officer led a final sword-swinging counterattack against the Soviets. He was killed by a hand grenade, and the rest of his men perished. The central outpost was now completely in Soviet hands.

The Soviets continued to proceed methodically. After a rainstorm on 14 August, a Soviet infantry battalion surrounded the remaining Japanese outpost near Hill 103, called *Ostraia* [Sharp] by the Soviets. The Japanese defenders slipped away during the night and contacted friendly units. With the fall of the last Japanese observation post, the Soviets had effectively blinded Japanese artillery. The surviving artillerymen were therefore divided into antitank suicide squads and 'special' (read 'suicide') attack units.[31]

The Japanese defenders never received word of the emperor's radio broadcast ending hostilities, and the fighting continued as it had on previous days. Under overcast skies and rain, the Soviets tried to overrun the remaining Japanese 15 cm artillery piece in the 2d Artillery Company's sector. Grenades and point-blank artillery fire forced the Soviet attackers to withdraw. That night about 15 Soviet medium tanks attacked the Japanese outpost protecting the entrance to the main underground fortress just north of Hill 103. The tanks shelled the entrance for about one hour before withdrawing.[32]

In a downpour on 16 August, the struggle for the central heights, Ostraia, continued. Farther west, Soviet tanks appeared that day, and about 30 attacked the 2d Infantry Company atop Hill 145. The company commander, a second lieutenant, had about 180 men – 100 infantry and the rest a 37 mm antitank squad. The 37 mm was obsolete and worthless against Soviet T-34 tanks, as shells just ricocheted off the Soviet armor plating. The Japanese second lieutenant led repeated counterattacks against the Soviet tanks, but the net result was to get himself and most of his men killed in the hopeless struggle.

By the end of 16 August, after a three-day struggle, the Soviets secured Ostraia, but only after the central heights had changed hands nine times.[33] The hilltop did hold out for another 11 days, but the Soviets surrounded and occupied the hill above the underground fort on 20 August. The Japanese survivors, after a last-ditch attempt to break out on 26 August, committed suicide with hand grenades and explosives near the underground entrance.[34]

The defense was now degenerating into a cat-and-mouse game. Soviet engineers and infantrymen held most of the ground underneath which the Japanese tenaciously held scattered fortified points. The Soviets searched for exhaust vents, and if they discovered one, poured gasoline into it and ignited the fluid. Carbon monoxide levels in the underground vaults reached dangerous proportions, and some garrison members and their dependents became violently ill.

As desperate as their situation was, the Japanese had no intention of giving up. They demonstrated this dramatically on 17 August when the Soviets sent a five-man delegation comprising captured Japanese into the fortress under a white flag. The delegation reported in bright sunlight to a Japanese first lieutenant and informed him that Japan had surrendered unconditionally two days earlier. The officer departed; when he returned, he told the delegation that Japanese soldiers could never surrender.[35] To punctuate his point, he suddenly drew his sword and beheaded one member of the surrender delegation.

The Soviets immediately pounded the Japanese positions with artillery and bomber attacks. Then Soviet assault groups led rifle companies in an attack against Hill 114, occupied by the 3d Infantry Company. Heavy fighting developed over the control of this summit. By nightfall the Soviets had already occupied the highest ground around Hill 114 and had brought in field artillery to fire directly into Japanese defensive positions. The Japanese counterattacked and once even seized the Soviet gun pits, but the superior Soviet strength drove the desperate defenders back. The Soviets then positioned self-propelled guns, rocket launchers, and other weapons previously unobserved by the Japanese near the slope of Hill 114. Their combined artillery bombardment, again coupled with air strikes, made it impossible for the Japanese defenders to leave their underground positions to defend the heights. Under this massive covering fire, Soviet riflemen took all of Hill 114 and then repositioned their own artillery weapons on the summit.[36]

That same day, the 4th Infantry Company, 15th BGU, defending the northernmost sector of the fortress and protecting the northern flank of the 2d Artillery Company's gun positions, was overrun. The 4th had held what the Soviets called *Severnyi Gorodok* (Northern Settlement) against Soviet attacks on 13 and 14 August. These company- and platoon-size Soviet attacks were most likely probes designed to fix the Japanese defenders and defenses for the main attack. With only about half his original 150 effectives still alive, the Japanese company commander had to abandon the northern salient and lead his survivors to the main Japanese fortifications. Most of the men, however, were killed or captured during their attempted escape. The company commander later died during captivity in the USSR.[37]

Around 2200 hours on 17 August, the Soviets succeeded in surrounding the 2d Artillery Company's positions. During this fighting, one Japanese 16 cm cannon gun turret was destroyed when its companion gun accidentally hit it while attempting to fire point-blank into the Soviet attackers. At dawn on 18 August, the Soviets launched a large-scale assault on the positions of the 2d Artillery. The Soviet 255th Rifle Battalion of the 109th Fortified Region, supported by self-propelled guns, tanks, and the fortified region's 97th Separate Artillery Battalion, resumed its attack on the positions. Covered by the tank and self-propelled direct fire, as well as by the direct fire of the 97th's guns, Soviet infantrymen tried to break into the underground vaults and destroy the gun turrets within. A vicious struggle ensued in which the Japanese were reduced to firing blank cartridges into the onrushing Soviet troops. Not willing to squander manpower to achieve the inevitable, the Soviets withdrew. During 17 August the Soviets had brought up two batteries of 203 mm guns to help reduce the fortified positions by direct fire. In all, 34 high-power guns joined in the reduction effort.[38]

The next day the Soviets continued their attacks, but the Japanese judged that Soviet losses on 18 August must have been considerable because the Soviets did not press their attacks with any great enthusiasm. Artillery and aircraft pounded the remaining Japanese pockets of resistance, and 'heavy tanks' (probably assault guns) reached the main entrance to the underground complex, where Soviet riflemen and machine gunners exchanged grenades and small arms fire with the Japanese defenders. Enemy shelling finally destroyed a portion of the thick concrete roof between the 2d Artillery Company and the command post. Communications were severed, and the passageway turned into a small lake because of a steady downpour through the gaping hole in the roof. The Soviets now controlled all of the top ground, and the Japanese scurried below, trying to strike back at their tormentors.

The fighting, to all intents, was over. On the night of 19 August, after Soviet probes against the central Japanese positions, several Japanese blew themselves to pieces to avoid the disgrace of being captured alive. Others were cut down by Soviet machine gunners as they tried to escape what had been transformed into a big underground tomb.

A few Japanese survivors watched as the Soviets collected Soviet dead in broad daylight on 20 August, apparently unconcerned that the Japanese were still prowling in the bowels of the forts. That night small parties of Japanese tried to escape. Some were successful, but most were not.

The Soviets proceeded methodically to finish off the Japanese still underground, including 600 non-combatants. The Japanese allege that the Soviets used some form of gas to eliminate these last pockets of resistance. Only on 22 August, following still more air strikes and artillery barrages, did the 109th Fortified Region finally declare that it had seized the center of Japanese resistance.[39]

CONCLUSIONS

The Japanese garrison at Hutou fought with stoic valor, but, despite their efforts, the result was a foregone conclusion. What the Soviets did, reducing the Hutou fortress, is not therefore the paramount consideration. How the Soviets took the fortress is important. The battle at Hutou provides an insight into Soviet tactics against a fortified strong point, and there is every reason to believe that they would employ similar tactics, should the need arise in a conventional war.

The Soviet troops who participated in the reduction of the Hutou fortress complex were well trained and thoroughly rehearsed for the operation. Their training exercises conducted just before the invasion conditioned the Japanese defenders to the sound of Soviet artillery fire. When that artillery fire was turned on the Japanese, they were uncertain whether it was the start of a shooting war or of an overexuberant local Soviet commander showing off. That initial confusion added to the Soviets' tactical surprise.

While the Soviet troops may have been well rehearsed, that did not mean their operations were stereotyped. Flexibility existed throughout the Manchurian operations. The use of artillery, for instance, illustrates how the Soviets tailored their forces to meet operational requirements. The Hutou attackers received more artillery support than the southern wing of 35th Army because Hutou was a fortified area. Conversely, they received less armor support than other 35th Army sectors because they were not expected to make a rapid advance. Theirs was to be a systematic destruction of an enemy position fortified in width and depth. At Hutou the artillery performed its job by disrupting and isolating the Japanese defenders and covering Soviet assault groups. The assault groups represent another aspect of Soviet task organization, which tailored specific units for specific missions. Throughout the Hutou fighting, Soviet tactics were highly refined and characteristic of Soviet tactics employed during the entire Manchurian campaign.

There were no massed frontal assaults or wave-type attacks. Soviet infantrymen flanked, enveloped, encircled, isolated, and then destroyed Japanese strong points. The Soviets were extremely frugal with their own lives but lavish with artillery and air support for their Hutou operation. Sheer Soviet manpower did not take Hutou. Soviet combined-arms forces worked well together during the fighting. As soon as the infantry identified significant Japanese targets, Soviet air, artillery, or self-propelled assault guns would bring fire to bear on those targets. The infantry also showed its initiative by skillful infiltration tactics, usually conducted at night, which isolated Japanese strong points at a cost of minimum Soviet casualties. The infiltrators also became spotters and observers to identify lucrative targets for their other combined arms to overcome. The Soviets also took advantage of the cover of darkness to position troops and weapons for early morning surprise assaults against Japanese fortifications. It is true that the Japanese opposition was inferior in every respect to its Soviet opponents. But the Soviets were able to accomplish all their objectives at Hutou in a relatively rapid manner without expending vast numbers of human lives. Soviet commanders appear to have judged the Japanese military situation accurately and conducted their operations with the skill and precision that only years of command instill.

DOCUMENTARY ADDENDUM

From a Report by the Commandant of the 109th Fortified Region Concerning the Combat Operations for the Capture of the Hutou Fortified Region during the Period from 9 through 19 August 1945.

18 September 1945

18 August 1945:

An artillery preparation was planned on the night of 18 August, which provided for allocation of the artillery groups' fires against groups of targets and in direct support of the 211th Battalion's attack by the 357th Separate Artillery Battalion, the 255th Battalion's by the 97th Separate Artillery Battalion, and the 1056th Rifle Regiment's by a mixed group (from the eastern slopes of *Shtabnaia* [Headquarters] Hill), and the determination of its duration depending on necessity.

The overall combat plan called for the seizure of the unnamed hill 0.5 kilometers east of *Ostraia* [Sharp] Hill by the 211th Battalion, Ostraia Hill by the 255th Battalion, the unnamed Hill 0.4 kilometers west of Ostraia Hill by the 1056th Rifle Regiment, and *Grob* [Coffin] Hill by the 105th Battalion, which were formed into assault groups equipped with explosives, fuel, and grenades.

The artillery preparation began according to plan at 0900 hours.

At 1000 hours an enciphered message with the following contents was received from Major General Comrade Vorontsov, the 35th Army chief of staff, on behalf of Major General Comrade Romanenko:

'At 0130 hours on 18 August 1945, I phoned Comrade Shtykov (the Member of the 1st Far Eastern Front's Military Council) and reported the following:

1. I congratulate you on your victory.

2. The Japanese emperor is issuing an order to his forces to cease resistance and lay down their weapons, as a result of which I order:

(a) Explain to the resisting Japanese through prisoners or other means that Japanese forces are laying down their weapons and that, if they do not lay down their weapons, they will be destroyed immediately.

(b) The army's mission is to finish with Hutou.

(c) ... Poli is taken. More than 2,000 prisoners and many trophies have been seized. The complete disarmament of Japanese forces has begun in other sectors of the front.

By order of Major General Romanenko, an appeal has been prepared to the officers and soldiers of the garrison of the Hutou Fortified Region. Accompanied by seven parliamentarians, including six civilians and one soldier from a number of Japanese prisoners with a prepared text (in Russian and in Japanese) it was sent to the central settlement, where an appeal with the following contents was signed.

"To all Japanese soldiers and officers of the Hutou Fortified Region:

On 17 August 1945, the Emperor of Japan ordered all Japanese forces to cease resisting the Red Army and lay down their weapons. A massive surrender of the Japanese Army has begun on all fronts.

I order:

Immediately cease resistance, lay down your weapons, and voluntarily leave your positions. I am explaining that voluntarily leaving your garrisons and laying down your weapons will guarantee your survival and return to Japan.

In the event of disobedience the garrison will be immediately and completely destroyed.

The period of leaving the garrison to fulfill this order is 1400 hours today.

The garrison will leave through the northern outskirts of the central settlement.

The commander of the Hutou Group of Forces
Colonel Vavin."'

At 1230 hours the artillery preparation ceased. At 1250 hours the parliamentarians were sent to the northern edge of the Central Settlement on the road to Ostraia Hill where they were shown the movement route and told to go forward.

When they reached the southern slope of Ostraia Hill, at 1320 hours they were met by four Japanese soldiers with a white flag, who led the parliamentarians to the entrance of the *poterna* [a gallery in the massive concrete and ferro-concrete fortification] on the eastern slope of Ostraia Hill.

At 1330 hours a Japanese lieutenant exited the *poterna*, took the packet, and said, "We do not wish to have anything in common with the Red Army", snatched the packet away, and chopped off the head of the old Chinaman who was offering him the packet. The remaining parliamentarians fled and reported the results to us through an interpreter.

The powerful artillery preparation resumed at 1400 hours.

After the artillery preparation, an assault group of the 255th Battalion under the command of Lieutenant Vasil'chuka, which had been prepared in advance and was reinforced by sappers and equipped with reserves of explosives and fuel, reached Ostraia Hill in one bound under fire from Pillbox No. 76 and began demolishing and stopping up the pillboxes within the *poterna* with fuel, all the while repelling constant counterattacks by small groups of enemy with grenades. Having fulfilled his mission, Lieutenant Vasil'chuka, the assault group commander, was killed in this fight. Immediately, the 255th Battalion, which had been provided with the requisite quantities of explosives and fuel for the demolition of the pillboxes and grenades for the conduct of night battle, arrived to reinforce the success on Ostraia Hill.

During the day, the 105th Battalion captured the northern part of Grob Hill, and Pillboxes Nos. 93, 92, 91, and 87, seized the *poterna's* main exits, and carried out demolition of the pillboxes and clearing of the occupied region. On the night of 19 August, it repelled a counterattack by a group of 60 enemy soldiers from the vicinity of Pillbox No. 85.

The 155th Reserve Rifle Regiment cleared the region of an enemy group and demolished pillboxes and the *poterna* on *Lesnaia* [Forest] Hill and the Eastern Settlement.

The 211th Battalion remained in its jumping-off position on the southeastern edge of the Central Settlement and conducted reconnaissance in the direction of the unnamed hill 0.4 kilometers east of Ostraia Hill.

The 1056th Rifle Regiment (less one battalion) captured the strong point on the unnamed hill 0.4 kilometers west of Ostraia Hill, wheeling its front to the northeast, and, by companies, the 2d Battalion of the 264th Rifle Division continued to clean out and demolish pillboxes on *Severnaia* [Northern], Shtabnaia, and Vulkan Hills.

The artillery remained in its previously occupied positions. The 265th Rifle Division and unit, which had returned from Hulin, concentrated in the region of the Hutou and Grafskii crossings (over the Ussuri River) for loading on trains at Iman Station.

At the end of the day, Major General Romanenko, the Member of the 35th Army's Military Council [commissar], left for the town of Mishan.

19 August 1945:

The units of the fortified region continued to fulfill their missions for the destruction of the Hutou Fortified Region's Northern center of resistance on the morning of 19 August 1945, supported by direct fire by the same artillery groupings.

Having completed clearing its occupied regions of small enemy groups, the 105th Battalion reached the northern outskirts of the Northern Settlement, then fought its way into it and raked it with small arms and machine gun fire, and was withdrawn to Grob Hill in order to avoid the effects of fire close to the attacking subunits from the south.

The 211th Battalion, supported by the 357th and 97th Separate Artillery Battalions and the 76th Battalion (less one battery) of the 264th Rifle Division, which was approaching at that time, fought its way into and occupied the unnamed hill 0.4 kilometers east of Ostraia Hill, and set about destroying pillboxes with the help of explosives and shut off all conduits connecting to the *poterna* with benzene and subsequently demolished them with hand grenades.

The 255th Battalion continued to destroy the caps [turrets] and pillboxes on Ostraia Hill with explosives and benzene in the same fashion as the 211th Battalion. While blowing up the pillboxes and caps [turrets] on Ostraia Hill, smoke was noticed rising from the caps and pillboxes that had already been demolished on an unnamed hill southwest of Ostraia Hill, where, up to then, the auxiliary command post of the fortified region's commandant had been located. This confirmed the presence of a large underground installation on the Ostraia Hill strong point and the hills adjacent to it. Soldiers with submachine guns chained to metal posts fastened to wood on the roof were firing toward our troops to the south.

After destroying pillboxes on the western slopes of Ostraia Hill and attacking from it along its northwestern slope, the 1056th Rifle Regiment (less one battalion), supported by two battalions of the 224th Separate Howitzer Artillery Brigade from a strong point in the region of the Western Settlement and a battery of SU-76 guns from the 264th Rifle Division, reached the southern outskirts, and then, on order, occupied the Northern Settlement. By companies, the 2d Battalion of the 1056th Rifle Regiment continued to probe the strong points on Severnaia, Shtabnaia, and Vulkan Hills.

While attacking along the road to the Northern Settlement, the 155th Reserve Rifle Regiment (less the 3d Battalion), reached its eastern outskirts, and after linking up with the 1056th Rifle Regiment, halted along that line. The training battalion continued to destroy pillboxes on Lesnaia Hill.

By 1600 hours on 19 August 1945, the battle for the Hutou Fortified Region was completed.

A specially created commission to investigate the losses suffered at strong point Sharp determined that more than 50 bodies of Japanese soldiers and non-commissioned officers were discovered in five dugouts, warehouses, and *poternas*. In addition, up to 80 women – supposedly the families of the officers – 50 men and 30 medical personnel. Some of the women were armed with daggers, grenades, and rifles. Up to 80 children's bodies from one to 12 years in age were found in one of the dugouts. Of the total number of discovered bodies, one-quarter were killed by firearms, one-half perished from suffocation (in gas masks), and one-quarter died from blast waves. No corpses were discovered in the pillboxes themselves. The bodies present were located in the *poternas*, cul-de-sacs, and dugouts. A great majority of the corpses were heaped in piles. A large quantity of ammunition, and a considerable amount of foodstuffs were discovered in the underground warehouses and dugouts. Evidently, the reserves were intended for a lengthy defense of the center of resistance.

Conclusion:

1. The conjecture and evidence of the prisoners concerning the assembly of all of the smashed remnants of Japanese forces in other strong points of the Hutou Fortified Region for the defense of the main strong point on Ostraia Hill are confirmed.

2. In an absolutely hopeless situation, the Japanese garrison of the strong point on Ostraia Hill rejected the humanity manifested to them – the proposal to cease resistance and lay down their weapons to escape wrongful losses, which simultaneously guaranteed their lives and their return to Japan.

3. The main and final enemy strong point in the Hutou Fortified Region has been taken and destroyed.

4. We must thrash the separate small groups of enemy snipers and riflemen who have scattered from the smashed strong points of the Hutou Fortified Region...

The commandant of the 109th Fortified Region
Colonel Vavin
The chief of staff of the 109th Fortified Region
Lieutenant Colonel Kachanov

Source: V. A. Zolotarev, ed., *Russkii arkhiv: Sovetsko–iaponskaia voina 1945 goda: Istoriia voenno–politicheskogo protivoborstva dvukh derzhav v 30–40–e gody: Dokumenty i materially v 2 t.*, T. 18 (7–1) [The Russian archives: The Soviet–Japanese War of 1945: A military–political history of the struggle between two powers in the 30s and 40s: Documents and materials in two volumes, Vol. 18 (7–1)] (Moscow: 'Terra', 1997), 357–9.

NOTES

1. 'Small Wars and Border Problems', 21.
2. Ibid. See also Yamanishi Sakae, 'ToManshu Koto yosai no gekito' [Eastern Manchuria: The fierce battle of the Hutou Fortress], *Rekishi to Jinbutsu* (August

1979), 99–100. In August 1945, Yamanishi was a second lieutenant in command of an outpost of the Hutou fortress.

3. Yamanishi, 'Koto yosai', 102.
4. *SoMan kokkyo*, 122. Also see Yamanishi, 'Koto yosai', 100.
5. *SoMan kokkyo*, 122.
6. Pechenenko, 'Armeiskaia', 42.
7. Ibid. and Vnotchenko, *Pobeda*, 94.
8. Boeicho Boei Kenshujo Senshishitsu [Japan Self Defense Forces, National Defense College Military History Department], ed., *Senshi sosho: Kantogun* (2) [Military history series: The Kwantung Army, Vol. 2] (Tokyo: Asagumo shinbunsha, 1974), 482.
9. Kusachi Teigo, *Sonohi, Kantogun wa* [That day, the Kwantung Army] (Tokyo: Miyakawa shobo, 1967), 97.
10. *SoMan kokkyo*, 148.
11. Vnotchenko, *Pobeda*, 137–42.
12. *SoMan kokkyo*, 137, 152. The difference results from the Japanese using Tokyo time and the Soviets Khabarovsk time.
13. Pechenenko, 'Armeiskaia', 45.
14. Ibid., 46, and *SoMan kokkyo*.
15. Pechenenko, 'Armeiskaia', 46, and Yamanishi, 'Koto yosai', 99. According to Soviet accounts, one battalion made the river crossing.
16. Boeicho, ed., *Senshi Sosho*, 395.
17. *SoMan kokkyo*, 167; Yamanishi, 'Koto yosai', 101–2.
18. *SoMan kokkyo*, 139; Vnotchenko, *Pobeda*, 204.
19. *IVMV*, 232.
20. Pechenenko, 'Armeiskaia', 46.
21. Yamanishi, 'Koto yosai', 102.
22. *IVMV*, 25.
23. Vnotchenko, *Pobeda*, 213.
24. *SoMan kokkyo*.
25. A Soviet rifle division contained a separate self-propelled (SP) artillery battalion equipped with 13 SU-76 self-propelled guns.
26. I. Tret'iak, 'Organizatsiia i vedenie nastupatel'nogo boia' [The organization and conduct of offensive battle], *VIZh*, No. 7 (July 1980), 42.
27. Vnotchenko, *Pobeda*, 213.
28. Ibid.
29. *IVMV*, 232.
30. Ibid.
31. *SoMan kokkyo*.
32. These tanks may have come from the 3d Battalion, 125th Tank Brigade, which had originally tried to spearhead the Soviet advance across the swampy Sungacha Valley. Finding it impossible to move in the marshes, this brigade and the 209th Tank Brigade were pulled back into reserve on 10 August. The 125th, less the 3d Battalion, later appeared at Mishan. The apparent lack of coordinated effort in support of the 15 August night attack supports the theory that these tanks came from units not originally attached to the 264th Rifle Division or to the 109th Fortified Region. These two units seem to have operated together, probably because of the extensive training they had undergone just before the invasion. See Pechenenko, 'Armeiskaia', 47, nn. 12 and 13.
33. *SoMan kokkyo*; Yamanishi, 'Koto yosai', 106–7.
34. Vnotchenko, *Pobeda*, 253.

35. According to the revised 1941 version of the Japanese Articles of War, troops who surrendered uninjured risked court-martial punishment. The Soviets were also impressed by the incident and later described it as a wholesale massacre in which 'prisoners were chopped up by the sabres of Japanese officers'. See ibid., 263.
36. Ibid., 285.
37. *SoMan kokkyo*, 174.
38. Ibid.
39. *IVMV*, 252.

6

The 39th Army's Envelopment of the Halung-Arshaan Fortified Region: Operations in Arid Mountains

TERRAIN CONSIDERATIONS IN WESTERN MANCHURIA

When the Kwantung Army formulated its plan for the defense of Manchuria, it paid primary attention to geographical terrain features in the region and the combat experiences of its previous wars against the Soviet Union. Both of these realities seemed to reveal clearly where and in what strength Soviet forces would deploy should they decide to invade Manchuria. The Japanese deployed their forces accordingly.

Even perfunctory Japanese consideration of terrain indicated that two major geographical features dominated the terrain in western Manchuria, and both would have a decisive impact on the course of any anticipated military operations. The first feature was the formidable Grand Khingan Mountain range, which had traditionally served as a barrier to invasion of Manchuria from the west. Although of only moderate height, the Grand Khingan Mountains were rugged and scarred with numerous gorges, jagged valleys, ravines, and dry streambeds. The few passes through them were narrow and winding, and, with precious few exceptions, the roads through the passes were scarcely more than animal paths and narrow tracks, suitable for caravans and a limited number of foot-soldiers, but not modern military vehicular or armored forces.

The second imposing terrain feature was the vast expanse of desert waste and steppe land that stretched westward from the Grand Khingans into Inner Mongolia and Mongolia, which reinforced the defensive value of the Grand Khingans themselves. While the desert was a barrier in its own right because of its frequent mesas, buttes, gullies, sand dunes, and dust and sand storms, the lack of both roads and water in the region compounded the problems of any large military force advancing through it. If either man or beast wished to cross the desert, they had to bring their water with them. If the force mastered the desert, they then had to negotiate the treacherous passes through the Grand Khingan barrier.

Based on their study of the geographical realities of western Manchuria, the Japanese concluded that there were only two feasible axes of advance that sizeable military forces could use to invade western Manchuria. The first ran parallel to the rail line and road emanating from the mining town of Handagai on the Mongolian border east of Tamsag-Bulag through the mountains between Halung-Arshaan and Wuchakou to the towns of Solun and Wangyemiao (Wulanhaote) east of the mountains. The second axis ran from Hailar in northwestern Manchuria eastward along the railroad and road to Yakoshih and then southeastward through mountain passes to Wunuerh (Wunoerh) to Pokotu.

The Kwantung Army also took into consideration its previous military experiences in the region, which also seemed to indicate that large forces could not operate in the region. During the so-called Khalkhin-Gol (Nomonhan) incident in August 1939, the Soviets had deployed a force of roughly 57,000 men into eastern Mongolia to engage two Japanese infantry divisions that a launched a minor incursion into Mongolian territory. The Japanese concluded that this was the largest force that the water resources and transportation network in the region could sustain. Based on the Nomonhan experience, Japanese planners assessed the Soviets could deploy roughly the same number of forces into eastern Mongolia in 1945 as they had in 1939.

Further, the Japanese recognized that the Soviets could deploy an even larger force eastward along the Trans-Siberian Railroad into positions adjacent to the railroad line into extreme northwestern Manchuria. However, based on their assessment of the Trans-Siberian Railroad's capacity, they believed this force would not exceed 150,000 men. Thus, in the Kwantung Army's view, the Soviets could mount an invasion of western and northwestern Manchuria with a force of up to 200,000 soldiers. Given the terrain and transportation network in the region, however, these forces would likely operate along only two major axes of advance described above.

The Kwantung Army constructed its defenses in western Manchuria accordingly. It built strong fortified regions along both major axes of advance through the Grand Khingan Mountains and manned each fortified region with at least one infantry division. It expected its forces along these two axes to delay any Soviet invasion and perhaps even successfully defend for an extended period of time while it mobilized and deployed the mass of its forces in central Manchuria. Since the success of the Japanese defense plan depended on the attrition of Soviet forces, it expected that attrition to be the greatest in the easily defensible regions of western Manchuria.

As they had in 1939, however, the Japanese woefully underestimated Soviet logistical and combat capabilities in August 1945. Ultimately, the Soviet Army deployed more than 350,000 men into eastern Mongolia and unleashed them against the Japanese along ten separate axes of advance. Thus, a defense that the Japanese perceived as more than adequate was in reality an open flank. The Japanese defense system in western Manchuria turned out to be the Kwantung Army's Achilles' heel.

While Kwantung Army planners largely dismissed the military value of western Manchuria because of its forbidding terrain, Soviet planners did not. In fact, Soviet military planners perceived the region's terrain as offering opportunities they could exploit to achieve surprise and win a quick victory. To Soviet planners, the most critical geographical feature in western Manchuria was the salient around Tamsag-Bulag in extreme eastern Outer Mongolia that pointed like a dagger toward the interior of Manchuria. While the point of the dagger was the closest point to central Manchuria, it also faced one of the two heavily defended axes of advance through the Grand Khingan Mountains, the route from Handagai past Halung-Arshaan and Wuchakou to Solun and the central Manchuria plain.

Based on their previous war experiences, the Soviets concluded that, if they planned carefully enough, they could deploy large forces into both the eastern extremity of Mongolia and the vast region southwest of Tamsag-Bulag. These forces could then pin down the relatively small Japanese force in the Halung-Arshaan and Wuchakou fortified regions, bypass it, and gain control over the main rail and road route into western Manchuria. More important still, if it advanced rapidly enough, the large force arrayed along the Inner Mongolian border to the south could attack across the deserts of Inner Mongolia and the Grand Khingan Mountains, and gain the Manchurian central valley by surprise, completely bypassing the heavily defended mountain pass through Halung-Arshaan and Wuchakou and pre-empting any subsequent Japanese defense in the west.

JAPANESE DEFENSES IN WESTERN MANCHURIA

The Japanese Third Area Army's 44th Army, commanded by Lieutenant General Yoshio Hongo, was responsible for defending western Manchuria south from Handagai to north of Jehol. Formed on 5 June 1945, Hongo's army consisted of three infantry divisions (the 63d, 107th, and 117th), one independent tank brigade (the 9th), one independent antitank battalion (the 29th), one raiding unit (the 2d), and a variety of supporting artillery and other units. Hongo's 63d Infantry Division was stationed along the railroad line from Liaoyuan (Shuangliao) westward to Kailu, and the 107th and 117th Infantry Divisions along the railroad line extending northwestward through

Taonan, Wangyemiao (Hsingan), and Solun to Wuchakou and Halung-Arshaan. The bulk of the army's supporting forces were still located in the Liaoyuan region in central Manchuria.

The Third Area Army's mission was:

> To exhaust the invading Soviet forces by carrying out harassing operations in the area between the western border and the Dairen–Hsinking Railway, but to avoid a major engagement; then to withdraw to the Tunhua area and destroy the enemy in the area east of the railway from prepared positions in the Tunghua [redoubt] area.[1]

Thus, the focus of the Third Area Army was clearly on the interior of Manchuria rather than its western border.

Within the area army's plan, the mission of Hongo's 44th Army was as follows:

> The Forty-Fourth Army and the 108th Division [at Jehol] will avoid a decisive battle and will exhaust the enemy's fighting strength and delay his advance. Should the enemy infiltrate and advance, these units will try to impair the enemy's fighting capability by attacking him from the rear.[2]

Since Hongo considered the narrow pass through the Grand Khingan Mountains from Handagai through Halung-Arshaan to Wuchakou as the most important and the only feasible axis of advance into western Manchuria, he defended that axis with two of his three divisions, the 107th and 117th Infantry Divisions. Hongo stationed the 107th Infantry Division in the sector extending from Handagai through the Grand Khingans to Wangyemiao and the 117th Infantry Division from Paichengtzu (Paicheng) southward through Taonan to Kaitung.

The most formidable defenses in the 44th Army's sector were the fortified regions along and forward of the main pass through the Grand Khingan Mountains between Halung-Arshaan and Wuchakou. The fortification ran parallel to the railroad line and road that ran throughout the pass and the Taoerh Ho (River), which formed another obstacle to lateral movement, especially in flood stage. The only road in the entire region suitable to support military operations was the Handagai–Wuchakou–Solun road. As formidable as these natural obstacles were, the primary obstacles to movement through the pass were the numerous and substantial fortifications and defensive field positions the Japanese had erected.

The Japanese erected their most important fortifications around or near Handagai, Iruse, Halung-Arshaan, and Wuchakou. These consisted of pillboxes, earthen dugouts, trenches, and, in the Wuchakou region, reinforced concrete field fortifications. A line of entrenchments protected the railroad running south from Halung-Arshaan, and additional field works covered the road junction south of Handagai. West of the road, in the hills adjacent to the border, the Japanese built observation posts and occasional field works manned by units ranging in size from squad to full battalion. The Japanese constructed a second line of field positions to the west of Wangyemiao, but it was still incomplete in August 1945. In short, an extensive and elaborate but exceedingly narrow system of Japanese fortifications defended the main axis of advance from Outer Mongolia into central Manchuria.

The Japanese 107th Infantry Division, commanded by Lieutenant General Koichi Abe, with headquarters at Wuchakou, manned these fortifications and positions along the rail line from the border to Wangyemiao (see Table 11). Subordinate to Hongo's 44th Army, whose mission was to cover enemy invasion routes into western Manchuria from Handagai to the south, the 107th Infantry Division defended the Handagai–Wangyemiao sector. The 117th Infantry Division, which was stationed at Paichengtzu and Taonan, and the 63d Infantry Division, which was situated to the southwest at Tungliao, backed up Koichi's division. The 2d Raiding Battalion stationed at Wangyemiao also supported the 107th Infantry Division.[3]

TABLE 11: JAPANESE 107TH INFANTRY DIVISION COMPOSITION, 9 AUGUST 1945

90th Infantry Regiment
177th Infantry Regiment
178th Infantry Regiment
107th Artillery Regiment
107th Engineer Regiment
107th Transportation Regiment
107th Signal Regiment
107th Reconnaissance Company

Source: Ota Hisao, Dai 107 shidan shi: Saigo made tatakatta Kantogun [The history of the 107th Division: The Kwantung Army that resisted to the last] (Tokyo: Taiseido Shoten Shuppanbu, 1979), 14, 24, 26, 72, 76–9.

By July 1945 the defensive plan of Hongo's 44th Army called for small units to defend along the border and the army's main forces to conduct a delaying action back into central Manchuria. Ultimately, Hongo hoped to withdraw the bulk of his forces into defenses in the redoubt area around Tunghua in southeastern Manchuria. Within the context of this plan, Hongo assigned his subordinate forces, including Abe's 107th Infantry Division, the following mission:

The 107th Division will secure the prepared positions in the vicinities of Wuchakou and Hsingen (Wangyemiao) and the rest of the commands will secure the key traffic points along the railroad line from Ssupingchieh (Ssuping)–Taonan Railroad and the Liaoyuan–Tungliao Railroad and check the enemy advance at these positions.

Positions will be organized at key traffic points and guerrilla warfare will be carried out with these positions as the bases of areas of approximately

20 kilometers radius. If the enemy detours around these positions, he will be attacked in the rear.

The artillery units presently under the direct command of the Army will become attached to the 63d and 117th Divisions to become the nuclei of the positions respectively in the Liaoyuan and Tungliao area and the Paichengtzu airfield. To counteract the action of enemy paratroops forces, it will employ its tanks as mobile pillboxes.

Defense positions at Wuchakou will be reformed so as to be adjustable to changes in strength.

Positions will be prepared in the Hsingen (Wangyemiao) area to thwart an enemy detour.[4]

Abe, the 107th Infantry Division's commander, stationed his 90th and 177th Infantry Regiments in defensive positions that protected the critical route from Handagai to Wuchakou. The 90th Infantry Regiment's 1st Battalion defended the Iruse strong point and manned forward outposts around the village of Handagai and in the region to the west along the Mongolian border. The 90th Infantry Regiment's 2d Battalion occupied a string of company-size defensive outposts west of Halung-Arshaan, the fortified region around Halung-Arshaan proper, and a vital railroad tunnel through the Grand Khingans. The 90th Infantry Regiment's 3d Battalion, together with the 177th Infantry Regiment's three battalions, defended the heavily fortified emplacements in the Wuchakou Fortified Region, security outposts on the approaches to Wuchakou, and the town of Wuchakou proper. The 107th Infantry Division's raiding battalion, which had been formed in July, was also stationed at Wuchakou. To the east, the division's 178th Infantry Regiment manned defensive positions at Solun, Wangyemiao, and other points along the railroad line between those major towns.[5] Finally, the 44th Army's 2d Raiding Battalion at Wangyemiao and the Manchurian 2d Cavalry Division at Solun were to support the 107th Infantry Division.

Although Abe's infantry division fielded over 14,000 men, it was seriously deficient in heavy weapons. In June 1945 Imperial General Headquarters had requisitioned half of its antitank guns for use in the defense of Japan and had also reduced the amount of weapons and equipment of the artillery regiment. Yet, given the nature of fixed defenses in the region adjacent to the Mongolian border and Japanese faith in terrain as an effective barrier to Soviet attack, the 44th Army felt its position to be relatively secure in August 1945.

There were, however, several serious if not fatal flaws in the Japanese assessment of their defensive capabilities. First, the fortifications in western Manchuria were far less formidable than the 44th Army assumed:

The prepared positions in the vicinity of Wuchakou, 80 kilometers in circumference, were too scattered. Readjustments of these defenses was undertaken by the 107th Infantry Division to adapt them to the strength of the division. Progress was so difficult, due to the total lack of fortifications materials – particularly explosives and rock drills – that at the time of the outbreak of the war, they amounted to nothing more than field positions. The division's front was a vast and barren plain with almost no trees. Late in July the Army dispatched the 47th Road Construction Unit to obtain timber from the forest along the Paichengtzu–Arshaan Railroad, particularly in the vicinity of Pailang. In August the Army assumed direct command of the 1st Transport Company of the 117th Division, and sent this company to Pailang to transport the timber. However, while this transport unit was in the vicinity of Hsingen, *en route*, Soviet Russia entered the war, and it returned to its original command. The Field Road Construction Unit also returned to its original station.[6]

Nor were Japanese intelligence assessments of Soviet military capabilities particularly accurate. As one staff officer later noted:

In general, however, enemy activities on the western front of Manchuria were not as conspicuous as those on the eastern front. Against the eastern front the Soviets were expected to hurl approximately eight infantry divisions, two tank divisions, and 1,000 planes. No such concentration was detected on the western front. In the immediate vicinity of the Forty-fourth Army border, there were absolutely no indications of a large concentration of troops even immediately prior to Soviet Russia's entry into the war.[7]

SOVIET MISSIONS AND TASKS

Vasilevsky's Far East Command assigned the task of invading western Manchuria to Marshal of the Soviet Union R. Ia. Malinovsky's Trans-Baikal Front. Vasilevsky's final directive dated 5 July 1945 ordered Malinovsky's *front* to 'deliver its main attack with a force of three combined-arms armies and one tank army from the south in the general direction of Changchun to envelop the Halung-Arshaan Fortified Region'.[8] The *front's* immediate mission was to smash the Japanese defenses, cross the Grand Khingan Mountains, and then capture a line from Tapanshang through Lupei to Solun with its main forces by the 15th day of the operation.

Operating in the general direction of Changchun, the 6th Guards Tank Army was to force the Grand Khingan Mountains by the tenth day of the operation, fortify the mountain passes, and hold them against enemy reserves until the arrival of the follow-on combined-arms armies. Subsequently, the *front's* main forces were to secure a line from Chihfeng, through Mukden, Ssupingchieh (Shantoiakou), and Changchun to Chalantun.

Malinovsky's operational concept required:

An impetuous advance to the mountains and rapid seizure of the passes and exit from the mountains by tank and motorized infantry, who would forestall the possibility of enemy reserves approaching the Khingans from the depths of Manchuria and facilitate the advance of our infantry.[9]

Therefore, success in the operation required Soviet forces to achieve surprise and operate with great speed throughout their subsequent advance.

Malinovsky ordered his 39th, 53d, and 17th Armies and the 6th Guards Tank Army to make the *front's* main attack and organized his shock grouping with the 39th and 17th Armies and the 6th Guards Tank Army in first echelon and the 53d Army in second echelon. Colonel General I. I. Liudnikov's 39th Army and Colonel General of Tank Forces A. G. Kravchenko's 6th Guards Tank Army were to spearhead Malinovsky's attack from the dagger pointed at the heart of Manchuria, the salient east of Tamsag-Bulag in eastern Mongolia.

Malinovsky assigned Liudnikov his mission when he visited the 39th Army's headquarters on 12 July 1945:

Make the main attack from the region southwest of Halung-Arshaan in the general direction of Solun. After enveloping the Halung-Arshaan Fortified Region from the south, the army's immediate mission was to reach the line of the Urlengui-Gol [Urgen Gol] (River) – a depth of 60 kilometers [37.2 miles]. Subsequently, [it was to] cut off enemy withdrawal routes southeast of the enemy's troop concentration at Solun by decisive attacks and capture the Solun region by the 15th day of the operation.[10]

This required Liudnikov's army to advance to a depth of 186–217 miles (300–350 kilometers) in a period of 15 days.

In addition, Malinovsky ordered Liudnikov to conduct a secondary attack northeastward toward Hailar with a force of no fewer than two rifle divisions to cooperate with the 36th Army and prevent Japanese forces at Hailar from supporting those at Solun. A third force of one rifle division was to attack directly against the right (northern) flank of the Japanese Halung-Arshaan Fortified Region.

To accomplish his assigned missions, Liudnikov's army consisted of three rifle corps, nine rifle divisions, two tank brigades, one tank division, and numerous attached supporting units. The army mustered a total strength of 502 tanks and self-propelled guns and 2,708 guns and mortars (see Table 12).[11]

TABLE 12: SOVIET 39TH ARMY COMPOSITION, 9 AUGUST 1945

39th Army – Colonel General I. I. Liudnikov

5th Guards Rifle Corps: Lieutenant General I. S. Bezuglyi
  17th Guard Rifle Division: Major General A. P. Kvashnin
  19th Guards Rifle Division: Major General P. N. Bibikov
  91st Guards Rifle Division: Major General V. I. Kozhanov
94th Rifle Corps: Major General I. I. Popov
  124th Rifle Division: Major General M. D. Papchenko
  221st Rifle Division: Major General V. N. Kushnarenko
  358th Rifle Division: Major General P. F. Zaretsky
113th Rifle Corps: Lieutenant General N. N. Oleshev
  192d Rifle Division: Major General L. G. Basanets
  262d Rifle Division: Major General Z. N. Usachev
  338th Rifle Division: Major General L. N. Lozanovich
61st Tank Division: Colonel G. I. Voronkov
44th Tank Brigade: Lieutenant Colonel A. A. Smetanin
206th Tank Brigade: Lieutenant Colonel F. P. Solovei
735th Self-propelled Artillery Regiment
927th Self-propelled Artillery Regiment
1197th Self-propelled Artillery Regiment
5th Artillery Penetration Corps: Major General L. N. Alekseev
  3d Guards Artillery Penetration Division
    8th Guards Howitzer Artillery Brigade
    22d Guards Gun Artillery Brigade
    99th Heavy Howitzer Artillery Brigade
    43d Mortar Brigade
    50th Heavy Mortar Brigade
    14th Guards-Mortar Brigade
  6th Guards Artillery Penetration Division
    29th Guards Gun Artillery Brigade
    69th Light Artillery Brigade
    87th Heavy Howitzer Brigade
    134th Howitzer Artillery Brigade
    4th Mortar Brigade
    10th Guards-Mortar Brigade
139th Gun Artillery Brigade
55th Antitank (Tank Destroyer) Artillery Brigade
390th Gun Artillery Regiment
142d Gun Artillery Regiment
1143d Gun Artillery Regiment
629th Artillery Regiment
610th Antitank (Tank Destroyer) Regiment
555th Mortar Regiment
24th Guards-Mortar Brigade
34th Guards-Mortar Regiment
46th Guards-Mortar Regiment
64th Guards-Mortar Regiment
14th Antiaircraft Artillery Division
  715th Antiaircraft Artillery Regiment
  718th Antiaircraft Artillery Regiment

721st Antiaircraft Artillery Regiment
2013th Antiaircraft Artillery Regiment
621st Antiaircraft Artillery Regiment
63d Separate Antiaircraft Artillery Battalion
32d Engineer-Sapper Brigade

Weapons:
502 tanks and self-propelled guns
2,708 guns and mortars

Source: M. V. Zakharov, ed., *Final: istoriko-memuarny ocherk o razgrome imperialisticheskoi iapony v 1946 godu* [Finale: A historical memoir-survey about the rout of imperialistic Japan in 1945] (Moscow: 'Nauka', 1969), 399–400.

Liudnikov deployed the 39th Army's forces into assembly areas east of Tamsag-Bulag in extreme eastern Outer Mongolia at the base of the salient jutting sharply into western Manchuria. To the east loomed the central sector of the Grand Khingan Mountains and, just beyond, the heavily fortified pass running northwest to southeast through the mountains from Handagai to Wuchakou. The mountains south of the Halung-Arshaan pass, which were 62 miles (100 kilometers) wide from east to west, ranged in elevation from 3,936 to 4,592 feet (1,200 to 1,400 meters), 656–984 feet (200–300 meters) above the high desert lowlands where Liudnikov's forces were forming for their attack. The mountains north of the pass rose to elevations as high as 5,904 feet (1,800 meters) and broadened to 124 miles (200 kilometers) in width.

Both north and south of the Halung-Arshaan pass, the western approaches to the mountains offered good visibility to advancing forces, since the mountains' western slopes were devoid of any trees except for thin groves near springs and along the valleys of the small but usually dry streams that drained the mountains. North of the pass, however, poor sandy and rocky soil conditions, the extensive width of the mountain range, and numerous scattered wooded areas, particularly on its eastern slopes, made vehicular movement virtually impossible, particularly during the rainy season in August and September. While the mountains south of the pass were more trafficable, numerous gullies, narrow valleys, and defiles scarred the mountain massif and the slopes of the passes through it.

THE 39TH ARMY'S OPERATIONAL PLANNING

In accordance with Malinovsky's orders, Liudnikov formulated a plan designed to exploit Japanese misperceptions regarding terrain conditions in western Manchuria, specifically, the judgment that any Soviet advance would have to be through the Halung-Arshaan pass (see Map 26). Liudnikov's ultimate aim was to structure his offensive to generate a rapid advance, bypass or overcome Japanese forward defenses, and deny Japanese forces the opportunity to regroup and construct a stronger defensive line deeper in Manchuria. First and foremost, his plan categorically ruled out any major frontal attack against the heavily fortified Japanese defenses in the Halung-Arshaan pass.

To accomplish these ambitious aims, Liudnikov hoped to generate and sustain an advance rate of up to 31–37 miles (50–60 kilometers) per day to enable the army to move forward in tandem with the 6th Guards Tank Army advancing on his right flank. This advance tempo would insure that his forces would be able to bypass the Halung-Arshaan pass by the seventh day of the operation and capture his objective, the line extending from Solun to Hailahai, halfway between Solun and Wangyemiao.

Liudnikov's final plan called for his army to conduct a two-stage and two-pronged offensive lasting six to seven days to fulfill the initial missions assigned him by Malinovsky.[12] During the first stage, two army shock groups were to bypass the forward Japanese defenses, the first advancing northward toward Hailar and the second crossing the Grand Khingan Mountains south of the Halung-Arshaan and Wuchakou fortified zone. The army's main attack force, which consisted of the 113th and 5th Guards Rifle Corps, was to march south and then east from the southern face of the Tamsag-Bulag salient through the small settlements of Dzurkin Harul on the Sel'dzin Gol (River) and Boto Nela on the Urgen Gol (River) to reach a line extending from two small villages of Tiikhonera and Kakusupera. At the same time, the army's smaller 94th Rifle Corps was to launch a secondary attack from the northern face of the Tamsag-Bulag salient toward the small hamlets of Ulan Koragan, Bain Chaumiao, and Tappi Bancha along the road (track) running northward toward Hailar. The first stage was to last for four days. Thereafter, during the second stage, which was to last another two to three days, the army's two attacking groups were to attack and capture Solun and Hailar.

To generate the required high rate of advance, Liudnikov formed his army into a single echelon operational formation with two corps attacking abreast in the south and the third corps attacking to the north. On the army's main attack axis toward Solun, Voronkov's 61st Tank Division was to lead the advance as the army's mobile group, followed by Oleshev's 113th Rifle Corps and Bezuglyi's 5th Guards Rifle Corps advancing on a broad front of 28 miles (45 kilometers). Liudnikov required each of his rifle corps and forward rifle divisions to lead their advance with forward detachments. The rifle corps employed reinforced tank brigades for this purpose and the rifle divisions employed truck-mounted rifle battalions supported by self-propelled artillery, antitank, and artillery battalions, and two guards-mortar battalions.

The unique aspect of Liudnikov's operational formation along the army's main attack axis was that armor or mobile forces led the advance at every

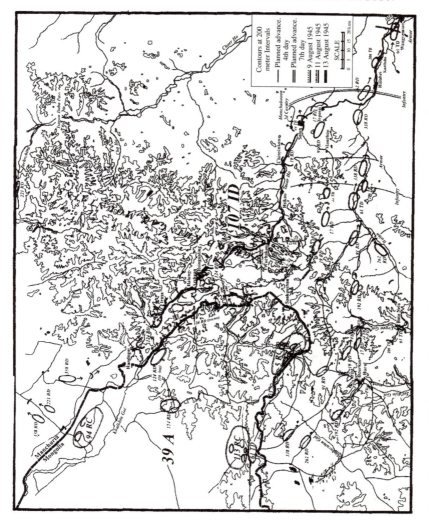

Map 26. Soviet 39th Army's Plan and Operations (Overview)

level of command. A tank division led the army's advance, the tank brigades led the rifle corps, and the tailored rifle battalions and self-propelled artillery battalions led the forward rifle divisions. These mobile forward detachments functioned like numerous awls penetrating wood to prepare the way for many screws. The massive columns of Oleshev's and Bezuglyi's rifle corps followed hard on the heels of the forward detachments, all marching in pre-combat column formation.[13]

Along the 39th Army's secondary attack axis, Popov formed his 94th Rifle Corps in a single echelon with Zaretsky's 358th Rifle Division on the left and Kushnarenko's 221st Rifle Division on the right. Papchenko's 124th Rifle Division, assigned to the 94th Rifle Corps' reserve, received orders to attack the Japanese Halung-Arshaan Fortified Region in support of the army's main attack.

Malinovsky provided Liudnikov's army with significant armor and artillery reinforcements so that it could both maintain its high rate of advance and, at the same time, pummel the Japanese fortified regions into submission. Since Liudnikov planned to bypass most of the Japanese fortified regions and centers of resistance in his sector, there was no need to mass artillery fires or create regimental, division, or corps artillery groups. Instead, Liudnikov allocated most of his army's artillery to his subordinate rifle corps and rifle divisions by attaching one artillery penetration division and one guards-mortar regiment in support of each rifle corps operating along the main attack axis. This measure concentrated 1,914 guns and mortars along the army's main attack axis and 2,586 guns and mortars in the army's sector as a whole.[14]

Most of the 39th Army's artillery advanced in march-column formation, either integrated within or following the divisions' and corps' march-columns. However, since the difficult terrain restricted column movement, especially of heavy equipment, much of the artillery lagged well behind the advancing tanks and infantry. This meant that the army was not able to conduct any systematic artillery preparation before the attack. Instead, the artillery was employed primarily to fire on-call missions in support of the advancing rifle divisions or corps and their forward detachments.

Marshal of Aviation S. A. Khudiakov's 12th Air Army was to support the army's advance with the 246th Fighter Aviation Division, less one regiment. On the first day of the operation, the division's aircraft were to bomb Solun, Hailar, and the Halung-Arshaan Fortified Region and all Japanese airfields in the region.[15] Each corps also received heavy engineer support to prepare and maintain the almost non-existent road network, to help negotiate the passes through the Grand Khingan Mountains and water obstacles east of the mountains, and support the infantry reducing Japanese fortified positions (see Table 13).

TABLE 13: ALLOCATION OF SUPPORTING ARMS TO 39TH ARMY'S
SUBORDINATE FORCES

113th Rifle Corps
    206th Tank Brigade
    69th Light Artillery Brigade
    134th Howitzer Artillery Brigade
    87th Heavy Howitzer Artillery Brigade
    29th Guards Gun Artillery Brigade
    4th Mortar Brigade
    10th Guards-Mortar Brigade
    1 regiment light antiaircraft artillery
    203d Engineer-Sapper Battalion
TOTAL: 860 guns and mortars
        112 tanks and self-propelled guns

5th Guards Rifle Corps
    44th Tank Brigade
    8th Howitzer Artillery Brigade
    99th Heavy Howitzer Artillery Brigade
    22d Guards Gun Artillery Brigade
    50th Heavy Mortar Brigade
    43d Mortar Brigade
    14th Guards-Mortar Brigade
    65th Guards-Mortar Regiment
    1 regiment light antiaircraft artillery
    230th Engineer-Sapper Battalion
TOTAL: 830 guns and mortars
        119 tanks and self-propelled guns

61st Tank Division
    164 tanks

94th Rifle Corps
    1142d Gun Artillery Regiment
    390th Gun Artillery Regiment
    629th Gun Artillery Regiment
    610th Antitank Regiment
    46th Guards-Mortar Regiment
    228th Engineer-Sapper Battalion
TOTAL: 508 guns and mortars
        47 tanks and self-propelled guns

Army Artillery Group
    139th Army Gun Artillery Brigade
    1143d Gun Artillery Regiment
    55th Antitank Brigade (less one regiment)
    621st Antiaircraft Artillery Regiment
    63d Antiaircraft Artillery Battalion
TOTAL: 224 guns and mortars

Artillery Reserve
    164 guns and mortars

Tank Reserve
13 tanks and self-propelled guns

Engineer Reserve
One pontoon-bridge battalion
One engineer-sapper battalion

ARMY GRAND TOTAL: 2,586 guns and mortars
455 tanks and self-propelled guns

Sources: I. I. Liudnikov, *Cherez Bol'shoi Khingan* [Across the Grand Khingans] (Moscow: Voenizdat, 1967), 51–2, and I. I. Liudnikov, *Doroga dlinoiu v zhizn* [The long road in life] (Moscow: Voenizdat, 1969), 168.

Malinovsky visited Liudnikov at the 39th Army headquarters on 2 August, approved Liudnikov's plan, and ordered him to deploy his army forward into its jumping-off positions. His army began the 75–81-mile (120–130-kilometer) march forward that evening. Oleshev's 113th Rifle Corps, with its attached units, marched forward in two columns and completed its deployment into its jumping-off positions near Ara Bulagin Obot along the southern flank of the Tamsag-Bulag salient at 0800 hours on 4 August. Bezuglyi's 5th Guards Rifle Corps marched in three columns and occupied its jumping-of positions east of the 113th Rifle Corps's positions by 0600 hours on 6 August.

On the northern flank of the Tamsag-Bulag salient, Popov's 94th Rifle Corps (less the 124th Rifle Division) concentrated in the region of Herimpt Nur at 0600 hours on 3 August. At the same time, Papchenko's 124th Rifle Division deployed into jumping-off positions near Derkin Tsagan Obo just across the border from Handagai and Halung-Arshaan at 0600 hours on 5 August. The army's remaining supporting forces completed their forward redeployment by nightfall on 6 August. All of the redeploying units used the occasion of the long march forward to conduct training and to practice water discipline.[16]

By late evening of 8 August, all of Liudnikov's forces had occupied their designated jumping-off positions and were prepared to attack. The advance across the border into the desert darkness was scheduled to commence two hours after the army's receipt of the code word *'Molniia'* [lightning] from Liudnikov. At 2100 hours on 8 August (Trans-Baikal time), Army General M. V. Zakharov, the Trans-Baikal Front's chief of staff, notified Liudnikov of the exact H-hour for the attack and included precise instructions concerning the army's actions during the initial hours of the attack.

According to Zakharov's instructions, Liudnikov was to initiate the attack in time-phased sequence. The army's reconnaissance detachments, the rifle divisions' forward detachments, and road regulators of the commandant's service, which were to control the movement of vehicular traffic, were to cross the Mongolian–Manchurian border precisely at 0005 hours on 9 August. The army's main forces were to begin their march toward the border at

0430 hours and cross the border from the march without halting for any reason. The 246th Fighter Aviation Division's aircraft and other reconnaissance aircraft were to begin flying their missions at 0530 hours. Army radio nets were to go on the air at daybreak, but to do so only if other means of communication were unavailable. Finally, all of the army's subordinate formations and units were to submit progress reports to their parent formations and the *front* headquarters every four hours, beginning at 0600 hours on 9 August.[17]

As of midnight on 8 August, *front* and army reconnaissance and intelligence organs indicated that only small Japanese security outposts manned the border; Japanese units appeared unaware of impending hostilities. Unlike other regions in Manchuria, the weather in the 39th Army's was clear, and conditions for opening the attack seemed excellent.

As indicated by a Japanese 44th Army after-action report, the Trans-Baikal Front's intelligence appreciation was essentially correct:

> After the middle of July, an increasing number of reports of enemy activities along the western front – a vast desert area – were received, particularly as regards the movement of motor vehicles. Also reported were frequent border crossings by motor vehicles from Outer Mongolia into Inner Mongolia. Although Inner Mongolia was under Japanese influence, its barrenness rendered it a no-man's land, and such crossings into Inner Mongolia had not been previously observed.
>
> It was estimated from these various reports that Soviet Russia must have some kind of reconnaissance plan, and it was evident that it had made considerable preparations for operations. This belief was later supported by the fact that early in the morning of 8 August the enemy at the border of the 107th Division in Arshaan issued an order stating in plain text: 'Launch the offensive when attack preparations have been completed.' Furthermore, during operations the enemy seemed prepared for crossing of the Tungliao area, which had been flooded by our forces, since the crossing was spearheaded by amphibious tanks, as was also the crossing of the Liao River in the vicinity of Hsinmin.[18]

By this time, however, the die had already been cast.

THE 39TH ARMY'S ATTACK

At H-hour, precisely 0005 hours on 9 August (Trans-Baikal time), the forces of Liudnikov's 39th Army crossed the Mongolian–Manchurian border on a front of over 249 miles (400 kilometers) without any artillery or aviation preparation (see Map 26). The army's forward detachment, Voronkov's 61st Tank Division, and rifle corps' forward detachments, Smetanin's and

Solovei's 44th and 206th Tank Brigades, preceded the army's main body at a distance of 12–18.6 miles (20–30 kilometers). The reconnaissance and forward detachments from the rifle corps' first echelon rifle divisions followed the corps' forward detachments 9.3–18.6 miles (15–30 kilometers) in front of the rifle divisions' main bodies. In turn, a rifle regiment in march-column formation led the advance of each rifle division as the division's advanced guard. The attached artillery marched in column formations parallel to the rifle divisions, prepared at a moment's notice to provide artillery support for the forward detachments and advancing infantry. As this imposing force advanced into the night, Soviet aircraft pounded Japanese military facilities at Solun, Wangyemiao, and Hailar. Had darkness not obscured the view, Liudnikov's advancing host would undoubtedly have been an awesome sight.

Despite the rugged terrain and lack of roads, Liudnikov's forces made excellent progress on the first day of the offensive. As the army commander recalled, the complete absence of any Japanese resistance and the clear weather more than compensated for the ruggedness of the terrain:

> The day turned out to be sunny and clear. From the observation point on Mount Salkhit, we could distinctly see how the tank division and tank brigades were moving forward decisively. We could see the command posts of corps commanders Bezuglyi and Oleshev and their deployed forces. I watched the columns of forces for more than an hour. Soldiers, tanks, and guns passed through the hills hidden in the thick and high grass, only to appear again on the slopes. And then the sun rose. The figures of men, military vehicles, and the contours of the hills opened up before us as if we were on morning maneuvers.[19]

All of the 39th Army's forces advanced in march-column formation on 9 August, by day's end covering far more territory than called for in the original plan. Along the main attack axis toward Solun, Voronkov's 61st Tank Division advanced 52 miles (100 kilometers), capturing crossing sites over the Urgen Gol (River) at Boto Nela. Meanwhile, Smetanin's and Solovei's 44th and 206th Tank Brigades thrust forward 47 miles (75 kilometers), reaching the Sel'dzin Gol (River) near Dzurkin Harul, and the western bank of the Urgen Gol (River), north of Boto Nela. The rifle corps' lead elements trailed 16 miles (25 kilometers) behind (see Map 27).

Despite the favorable weather, by day's end on 9 August the adverse effects of the rugged terrain on the pace of the advance compelled Liudnikov's staff to modify the composition and structure of the army's march-column formations. First, because of the superior mobility of the tracked vehicles, those in the rifle divisions' forward detachments far outdistanced the detachments' wheeled vehicles, which were transporting ammunition, fuel, and other supplies. Second, the extreme daytime heat drastically increased vehicle

Map 27. Soviet 39th Army's Operations (Dzurkin–Harul Axis)

fuel consumption, which was difficult to remedy since the fuel trucks lagged far behind.

The two rifle corps commanders tried to solve this problem by forming new divisional forward detachments, each consisting of a single self-propelled artillery battalion with only minimal support. However, the worsening fuel shortage stymied this innovation as well. Finally, by pooling all available fuel, the rifle divisions created replacement forward detachments formed around the nuclei of each of the divisions' self-propelled artillery batteries.[20] This expedient proved feasible since the army encountered little or no Japanese resistance.

Despite the army's spectacular advance, as Liudnikov noted, the hot weather exacted a toll on both men and machines:

The soldiers advanced from hill to hill under the blazing sun, rejoicing at the breath of each breeze. Upwards and downwards – to them the hills seemed without end, and they concealed the distances. The contours of every height and depression were missing on our topographical maps. The corps commanders, Generals Bezuglyi and Oleshev, reported that the forces were moving forward without delay just as planned. Every vehicle speedometer confirmed this fact. The speedometers read 50 kilometers – as much as the infantry covers in a single day. However, the designated objective line on the map was still far distant. Accordingly, we shortened our rest stops. We began to regard the 'Manchurian' kilometer as rather special.

The soldiers marched on. While on the march we scattered individual combat groups of Japanese covering the ravines and passes, and we destroyed enemy fortified points. The sun blazed unmercifully. The temperature during the day reached 35 degrees Centigrade (95 degrees Fahrenheit). The doctors became alarmed lest heat stroke occur. There was little water. Life-giving moisture was dear to every throat. The soldiers knew that as soon as you snatched at the water bottle, your thirst was stronger. The soldiers endured. The vehicles could not stand it – boiling water seethed in the radiators and motors overheated. That was why we had a reserve of water – primarily for the equipment.

Finally, the Grand Khingans loomed up in front of the columns of forces. There was utter silence in the mountains. There was every indication that we reached them before the Japanese. We had to storm them immediately.[21]

The arduous march confirmed the Soviet doctors' worse fears. Despite the intensive desert training that the army's forces had undergone while they were making their long march across eastern Mongolia into assembly and jumping-off positions, the relentless sun took a grievous toll on the soldiers. From 30 to 40 men in each division suffered heat stroke each day. The water canteens the men were carrying proved inadequate in such harsh conditions, since they were too fragile and broke under the slightest blow. Eventually, 30–40 per cent of the troops lacked the necessary water reserves.[22]

Despite these hardships, the troops of Oleshev's and Bezuglyi's rifle corps reached the western foothills of the Grand Khingan Mountains by the end of the first day of the operation, encountering only negligible Japanese resistance. If they could endure one more day's march, the mountains would be behind them, and the Japanese fortified regions would be bypassed.

While the main body of Liudnikov's army was struggling its way across the Grand Khingan Mountains south of Wuchakou, on the morning of 9 August, the main shock force of Popov's 94th Rifle Corps was advancing northeast-ward past the 1939 battlefield at Khalkhin-Gol toward the southern approaches to Hailar (see Map 28). Also marching in column formation, Kushnarenko's 221st and Zaretsky's 358th Rifle Divisions covered more than 25 miles (40 kilometers) on the first day, while their forward detachments defeated small groups of Japanese machine guns and scattered detachments of Manchukuoan cavalry and captured sites crossings over the Hui Gol (River), 62 miles (100 kilometers) southwest of Hailar.[23]

While Popov's main force was marching on Hailar, Papchenko's 124th Rifle Division occupied jumping-off positions south of the Khalkhin-Gol (River) and prepared to attack the northern sector of the Japanese Halung-Arshaan Fortified Region early on 10 August. The rifle division's reconnaissance patrols had already crossed the frontier and engaged Japanese security posts at several points along the border west of Arshaan and Wuchakou.

General Hongo's 44th Army received first word of the Soviet attack at 0200 hours on 9 August, when the Japanese Third Area Army reported: 'the Soviets [have] penetrated the Heiho, Tungning, Hutou, and Manchouli fronts, and [have] bombed Mutanchiang, Manchouli, Hailar, Hsinking (Changchun), and other places'.[24] Hongo immediately declared a state of emergency and at 0300 hours implemented the army's wartime defense plan. At 0500 hour a telephone report from the chief of staff of the 107th Infantry Division con-firmed the Soviet attack, clearly indicating that the 107th Infantry Division realized the dilemma it faced:

> The enemy strength on the Arshaan Front is approximately one sniper [rifle] division with tanks, and is gradually increasing. Scores of enemy tanks are crossing the border in the sector south of Sankuoshan and are making a detour around the rear of the division. The enemy radio, located in front of our positions, transmitted an order to attack and advance as soon as prepa-rations are completed. The division considers this to be an earnest attack by the Soviet Army and will smash the enemy in front of its position.[25]

Within a matter of hours, the army had enough information upon which to base a frightening assessment:

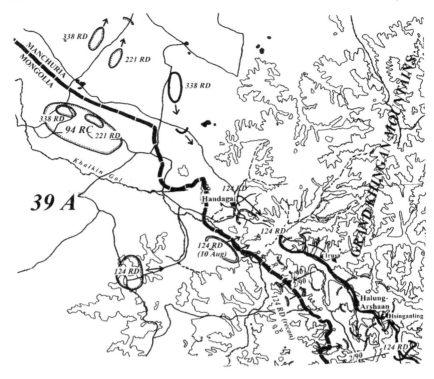

Map 28. Soviet 39th Army's Operations (Halung-Arshaan Axis)

Other information received on 9 August concerning the enemy situation in front of the Army was as follows:

'Approximately 1,000 tanks and vehicles are advancing east on the East Uchumuchin–Lichuan road.

A mechanized unit (approximately 1,000 tanks and vehicles) covered by three fighter planes is advancing southeastwardly on the East Uchumuchin Kailu road.

About one division of the Outer Mongolian cavalry is advancing on the West Uchumuchin–Linhsi road.'

Information obtained by the Army on enemy movements elsewhere on the western front indicated that the strength of the enemy advancing south on the Chilalin–Hailar road appeared to be one mechanized division, and that the enemy advancing eastward on the Manchouli–Hailar road, approximately two divisions.[26]

The 44th Army's intelligence appreciation was essentially accurate in that it noted Soviet intentions to pin down Japanese forces at Halung-Arshaan and bypass the fortified region to the south with the bulk of its forces. The problem for Hongo was how to defend against this multiple threat. For the time being, he ordered his 117th and 63d Infantry Divisions, in the army's rear area, to undertake prudent defensive measures, but, as after-action reports indicate, he could do little to assist the beleaguered 107th Infantry Division.

Two reconnaissance planes were attached to the Army from Third Area Army for liaison purposes and were assigned to Ssupingchieh airfield. The Army endeavored to maintain contact with the 107th Division by telegraph, but failing to receive a response due to the division's defective sending set, the Army had no alternative but to continue sending messages. (We were later informed that the 107th Division's telegraph receiver was functioning normally and could receive the Army's transmissions but that its transmitter was out of order.)[27]

Nor, as the after-action report noted, did the situation at 44th Army headquarters change appreciably the following day:

There was no change on 10 August in the enemy situation on the western front. The enemy forces in front of the 107th Division appeared to be about two divisions, but they did not press the attack. On other fronts, the enemy in eastern Manchuria made a rapid advance and was nearing the Muleng sector. The Hailar front was under attack by the enemy. The Aihun and Hutou fronts reported that Japanese forces were resisting the enemy and carrying out vigorous raiding attacks at border positions.[28]

At 0900 hours on 10 August, the Third Area Army finally issued fresh orders to Hongo's forces:

The 107th Division, 117th Division, and 9th Independent Tank Brigade will move to Hsinking (Changchun) and be commanded by the Thirtieth Army commander; the Army Headquarters, the forces directly assigned to the command, and the 63d Division will move to the vicinity of Mukden. The 108th Division, 136th Division, 130th Independent Mixed Brigade, and 1st Tank Brigade will be placed under your command.[29]

This wholesale alteration in the Japanese command and control structure in western and central Manchuria did little more than increase the paralysis already affecting Japanese forces throughout the Third Area Army's operational sector. Nevertheless, at 1000 hours Hongo issued new orders in an attempt to restore some semblance of order to the deteriorating situation:

The 107th Division will check the enemy advance at its present position, then destroy the Paichengtzu–Arshaan Line, Hsinganling Tunnel, and other technical objects to obstruct his advance, and will then redeploy to the vicinity of Hsinking [Changchun] as soon as possible [to] be placed under the command of the Thirtieth Army commander.

The 117th Division will dispatch an element to the vicinity of Paichengtzu (Paicheng) to cover the withdrawal of the various units in the Paichengtzu–Arshaan Line area. The division's main body will quickly move to the vicinity of Hsinking (Changchun), where it will be placed under the command of the Thirtieth Army commander.

The 63d Division will move rapidly to the vicinity of Mukden. One engineer company will be attached to the Army at Liaoyuan.[30]

This order essentially concentrated the bulk of the Third Area Army's 44th and 30th Armies in central Manchuria, leaving the 107th Infantry Division utterly isolated in its fortified positions along the western border. Late on 10 August, the Soviets only increased that isolation by severing all telephone communications between the beleaguered division and its parent army. Thereafter, higher Japanese headquarters had no idea what the 107th Infantry Division was up to. The last transmission concerning its dilemma came from the 117th Infantry Division:

The 117th Division reported on the afternoon of 10 August that approximately 1,000 enemy tanks were advancing to Lichuan [Tuchuan] and that the division had dispatched one infantry battalion and the Independent Antitank Battalion to the vicinity, about 30 kilometers [19 miles] west of Taonan, to check the enemy advance. At the same time, the report added, the division was attempting to concentrate its strength in the vicinity of Taonan.[31]

What Soviet accounts do make clear is that the 107th Infantry Division resisted vigorously in the fortified region and along the rail line eastward toward Solun and Wangyemiao. In fact, even after those uneven battles, the bulk of the division was able to disengage and fight effective delaying and harassing actions against the Soviets well after the other Japanese forces in the region to the east had capitulated.

The advancing columns of Liudnikov's 39th Army struggled across the Grand Khingan Mountains south of Wuchakou from 10 to 14 August, encountering minimal Japanese resistance but suffering to an increasing extent from the rugged terrain conditions and, later, from deteriorating weather. The weather did cooperate with Liudnikov's forces during the first few days of the offensive. The oppressive 95° Fahrenheit (35° Centigrade) heat of 9 August gave way to more moderate temperatures of between 66° and 71° Fahrenheit (19° and 22° Centigrade) on subsequent days. While short periods of drizzling rain interrupted the long periods of sunlight from 12 through 14 August, beginning on 15 August torrential rains struck, dramatically interfering with Liudnikov's advance, particularly, the rapid advance of his tracked and wheeled vehicles.

During their passage of the mountains, Liudnikov's forces had moved in multiple columns along numerous valleys and ravines. The dry and sandy soil conditions in the region permitted the forces to advance fairly rapidly along four or five parallel tracks. However, after crossing the mountains, the forces entered a region characterized by virgin black soil, which, when moist, made movement in neat march-columns practically impossible without extensive engineer or sapper support. As was the case in eastern Manchuria, the engineers and sappers built and maintained the crude roads by laying thick beds of gravel over the soft black soil. It was, however, a very laborious, tedious, and time-consuming task.[32]

The increasing number of water barriers east of the Grand Khingans also proved to be a problem. West and in the mountains, the Sel'dzin Gol and Siaburutan Gol (Rivers) were totally dry and completely passable in early August, even though the dried-up swamps on the rivers' banks were difficult for wheeled vehicles to negotiate. However, east of the mountains, the bed of the Urgen Gol was half full of water, 26 feet (8 meters) wide, and up to 7 feet (2.1 meters) deep. The engineers had to construct six bridges across this formidable obstacle in order that Liudnikov's two rifle corps could cross it.

The passage across the Grand Khingan Mountains also consumed immense quantities of fuel. As already mentioned, the intense heat increased the fuel consumption by a factor of 50 per cent. Even more vexing were the dead ends, detours, false starts, and other impediments to smooth and continuous move-ment along the fragile, winding, and complex network of mountain tracks. In short, individual units found it exceedingly difficult to locate and stay on their proper routes. As Liudnikov noted, existing maps of the region proved particularly inaccurate and unreliable:

The roads in these regions ... were few in number and even unmarked, gorges and swamps were incorrect [on maps]. All of this hindered the orientation and movement of the columns to a significant degree. Thus, one of our divisions determined its movement route on a map. In the end, the unit ended up in a labyrinth of blind mountain valleys, which were not shown on the map. Later, an officer from the army staff flying a PO-2 [reconnaissance] aircraft located the division and put it on the correct course.[33]

The division to which Liudnikov was referring was Major General L. G. Basanets' 192d Rifle Division, which essentially remained lost in the rugged mountainous region for two entire days during the crossing. Obviously, when the two rifle corps emerged from the mountains, Basanets' division was in second echelon.

Despite all of the difficulties they encountered while mastering their crossing of the barren and rugged mountains, Oleshev's and Bezuglyi's rifle corps, with Voronkov's tank division still in the lead, reached the Japanese 107th Infantry Division's left flank and rear by 12 August (see Map 29). The road to Solun and Wangyemiao was wide open to further Soviet advance, and, with no other combat troops available to contest the Soviet advance, there was very little the Japanese could do to counter the threat. The full attention of Abe's 107th Infantry Division was riveted to its front and right flank, where Papchenko's 124th Rifle Division and other elements of Popov's 94th Rifle Corps were closing in on the Japanese division's defensive positions.

Hongo's 44th Army kept track of the deteriorating situation, but nothing it did seemed to improve the situation:

Reports were received on 11 August that enemy tanks had attacked Lichuan [Tuchuan], some 95 kilometers west of Taonan, and that the prefectural government office and other buildings had been set afire. Later, a patrol indicated that this tank force had stopped at Lichuan [Tuchuan] and that it showed no indications of making further advances. The Army was not able to determine whether the enemy tank unit would advance northward to Hsingan [Wangyemiao] and cut the 107th Division's retreat or attempt an attack on Taonan after replenishment and servicing. In either event, the Army feared that the tank force would seriously hinder the planned withdrawal, and requested the Third Area Army headquarters to deliver an air strike.

The Area Army's answer was to direct the Forty-fourth Army to use the 117th Division to attack the enemy mechanized unit and later withdraw. Since an orderly retreat of the division would be impossible if it launched an attack, Forty-fourth Army instead directed the 117th Division to put out rear guards while effecting the withdrawal of the main body promptly. It also instructed the 117th Division to destroy military installations,

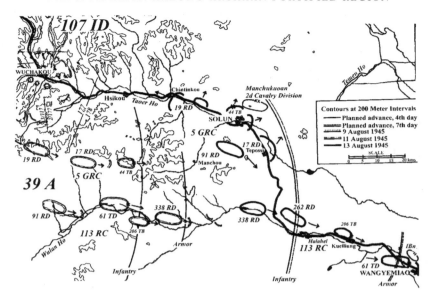

Map 29. Soviet 39th Army's Operations (Wuchakou–Wangyemiao Axis)

including the airfield and fuel dumps, in the vicinity of Taonan during its withdrawal.[34]

What the 44th Army did not understand was that the force on the western outskirts of Lichuan (Tuchuan) was the forward detachment of the 6th Guards Tank Army's 7th Mechanized Corps, whose objective was Taonan rather than Wangyemiao. Furthermore, the army also remained essentially unaware that the bulk of Liudnikov's 39th Army was bearing down on Wangyemiao surreptitiously and with a vengeance. It did, however, have at least hints that all was not well with the 107th Division and its immediate rear area:

> The enemy situation along the front of the 107th Division near the border was totally obscure ... During the day [11 August] a minor problem arose regarding the withdrawal of the Military Police Unit at Hsingan (Wangyemiao). The chief of that unit phoned Army headquarters stating: 'The Paichengtzu [Paicheng]–Arshaan Railway has been cut in the vicinity of Pailang and the enemy units are steadily closing in on Hsingan (Wangyemiao). Therefore, it is desirable that a withdrawal order be issued to us immediately'...
>
> At about 2100 hours [12 August], the chief of the Hsingan (Wangyemiao) Special Service Agency arrived in Liaoyuan and reported that the 2d Raiding Unit, which operated under its control, was in action near Hsingan, adding that the Special Service Agency was itself preparing to carry out guerrilla warfare.[35]

The forces that the 2d Raiding Detachment was engaging north of Wangyemiao were the deep reconnaissance elements, probably including *spetznaz* [special designation] teams, operating well forward of Liudnikov's 39th Army, whose forward elements were about to descend upon the railroad from Solun southward to Wangyemiao.

Throughout 10 and 11 August, the two rifle divisions in the main shock group of Popov's 94th Rifle Corps, with Lieutenant General G. K. Kozlov, Liudnikov's deputy, in overall charge, brushed aside small Japanese security detachments north of the border and pushed on northward towards Hailar (see Map 28). By the evening of 11 August, Kozlov's forces reached positions just south of Bualuto, 7.5 miles (12 kilometers) northeast of Dunda-Khana, which was situated about halfway along the road from the border to Hailar, while the force's forward detachment penetrated to the southern outskirts of the town.

With Hailar already firmly invested and bypassed by the Trans-Baikal Front's 36th Army, the services of the 94th Rifle Corps were no longer needed along this axis. Therefore, Popov assigned fresh missions to his two rifle divisions.[36] Kushnarenko's 221st Rifle Division was to sweep eastward along the valleys of the Taehrhsu and Taehrchi Rivers, cross the Grand Khingan Mountains through Tagan-Tabe Pass, and advance toward Lusun Tsihi (Langfeng) on the Cholo Ho (River). Thereafter, the division was to advance southward along the Cholo Ho and sever the communications between linking Japanese forces at Hailar, Pokotu, and Wangyemiao. At the same time, Zaretsky's 358th Rifle Division was to reverse its course, wheel directly southward toward the Halung-Arshaan Fortified Region, and assist Papchenko's 124th Rifle Division in the reduction of the Japanese fortified region, which was now almost cut off from other Japanese forces to the east.

While Liudnikov's main force was enveloping the Halung-Arshaan Fortified Region from the south, early on 10 August, Papchenko's rifle division launched a direct assault against the 107th Infantry Division's 90th Infantry Regiment, which occupied defenses in the fortified region's northern and western sectors, with two rifle regiments. Simultaneously, Colonel D. M. Lelekov's 622d Rifle Regiment, the third regiment in Papchenko's division, crossed the Khalkhin-Gol between Handagai and Iruse and attacked Japanese outposts north of the river. Intense, desperate, and often hand-to-hand small-unit fighting soon erupted throughout the rifle division's attack sector.

Northwest of Mount Mana-Ula, the northern anchor of the fortified region, nine soldiers from the 1st Company, 1st Battalion, 90th Infantry Regiment, defended a four-embrasure machine gun pillbox. Several external machine gun positions and trenches surrounding the hilltop and an extensive network of barbed wire entanglements protected the pillbox, which was situated on a hilltop. The small Japanese force was armed with two machine guns, grenades, and nine rifles. Lelekov decided to envelop the outpost with a battalion advancing from the northwest and one from the southeast.

While three 76 mm and 45 mm guns engaged the outpost with direct fire from the southeast, a group of submachine gunners with grenades formed an assault group to strike the pillbox from the front. Every fifth man carried an overcoat and cloak-tent in order to overcome the barbed wire. In addition, the regiment's antitank rifle company also conducted direct fire on the pillbox from the south and southeast prior to the assault to distract the Japanese defenders and protect the assault group as it maneuvered into its jumping-off positions for the attack.

A salvo from the artillery signaled the beginning of the infantry assault. The assault group advanced, firing its weapons as the Japanese turned their attention to the artillery fire. When the assault group moved through the barbed wire and approached the trenches, the Japanese turned their fire on them – but too late. The assault group captured the pillbox in hand-to-hand fighting, providing an example of the sort of fighting that was to continue for several more days. Typically, the Japanese fought to the last man, while the Soviets claimed a loss of only four wounded.[37] The emphasis on firepower and maneuver to conserve manpower characterized Soviet reduction of these Japanese fortified positions.

Papchenko's troops penetrated ever deeper into the fortified region, systematically reducing Japanese outposts one after the other on 10 and 11 August. After briefly turning northward to clear the remnants of Japanese forces out of Handagai, his division pushed on toward Iruse, Arshaan, and Wuchakou on 12 August. That evening the Japanese counterattacked from the northeast and southeast of Arshaan, but the division's forces drove them off and continued their advance southeastward toward Wuchakou. The overall objective of this maneuver was to catch the Japanese 107th Infantry Division between the advancing pincers of Papchenko's rifle division and the lead elements of Bezuglyi's 5th Guards Rifle Corps, which were about to advance into Solun from the southwest.

The lead elements of Bezuglyi's 5th Guards and Oleshev's 113th Rifle Corps completed their eastward march along and north of the Wulan Ho on 12 August, and emerged from the hills just southwest of Solun and Tepossi (see Map 29). At the same time, the forward detachment of Bezuglyi's corps reached and assaulted the railroad station at Hailahai, where it encountered and destroyed a train transporting a battalion of Japanese infantry southward from Solun.

However, even though the road to Solun seemed to be wide open, the main forces of both Bezuglyi's and Oleshev's corps experienced unanticipated problems with the terrain, and that forced them to halt and regroup in order to concentrate sufficient forces to seize the city. The valleys of the Wulan Ho and other rivers protecting the approaches to both Solun and the rail line were near or above flood stage, and the roads running along and across these valleys had become swampy, muddy tracks. Bezuglyi's and Oleshev's vehicles sank into the swampy valley floors, and, when they tried to bypass the deteriorated roads, the rocky crags along the valley sides restricted their movement. These road conditions slowed the units and forced them to deploy into single column formation. Since the overworked engineers and sappers fell behind in their roadwork, the soldiers in entire combat units had to join in the task of laying gravel roads capable of supporting the weight of the vehicles.

Soviet forces resorted to all sorts of improvised measures to restore the roads or construct new ones. Guards-mortar units even used their rocket launching ramps to surface the roads. Teams of tractors and even tanks combined to tow the guns and heavy equipment through the muck, and groups of tractors were left at each bottleneck to facilitate movement of the following unit. Even after being repaired, however, the roads once again deteriorated after the passage of each unit's lead elements, forcing the follow-on units to construct new bypasses. This entire process lengthened the army's marching columns to tens of kilometers. Artillery units suffered more than other types of forces because they had to detach their vehicles to assist the advancing infantry.[38] Despite these daunting challenges, the two rifle corps' forward infantry elements still maintained a rate of advance of about 25 miles (40 kilometers) per day, and tank units and tractors carrying infantry managed rates of from 31 to 50 miles (50 to 80 kilometers) per day.

The 5th Guards Rifle Corps was finally able to regroup and concentrate its forces into position southwest of Solun on the afternoon of 12 August, and Bezuglyi ordered his forward detachments, Smetanin's 44th Tank Brigade, and his lead rifle divisions, Bibikov's 19th Guards and Kvashnin's 17th Guards, to resume their advance on the city. Bibikov's division maneuvered to cut the railroad line west of Solun, while Smetanin's tank brigade and Kvashnin's division struck at Solun proper and the stretch of rail line to the south. That evening, after an artillery and aviation preparation, Bezuglyi's troops occupied the bulk of the city. The defending Japanese, probably from the 107th Infantry Division's 178th Infantry Regiment and the 2d Manchurian Cavalry Division, counterattacked repeatedly on the evening of 12 August and the morning of 13 August, but to no avail, before falling back into the hills northeast of the city.[39] Bezuglyi's forces pursued the Japanese, advancing southeast along the railroad line from Solun toward Tepossi.

On the same day, Bezuglyi's second forward detachment, consisting of the 735th Self-propelled Artillery Regiment, one battalion of the 45th Artillery Regiment, the 7th Antitank Artillery Battalion, and the 508th Self-propelled Artillery Battalion, approached Tepossi from the west. As the forward detachment entered the city, it intercepted a Japanese vehicular column withdrawing from Solun, drove off the Japanese, and captured the sorely needed fuel supplies that it was transporting.[40] After joining the rest of Bezuglyi's forces, which were arriving from Solun, the 735th Self-propelled Artillery Regiment continued its pursuit south along the rail line from Tepossi.

While Bezuglyi's main forces were clearing Japanese forces from Tepossi, Smetanin's 44th Tank Brigade and Kvashnin's 17th Guards Rifle Division finished capturing the remainder of Solun city by seizing the railroad station at 1000 hours on 13 August. Bibikov's 19th Guards Rifle Division, led by the 61st Guards Rifle Regiment and 508th Self-propelled Artillery Battalion, advanced westward from Solun toward Chinyinkou Station (Hsikou). *En route* they engaged yet another unit from the Japanese 107th Infantry Division and forced it to retreat northward from the railroad line.[41]

By virtue of Bezuglyi's dash to Solun, a pincer formed by Bibikov's 19th Guards Rifle Division west of Solun and Papchenko's 124th Rifle Division east of Wuchakou had trapped the bulk of Abe's 107th Infantry Division along the railroad line. Papchenko's rifle division had passed through Wuchakou, bypassed and encircled the Japanese fortified positions outside the city, and advanced eastward along the railroad to Hsikou on 12 and 13 August. Faced by deadly threats from both east and west, after two days of heavy fighting, the remnants of the 90th and 177th Infantry Regiments of Abe's 107th

Infantry Division had no choice but to withdraw northward into the mountains. They did so on 15 August, after which they regrouped to carry out guerrilla operations as mandated by the 44th Army's previous order.

While Bezuglyi's 5th Guards Rifle Corps was capturing Solun, Oleshev's 113th Rifle Corps and Voronkov's 61st Tank Division continued their march eastward along the Wulan Ho valley through Hailahai and Kueiliuho toward Wangyemiao. The continuing fuel shortage and abysmal road conditions forced Liudnikov's army and Oleshev's rifle corps to rely ever more heavily on forward detachments to sustain their forward momentum. Elements of the 61st Tank Division and the rifle corps' self-propelled artillery regiments and battalions led the advance, with the army's force units lagging far behind. To insure close control over the pursuit, Liudnikov ordered the commanders and staffs of his subordinate corps, divisions, and regiments to remain at least within 6.2 miles (10 kilometers) of their forces' main bodies.[42]

Far to the army's rear, on 14 August Smetanin's 44th Tank Brigade and elements of Kvashnin's 17th Guards Rifle Division repelled yet another desperate Japanese counterattack 3.7 miles (6 kilometers) northwest of Solun, and elements of Bezuglyi's 5th Guards Rifle Corps fought off similar Japanese counterattacks south of Solun. All the while the pincer formed by Papchenko's 124th Rifle Division and Bibikov's 19th Guards Rifle Division continued to squeeze Japanese forces caught in the narrowing corridor along the railroad west of Solun. By this time the lead elements of Voronkov's tank division and Oleshev's 113th Rifle Corps were assaulting Japanese defenses northwest of Wangyemiao, completing the clearing of Japanese forces on 15 August. The main bodies of both Bezuglyi's and Oleshev's rifle corps entered Wangyemiao city on 16 and 17 August.[43]

With Solun and Wangyemiao in the hands of Liudnikov's 39th Army, the envelopment of the Japanese Halung-Arshaan and Wuchakou Fortified Regions was complete. Liudnikov's forces had fulfilled their principal mission of cutting the withdrawal routes of the Japanese 107th Infantry Division from the border fortified region and preventing it from rejoining other Japanese forces in central Manchuria. The relentless pressure exerted by Papchenko's rifle division's advance directly against the fortified region combined with the effects of Bezuglyi's massive envelopment forced Abe's 107th Infantry Division to withdraw slowly northeastward ever deeper into the mountains. Once there, it ultimately ran into the forces of Kushnarenko's 221st Rifle Division, which was just completing its long trek southeastward through the Grand Khingans.

While the main force of Liudnikov's 39th Army was completing its envelopment of the Japanese 107th Infantry Division west of Solun, Popov's 94th Rifle Corps was continuing its southward advance along diverging axes on both sides of the Grand Khingan Mountains (see Map 28). Before splitting their forces, on 12 August Popov and deputy army commander Kozlov received a delegation from General Houlin, the commander of the Manchukuoan 10th Military District who presented the two Soviet commanders with a message that read:

> During the bombing of Hailar by Red Army aircraft, the forces subordinate to me withdrew to the vicinity of Shinho, and at present 1,000 cavalry troops are located here. Just now, that is, at 0600 hours on 12 August, we learned that forces led by you had entered the village of Ulan-Harchanin and, therefore, I am hastening to inform you about my wish to surrender to your protection with all of my military forces.[44]

Houlin and his band of 1,000 cavalrymen, which the Trans-Baikal Front's 36th Army had driven from Hailar the day before, surrendered to Kozlov's force late on 12 August.

After Kozlov's force split into two groups and reversed its course to the southeast and south, Zaretsky's 358th Rifle Division headed due south towards the Halung-Arshaan Fortified Region, where it arrived on 14 August, just in time to assist the 124th Rifle Division in liquidating the final Japanese strong points in the region. After its eastward passage of the Grand Khingan Mountains, Kushnarenko's 221st Rifle Division wheeled south along the valley of the Cholo Ho and, after 15 August, cut the withdrawal routes of Abe's 107th Infantry Division. With no hope remaining, Abe surrendered his division to Kushnarenko's force on 30 August at Chalai (Chalaitochi), 31 miles (50 kilometers) southwest of Tsitsihar.[45] Abe's surrender essentially brought the 39th Army's offensive to a victorious end.

CONCLUSIONS

After six days of operations, by 15 August Liudnikov's 39th Army had enveloped, bypassed, and reduced the mighty Japanese Halung-Arshaan Fortified Region, captured Solun and Wangyemiao, leaving the approaches to Taonan and Changchun wide open. In this brief period, Liudnikov's army had accomplished what Far East Command planners had expected would take nearly three times as long to accomplish. Simply concentrating so large and complex a force in such difficult terrain required prodigious feats of planning to overcome daunting deployment and logistical problems. Liudnikov's offensive plan itself was imaginative because it capitalized on the erroneous assumptions of Japanese planners that the Soviets must directly overcome Japanese defenses on the only 'feasible' avenue of approach into western Manchuria.

In fact, Liudnikov's army paid only passing attention to that approach by assigning only one rifle division to deal with it. Instead, Liudnikov committed the bulk of his army along axes of advance of his own creation. He deliberately selected axes through the trackless desert and mountain region south of the Japanese fortified region and to its north and east. This successful, though difficult, maneuver left the Japanese 107th Infantry Division dangling in mid-air, isolated from supporting Japanese units, and unable to conduct an orderly withdrawal to the main Japanese defensive positions to the rear. Finally, when the 107th Infantry Division finally managed to withdraw to the northeast there was literally nowhere for it to go. The futile hegira of Abe's division ended with its surrender to peripheral Soviet forces.

In its shape and form, the 39th Army's attack resembled that of Kravchenko's 6th Guards Tank Army in some respects. Although Liudnikov's objectives were not as deep as Kravchenko's, his forces had to negotiate terrain quite similar to that traversed by the 6th Guards Tank Army. Like the 6th Guards Tank Army, Liudnikov's army relied heavily on armor to spearhead his advance and to impart momentum to the army's entire advance. Like the 6th Guards Tank Army, the 39th Army also experienced serious fuel and logistical problems and had to rely on small task–organized forward detachments to maintain the momentum of its advance.

Unlike the 6th Guards Tank Army, however, the 39th Army was encumbered with a preponderance of infantry units and heavy weaponry and, as a result, constantly faced the problem of coordinating rates of advance of its infantry, tanks, and artillery. Of necessity, the 39th Army employed a wide variety of innovations and field expedients to maintain a proper balance of the two ingredients, at least in its forward elements. Unlike the case with the 6th Guards Tank Army, whose advance was largely unopposed, Liudnikov's army encountered spotty but fiercely determined Japanese resistance. Liudnikov's forces, however, were able to maneuver skillfully and project enough forces into the Japanese rear areas to overcome that opposition without significant Soviet losses. Throughout the entire offensive operation, and in particular, in its combat engagements with Japanese units and in its reduction of Japanese fortified points, the army stressed use of firepower rather than manpower to achieve success.

While the 39th Army's deep advance proved successful, it also encountered numerous vexing problems. Navigation across the Grand Khingan Mountains was difficult because of inadequate maps and an absence of good reconnaissance, the latter having been sacrificed to maintain surprise. Consequently, Basanets' 192d Rifle Division remained lost in the mountains for over two days. Given the poor terrain and spotty Japanese resistance, Liudnikov was able to employ his massive artillery to good effect only while reducing the Halung-Arshaan Fortified Region. Elsewhere, the artillery accompanying the army's main force experienced great difficulty in crossing the mountainous region and swampy valleys and, therefore, lagged well behind the rest of the army and was never brought to bear against the Japanese.

The army also suffered from acute fuel shortages throughout its long advance because tank and other mobile forces units consumed far more fuel than anticipated. As a result, the fuel problems persisted thereafter, requiring Liudnikov to severely truncate the size and strength of his forward forces. Only the seizure of Japanese aviation fuel at Tepossi and fuel delivery by air permitted the army to continue its operations to Wangyemiao. Like the 6th Guards Tank Army, the 39th Army also used aircraft extensively to deliver fuel to forward units.

The 39th Army and Trans-Baikal Front also severely underestimated the amount of engineer support necessary to sustain high-speed operations over such difficult terrain. The two engineer brigades organic to the army were woefully inadequate to handle the army's varied engineer needs. The additional engineer brigade attached to the army at the beginning of the operation never caught up and lagged far behind the advancing units throughout the duration of the operation. Finally, neither organic engineer brigade had sufficient vehicular transport to operate effectively and they simply were not able to conduct the extensive engineer reconnaissance required in such a region.

The army's broad front and the extraordinary depth of operations also severely taxed the army's communications system. Lack of vehicular transport hindered the installation of ground communications by land-line, and the long distances made radio communication erratic, although army use of aircraft to relay or deliver messages alleviated some of the communications problems.

These difficulties, however, were a direct product of the army's audacious offensive plan, and Liudnikov's army was successful in spite of them. Even with these problems, as a whole, the army sustained a rate of advance of 25 miles (40 kilometers) per day. As a result, its achievements, along with those of Kravchenko's 6th Guards Tank Army, utterly destroyed Japanese hopes for a successful defense in western Manchuria.

NOTES

1. *JM 155*, 4.
2. Ibid.
3. Ibid., 82–4.
4. Ibid., 86.
5. Ota Hisao, *Dai 107 shidan shi: Saigo made tatakatta Kantogun* [The history of the 107th Division: The Kwantung Army that resisted to the last] (Tokyo: Taiseido Shoten Shuppanbu, 1979), 14, 24, 26, 72, 76–9.
6. *JM 155*, 90.
7. Ibid., 100.
8. *IVMV*, 2:199.
9. Vnotchenko, *Pobeda*, 85.
10. *IVMV*, 2:202.

11. Vnotchenko, *Pobeda*, 88, and Sidorov, 'Boevoe', 14.
12. I. I. Liudnikov, *Cherez Bol'shoi Khingan* [Across the Grand Khingans] (Moscow: Voenizdat, 1967), 48–9.
13. Ibid., 49.
14. Vnotchenko, *Pobeda*, 104; Sidorov, 'Boevoe', 14; and Liudnikov, *Cherez*, 51.
15. Vnotchenko, *Pobeda*, 113, and Liudnikov, *Cherez*, 41.
16. Liudnikov, *Cherez*, 53–4.
17. Ibid., 55; I. Liudnikov, '39-ia armiia v Khingano–Mukdenskoi operatsii' [The 39th Army in the Khingan–Mukden operation], *VIZh*, No. 10 (October 1965), 71; and Liudnikov, *Doroga*, 171.
18. *JM 155*, 101.
19. Liudnikov, *Doroga*, 171.
20. Vnotchenko, *Pobeda*, 116–17.
21. Liudnikov, *Doroga*, 172.
22. Liudnikov, *Cherez*, 58–9.
23. Ibid., 68–9.
24. *JM 155*, 101.
25. Ibid., 101–2.
26. Ibid., 102.
27. Ibid., 103.
28. Ibid.
29. Ibid.
30. Ibid., 104.
31. Ibid., 105.
32. Liudnikov, *Cherez*, 61.
33. Liudnikov, '39-ia armiia', 73, and Liudnikov, *Doroga*, 173.
34. *JM 155*, 106.
35. Ibid., 109. The Special Service Agency was responsible for carrying out espionage and counter-intelligence activities throughout Manchuria.
36. Liudnikov, *Cherez*, 69.
37. Ibid., 68–76.
38. Ibid., *Cherez*, 59–60.
39. Vnotchenko, *Pobeda*, 195; Liudnikov, '39-ia armiia', 72–3.
40. Vnotchenko, *Pobeda*, 196; Liudnikov, *Cherez*, 63–7.
41. Liudnikov, '39-ia armiia', 73; Liudnikov, *Cherez*, 67.
42. Liudnikov, *Cherez*, 68.
43. Vnotchenko, *Pobeda*, 196–7.
44. Liudnikov, *Doroga*, 173, and Liudnikov, *Cherez*, 69–70.
45. Liudnikov, *Cherez*, 101.

7

The 36th Army's Advance to Hailar: A Forward Detachment's Deep Operations

TERRAIN CONSIDERATIONS IN NORTHWESTERN MANCHURIA

When planning military operations against the Kwantung Army's defenses in northwestern Manchuria, the Trans-Baikal Front's staff officers faced a significantly different set of terrain conditions than Soviet forces faced in other operational sectors in Manchuria. To achieve success elsewhere in Manchuria, Soviet forces first had to overcome major terrain obstacles such as deserts, mountains, or swamps. Fortunately for the Far East Command, Japanese planners frequently chose not to defend these terrain obstacles because they were convinced large Soviet forces could not operate through them.

In northwest Manchuria, however, the most significant terrain obstacles to an invasion, the Grand Khingan Mountains, were located 186 miles (300 kilometers) east of the Soviet–Manchurian border. In order to reach the Grand Khingans, any invading Soviet force would first have to traverse the broad and arid Barga Plateau region, which extended from the Argun River, a tributary of the Amur River forming the Soviet–Manchuria border in the west, eastward to the town of Yakoshih in the foothills of the Grand Khingans. The Hailar Ho (River), which ran eastward through the central part of this plateau from Yakoshih to Manchouli at the extreme northwestern tip of Manchuria, divided the plateau into two distinct parts.

To complicate matters further for any would-be invader, the Kwantung Army constructed and garrisoned several large fortified regions along the river to defend against an enemy incursion across the plateau. Thus, before penetrating into central Manchuria, any invading force had to cross the plateau and capture the passes through the Grand Khingans.

Aside from its vastness, the Barga plateau contained few major natural terrain obstacles. Bounded on the north by the Argun River, on the south by the Khalkhin-Gol [River], and on the east by the Grand Khingans, the plateau region formed a salient jutting northwestward between Siberia and Outer Mongolia. Occasional buttes, rocky hills, and dry streambeds punctuated the plateau's usually flat relief and vegetation on the plateau was limited to steppe grass and occasional patches of dense brush. The most important terrain feature was the Hailar Ho, which flowed from east to west across the center of the plateau. The important Chinese Eastern Railroad line, which connected the city of Chita in Siberia with the cities of Tsitsihar and Harbin in north-central and central Manchuria ran along the banks of this river, and the only major road in the region ran parallel to the rail line.

The few significant towns in the region were also located along these meager communications routes. Chalainor and Manchouli were located at the northeast terminus of the railroad, adjacent to the Soviet border, and Hailar, the key strategic objective in the heart of the plateau region, was located on a river of the same name. Farther east, the town of Yakoshih was situated at the western base of the Grand Khingans, where the rail line and road entered passes through these mountains.

The main northwest to southeast rail line, with its associated road and population centers, was the principal axis of advance across the plateau to the Grand Khingans. The Soviet Army had used this approach during its punitive expedition against the Chinese in 1929. Drawing on the historical record, the Japanese constructed their defenses exclusively along this route.[1] Unlike other areas of Manchuria, however, the plateau had alternate trafficable approaches. Although it lacked a good road network, the soil conditions and terrain permitted relatively easy movement of forces along the numerous hard tracks and trails that crisscrossed the plateau. The only major obstacles to off-road movement were the swamps along the Argun River, occasional bogs (some dry) along the riverbeds, and large sandy areas primarily south of Hailar toward the Khalkhin-Gol.

The climate of northwestern Manchuria was much dryer than that of other areas of Manchuria. During August, one could expect only occasional showers and thunderstorms. The average daytime temperature of 86° Fahrenheit (30° Centigrade), however, made adequate water supply a major concern for any force operating in the region.

Given the geographical configuration of the northwest and the wide expanse forces would have to cross in order to penetrate into central Manchuria, the Soviet Far East Command decided to conduct only supporting attacks into the region. The aim of these attacks was to occupy the plateau as quickly as possible, capture the passes through the Grand Khingans, and prevent as many of the Japanese forces as possible from withdrawing to join their comrades to the south.

To accomplish these ends, Malinovsky's Trans-Baikal Front sought to neutralize Japanese defenses at Hailar by conducting a rapid deep offensive thrust to cut the rail line east of the city and isolate Japanese forces defending the town as well as the Chalainor-Manchouli Fortified Region, located farther west along the border. While second echelon forces liquidated the Japanese defenders in Hailar, the bulk of Soviet forces would march eastward and capture the passes through the Grand Khingan Mountains.

JAPANESE DEFENSES IN NORTHWESTERN MANCHURIA

The Japanese 4th Separate Army, commanded by Lieutenant General Uemura Mikio, with its headquarters at Tsitsihar, was responsible for defending north-central and northwestern Manchuria. Prior to May 1945, Uemura's army had been subordinate to the Kwantung Army's Third Area Army and had been responsible for defending the Amur River sector, with its headquarters at Sunwu. After May, when the Kwantung Army concentrated the bulk of its forces in central Manchuria, the 4th Army was directly subordinate to the Kwantung Army, and its mission expanded to include the defense of all of northern Manchuria from the Nomonhan and Manchouli sector in the west to the Sunwu region in the northeast.

In early August 1945, Uemura's army consisted of three infantry divisions, four independent mixed brigades, and a variety of supporting units (see Table 14).

TABLE 14: COMPOSITION AND DISPOSITIONS OF JAPANESE
4TH SEPARATE ARMY, 9 AUGUST 1945

Force	Location
4th Separate Army:	Tsitsihar
119th Infantry Division	Hailar
80th Mixed Independent Brigade	Hailar
123d Infantry Division	Sunwu
135th Independent Mixed Brigade	Aihun
149th Infantry Division	Tsitsihar
131st Mixed Independent Brigade	Harbin
136th Independent Mixed Brigade	Nencheng

Source: 'Record of Operations Against Soviet Russia on Northern and Western Fronts of Manchuria and in Northern Korea (August 1945)', *Japanese Monograph No. 155* (Tokyo: Military History Section, US Army Forces Far East, 1954), 172–5.

The 4th Separate Army's defense plan protected two main potential axes of advance, the first southward from the Amur River near Sunwu into the Harbin region and the second southeastward from Manchouli along the Chinese Eastern Railroad:

On the western front where the enemy was expected to advance along the Manchouli–Hailar–Wunoerh–Pokotu axis, a force deployed in positions in the Hailar region was to check the enemy advance as long as possible; thereafter, a defense in depth was to be carried out in the mountain fortifications near Wunoerh, with the Pokotu sector as the rear line.[2]

To defend the region northwest of the Grand Khingans, the 4th Separate Army stationed Lieutenant General Kiyonobu Shiozawa's 119th Infantry Division and the 80th Independent Mixed Brigade at Hailar and its adjacent Hailar Fortified Region. The 119th Division was one of the best equipped units of the Kwantung Army. It had almost all its authorized arms and equipment, although it did lack heavy infantry weapons and grenade launchers. The same could not be said of the 4th Army's other divisions and mixed brigades:

In almost every command, the units commanders up to and including those of battalion level were draftees, with little or no combat experience. Many of the battalion commanders were too young for their commands. Most of the troops were also draftees, mobilized in Manchuria; many were old or physically unfit. Since the training period was short, their fighting capabilities had not been developed.

At the time the war started the divisions and brigades formed in July had about two-thirds of their authorized strength; some of the draftees were still en route to join their units.

Fourth Army's units were in no better shape as regards supplies and equipment. In general, Fourth Army's stocks of provisions and ammunition (except antitank explosives) were adequate, but the stockpiling of these supplies in fortified positions where they were most needed lagged behind schedule.

The 149th Division and the 131st, 135th, and 136th Brigades, organized in July, were extremely short of arms and equipment; the 149th Division, for example, did not have a single artillery piece. The comparatively older 119th and 123d Divisions, however, had almost their complete authorization of arms and equipment, although they lacked infantry heavy weapons and grenade launchers. The shortages of weapons had the effect of reducing the fighting capability of each division to that of an infantry regiment.[3]

As in the case of its other divisions, the Japanese rated the 119th Infantry Division's fighting capacity to be significantly less than that of a prewar standing line combat division. That was why it reinforced the division with the 80th Independent Mixed Brigade. In the event of war, the 119th Infantry Division was to fall back and defend the passes through the Grand Khingan Mountains from Yakoshih to Pokotu.[4]

The 80th Independent Mixed Brigade (IMB) defended Hailar and provided smaller forces to garrison the Chalainor-Manchouli Fortified Region and border posts scattered along the Soviet and Mongolian borders north and south of the city. The brigade consisted of five infantry battalions, a raiding battalion, an artillery battalion, and a few support units. Its most important defensive position was the Hailar Fortified Region, a series of five strong centers of resistance located on the hills and plateau around the city. The brigade stationed at least a battalion of infantry with artillery support in all but one of these centers and an infantry company in the fifth.

Two companies of the 80th Brigade manned two smaller fortified regions at Manchouli and Chalainor, at the western terminus of the Chinese Eastern Railroad, while a platoon-size force based at Sanho (Dragotsenka) manned outposts along the Manchurian side of the Argun River. Far to the southwest, another platoon-size force manned similar defensive outposts to the south on the Mongolian border near Nomonhan on the Khalkhin-Gol (River).

Because the 80th Independent Mixed Brigade numbered only about 6,000 men, auxiliary units assisted the Japanese in their defensive tasks.[5] The Manchurian 10th Military District at Hailar included two cavalry regiments (the 50th and 51st) and several smaller cavalry units in the immediate Hailar region.[6] Other small Manchurian units were stationed at Manchouli and along the Mongolian border. Weaker regional forces, primarily cavalry, which also included a few score of Russian *émigré* Cossacks, were also stationed in the region northeast of Hailar.

The Japanese fortifications around Hailar were formidable. Like the Suifenho and Hutou fortified regions in eastern Manchuria, many of its strong points consisted of ferro-concrete pillboxes and gun emplacements supported by a vast network of bunkers, trenches, and barbed wire obstacles. However, some of the fortifications had suffered from neglect, and the fortifications in the Grand Khingan passes to the east were incomplete and left much to be desired:

Most of the operational preparations made in earlier years had been intended for offensive or holding operations, and were not adequate for delaying operations with reduced troop strengths. This was especially the case with fortifications. Therefore the Army planned to construct new fortifications and to remodel certain of the old fortifications to meet the needs of the delaying plan. Work was to start in the middle of May ...

On the western front, positions at Wunoerh had been under construction by the Kwantung Army since 1943. Since these were huge positions designed for use by about three divisions, plans were made to reduce their size so that they could be used by one division, and to decrease their depth. In the interior, positions were to be constructed for troops deployed in the vicinities of Tsitsihar and Nencheng.

Work on these construction projects did not progress according to schedule. Principally responsible for the delay was the shortage of materials, aggravated by the reduced capabilities of construction crews – which included officers and NCOs – resulting from reorganization of some units and transfer of others. After the Soviet build-up in the Far East began, the Army Commander attempted to accelerate the construction program, but by the time the war started only field fortifications had been constructed. In the areas occupied by units organized in July, furthermore, only preparatory reconnaissance of terrain had been made.[7]

Given the dilapidated condition of Japanese defenses elsewhere in the 4th Army's sector, it was vitally important for advancing Soviet troops to neutralize the Hailar Fortified Region and to do so as rapidly as possible.

SOVIET MISSIONS AND TASKS

Malinovsky, the Trans-Baikal Front commander, assigned to Lieutenant General A. A. Luchinsky's 36th Army the task of neutralizing Japanese forces and their auxiliaries in northwestern Manchuria and capturing the important passes through the Grand Khingan Mountains into north-central Manchuria. In his 28 June directive, Malinovsky ordered Luchinsky, in cooperation with the left wing of Liudnikov's 39th Army, to prevent Japanese forces from withdrawing into the Grand Khingan Mountains and to crush Japanese forces at Hailar and in the Hailar Fortified Region.

Initially, Luchinsky was to deliver his main attack with the bulk of his forces from the Duroy and Staro-Tsurukhaitui sector along the Argun River southward toward Hailar. Subsequently, the army was to isolate and bypass the Hailar Fortified Region, exploit rapidly eastward, cross the Grand Khingan Mountains, and capture the cities of Chalantun (Putehachi) and Tsitsihar. In addition, Luchinsky was to conduct a secondary attack to seize the Chalainor–Manchouli Fortified Region during the first stage of the offensive (see Map 30).[8]

Later, in July, Malinovsky refined Luchinsky's mission based on the Far East Command's guidance and issued Luchinsky his specific orders. The fresh orders, which still required Luchinsky's army to attack decisively to envelop the Hailar Fortified Region from the northeast, destroy the Japanese at Hailar, and prevent the Japanese from withdrawing to the Grand Khingan Mountains, ordered his army to capture Chalainor, Hailar, and Yakoshih by the tenth day of the operation.

Specifically, Malinovsky ordered Luchinsky to form a strong shock group consisting of no fewer than five rifle divisions subordinate to the army's 2d and 86th Rifle Corps and employ the shock group to launch his main attack on the army's left flank. The shock group's missions were to:

• assault across the Argun River and capture the ridge of the Hairukan Hills;

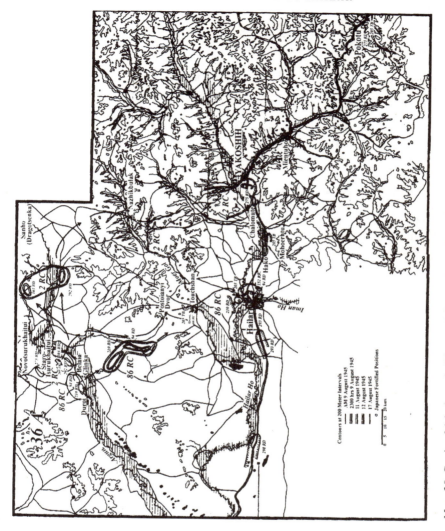

Map 30. Soviet 36th Army's Plan and Operations (Overview)

- exploit the army's success, reach the Hailar Ho (River), and capture the northern portion of the Hailar Fortified Region;
- penetrate the Hailar Fortified Region by conducting the main attack from the northeast and complete the destruction of the enemy Hailar grouping, while preventing it from withdrawing to the peaks of the Grand Khingans.
- [create a secondary grouping (an operational group) on the army's right flank] with the mission of penetrating the Manchouli–Chalainor Fortified Region and capturing the Manchouli and Chalainor line;
- pursue the enemy, capture the Bain-Tsagan-Obo Heights, and reach the line of the Imin Gol (River) [east of Hailar].[9]

Malinovsky's plan required Luchinsky's army to conduct its attack along a 155-mile (250-kilometer) front separated by a distance of 62–76 miles (100–120 kilometers) from the Trans-Baikal Front's adjacent 39th Army. In addition, Luchinsky's main and secondary attack sectors were 62 miles (100 kilometers) apart, although they did ultimately converge on Hailar.

THE 36TH ARMY'S OPERATIONAL PLANNING

To perform these missions, Luchinsky's army had two rifle corps headquarters, seven rifle divisions, two fortified regions, and a variety of supporting forces.[10] To permit the army to operate rapidly to the depths of the Japanese defenses, Malinovsky attached a tank brigade and two tank battalions and sufficient artillery to reduce the fortified regions in its sector to his force. The Trans-Baikal Front also attached a substantial quantity of engineer and bridging units to his army so that it could conduct a speedy and effective crossing of the Argun River (see Table 15).[11]

Luchinsky and his staff prepared his army's initial offensive plans during early July. Although *front* and army intelligence organs developed a fairly accurate estimate of the composition and strength of Japanese forces in the region, the prohibition on Soviet troops operating within 12.4 miles (20 kilometers) of the border to preserve the element of surprise made detailed and accurate reconnaissance of Japanese positions difficult. Therefore, Luchinsky relied primarily on reconnaissance reports from *front* headquarters and on information obtained from Soviet fortified regions and border detachments stationed along the frontiers. After he had completed his preliminary planning in mid-July, Vasilevsky and Malinovsky visited his headquarters, where, together, they conducted a reconnaissance of the border region in the 36th Army's main attack sector from Otpor Station to Staro-Tsurukhaitui. Based on this reconnaissance, Luchinsky's superiors approved his plan.[12]

According to Luchinsky's final plan, five rifle divisions and one tank brigade were to conduct the 36th Army's main attack across the Argun River

TABLE 15: SOVIET 36TH ARMY'S COMPOSITION, 9 AUGUST 1945

36th Army − Lieutenant General A. A. Luchinsky

2d Rifle Corps: Major General D. E. Petrov (Lieutenant General A. I. Lopatin)
   103d Rifle Division: Major General V. A. Solov'ev
   275th Rifle Division: Colonel K. F. Maiorov
   292d Rifle Division: Major General N. I. Poliansky
86th Rifle Corps: Major General G. V. Revunenkov
   94th Rifle Division: Major General I. V. Zamakhaev
   210th Rifle Division: Colonel N. I. Baniuk
Operational Group: Lieutenant General S. S. Fomenko
   293d Rifle Division: Colonel S. M. Sgibnev
   298th Rifle Division: Colonel S. I. Guzenko
   31st Fortified Region
   32d Fortified Region
205th Tank Brigade: Lieutenant Colonel N. A. Kurnosov
33d Separate Tank Battalion
35th Separate Tank Battalion
68th Separate Armored Train
69th Separate Armored Train
6th Machine gun-Artillery Brigade (renamed the 1st on 1 August)
15th Machine gun-Artillery Brigade (renamed the 2nd on 1 August)
259th Howitzer Artillery Regiment
267th Gun Artillery Regiment
1233d Gun Artillery Regiment
1146th High-power Howitzer Artillery Regiment
1912th Antitank (Tank Destroyer) Artillery Regiment
32d Guards-Mortar Regiment
176th Mortar Regiment
177th Mortar Regiment
190th Mountain Mortar Regiment
7th Antiaircraft Artillery Division
   465th Antiaircraft Artillery Regiment
   474th Antiaircraft Artillery Regiment
   602d Antiaircraft Artillery Regiment
   632d Antiaircraft Artillery Regiment
120th Separate Antiaircraft Artillery Battalion
405th Separate Antiaircraft Artillery Battalion
68th Engineer-Sapper Brigade

Source: M. V. Zakharov, ed., *Final: istoriko-memuarny ocherk o razgrome imperial-isticheskoi iapony v 1945 godu* [Finale: A historical memoir-survey about the rout of imperialistic Japan in 1945] (Moscow: 'Nauka', 1969), 399–400.

between Duroy and Staro-Tsurukhaitui in the direction of Hailar. Under the control of Lopatin's 2d and Revunenkov's 86th Rifle Corps, this force was to envelop Hailar from the northeast, sever Japanese withdrawal routes to Yakoshih, and destroy Japanese units in the Hailar Fortified Region. A strong forward detachment, organized around a nucleus of Kurnosov's 205th Tank Brigade and commanded by the deputy commander of the 86th

Rifle Corps, Major General V. A. Burmasov, was to spearhead the main attack along the Hailar axis to capture crossing sites for the army over the Moerh Gol (River), 20 miles (32 kilometers) north of Hailar, by the evening of 9 August (see Table 16). By that time, the advanced party of Burmasov's forward detachment was to capture the railroad bridge across the Hailar Ho (River), while two reconnaissance detachments were to seize other crossing sites over the river east of Hailar.

TABLE 16: COMPOSITION OF THE 36TH ARMY FORWARD DETACHMENT, 9 AUGUST 1945

36th Army Forward Detachment – Major General V. A. Burmasov
205th Tank Brigade: Lieutenant Colonel N. A. Kurnosov
152d Rifle Regiment (94th Rifle Division) – truck mounted
158th Antitank (Tank Destroyer) Battalion
1st Battalion, 32d Guards-Mortar Regiment
97th Light Artillery Regiment
791st Self-propelled Artillery Battalion (SU-76), 94th Rifle Division
465th Antiaircraft Artillery Regiment
1st Battalion, 176th Mortar Regiment
1st Company, 124th Sapper Battalion

Source: L. N. Vnotchenko, *Pobeda na dal'nem vostoke: Voenno-istoricheskii ocherk o boevykh deistviiakh Sovetskikh voisk v avguste–sentiabre 1945g.* [Victory in the Far East: A military-historical survey about the operation of Soviet forces in August–September 1945] (Moscow: Voenizdat, 1971), 178–9.

Simultaneously with the 36th Army's main attack, an operational group of two rifle divisions and two artillery machine gun brigades commanded by Lieutenant General S. S. Fomenko was to penetrate the Chalainor-Manchouli Fortified Region and pursue the retreating Japanese eastward along the rail line to Hailar, there joining the army's main force.[13]

An army artillery group of seven artillery battalions and two artillery destruction groups of three artillery battalions each were to provide necessary firepower to support the crossing of the Argun River and the reduction of Japanese fortified positions. A ten-minute artillery preparation was to precede the operational group's assault against Japanese defenses in the Chalainor-Manchouli Fortified Region, but, to ensure surprise, Luchinsky planned no preparation before the assault across the Argun River.[14]

Luchinsky also took care to provide the forward detachment with sufficient artillery to facilitate its advance deep into the Japanese rear. One bomber aviation division from the 12th Air Army was to provide air support for the operation by conducting bombing sorties against the Japanese fortified regions, airfields, and troop concentrations.[15] The 36th Army possessed only limited armor resources in the form of one tank brigade and two separate tank battalions. While Kurnosov's 205th Tank Brigade was to form the nucleus of the army's forward detachment, the 33d and 35th Tank Battalions provided only infantry support.[16]

The Trans-Baikal Front attached a significant quantity of engineer and sapper forces to Luchinsky's army to prepare approach routes and protect the army's forward deployment to the border region. More important still, the additional engineer support was essential to support the two rifle corps' crossing of the Argun River and the reduction of Japanese fortified positions at and around Hailar. These engineer reinforcements included the 68th Army Engineer-Sapper Brigade, consisting of the 295th, 296th, 297th, and 298th Engineer-Sapper Battalions, the 2d and 17th Separate Motorized Pontoon-Bridge Battalions, and the 12th Separate Motorized Pontoon-Bridge Regiment.

The bridging units were to provide the 2d and 86th Rifle Corps with direct bridging support. Luchinsky's chief of engineers was responsible for concentrating all of the army's bridging equipment on the northwestern bank of the Argun River by the late evening of 8 August. To support the preliminary assault crossings before the construction of the heavier bridges, the Trans-Baikal Front attached a company of American-made DUKWs (light amphibious vehicles) from the 653d Large Amphibious Vehicle Battalion to the 36th Army.[17]

As in the other sectors of the Trans-Baikal Front, the absence of water in the arid steppe land in northwestern Manchuria posed a potentially serious problem to Luchinsky's army, particularly in the region between the Argun River and Hailar. Therefore, Malinovsky attached the *front's* 90th Separate Field Water Supply Company to Luchinsky's army and assigned it the mission of locating and maintaining water sources and storing any water it found. This company formed reconnaissance groups of four to six men each under an experienced engineer officer who, with a vehicle and survey equipment, were to accompany the advancing forces and search for sources of water. Unfortunately, their lack of accurate maps of the region and shortages in drilling equipment hindered their subsequent operations. When the company's teams located water sources, they established water supply points that were then maintained jointly by a battalion from the army's engineer-sapper brigade and a company from each rifle corps or from each rifle division's sapper battalion. Once established, the army maintained water supply points 9.3–25 miles (15–40 kilometers) apart in the army's concentration areas and on its major axes of advance.[18]

Luchinsky had to address and solve two other major problems before his forces could expect to attack successfully across the Argun River even if, as expected, the Japanese resistance proved to be light. First, he had to deploy his main attack force into jumping-off positions located in the marshy and sandy region west of the Argun River, between Staro-Tsurukhaitui and Duroy. Second, once they were in their jumping-off positions, these forces had to cross the Argun River, which was 492 feet (150 meters) wide. Worse still, in some places the Argun River's adjacent flood plain was 7.5 miles (12 kilometers) wide, and patches of swampland extended to depths of from 2.5 to 3 miles (4 to 5 kilometers) on either side of the river, making the river difficult for forces to approach.

To overcome these obstacles, the army's 68th Army Engineer-Sapper Brigade worked laboriously to build corduroy approach roads to all prospective crossing sites. The lack of trees on the Soviet side of the border forced the engineers, who were working under the personal supervision of Lieutenant General A. D. Tsirlin, the chief of the Trans-Baikal Front's Engineer forces, to dismantle the wooden houses at Staro-Tsurukhaitui and use that material to construct roads.

While the engineers were building 12.4–15.5-mile-(20–25-kilometer) long approach roads to the river's northwestern bank, they also camouflaged the roads and dug foxholes and shelters for tanks and vehicles. With advice from corps and divisional sappers, the combat forces themselves camouflaged the troop positions, weapons, and other equipment in the force concentration areas.[19] All force movements into these concentration areas and jumping-off positions occurred under cover of darkness with strict light discipline. Even though the persistent usual July and August fog complicated the forward movement, all of the shock group's forces and their supporting bridging equipment managed to occupy their designated jumping-off positions by the evening of 8 August.

In the sector of Revunenkov's 86th Rifle Corps on the right flank of the army's main attack sector, the troops of Zamakhaev's 94th and Baniuk's 210th Rifle Divisions occupied jumping-off positions between the villages of Duroy and Belaia Glinka late on 8 August. Bridging equipment and 30 assault boats from the 2d Separate Motorized Pontoon-Bridge Battalion, which was to support the corps' assault crossing, were already in position.

Lopatin's 2d Rifle Corps, consisting of Solov'ev's and Poliansky's 103d and 292d Rifle Divisions, deployed forward to jumping-off positions on the banks of the Argun between Staro-Tsurukhaitui and Belaia Glinka on Revunenkov's left, with the 17th Separate Pontoon-Bridge Battalion in direct support. In addition to its bridges and assault boats, the pontoon-bridge battalion also had the 30 large amphibious vehicles of the 653d Amphibious Vehicle Battalion attached. The 12th Separate Pontoon-Bridge Regiment deployed to the rear of the two rifle corps to assist the passage of the army's heavier artillery units across the river.

Burmasov's forward detachment, which was formed around the nucleus of Kurnosov's reinforced 205th Tank Brigade, moved forward from its assembly areas toward the Argun River late on the evening on 8 August. Its orders required it to concentrate at Pad Klimechi, just to the rear of the forward rifle divisions, by 0600 hours the following morning. Once in its forward concentration area, Burmasov's detachment was to begin its advance immediately after the rifle corps' advanced battalions captured bridgeheads over the Argun River and the bridging was in place. After conducting a passage of lines through the advancing infantry, it was to exploit southward toward Hailar at maximum speed.

On Luchinsky's extreme right flank, Fomenko's operational group, consisting of Sgibnev's 293d and Guzenko's 298th Rifle Divisions with two machine gun-artillery brigades in support deployed opposite the Japanese Chalainor-Manchouli Fortified Region. Luchinsky's reserve, Maiorov's 275th Rifle Division, occupied positions to the rear of the 2d Rifle Corps with orders to support and, if necessary, reinforce Lopatin's advance.[20]

Each of the rifle corps and rifle divisions deployed in the army's main attack sector created special assault groups to engage and destroy Japanese strong points, block Japanese counterattacks, and clear obstacles from the path of the advancing main body. The assault groups at division level consisted of attack, blockading, and security subgroups. The attack subgroups, which were designed to assault enemy strong points, consisted of from one to two rifle platoons, a T-34 tank, and one or two artillery pieces. The blockading subgroup, whose mission was to protect the attack subgroups' flanks, consisted of one or two infantry or sapper platoons, and the security subgroup, which protected and supported the blocking subgroups, contained riflemen and submachine gunners. Each subgroup carried high explosives for demolishing bunkers.

Each attacking rifle corps, rifle division, and rifle regiment also formed a mobile obstacle detachment containing of sapper squad or sapper company, each equipped with mines, whose mission was to lay mines and other obstacles on its parent force's flanks. Finally, a battalion of the army engineer-sapper brigade equipped with four vehicles and 600 antitank and 600 antipersonnel mines performed the same function at army level. In the operational group's sector, for two days before the attack, engineers of the two rifle divisions cleared mines and obstacles from their front. In all, they cut a total of 17 corridors through the dense Japanese obstacle network.[21]

THE 36TH ARMY'S ATTACK

At 0020 hours on 9 August (Trans-Baikal time), assault detachments from local border guards units and the reconnaissance teams and detachments from the 2d and 86th Rifle Corps' attacking rifle divisions began crossing the Argun River and clearing Japanese outposts on the south bank (see Map 30). To the west, the army artillery group fired an intense ten-minute preparation against Japanese fortified positions in the Chalainor-Manchouli sector to pave the way for Fomenko's operational group to begin its advance.

Along the Argun River, in total darkness and dense fog, an advanced battalion from each first echelon rifle division crossed the swollen river on assault boats and makeshift rafts, as engineers struggled to complete constructing roads to the river's northwestern bank along which the engineers could bring their heavy bridging equipment forward. The reconnaissance teams and assault groups quickly seized the far bank of the river to a depth of 0.6–1.2 miles (1–2 kilometers), and at 0200 hours the engineers completed their work on the vital approach roads to the river.

One hour later the 17th Separate Motorized Pontoon-Bridge Battalion threw a 30-ton, 98-foot- (30-meter) long bridge across the river, while the corps' and rifle divisions' sapper battalions deployed five assault crossing sites and one ferry crossing using organic bridging equipment. On the left flank of Lopatin's 2d Rifle Corps, near Staro-Tsurukhaitui, the 653d Large Amphibious Vehicle Battalion transported two rifle regiments across the river within 25 minutes. In accordance with the engineer support plan, army engineers then floated five pontoon bridges across the river. These included two 9-ton, one 16-ton, and one 30-ton pontoon bridge within two and one-half hours, and one 60-ton within four hours.

This efficient bridging operation made it possible for the two rifle corps to cross the Argun River completely within only 13 hours.[22] Once the two rifle corps' main bodies were across the river, Lopatin's and Revunenkov's corps formed their rifle divisions in three march-columns to begin the advance southward toward Yakoshih and Hailar. A mobile, armor-heavy forward detachment led each march-column.

However, the most important role during the exploitation phase of the operation fell to Burmasov's forward detachment. At 0600 hours, Kurnosov's 205th Tank Brigade moved out of its assembly area at Pad Klimechi and began crossing the Argun River (see Map 31). Burmasov's orders were to pass through Revunenkov's advancing infantry, lunge southward along the road from Staro-Tsurukhaitui to Hailar, and capture crossing sites over the Moerh Gol at Touchshan by nightfall on 9 August. At the same time, the forward detachment's advanced detachment was to capture the railroad bridge over the Hailar Ho into Hailar, and reconnaissance teams were to seize crossings over the river further to the east and hold them until the main force reached the region.

Kurnosov's tank brigade completed crossing the Argun at 1500 hours on 9 August and, led by a reinforced tank platoon, struck southward at maximum speed in pre-combat march-column formation. Meeting virtually no Japanese opposition, the main body of the 205th Tank Brigade reached the settlement at Postoianyi Dvor in the Burkhata Valley, halfway from the Argun River to Hailar, at 2000 hours. At the same time, its reconnaissance detachment reached the Moerh Gol (River), where Luchinsky issued the reinforced tank brigade new instructions to conduct a night attack on Hailar and, if possible, capture

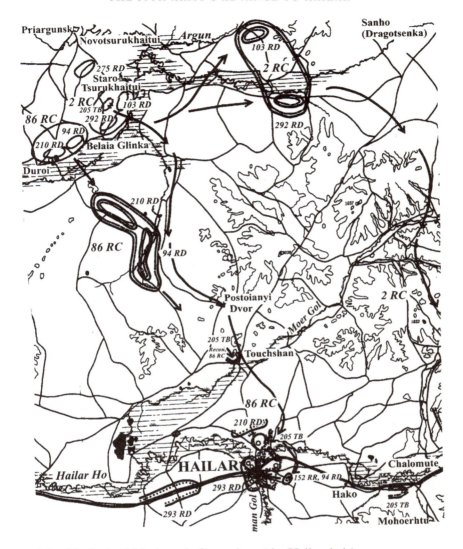

Map 31. Soviet 36th Army's Operations (the Hailar Axis)

the city and fortified region by the morning of 10 August. In addition, Luchinsky ordered Burmasov's forward detachment to 'conduct an active reconnaissance to positions along the Mohoerhtu and Charomute Rivers to the east'.[23]

Burmasov ordered his forward detachment to continue its advance throughout the night of 9 August. Soon after, the reconnaissance detachment, which had bypassed the Japanese fortifications north of Hailar, reported that the main rail bridge over the Hailar Ho was intact and defended by only a platoon of Japanese troops. Burmasov immediately ordered the reconnaissance detachment to attack, and the bridge fell into Soviet hands by 2130 hours. The remainder of Kurnosov's 205th Tank Brigade soon joined its reconnaissance detachment on the south side of the river.

Leaving a motorized rifle battalion to contain Japanese forces on Anbo Shan (hill) north of the city, Burmasov ordered a general night attack on the town of Hailar and the adjacent fortified region (see Map 32). Specifically, he ordered the 205th Tank Brigade 'to envelop the center of resistance on "Eastern Hill" and attack Hailar from the northeast, securing the railroad station and workers' settlement, and then the center of the town'.[24] The reinforced 152d Rifle Regiment was to envelop Hailar from the east and south and capture the southern portion of the town.

Kurnosov maneuvered his tank brigade around the northeast outskirts of the town and launched his assault at 2300 hours, capturing both the railroad station and the workers' settlement in the town's outskirts. However, heavy Japanese artillery fire from Mount Oboto, 6.2–7.5 miles (10–12 kilometers) northwest of the city, and from positions overlooking Hailar from the west and southwest brought the tank brigade's advance to an abrupt halt. Although repeated Japanese counterattacks failed to drive the brigade out of its newly won positions, Kurnosov lacked sufficient infantry to resume his attacks.

Meanwhile, the 152d Rifle Regiment, which was supposed to attack the southern outskirts of Hailar 30 minutes after the 205th Tank Brigade began its assault, failed to do so because it was unable to complete its complicated night march until early on the morning of 10 August. Once it finally joined the fray, it quickly captured the eastern and southern portions of the town before it too was halted by the heavy Japanese fire from the nearby fortified region.[25]

Kurnosov's tank brigade and the single rifle regiment struggled to maintain their footholds in Hailar town all day on 10 August against heavy Japanese artillery fire and frequent infantry counterattacks. By late afternoon, however, it was apparent that this small force would not be able to clear Japanese forces from the town, much less the fortified region. Therefore, Luchinsky ordered Revunenkov's 86th Rifle Corps, which was still marching southward from the Argun River, to issue sufficient trucks to Zamakhaev's 94th Rifle Division so that it could quickly move a force forward to reinforce Burmasov's forward

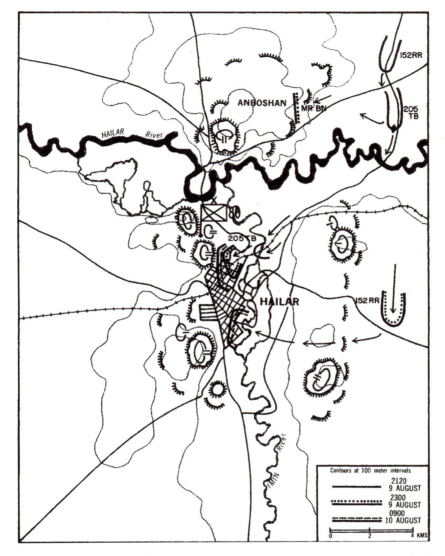

Map 32. Soviet 205th Tank Brigade's Assault on Hailar, 9–10 August 1945

detachment. This expedient worked, and at 2400 hours on 10 August, the 3d Battalion, 9th Rifle Regiment of Zamakhaev's 94th Rifle Division joined Burmasov's forward detachment in the fight for Hailar.[26]

At this point, the dramatic forced march of Burmasov's forward detachment and Kurnosov's 205th Tank Brigade came to an end. In less than 12 hours, the brigade had raced 62 miles (100 kilometers) ahead of the army's main shock group, captured vital crossing sites over the Hailar Ho, and established a significant foothold in the city. From this time forward, Revunenkov's 86th Rifle Corps would take over the difficult task of rooting Japanese forces from their remaining defensive fortifications around the town. Once relieved from the fight in Hailar town, Kurnosov's tank brigade quickly moved eastward to lead the 36th Army's advance to and through the Grand Khingan Mountains.

While Luchinsky was reinforcing Burmasov's forces at Hailar, Lopatin's 2d Rifle Corps advanced roughly 37 miles (60 kilometers) eastward from the Argun River and then wheeled southward, clearing Japanese outposts from the Sanho (Dragotsenka) region. Then on 11 August Lopatin's divisions advanced slowly southward in march-column formation through the western foothills of the Grand Khingan Mountains and the small village of Nazhikbulak toward Yakoshih (see Map 33). All the while, the remainder of Revunenkov's 86th Rifle Corps moved southward to reinforce its forward battalion at Hailar.

To the west, at the terminus of the Chinese Eastern Railroad, Fomenko's operational group cleared Japanese forces from the fortified region at Manchouli and Chalainor on 11 and 12 August, killing over 450 Japanese troops and their auxiliaries and capturing 100 more. The remnants of the Japanese force withdrew toward Tsagan Station and Hailar with Fomenko's forces in pursuit.[27]

Luchinsky's audacious offensive had taken the Japanese defenders at the Hailar and Manchouli-Chalainor Fortified Regions completely by surprise and, as Japanese after-action reports noted, rendered much of their defense ineffective or utterly superfluous:

Before dawn on 9 August, Army Headquarters was notified by Kwantung Army of the Soviet invasion of Manchuria. The Army commander immediately notified all subordinate commands, ordering them to put their pre-arranged emergency plans into effect. At the Army headquarters, a check of personnel showed about one-fourth of the officers were on duty at the time. (Headquarters had been operating during the preceding week on an around-the-clock schedule, fearing that an invasion was imminent.)

Reports from the border indicated that Soviet armored units had carried out simultaneous invasions of the Manchouli area and along the Outer Mongolian border in general before dawn of 9 August, and were advancing

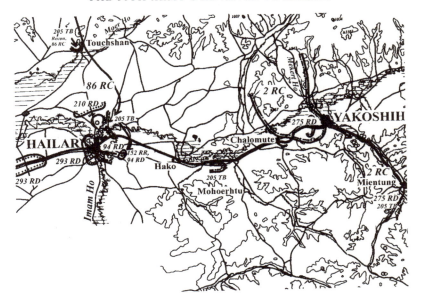

Map 33. Soviet 36th Army's Operations (the Hailar–Yakoshih Axis)

213

toward Hailar. In the Amur River area, reports indicated, the Soviets had not yet begun to cross the river ...

On Fourth Army's western front, the garrison unit at Manchouli was taken by surprise by the Soviet invasion on 9 August. It fought desperately as it retreated toward Hailar, meanwhile suffering heavy losses.[28]

In accordance with the 4th Army's orders, the 80th Independent Mixed Brigade at Hailar conducted a stoic but futile defense against, first, the 205th Tank Brigade, and, later, the 94th Rifle Division. Zamakhaev's rifle division began what it hoped would be its final assault on Japanese defenses at Hailar at 1200 hours on 11 August with heavy air and artillery support. However, the Japanese garrison held out stubbornly, inflicting costly losses on the Soviet infantry. The Japanese 4th Army's account recorded its perspective on the defense of Hailar:

> At the permanent fortifications in the Hailar sector the 80th Independent Mixed Brigade fought an all-out engagement with the enemy advancing from the Manchouli and Sanho sectors.
> The 119th Division, which had been deployed in the Hailar positions, immediately upon the outbreak of hostilities began withdrawing its main body by rail to the Wunoerh positions. On the 13th, the enemy confronted outpost positions in this sector, and, when the war ended was engaging the defenders.[29]

While Burmasov's forward detachment was conducting its impetuous dash to Hailar, early on 9 August, Uemura, the 4th Separate Army commander, ordered Shiozawa's 119th Infantry Division to withdraw and deploy eastward to defend the Wunoehr Fortified Region, which protected the Grand Khingan Mountain pass between Yakoshih and Pokotu. Barely escaping the deep thrust of the 205th Tank Brigade, the 119th Infantry Division entrained and left Hailar during the afternoon and evening of 9 August and successfully occupied its defensive positions in the Grand Khingans.[30]

At the same time, the Manchurian cavalry forces subordinate to the 10th Military District managed to escape southward from Hailar before the Soviet trap slammed shut. However, the cavalry ran into the advancing columns of the 39th Army's 94th Rifle Corps and surrendered only days later.

At Hailar proper, after the 80th Independent Mixed Brigade resisted successfully for four days, Luchinsky allocated additional forces to the fight to snuff out all Japanese resistance once and for all. By 15 August, his assault group at Hailar consisted of Zamakhaev's 94th and Sgibnev's 293d Rifle Divisions from Revunenkov's 86th Rifle Corps and the 6th and 15th Machine gun-Artillery Brigades, supported by gun, howitzer, mortar, high-power howitzer regiments, tanks, and concentrated bomber strikes. Attacking on 16 August, this combined force smashed all remaining Japanese resistance by 18 August. By Japanese count, the 4th Separate Army lost 200 dead at Manchouli and Chalainor and another 1,000 dead in and around Hailar plus uncounted prisoners-of-war.

While Zamakhaev's 94th Rifle Division was attempting to reduce Japanese defenses at Hailar, Lopatin's 2d Rifle Corps, spearheaded by Kurnosov's 205th Tank Brigade, which had just returned from Hailar via Hako Station, pursued the Japanese 119th Infantry Division to the outskirts of Yakoshih (see Map 33). There, the Japanese division's rear guard occupied delaying positions, supported by a small force of White Russian Cossacks, who had emigrated to the region after the Russian Civil War.

When Japanese resistance stiffened on the outskirts of Yakoshih, Lopatin deployed his reserve, Maiorov's 275th Rifle Division, to reinforce Kurnosov's forward detachment. Together, on 13 August they smashed Japanese defenses at Yakoshih, forcing the Japanese forces southward toward the Wunuerh Fortified Region in the pass through the Grand Khingans. During the fight for Yakoshih, Luchinsky claimed the Cossack force surrendered, presenting him with 30 combat standards of former units in the Tsarist Army, including 'one Georgiev standard received by the 1st Chita Regiment of Trans-Baikal Cossacks for distinguishing itself in battle during the Russo–Japanese War of 1904–1905'.[31]

After the brief engagement at Yakoshih, Shiozawa's 119th Infantry Division resumed its retreat along the railroad line through the Grand Khingan Mountain pass toward the Wunuerh Fortified Region. During Lopatin's pursuit, Japanese forces made a feeble attempt to halt the advancing Soviet tide at Wunuerh but were driven back by a combined assault by Maiorov's 275th Rifle Division and 205th Kurnosov's Tank Brigade. Lopatin's corps pursued vigorously, reaching and capturing Pokotu on 17 August, where he reported capturing 4,900 Japanese officers and men, nine tanks, five guns, 20 machine guns, and 4,000 rifles, most from the 119th Infantry Division, which had already lost 1,000 killed on the march through the mountains from Yakoshi to Pokotu.[32]

By day's end on 18 August, Luchinsky and his headquarters staff had deployed forward to Pokotu to plan the final drive toward Tsitsihar on the Nonni River. There they learned that the Japanese Emperor had ordered the Kwantung Army to lay down its arms and capitulate. Luchinsky later recalled:

In connection with the sharply changing situation, we had to hasten with the seizure of the principal command and control points in the country. For the capture of Tsitsihar, where the headquarters of the Japanese 4th Army was located, a forward detachment was send forward – the 982d Rifle Regiment mounted on trucks. The 36th Army's forward units reached Tsitsihar on 19 August ...

By this time, on the Trans-Baikal Front's left wing at Hailar, our 86th Rifle Corps defeated the Japanese 80th Separate Brigade and captured 3,800 soldiers and officers together with their commander, General Nomura ...

After 19 August, Japanese forces ceased organized resistance everywhere and surrendered massively. At Pokotu Station alone, about 20,000 enemy soldiers and officers lay down their arms.[33]

Immediately after capturing Tsitsihar, on 20 August Luchinsky received fresh orders from Malinovsky 'to concentrate one of the 36th Army's rifle corps in the Ssipingai (Ssuping), Hsifeng, and Hunchulin (Huaite) regions by 24 August and relocate the army headquarters and one rifle division to Changchun'. Luchinsky's forces managed to make the 310–373-mile (500–600 kilometer) movement to its designated objectives using commandeered Chinese railroad trains to carry the troops across the flooded plain along the banks of the Nonni River.

Luchinsky's headquarters and one battalion of the 310th Rifle Division left Tsitsihar by train on 22 August and entered Harbin that evening, where he made contact with General Beloborodov, the commander of the 1st Far Eastern Front's 1st Red Banner Army. The next day, Luchinsky's small task force reached Changchun. By 26 August, all of Luchinsky's subordinate forces had reached their designated objectives, while the toll of surrendered Japanese soldiers and officers reached 77,897.[34] For Luchinsky and his troops, the Manchurian campaign was at an end.

CONCLUSIONS

Luchinsky's 36th Army accomplished all of the tasks Malinovsky had assigned to it, some in spectacular fashion. The army's assault across the Argun River and the subsequent audacious southward dash by Burmasov's forward detachment clearly caught the Japanese 4th Army by surprise. However, while Kurnosov's 205th Tank Brigade achieved most of its objectives, it failed to seize the entire Hailar Fortified Region from the march, and it failed to prevent the Japanese 119th Infantry Division from escaping the town. Nevertheless, the brigade's deep thrust covered an extensive distance in a very short time and did manage to isolate the Japanese 80th Independent Mixed Brigade in the Hailar Fortified Region. In the final analysis, however, the Japanese brigade had no intention of abandoning its position, since, like other Japanese units manning fortified regions, its orders were to defend and, if necessary, die to the last man.

Ultimately, the 80th Independent Mixed Brigade's decision to stand and die tied down two of Luchinsky's rifle divisions and much of the 36th Army's supporting artillery. The ensuing fight for Hailar was prolonged, fierce, and bloody. Japanese resistance in the fortified region lasted until 18 August and the 36th Army's forces finally snuffed out the determined resistance only by using bombers, artillery, and infantry sapper assault units to reduce the fortified zone pillbox by pillbox.

By successfully escaping eastward, the Japanese 119th Infantry Division managed to delay the 36th Army's advance through the Grand Khingan Mountain pass for four days before Luchinsky's forces finally managed to penetrate to Pokotu on the eastern fringe of the mountains. By this time, however, the Kwantung Army's defenses throughout Manchuria had collapsed irreparably. The Emperor's surrender order only confirmed the catastrophic defeat the Kwantung Army had already suffered.

During the 36th Army's offensive, Kurnosov's 205th Tank Brigade conducted the deepest independent operation by a unit of its size in the Manchurian campaign. Despite the mixed results, its feat illustrates the innovative manner in which the Soviets tailored and employed forward detachments throughout the campaign. That the brigade did not totally succeed in its mission is the result less of its omissions than of the rapid reaction of the 119th Infantry Division during its hurried escape from the advancing Soviet dragnet.

NOTES

1. For details see Iu. M. Shchen'kov, 'Man'chzhursko–Chzhalainorkaiia operatsiia 1929' [The Manchurian–Chalainor Operation 1929], *Sovetskaia voennaia entsiklopediia*, T. 5 [Soviet military encyclopedia, Vol. 5] (Moscow: Voenizdat, 1978), 127–8.
2. *JM 155*, 174–5,180.
3. Ibid., 179–80.
4. Ibid., 175.
5. Boeicho, *Senshi sosho*, 485–6.
6. Ranseikai, ed., *Manshukokugunshi* [History of the Manchukuoan Army] (Tokyo: Manshukokugun kankokai, 1970), 785.
7. *JM 155*, 175–6.
8. Vnotchenko, *Pobeda*, 69.
9. *IVMV*, 2:202; A. I. Radzievsky, ed., *Armeiskie operatsii: primery iz opyta Velikoi Otechestvennoi voiny* [Army operations: examples from the experience of the Great Patriotic War] (Moscow: Voenizdat, 1977), 101. An operational group was a temporary grouping of forces designated to operate along a separate axis from *front* or army forces or a temporary grouping assigned a special mission.
10. Zakharov, *Final*, 398.
11. Vnotchenko, *Pobeda*, Appendix 2, lists Petrov as the commander of the 2d Rifle Corps. The articles by Luchinsky and Loskutov name Lopatin as the 2d Rifle Corps commander.
12. A. A. Luchinsky, 'Zabaikal'tsy na sopkakh Man'chzhurii' [Trans-Baikal troops in the hills of Manchuria], *VIZh*, No. 8 (August 1971), 68.

13. Radzievsky, *Armeiskie*, 104, and Vnotchenko, *Pobeda*, 178–9.
14. Sidorov, 'Boevoe', 15–17.
15. Vnotchenko, *Pobeda*, 113.
16. Zakharov, *Final*, 398.
17. V. Sidorov, 'Inzhenernoe obespechenie nastupleniia 36-i armii v Man'chzhurskoi operatsii' [Engineer support of the 36th Army's offensive in the Manchurian operation], *VIZh*, No. 4 (April 1978), 97.
18. Ibid., 97–8.
19. Ibid. and Luchinsky, 'Zabaikal'tsy', 68–9.
20. Luchinsky, 'Zabaikal'tsy', 70; Sidorov, 'Inzhenernoe', 98; and Vnotchenko, *Pobeda*, 179.
21. Sidorov, 'Inzhenernoe', 98.
22. Vnotchenko, *Pobeda*, 178–9, and Sidorov, 'Inzhenernoe', 98–9.
23. Radzievsky, *Armeiskie*, 102, and Vnotchenko, *Pobeda*, 179.
24. Vnotchenko, *Pobeda*, 179.
25. *IVMV*, 2:221; Radzievsky, *Armeiskie*, 102; and Vnotchenko, *Pobeda*, 180–1.
26. Radzievsky, *Armeiskie*, 102.
27. *JM 155*, 184.
28. Ibid., 180–1, 184.
29. Ibid., 185.
30. Ibid.
31. Luchinsky, 'Zabaikal'tsy', 72.
32. Ibid. and *JM 155*, 185.
33. Luchinsky, 'Zabaikal'tsy', 72–3.
34. Ibid., 73.

8

The 15th Army's Advance to Chiamussu: Joint Ground and Riverine Operations

TERRAIN CONSIDERATIONS IN NORTHEASTERN MANCHURIA

While the Trans-Baikal and 1st Far Eastern Fronts were conducting the Far East Command's main attacks against Kwantung Army forces in eastern and western Manchuria, Army General M. A. Purkaev's 2d Far Eastern Front launched secondary attacks against Japanese forces in northern Manchuria. The 15th Army's initial attack southward along the Sungari River toward Chiamussu and the 2d Red Banner Army's subsequent assault of Japanese defensive positions near Sunwu sought to tie down Japanese forces in northern Manchuria and prevent them from reinforcing the Kwantung Army's beleaguered main forces to the south.

To conduct these offensives successfully, Purkaev's forces had to overcome several daunting terrain obstacles. The most formidable of these barriers was the extensive river network separating northern Manchuria from the Soviet Maritime Provinces. Furthermore, the wide expanse of marshy terrain bordering these rivers and the heavily wooded Lesser Khingan Mountains to the south blocked the passage of Purkaev's forces southward from the Amur River and adjacent swamps into central Manchuria.

The 2d Far Eastern Front's operational sector stretched 1,553 miles (2,500 kilometers) from the northernmost point in Manchuria, north of Blagoveshchensk, southeastward and eastward along the Amur River to Khabarovsk, and then southward along the Ussuri River to just north of Iman. Along its entire front, the 2d Far Eastern Front's forces faced the imposing Amur and Ussuri Rivers, neither of which was fordable and both of which had broad floodplains spanning many kilometers inundated by water in varying depths.

Considered as a whole, the territory south of the Amur and Ussuri Rivers opposite the 2d Far Eastern Front constituted two distinct sectors, each characterized by a unique set of challenging terrain conditions. In the northern half of the 2d Far Eastern Front's sector, north and south of Blagoveshchensk, the Amur River ran through a narrow flood plain averaging 6.2 miles (10 kilometers) in width. Here the land south of the Amur River rose sharply, first into the lightly wooded foothills of the Lesser Khingan Mountain range, which were 12.4–18.6 miles (20–30 kilometers) deep, and then into the heavily forested mountains themselves. The wider flood plain north of the river, which extended 12.4–18.6 miles (20–30 kilometers) from the river's northern bank, posed a major obstacle to forces seeking to deploy to or across the river.

In the southern portion of the 2d Far Eastern Front's sector, west and south of Khabarovsk, the extensive flood plains of the Amur and Ussuri Rivers stretched from 62 to 78 miles (100 to 125 kilometers) south and west of the rivers. Compounding the terrain problems in this sector, the Sungari River and its tributaries, each with its own flood plain, flowed northeastward across the flood plain into the Amur River. The vast flood plain south of the Amur River formed a rectangle of swampy and marshy terrain punctuated by occasional low hills rising from the swamps bounded on the north by the Amur River, on the east by the Ussuri River, on the south by the Hataling Mountains and Wanta Shan, and on the west by the Lesser Khingan Mountains. This rectangle measured 186 miles (300 kilometers) from east to west and 62 miles (100 kilometers) from north to south.

Vasilevsky's Far East Command ordered Purkaev's 2d Far Eastern Front to launch its supporting attack across this flooded region. Of necessity, Purkaev's operational plan was designed to take maximum advantage of the limited number of communication routes through the region, ground and water alike.

The most important communications artery traversing the region was the Sungari River, which flowed from Harbin in north-central Manchuria eastward and then northeastward through a broad pass between the Lesser Khingan and Hataling Mountains, and across the western half of the swampy rectangle into the Amur River. Most major towns north of the pass between the two mountain ranges were on the eastern bank of the Sungari River, the largest being the river ports of Chiamussu, Fuchin, and Tungchiang. A frail and patchwork network of roads paralleled the Sungari's eastern bank, but at times of high water during July and August of each year, the roads were often flooded and impassable. Virtually no roads existed farther east into the swamplands that stretched from the Sungari River to the Ussuri River. There were also few trafficable roads in the salient formed by the Amur and Ussuri Rivers. The only other sizeable populated points in the region, the mining towns of Lienchiangkou, Hsingshanchen, and Hokang and the Amur port of Lopei, were nestled either in the eastern foothills of the Lesser Khingan Mountains north of Chiamussu or along the southern bank of the Amur River.

The only suitable exit route southward from this basin or axis of advance into central Manchuria was up the Sungari River to Chiamussu and through the 93-mile (150-kilometer) gap that the Sungari River cut through the mountains to Harbin. However, the harsh terrain along this 155–86-mile (250–300-kilometer) stretch of river, swamps, and mountain passes dictated that it be only a secondary attack axis. Secondary or not, for their offensive to succeed, Purkaev's forces had to master the terrain and overcome the Japanese who defended it.

JAPANESE DEFENSES IN NORTHEASTERN MANCHURIA

The Japanese force responsible for defending this sector of northern Manchuria was the 134th Infantry Division, commanded by Lieutenant General Jin Izeki, whose headquarters was at Chiamussu. Because of its relatively isolated position, Izeki's infantry division was directly subordinate to Kita's First Area Army. Configured like a normal triangular infantry division, the bulk of the division's 365th, 366th, and 367th Infantry Regiments and divisional support units were stationed at Chiamussu, Hsingshanchen, and Fuchin, respectively. Smaller elements of the division manned security outposts along the southern bank of the Amur River and a series of small, fortified positions blocking access into the area or up the Sungari River.

Small fortified regions manned by only platoons and companies were located at Mingshanchen, Tungchiang, Chiehchingkou, and Fuyuan on the southern bank of the Amur. Larger, permanent, and more formidable fortified regions, each manned by up to a battalion of Japanese infantry and varying numbers of Manchukuoan troops, were situated at Fenghsiang, Hsingshanchen, and Fuchin, where they could dominate the lowlands and axes of advance from Lopei to Chiamussu and southward up the eastern bank of the Sungari River from its confluence with the Amur River.

About 19 miles (30 kilometers) wide and 7.5 miles (12 kilometers) deep, the Fuchin Fortified Region consisted of two centers of resistance, one adjacent to the town itself and the other on the Wuerhkulishan, an imposing rocky hill mass west of the town. At Fuchin a mixed force of 1,200 Japanese and Manchurians manned 156 reinforced concrete and log pillboxes protected by more than 31 miles (50 kilometers) of trenches and antitank obstacles. Japanese forces defending Fuchin consisted of the 2d Battalion of the 134th Infantry Division's 367th Infantry Regiment, an infantry battalion from the Japanese Sungari River Flotilla, and a security battalion. In addition, the 7th Manchurian Infantry Brigade kept the bulk of its force in the city, with the remainder downriver at Tungchiang.

North of Chiamussu, the 14th Border Guard Unit manned the Fenghsiang Fortified Region and its lesser installations forward at Yenhsingchen, which loomed over the Amur River. The 2d Battalion of the 134th Infantry Division's 366th Infantry Regiment manned the Hsingshanchen Fortified Region in the hills just north of Hokang. Overall, a force of roughly 25,000 Japanese soldiers and their Manchurian auxiliaries protected the approaches to Chiamussu, including roughly 14,000 assigned to Izeki's infantry division and another 1,500 in the 14th Border Guard Unit. Although some of these forces defended the extensive fortifications along the limited number of axes of advance through the region, the bulk of Izeki's forces were in the Chiamussu region.[1] This was understandable, since his division's mission was to only delay any Soviet advance into northern Manchuria.

SOVIET MISSIONS AND TASKS

In conjunction with his overall offensive plan, Vasilevsky ordered Purkaev's 2d Far Eastern Front to conduct a series of assaults against Japanese defenses in northern Manchuria, both to divert Japanese attention from the Far East Command's main attacks and, ultimately, to expel Japanese forces from the region. These assaults were to take place in two stages. First, simultaneously with the 1st Far Eastern and Trans-Baikal Fronts' offensives against eastern and western Manchuria, Purkaev's forces were to attack south and west across the Amur River, clear Japanese forces from the Sungari River region, and advance through Chiamussu to Harbin, where they were to link up with lead elements of Meretskov's 1st Far Eastern Front. Second, once the Soviet assaults into eastern and western Manchuria were successfully under way, Purkaev was to conduct yet another attack, this time further north, to clear Japanese forces from the Aihun and Sunwu region across the Amur River from Blagoveshchensk and advance toward Tsitsihar to link up with the forward elements of Malinovsky's Trans-Baikal Front.[2]

Purkaev directed Lieutenant General S. K. Mamonov's 15th Army to conduct his *front's* initial offensive:

> In cooperation with two brigades of the Amur Flotilla, the 15th Army will force the Amur River in the region of the mouth of the Sungari River, destroy the enemy defending the Sungarian and Fuchin Fortified Regions, and subsequently advance on Fuchin with its main force on the eastern bank of the Sungari. Then develop the offensive in the direction of Chiamussu and Harbin. Defend along the [remainder] of the *front's* 240 kilometer [149 mile] sector with a portion of your forces.[3]

To accomplish this task, Mamonov's army included three rifle divisions, one fortified region, and three tank brigades, totaling 1,433 guns and mortars, 18 multiple rocket launchers, and 164 tanks and self-propelled guns (see Table 17).[4]

TABLE 17: SOVIET 15TH ARMY COMPOSITION, 9 AUGUST 1945

15th Army – Lieutenant General S. K. Mamonov

34th Rifle Division: Major General S. V. Kolomiets
361st Rifle Division: Lieutenant Colonel A. K. Oganezov
388th Rifle Division: Colonel N. F. Mulin
4th Fortified Region
102d Fortified Region
165th Tank Brigade: Lieutenant Colonel S. G. Myslitsky
171st Tank Brigade: Lieutenant Colonel V. S. Potapov
203d Tank Brigade: Lieutenant Colonel R. A. Ushillo
21st Antitank (Tank Destroyer) Artillery Brigade
52d Gun Artillery Regiment
145th Gun Artillery Regiment
1120th Gun Artillery Regiment
1121st Gun Artillery Regiment
1637th Gun Artillery Regiment
424th Howitzer Artillery Regiment
1632d Antitank (Tank Destroyer) Artillery Regiment
1633d Antitank (Tank Destroyer) Artillery Regiment
183d Mortar Regiment
470th Mortar Regiment
85th Guards-Mortar Regiment
99th Guards-Mortar Regiment
73d Antiaircraft Artillery Division
   205th Antiaircraft Artillery Regiment
   402d Antiaircraft Artillery Regiment
   430th Antiaircraft Artillery Regiment
   442d Antiaircraft Artillery Regiment
1648th Antiaircraft Artillery Regiment
29th Separate Antiaircraft Artillery Battalion
46th Separate Antiaircraft Artillery Battalion
302d Separate Antiaircraft Artillery Battalion
505th Separate Antiaircraft Artillery Battalion
10th Pontoon-Bridge Brigade
21st Motorized Assault Engineer-Sapper Brigade
101st Separate Engineer Battalion
129th Separate Engineer Battalion

Weapons:
164 tanks and self-propelled guns
1,433 guns and mortars

Source: M. V. Zakharov, ed., *Final: istoriko-memuarny ocherk o razgrome imperialisticheskoi iapony v 1945 godu* [Finale: A historical memoir-survey about the rout of imperialistic Japan in 1945] (Moscow: 'Nauka', 1969), 401–3.

Like his counterparts in other *fronts*, Purkaev assigned significant artillery reinforcements to Mamonov's army to enable it to reduce the Japanese fortified regions in its sector. An army artillery group consisting of the 52d, 145th, and 1120th Gun Artillery Regiments cooperated closely with gunboats of the Amur Military Flotilla to deliver suppressive fire on Japanese defensive positions during the actual crossing of the Amur River. Regimental and divisional artillery groups supported their parent forces throughout the offensive except when terrain conditions hindered their forward deployment. Overall, a total of 12 artillery regiments, one tank destroyer brigade, one antiaircraft artillery division, one antiaircraft artillery regiment, and four antiaircraft artillery battalions supported the 15th Army's subsequent advance.[5]

Although rich in artillery, the 15th Army received only limited armor assets because of poor road trafficability in the region. Purkaev's chief of armor and mechanized forces reinforced the 15th Army with just three tank brigades and four self-propelled artillery battalions and ordered that these be employed as forward detachments to lead the advance of each rifle division and to provide direct fire support to these divisions when they engaged Japanese fortified positions.[6] Finally, Colonel General of Aviation P. F. Zhigarev's 10th Air Army, which was supporting the 2d Far Eastern Front as a whole, allocated 45 per cent of its aircraft to support the 15th Army's attack.[7]

Because the 15th Army required substantial heavy engineer support to cross the Amur River and reduce several Japanese fortified regions, Purkaev attached an entire motorized assault engineer-sapper brigade, two separate engineer battalions, and a pontoon-bridge battalion to Mamonov's army. Once attached, these units built and improved movement routes into the army's assembly areas and jumping-off positions and upgraded the load-bearing capacity of bridges. Within three months the engineers constructed 165 miles (266 kilometers) of corduroy or dirt roads and repaired another 880 miles (1,417 kilometers) of roadway. Army engineers also created three separate river-crossing sectors across the Amur River and built up to 20 camouflaged observation posts in each regimental sector along the river.[8]

To facilitate the army's assault crossing of the Amur River and subsequent advance up the water-logged Sungari River valley, the Far East Command subordinated the Amur River Flotilla to Purkaev's command. The flotilla, which was commanded by Rear Admiral N. V. Antonov and was headquartered in Khabarovsk, consisted of three brigades of armored cutters, gunboats, and minesweepers stationed on the Amur River, plus several smaller units operating on tributaries of the Amur River, on the Ussuri River, and on Lake Khanka.[9] Purkaev directed most of this force to support Mamonov's 15th Army, specifically, the 1st and 2d Brigades of River Ships. He also assigned the 4th Fighter Aviation Regiment and the 10th Separate Aviation Detachment to support the 15th Army's operations (see Table 18).

Mamonov's operational plan was similar in concept to those of other army commanders in the Far East Command (see Map 34). While he selected the Sungari River corridor as his army's main axis of advance, he also planned to apply as much pressure as possible along the entire Japanese defensive front by exploiting virtually every feasible axis of advance in his sector.

TABLE 18: COMPOSITION OF AMUR MILITARY FLOTILLA FORCES
SUPPORTING 15TH ARMY, 9 AUGUST 1945

*Amur Flotilla: Khabarovsk – Rear Admiral N. V. Antonov (1st Brigade deployed to
Leninskoe and 2d Brigade to Nizhne-Spasskoe on 8 August)*

1st Brigade of River Ships: Captain 1st Rank V. A. Krinov
  Monitors (gunships) *Lenin, Krasnyi Vostok* [Red East], and *Sun Yat Sen*
  1st Division of River Minesweepers
  1st Detachment of Armored Cutters
  5th Detachment of Armored Cutters
  1st Detachment of Cutter-Minesweepers
  2d Detachment of Cutter-Minesweepers
  1st Detachment of Mine-Cutters
  2 floating batteries
2d Brigade of River Ships: Captain 1st Rank L. B. Tankevich
  Monitors *Sverdlov* and *Dal'nevostochnyi Komsomolets* [Far-eastern Komsomol]
  2d Division of River Minesweepers
  2d Detachment of Armored Cutters
  3d Detachment of Armored Cutters
  3d Detachment of Cutter-Minesweepers
  2 floating batteries
45th Fighter Aviation Regiment
10th Separate Aviation Detachment

Source: V. M. Bagrov and N. F. Sungorkin, *Krasnoznamennaia amurskaia flotiliia* [The
Red Banner Amur Flotilla] (Moscow: Voenizdat, 1976), 155–7.

Oganezov's and Mulin's 361st and 388th Rifle Divisions were to conduct the
15th Army's main attack by assaulting across the Amur River near Leninskoe
and Voskresenskoe in the center of the army's sector, supported by boats and
ships of the Amur Military Flotilla's 1st Brigade, to seize bridgeheads on the
river's southern bank.

  Once the infantry had secured the bridgeheads, the Amur Flotilla was to
ferry Potapov's 171st Tank Brigade and additional supporting artillery
across the river. Then the two rifle divisions, with Potapov's tank brigade
serving as their forward detachment, were to capture Tungchiang, advance
up the eastern bank of the Sungari River to overpower the Japanese defenses
at Fuchin, and then move southwestward along the river to capture
Chiamussu. The Amur Flotilla's 1st Brigade was to cooperate closely with
the two divisions throughout the offensive by conducting amphibious landing operations whenever and wherever necessary to facilitate the advance by
the infantry and armor along the difficult overland route.

  On the left flank of Mamonov's army, the Amur Military Flotilla's 2d
Brigade was to transport the 388th Rifle Division's 630th Rifle Regiment
across the river from Nizhne-Spasskoe, 40 miles (65 kilometers) west of
Khabarovsk, so that it could assault and capture the small Japanese strong
point at Fuyuan. The regiment was then to advance southwestward to seize

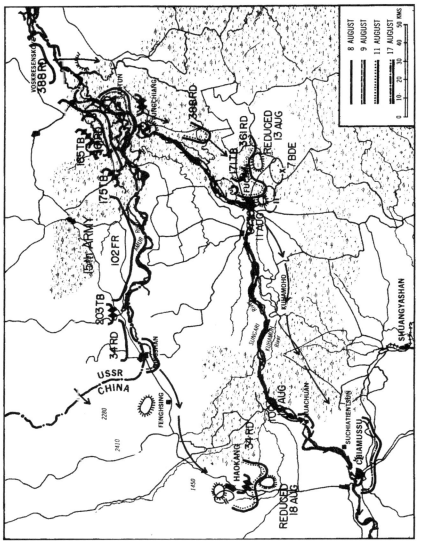

Map 34. Soviet 15th Army's Plan and Operations, 9–17 August 1945

other Japanese strong points and security outposts on the southern bank of the Amur as far southwest as the mouth of the Sungari River.

On Mamonov's right flank, in close coordination with ships of the Amur Flotilla's 1st Brigade, Kolomiets' 34th Rifle Division, Ushillo's 203d Tank Brigade, and the 102d Fortified Region's artillery and machine gun battalions were to assault across the Amur River from the Blagoslovennoe region and capture Mingshanchen. After securing the bridgehead on the river's southern bank, this force was to advance southward, reducing Japanese fortified regions and other defensive positions between Lopei and Chiamussu. Ultimately, Kolomiets' rifle division was to assault Japanese defenses around Chiamussu from the north while the 15th Army's main body attacked the city from the east in yet another pincer movement so characteristic of Soviet operations during the Manchurian campaign.[10]

The assault groups of Mamonov's army were in their jumping-off positions, and the Amur Military Flotilla's ships and assault boats were in position to transport then across the Amur River by late evening on 8 August. To support the assault, the Amur Flotilla's 1st Brigade had displaced to Leninskoe and the 2d Brigade to Nizhne-Spasskoe, and Mamonov had established a joint command post at Leninskoe from which he could coordinate the actions of both forces. In addition, Mamonov created a floating command post and naval repair base on the surface of the Amur River in his army's sector.[11]

The 15th Army planned to precede the amphibious assault with a 50-minute artillery preparation to destroy Japanese security outposts and soften up Japanese defensive positions on the river's southern bank. At the same time, aircraft from the 10th Air Army prepared to employ numerous sorties by fighter aircraft to protect the infantry assault crossing and bomber sorties to strike Japanese fortified positions, troop garrisons, and communications links to the depth of the Japanese defensive zone.

THE 15TH ARMY'S ATTACK

At 0100 hours on 9 August, the 15th Army's shock groups began their assault by dispatching border guards units, reconnaissance detachments, and advanced battalions from the rifle divisions' first echelon rifle regiments across the river on small boats to secure tactically important islands in the river and Japanese outposts on the river's southern bank (see Map 35). Boats and cutters assigned to the Amur Flotilla's 1st Brigade transported the 2d Battalion of the 361st Rifle Division's 394th Rifle Regiment across the river to Tartar Island, 12.4 miles (20 kilometers) down the Amur from the mouth of the Sungari.

The soldiers awaited the signal. Red rockets flashed across the pitch darkness. The battalion silently boarded and settled down in the boats of the Amur Flotilla and headed towards the island. Under the cover of the darkness of night and pouring rain, the battalion successfully forced the Amur and landed on the island.[12]

After a short but intense fight, by 0800 hours the rifle battalion had overcome the small Japanese security outpost and secured the entire island as an intermediate staging area for the larger assault crossing (see Map 34). Mamonov's riflemen achieved similar success in the remainder of the army's main attack sectors, and, by the morning of 9 August, all of the larger islands in the river were in Soviet hands.

During the morning of 9 August, Oganezov's 361st Rifle Division secured a foothold on the river's southern bank with his advanced battalion, and, shortly thereafter, the Amur Flotilla's 1st Brigade ferried three reinforced rifle battalions of his 394th Rifle Regiment across the river to reinforce this lodgment. By nightfall of 9 August, the rifle regiments had captured the Japanese defensive positions at Santun, just east of the mouth of the Sungari River, and had begun moving southward toward the Japanese defenses at Tungchiang. By this time, however, Izeki, the commander of the Japanese 134th Infantry Division, had already ordered his forces to withdraw southward to Chiamussu. Therefore, only small Japanese rearguard forces and Manchurian units resisted the subsequent Soviet advance along the Sungari.

All night on 9–10 August, boats and barges of the Amur Flotilla shuttled back and forth across the Amur River, transporting the main force of Oganezov's rifle division and its artillery and rear services across the river to the Santun and Tungchiang regions. On the 361st Rifle Division's left flank, two rifle regiments of Mulin's 388th Rifle Division also crossed to the southern bank of the river.[13]

The Amur Flotilla's 1st Brigade was responsible for organizing the complex crossing operation. The brigade employed assault boats and river cutters to carry the riflemen across the river and 60-ton rafts, each supported by three pontoons, to transport the heavier weapons and equipment. Each raft could carry a load of either one T-34 and two T-26 tanks, two T-34s and six T-26s tanks, or one T-34 tank and three trucks, and each run across the river took four to five hours to complete because of the swift river currents. The limited number of rafts available to the flotilla meant that it required two to three days to transport a single tank brigade across the river.

The tanks of Potapov's 171st Tank Brigade, for example, took 30 hours to cross the river, and it took a total of four days to transport the entire brigade with its rear services across the river.[14] This complicated subsequent operations, since by the time the tank brigade's rear services were across the river, its forward elements were already more than 62 miles (100 kilometers) to the

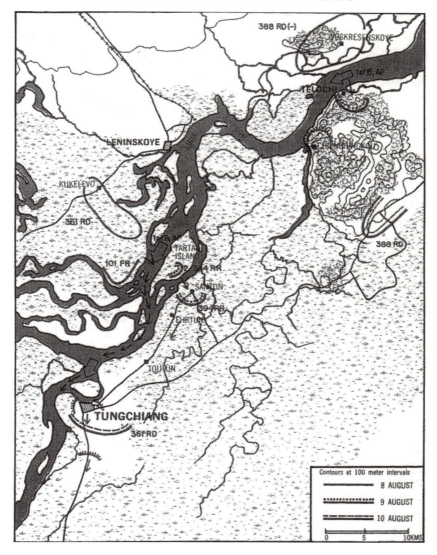

Map 35. Soviet 15th Army's Assault Across the Amur River, 9–10 August 1945

south accompanying the advancing infantry. Furthermore, the wretched road conditions guaranteed that the brigade's rear service elements would take days to catch up with the brigade's forward elements. The resulting absence of logistical and maintenance support further limited the ability of Potapov's tank brigade to function effectively as a forward detachment.

The 15th Army's overall shortage of pontoon-bridging units and other river-crossing equipment also forced the army to rely heavily on commercial steamships and barges to transport its men and equipment across the Amur River. The steamships *Astrakhan, Groznyi, Donbas, Kokkinanki, Sormovo,* as well as other smaller ships augmented the flotilla's organic ships and boats, and the steamships *Chicherin, Ostrovskii,* and *Kirov,* which were equipped to function as hospital ships, carried wounded troops back from the fighting on the south side of the river.

To facilitate a more effective crossing operation and better exploit the scarce crossing equipment, the 15th Army and Amur Flotilla organized three separate crossing sectors. The first sector consisted primarily of ships from the Amur Flotilla, the second comprised the steamships, and the third relied on army pontoon units. A special operational group formed by the 15th Army controlled the crossing operation overall, and a representative of the operational group supervised crossing operations in each sector. Despite the river crossing difficulties, however, sufficient forces were across the Amur River by the morning of 10 August to sustain subsequent operations.[15]

In the army's main attack sector, while the Amur Flotilla's gunboats cut through the murky waters of the Amur toward the town of Tungchiang and prepared to bombard Japanese positions, the troops of Oganezov's 361st Rifle Division advanced on Tungchiang by road from the north. To their surprise, when the riflemen reached the town, they discovered that the Japanese garrison had already abandoned Tungchiang the night before and had retreated south to join Japanese forces in the stronger fortified region at Fuchin.[16] While the Japanese 134th Infantry Division as a whole withdrew southward in accordance with the Kwantung Army's orders, several of the division's infantry battalions and the associated Border Guard Unit and Manchukuoan auxiliaries also followed orders to man to the death the defenses in the region.

After capturing Tungchiang, Oganezov's and Mulin's 361st and 388th Rifle Divisions regrouped and began their southward advance toward Fuchin (see Map 36). Potapov's 171st Tank Brigade (minus its rear elements), with infantry mounted on its tanks, led the advance. At 1500 hours on 10 August, Mamonov issued a new directive, ordering Oganezov's rifle division and the Amur Flotilla to capture Fuchin by 0800 on 11 August with an amphibious assault in coordination with the tediously slow ground advance along the Sungari River's southern bank.

Specifically, Mamonov's directive required the Amur Flotilla's 1st Brigade to land two reinforced rifle battalions and an assault rifle company from

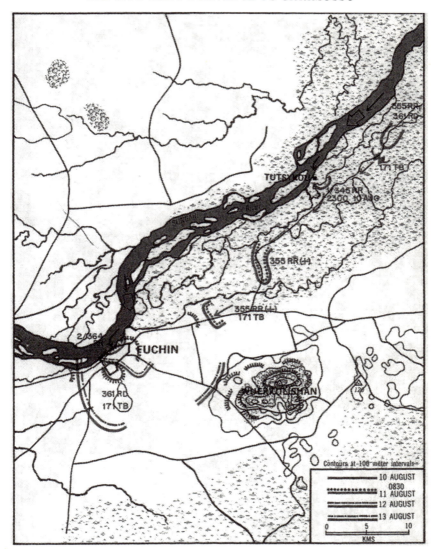

Map 36. The Battle of Fuchin, 10–13 August 1945

Oganezov's rifle division on the right (eastern) bank of the Sungari near Fuchin. These forces were to assault the town proper in coordination with an attack on the town from the northeast by the lead elements of Potapov's 171st Tank Brigade and Oganezov's 361st Rifle Division. Since the lack of time made it impossible to work out a thorough plan, prepare necessary written orders, and properly train the rifle battalions in assault techniques, all orders were issued orally, and the assault battalions conducted hasty training in amphibious assault techniques during the brief few hours before the attack.[17]

The Amur Flotilla's 1st Brigade formed two special naval detachments to conduct and support the amphibious assault. These consisted of a reconnaissance patrol detachment, which consisted of one monitor gunship, three armored cutters, and three cutter-minesweepers, and a covering detachment, which included two monitors and three armored cutters. The reconnaissance patrol detachment was to reconnoiter Japanese positions and land the first echelon of the amphibious assault force, and the covering detachment, located 9.3 miles (15 kilometers) behind, was to support the reconnaissance detachment and land the second echelon of the landing force.

At 1630 hours on 10 August, the reconnaissance patrol detachment sailed with the 3d Battalion of the 361st Rifle Division's 364th Rifle Regiment on board the monitor *Sun Yat Sen*, and the assault company on board the three armored cutters. The covering detachment, which was carrying the 1st Battalion of the division's 345th Rifle Regiment, departed three hours later. During the 43-mile (70-kilometer) journey upriver, lookouts on board the ships watched carefully for the presence of mines and other obstacles in the river. Fortunately for the small and fragile force, in their haste to withdraw to Fuchin, Japanese forces had not had time to sow mines or other obstacles in the river.[18]

At 2200 hours on 10 August, the detachments reached the village of Tutsykou, 23 miles (37 kilometers) north of Fuchin, dropped anchor, and landed the 1st Battalion of the 345th Rifle Regiment. The armored cutters then set off southward to reconnoiter the river channel near Fuchin and the Japanese firing points covering the river. The cutters searched the channel and found it clear of mines. Darkness, however, prevented them from determining the exact configuration of Japanese defenses in and around the town. Also due to the darkness, however, the Japanese failed to detect the cutters, which returned without incident to Tutsykou. Based on this reconnaissance, Oganezov, who was also functioning as the landing force commander, ordered the 1st Battalion of his 346th Rifle Regiment, which was already on shore, to join up with lead elements of his rifle division advancing along the land route and attack Fuchin from the northeast.[19] At the same time, the regiment's second battalion and the division's assault company were to conduct their amphibious assault into Fuchin at dawn in coordination with the attack by the division's main force.

The three armored cutters and minesweepers of the Amur Flotilla's 1st Brigade, followed by the monitors, approached Fuchin at 0700 hours on 11 August. Twenty minutes later the cutters opened fire on Japanese positions. The Japanese returned heavy fire with mortars, artillery, and machine guns, but the effectiveness of the fire was limited because the Japanese possessed no artillery greater than 75 mm. The 130 mm guns of the Soviet monitors *Krasnyi Vostok*, *Lenin*, and *Sun Yat Sen* and the multiple rocket launchers of the armored cutters systematically silenced the outgunned Japanese shore firing positions. While doing so, the monitors reportedly destroyed five concrete and 12 wooden pillboxes, six mortar batteries, and several ammunition warehouses, and the armored cutters destroyed another ten firing points with direct naval gunfire.

During the artillery duel, which lasted one hour, the armored cutters successfully landed the assault company, and at 0830 hours the entire 3d Battalion of the 364th Rifle Regiment landed from the monitor *Sun Yat Sen*. After securing a bridgehead on the river's southern shore, the small force moved on the town itself but was halted in its tracks on the town's outskirts by heavy Japanese artillery fire and infantry counterattacks, which it managed to repel only with the aid of heavy gunfire from the monitors. Only the timely arrival of the lead elements of Potapov's 171st Tank Brigade and the main body of Oganezov's rifle division finally smashed the determined Japanese resistance. At about 0900 hours, the bulk of the defending Japanese and Manchukuoan forces withdrew into the fortified military settlement in the southwestern sector of Fuchin and the Wuerhkuli Shan Fortified Region in the hills southeast of the city. The fight for the fortified camp, which continued well into 12 August, was particularly intense:

The Japanese had strongly fortified the town as part of the Fuchin Fortified Region by creating permanent firing positions on its outskirts. They had constructed pillboxes in the stone buildings and erected 20-meter-[66-foot] high metal watchtowers around the town, upon which they placed armored cupolas with embrasures from which heavy machine guns could conduct all-round fire. The 2d Battalion of the Sungari Naval Flotilla's infantry regiment, the 25th Security Battalion, and other subunits and detachments of Manchurian troops defended the town and the fortified region.[20]

The riflemen of Oganezov's 361st Rifle Division, supported by the tanks of Potapov's tank brigade, slowly cleared Fuchin of its defenders in intense house-to-house fighting. By 1200 hours on 11 August, a battalion of Oganezov's 455th Rifle Regiment captured the town's center but was unable to seize the remainder of the town. The Japanese launched several unsuccessful counterattacks overnight on 11–12 August, and the next day the Soviet infantry resumed its attacks, this time supported by monitors. However, once again, the small Soviet force achieved only limited success. The main body of Oganezov's 361st Rifle Division and Potapov's tank brigade finally reached Fuchin on 13 August and immediately joined the fight. By nightfall, Japanese resistance had collapsed and the town was in Soviet hands even though Japanese forces continued to resist in the hilltop fortress southeast of town. With Fuchin in Soviet hands, Mamonov immediately ordered his main shock group to continue its march toward Chiamussu.

While Mamonov's two rifle divisions and tank brigade advanced southward along the Sungari River, his secondary attacks struck Japanese defenses on his army's right and left flanks. On the 15th Army's right flank, Kolomiets' 34th Rifle Division and Ushillo's 203d Tank Brigade crossed the Amur River early on 9 August and captured Japanese defensive positions at and around Mingshanchen. The next day Kolomiets' rifle division advanced southward along the Lopei–Chiamussu road, leaving a portion of its forces behind to blockade the Japanese fortified positions at Fenghsiang, while the division's main body moved southward over waterlogged roads to invest the larger Japanese fortified region at Hsingshanchen. A heavy Soviet air and artillery bombardment against Japanese defenses at Hsingshanchen ultimately forced the Japanese to withdraw into the hills west of the fortified region or southward to Chiamussu. By day's end on 13 August, the lead elements of Kolomiets' rifle division had pushed slowly southward toward Japanese positions at Lienchiangkou, which protected the northern bank of the Sungari River directly across the river from Chiamussu.[21]

On the 15th Army's left flank, the 630th Rifle Regiment of Mulin's 388th Rifle Division was to cooperate closely with the Amur Flotilla's 2d Brigade to capture Japanese defenses on the south bank of the Amur River southwest of Khabarovsk.[22] The most important of these Japanese defensive positions were at and around the small river village of Fuyuan. Destruction of the Japanese garrison at Fuyuan and adjacent defensive outposts would insure safe, continuous Soviet passage up and down the Amur River. At 0320 hours on 9 August, the gunship *Proletarii* [Proletariat], the 2d Detachment of Armored Cutters, and the 3d Detachment of Minesweepers left Nizhne-Spasskoe with troops from the 630th Rifle Regiment's 1st Battalion on their decks. The monitors *Sverdlov* and *Dal'nevostochnyi Komsomolets* and the 3d Detachment of Armored Cutters took up firing positions near Malankin Island to support the amphibious landing at Fuyuan.

As the amphibious assault detachment and ships approached the shore, the monitors and cutters opened fire on Japanese firing positions in the Fuyuan Fortified Region, and landing parties went ashore near the wharves at the western and eastern ends of the town. Initially, the unsuspecting Japanese offered only light resistance, but as the 630th Rifle Regiment's 1st Battalion advanced, the resistance stiffened measurably. Yak-9 aircraft of the 10th Air Army's 307th Fighter Aviation Regiment provided air cover until it was clear that no Japanese aircraft would intercede. Closer to the town's center, two detachments of Soviet sailors also went ashore to support the 1st Battalion. This combined force proved too strong for the weak defenders, and all Japanese resistance ceased by 0800 hours.

After capturing the town, one company of the 630th Rifle Regiment's 1st Rifle Battalion garrisoned Fuyuan, while the remainder of the battalion re-embarked aboard the ship. This time the Amur Flotilla's 2d Brigade was to move the small assault force upstream toward the mouth of the Sungari River to seize the three small Japanese defensive outposts at Chinteli, Otu, and Kaintsi. *En route*, the brigade picked up the 630th Rifle Regiment's 2d Battalion. However, when the brigade's ships reached Chinteli at 1000 hours on 10 August, it found the village already in Soviet hands, having fallen to the crew of an armored cutter and several soldiers who had crossed the river and captured the village on their own initiative the night before.

After picking up 630th Rifle Regiment's 3d Battalion at the village of Pokrovskoe, the flotilla's 2d Brigade moved on to Otu, only to find it also in Soviet hands. Continuing upriver, the brigade reached the larger outpost at Kaintsi at 1925 hours on 10 August. The monitor *Sverdlov* and three armored cutters landed assault parties at the mouth of the Kaintsi River, while the monitor *Dal'nevostochnyi Komsomolets* landed a rifle company north of Kaintsi village. Once again most of the Japanese defenders had already withdrawn from the village, and the few that remained fled after hearing the first salvo of rockets from the armored cutters.

Thus, by day's end on 10 August, the 630th Rifle Regiment and Amur Flotilla's 2d Brigade had cleared Japanese forces from the entire southern bank of the Amur River in the 124-mile (200-kilometer) sector from Khabarovsk to the mouth of the Sungari River. The brigade left garrisons behind in each of the captured villages, while transporting the 15th Army's support echelons across the Amur River at Leninskoe. After completing this task on 13 August, Antonov's Amur Flotilla command group, which was *en route* up the Sungari River to Fuchin, ordered the 2d Brigade to reinforce the 1st Brigade along the Sungari River. It also ordered a battalion of gunboats and a detachment of armored cutters from the Ussuri River naval force, a battalion of armored cutters, and the monitor *Aktivnyi* [Active], and the gunboat *Krasnaia Zvezda* [Red Star], which belonged to the Zee-Bureisk Brigade, to join the 1st Brigade at Fuchin. Antonov and Mamonov hoped that this concentrated naval power would help compensate for the flooded terrain that was slowing down the Soviet ground force advance along the southern bank of the Sungari River.

Faced with the sudden Soviet attack, as early as the evening of 9 August Kita's Japanese First Area Army ordered Izeki's 134th Infantry Division to fall back on Chiamussu and, if necessary, to Fangcheng. By 12 August the bulk of the 134th Infantry Division had concentrated at Chiamussu, leaving only a rear guard and Manchukuoan units to defend in the fortified regions. After Mamonov's main shock group captured Fuchin and began advancing on Chiamussu from the northeast, Izeki assigned responsibility for defending Chiamussu to the 7th Manchukuoan Infantry Brigade and withdrew his division southward up the Sungari River to Fangcheng.[23]

Meanwhile, early on 11 August, Purkaev had already ordered Mamonov to commence a concerted attack on Chiamussu:

Combat Order of the 2d Far Eastern Front Commander to the 15th Army Commander Concerning an Offensive in the Direction of Chiamussu

0140 hours 11 August 1945

In connection with the enemy withdrawal in front of the 2d Far Eastern Front's forces, I ORDER:

On the morning of 11 August 1945, the 15th Army will continue a decisive offensive along the Lopei, Hsingshanchen, and Chiamussu and Tungchiang, Fuchin, and Chiamussu axes with mobile (tank) units, reinforced by infantry assault forces, in the first echelon along both axes.

The army's mission is to capture Hsingshanchen and Fuchin by 11 August and Chiamussu by 12 August.

Purkaev
Shevchenko
Leonov[24]

Although Mamonov's army had accomplished the first part of this mission by day's end on 12 August, the second task Purkaev assigned to him still eluded his grasp. With his ground operations bogged down in the soggy ground, Mamonov decided to rely more heavily on amphibious assaults to snatch the prize of Chiamussu.

Oganezov, the commander of the 361st Rifle Division, met with Captain 1st Rank V. A. Krinov, the commander of the Amur Flotilla's 1st Brigade, at Fuchin on 13 August to plan their subsequent joint advance on Chiamussu. High water made the few roads along the southern bank of the Sungari treacherous, if not utterly impassable, even for a limited offensive without significant engineer support. Complicating matters, fuel shortages hindered the forward movement of Potapov's 171st Tank Brigade. Facing these problems, the respective commanders decided to capture Chiamussu by an amphibious operation.

Specifically, the two commanders planned a series of successive assault landings along the banks of the Sungari River to threaten Japanese withdrawal routes and facilitate the movement of the division's main force, which

was to advance overland along the single road parallel to the southern bank of the river. Antonov then approved the plan and ordered the Amur Flotilla's 1st and 2d Brigades to transport assault-landing detachments to the Chiamussu region and to cooperate with the 15th Army's ground units in capturing Chiamussu no later than day's end on 15 August:
According to the plan,

> The 1st Brigade was to land one reinforced battalion at Kekhoma [Kuhomo Ho] and Sansinchen (Hsincheng)], 85 kilometers [53 miles] and 70 kilometers [43 miles] below Chiamussu, to capture the towns and support the movement of the battalions along the shore and the seizure of Chiamussu. The 2d Brigade would follow the ships of the 1st Brigade and land the 632d Rifle Regiment in the immediate vicinity of Chiamussu.[25]

At 0535 hours on 14 August, the ships of the 1st Brigade, carrying two rifle battalions from the 349th Rifle Regiment of Oganezov's 361st Rifle Division, and a mixed detachment from the 83d Rifle Regiment of Kolomiets' 34th Rifle Division, headed upriver toward the two landing sites (see Map 37). When they reached the designated landing sights, however, they found that the Japanese had abandoned both, but high water still blocked the roads from these towns to Chiamussu. Consequently, the ships re-embarked the troops and sailed on, this time landing their troops at Sustun [Huachuan], only 25 miles (40 kilometers) from Chiamussu.

While the riverine force was searching for an appropriate landing site, the main force of Kolomiets' 34th Rifle Division and Ushillo's 203d Tank Brigade, which were still operating toward Chiamussu from the north, finally assaulted and overcame Japanese defenses at Lienchiangkou, across the Sungari River from Chiamussu. However, several attempts by this force to cross the river on makeshift rafts failed because of stiff Japanese resistance and the treacherous river currents. Because Kolomiets' efforts to cross the Sungari River failed, and Oganezov's 361st Rifle Division task force on the south bank of the river was still advancing at a painfully slow pace, on 15 August Purkaev decided to employ the Amur Flotilla in a direct assault on Chiamussu proper.

That evening, as the flotilla's ships began moving toward Chiamussu, the Japanese released logs and burning barges into the river in an attempt to block their movement.[26] Dodging the obstacles, the armored cutters and monitors approached Chiamussu the next morning only to find that the withdrawing Japanese had set fire to most of the buildings and warehouses in the city. At 0630 hours on 16 August, the 1st Detachment of Armored Cutters, supported by the monitor *Lenin*, landed a reconnaissance detachment of sailors under Captain S. M. Kuznetsov directly into the city's docks. The detachment soon captured the entire wharf area and, after being reinforced by another reconnaissance detachment, pushed on to capture the city's police station.

The remainder of the 632d Rifle Regiment followed the reconnaissance detachments and finally snuffed out the remaining Japanese resistance in the city. Meanwhile, reports reached the Amur Flotilla that the 7th Manchukuoan Infantry Brigade at Myngali, 4.3 miles (7 kilometers) east of Chiamussu, was ready to surrender to Soviet forces. At 1100 hours on 16 August, the 3d Detachment of Armored Cutters landed two automatic weapons companies from the 632d Rifle Regiment at Myngali, and within minutes the small detachment accepted the surrender of the 3,500-man Manchukuoan force. By nightfall, Oganezov's rifle division and Potapov's tank brigade had entered Chiamussu, and both the city and its surrounding region were firmly in Soviet hands. The next day, the lead elements of Mulin's and Kolomiets' 388th and 34th Rifle Divisions also entered the city, thus accomplishing Mamonov's principal mission. Soon after, Purkaev announced the heartening news to Vasilevsky:

Combat Report by the 2d Far Eastern Front Commander to the Supreme Commander of Soviet Forces in the Far East Concerning the Capture of Chiamussu

1338 hours 17 August 1954

I am reporting:
The 2d Far Eastern Front's forces have fulfilled the mission assigned by *Stavka* of the Supreme High Command's Directive No. 11112 concerning the Sungarian offensive on 17 August (the eighth day of the operation).
At 1000 hours on 17 August 1945, the *front's* forces, in cooperation with the Red Banner Amur Flotilla, have destroyed the remnants of the enemy in the military settlement southwest of Chiamussu and have completely cleared the city of Chiamussu and the airfield.
The offensive toward Sansing (Ilan) is continuing.

Purkaev
Leonov
Shevchenko[27]

The next day, Mamonov's forces continued their pursuit of Izeki's withdrawing infantry division up the Sungari River along the narrow river valley through the mountains toward Sansin Ilan (Sansing) and Harbin. The Japanese First Area Army was unable to keep track of its isolated division during its retreat to Chiamussu and thereafter southward along the river:

Information from the 134th Division in the north sector of the Area Army's front was meager on the 10th. A report from the Chiamussu signal station, however, confirmed earlier reports that the division was withdrawing to Fangcheng ...

238

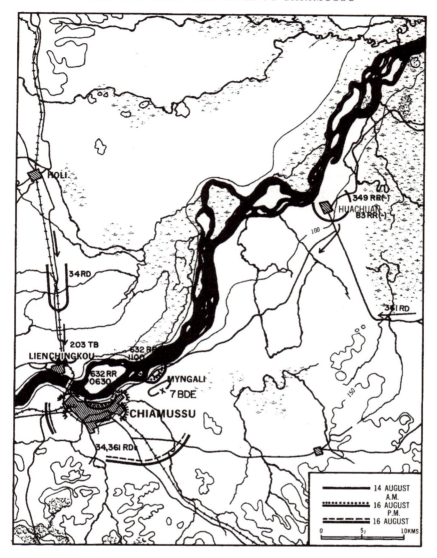

Map 37. The Fall of Chiamussu, 14–16 August 1945

According to rough estimates ... the 134th Division [retained] about two-thirds [of its pre-hostilities combat effectiveness] ...

Communications with the 134th Division were out since about 11 August because of the breakdown of the division's wireless. On 19 August one of the division's staff officers, Colonel Sato, arrived in Tunhua by airplane and was given a copy of the cease-fire order to take back to Fangcheng.[28]

Once again, Mamonov assigned the Amur Flotilla and 632d Rifle Regiment the task of seizing Ilan with yet another amphibious assault. Proceeded by a reconnaissance detachment of three armored cutters and the monitor *Sun Yat Sen*, which was carrying a reconnaissance detachment, the force conducted several landings north of Ilan against stiff Japanese resistance before capturing Ilan on 18 August, where it captured a reported 3,900 Japanese troops.[29] By this time Japanese forces were laying down their arms pursuant to the Emperor's cease-fire order. The 15th Army's Sungarian offensive was at an end as it linked up with forces of the 5th Separate Rifle Corps, which were advancing westward from Poli.

CONCLUSIONS

Over the course of seven days, the combined forces of Mamonov's 15th Army and Antonov's Amur Military Flotilla had crossed the Amur River and advanced 130 miles (210 kilometers) up the Sungari River to Chiamussu, at a rate of 18.6 miles (30 kilometers) per day despite the appalling terrain. Within nine days, but at a cost of strenuous effort, the flotilla managed to transport 91,000 men, 150 tanks and self-propelled guns, and 413 artillery pieces, along with 3,000 horses and 28,000 tons of supplies across the Amur River.[30]

Throughout the entire duration of the offensive, the flotilla's ships, with amphibious detachments aboard, served both as a riverine forward detachment and advanced guard for Mamonov's army and Purkaev's *front* as a whole. Operating far ahead of the main force, the ships and amphibious forces overcame the imposing terrain obstacles, generating and maintaining a surprisingly high tempo of advance in the region. By applying their limited combat power in timely fashion, the riverine forces maintained unrelenting pressure on withdrawing Japanese forces and, while doing so, easily overcame all Japanese fortified positions in the region.

The joint operations by the Amur Flotilla and 15th Army represent a classic case study in the conduct of flexible and effective joint amphibious operations. Much of the operations' success resulted from the close coordination of the flotilla's ships and the ground force and the ability of commanders to adapt quickly to ever-changing conditions in the area of operations. Soviet ground and naval commanders demonstrated sufficient initiative to maintain the momentum of the offensive until its successful conclusion.

NOTES

1. Boeicho, *Senshi sosho*, 438; *JM 154*, sketch no. 2, map no. 2, chart 3, gives 134th Infantry Division strength as 14,056 men; S. E. Zakharov *et al.*, *Krasnoznamennyi tikhookeanskii flot* [The Red Banner Pacific Fleet] (Moscow: Voenizdat, 1973), 206.
2. *IVMV*, 2:200.
3. Vnotchenko, *Pobeda*, 97.
4. Ibid.
5. Zakharov, *Final*, 400; Vnotchenko, *Pobeda*, 109; and Sidorov, 'Boevoe', 15.
6. Vnotchenko, *Pobeda*, 125; Krupchenko, *Sovetskie*, 320.
7. Vnotchenko, *Pobeda*, 117.
8. Ibid., 132; and *IVMV*, 2:208.
9. V. N. Bagrov and N. F. Sungorkin, *Krasnoznamennaia amurskaia flotiliia* [The Red Banner Amur Flotilla] (Moscow: Voenizdat, 1976), 156–7.
10. Ibid., 149–50.
11. Ibid., 151.
12. Vnotchenko, *Pobeda*, 230, claims the Soviets overcame light Japanese resistance on Tartar Island. Other sources deny the Japanese offered any resistance.
13. Zakharov *et al.*, *Krasnoznamennyi*, 203–4; Bagrov and Sungorkin, *Krasno*, 159–60; and Vnotchenko, *Pobeda*, 230.
14. Vnotchenko, *Pobeda*, 231–2.
15. Bagrov and Sungorkin, *Krasno*, 178–9.
16. Zakharov *et al.*, *Krasnoznamennyi*, 203–4; and Bagrov and Sungorkin, *Krasno*, 160. Vnotchenko, *Pobeda*, 233, mentions a 'two-hour bloody struggle' for Tungchiang.
17. Zakharov *et al.*, *Krasnoznamennyi*, 206–7.
18. Ibid.; Bagrov and Sungorkin, *Krasno*, 178–9.
19. Accounts of the assault on Fuchin are found in Vnotchenko, *Pobeda*, 233–5; Zakharov *et al.*, *Krasnoznamennyi*, 206–10; and Bagrov and Sungorkin, *Krasno*, 179–83.
20. Vnotchenko, *Pobeda*, 234.
21. Ibid., 232–3; Bagrov and Sungorkin, *Krasno*, 185.
22. Zakharov *et al.*, *Krasnoznamennyi*, 204–6, and Bagrov and Sungorkin, *Krasno*, 161–6.
23. *JM 154*, 9, 61, 63.
24. V. A. Zolotarev, ed., *Russkii arkhiv*, T. 18 (7–1), 350.
25. Zakharov *et al.*, *Krasnoznamennyi*, 210.
26. Details of the Chiamussu operation are from Vnotchenko, *Pobeda*, 235; Zakharov *et al.*, *Krasnoznamennyi*, 210–11; and Bagrov and Sungorkin, *Krasno*, 185–7.
27. Zolotarev, *Russkii arkhiv*, T. 18 (7–1), 353.
28. *JM 154*, 63, 72.
29. Vnotchenko, *Pobeda*, 266–7.
30. Bagrov and Sungorkin, *Krasno*, 168.

9

The Battle for Southern Sakhalin Island, 11–25 August 1945: Joint Ground and Amphibious Operations

CONTEXT AND TERRAIN

Simultaneously with the ground operations in Manchuria proper and the amphibious operations against the northern Korean coast, the Far East Command conducted active offensive operations against Japanese forces on southern Sakhalin Island and the strategically important Kuril Islands (see Map 38).

Sakhalin Island, which the Japanese call Karafuto, extends more than 559 miles (900 kilometers) from north to south and 19–62 miles (30–100-kilometers) from east to west. Encompassing an area of 30,116 square miles (78,000 square kilometers), the island is strategically located off the coast of the Soviet (Russian) Maritime Province's Amur District in the Far East. Although the island came under Russian control in the early nineteenth century, Japan seized control over the southern half of the island south of the 50th parallel in 1905 by virtue of its victory in the Russo-Japanese War.

The island, which is bordered on the north and east by the Sea of Okhotsk, on the south by La Perouse Straits, and on the west by the Tatar Strait, dominates the vital sea-lanes connecting Russia's Maritime Provinces with the Kamchatka Peninsula, Magadan in eastern Siberia, Russia's arctic ports, and the Pacific Ocean beyond. The island is separated from the Asian mainland by the Tatar Strait, which ranges in width from 6.2 miles (10 kilometers) in the north to about 174 miles (280 kilometers) in the south, and from the Japanese northern island of Hokkaido by the 30-mile-(48-kilometer) wide La Perouse Straits (see Map 39).

The island itself is principally heavily forested and mountainous, punctuated by numerous forest swamps and bogs. The Eastern and Western Mountain ranges traverse the island from north to south, rising to heights of as much

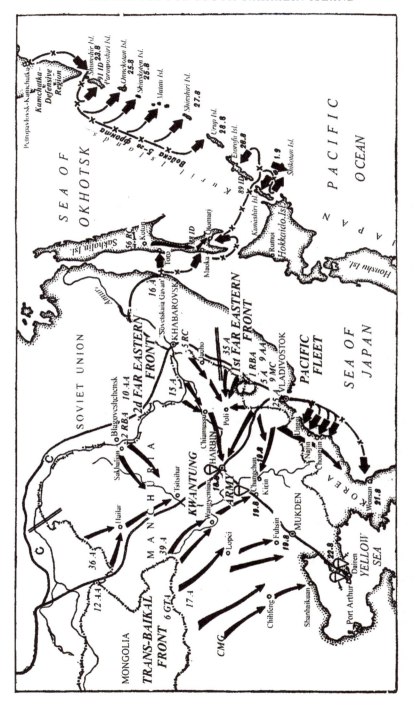

Map 38. Soviet Far East Command Operations in Manchuria, Southern Sakhalin Island, and Kuril Islands

as 1,975 feet (602 meters) in the north, 4,587 feet (1,398 meters) in the center, 3,500–3,700 feet (1,067–1,128 meters) in the narrow south central region, and 1,929 feet (588 meters) in the extreme south.

While most of the rivers on Sakhalin are short and radiate outward from the mountains directly to the adjacent seas, the Tym' and Poronai Rivers traverse the island's interior. The former extends 186 miles (300 kilometers) northward from the town of Tymovskoe into the Sea of Okhotsk, and the latter flows 155 miles (250 kilometers) southward from the island's center into Taraika Wan (Terpeniia Bay) on the southeastern coast. The only trafficable rail and road routes from north to south lie along the narrow valleys of these rivers, although a narrow road network hugs the seas along the eastern and western coasts.

Climatic conditions on the islands also vary in accordance with the mountainous terrain and the influence of the relatively cold Sea of Okhotsk and warm Sea of Japan. Generally, the northern and western portions of the island are dry, while the southern and eastern are wet. Sakhalin's abundant summer and fall rains often fill the island's river to overflowing.

While a few small ports existed on the Soviet controlled northern half of the island, the Japanese had constructed numerous ports in the south, many for principally military purposes. From north to south, these included Toro, Esutoru, Tomarioru, Maoka, and Honto on the western coast, Shikuka on Taraika Wan (Bay) along the southeastern coast, and Odomari on Aniwa Wan (Bay) in the south. The largest towns in the island's interior were Okha in the extreme north, Aleksandrovsk-Sakhalinskii midway between the island's north and south, Tymovskoe (Debinskoe) inland east of Aleksandrovsk, and Maoka, Odomari, and Toyohara in the extreme south.

The only axis of advance suitable for use by Soviet military forces was the railroad line and road extending from Tymovskoe in the north southward along the Poronai River through Koton to Shikuka on Taraika Wan (Bay). However, heavily forested mountains with numerous swamps and bogs flanked both sides of this narrow corridor. In addition, the Japanese constructed the formidable Haramitog (Koton) Fortified Region astride this axis.

JAPANESE DEFENSES

The Japanese Fifth Area Army, whose headquarters was situated at Sapporo on the island of Hokkaido, defended the southern half of Sakhalin Island with its 88th Infantry Division and various supporting units (see Table 19).

The division's 125th Infantry Regiment manned the Haramitog (Koton) Fortified Region near the Poronai River, which ran southward down the center of the island and blocked any Soviet advance down the river. Two battalions of the 88th Infantry Division's 25th Infantry Regiment protected the port of Maoka (Kholmsk) on the west coast of the southern half of

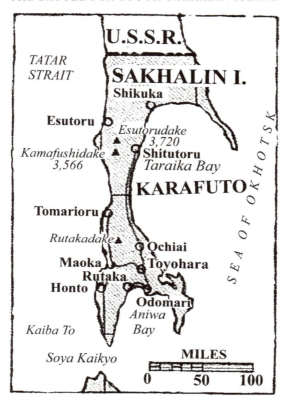

Map 39. Southern Sakhalin Island

TABLE 19: COMPOSITION AND DISPOSITIONS OF JAPANESE
88TH INFANTRY DIVISION, 9 AUGUST 1945

Force	*Location*
88th Infantry Division	
125th Infantry Regiment	Haramitog (Koton) Fortified Region
	(3 battalions)
25th Infantry Regiment	Maoka (2 battalions)
	Honto (1 battalion)
306th Infantry Regiment	Haihoro (20 km south of Honto) (1 battalion)
	Sakahama (20 km north of Ochaia) (1 battalion)
	Odomari (1 battalion)
88th Artillery Regiment	Haramitog, Maoka, and Haihoro (1 battalion
	each)
Strength:	
19,000 men plus 10,000 reservists	

the island, and one battalion the island's southwestern extremity. The division's 306th Infantry Regiment had its three infantry battalions stationed at Haihoro (Gastello), Sakahama (Dolinsk), and Odomari (Korsakov), respectively.

The division attached the artillery of its artillery regiment and its other heavy weapons to its regiments. In addition, border guard troops defended alongside the 88th Infantry Division, and the Fifth Area Army had several reserve units that could be mobilized to support the island's defense. Overall, the Japanese force on the island numbered 19,000 men and about 10,000 reservists, 5,400 of whom were defending the Haramitog Fortified Region. However, supporting ships of the Japanese Navy had been transferred to Manchurian ports, and thus were not available to assist in the defense.[1]

Because of its strategic location astride the principal potential Soviet invasion route, the Haramitog Fortified Region, which had been under construction since 1939, was the strongest and most important Japanese defensive position on the island: 7.5 miles (12 kilometers) wide and up to 10 miles (16 kilometers) deep, the fortified region contained a line of security outposts, a security belt and main and second defensive belts.[2]

The Haramitog Fortified Region's *security outposts* consisted of a series of observation posts located on Hills 274 and 237, 1.4–1.9 miles (2–3 kilometers) forward (north) of the security belt. The *security belt*, which ran east to west along the southern bank of the Kottongai Gava (River) 5 miles (8 kilometers) from the forward edge, consisted of two company and two platoon strong points containing a total of two ferro-concrete pillboxes, four earth and timber pillboxes, and 22 concrete embrasures protected by double barbed wire entanglements and a 0.6-mile-(1-kilometer) long open antitank ditch.

Although the strong points were not mutually supporting, each was organized for all-round defense. The strongest of them was strong point Honda, which covered the road southward toward the center of the main defensive belt. Two Japanese infantry companies and a border police detachment manned the security belt.

The *main defensive belt*, which ran north and northwest of Koton village, consisted of three centers of resistance and one company and three platoon strong points, which were concentrated to protect the fortified region's more vulnerable left flank (see Map 40). The Japanese also deployed another strong point 2.5 miles (4 kilometers) north of the Haramitog Pass to deceive the Soviets regarding the actual location of the forward edge.

The center of resistance on *Happo Hill*, which was 4.3 miles (7 kilometers) wide and 2.2 miles (3.5 kilometers) deep, consisted of seven company strong points equipped with 46 machine gun and eight artillery pillboxes and 70 bunkers manned by two infantry battalions. The Happo center of resistance was ideally situated to deliver flanking fire and counterattacks against any force attacking directly south along the road toward Koton.

The center of resistance on *Fugato Hill*, which was 2.5 miles (4 kilometers) wide and 1.9 miles (3 kilometers) deep, consisted of four company strong points with 22 earth and timber pillboxes, two ferro-concrete observation posts, and two concrete artillery firing positions. About 2.5 miles (4 kilometers) of open trenches and triple coil barbed wire entanglements surrounded this hill. The Fugato center of resistance, which was located due south of Happo Hill and was manned by one infantry battalion, increased the depth of the main defensive belt in this sector to 3.7 miles (6 kilometers), and its fires controlled the approaches to the Haramitog Pass.

The center of resistance at *Haramitog Pass*, which was 2.5 miles (4 kilometers) wide and 1.4 miles (2 kilometers) deep, contained four company strong point, six ferro-concrete artillery and machine gun pillboxes, 15 earth and timber pillboxes, and six artillery and six mortar positions. In addition, the Japanese dug an extensive network of open trenches and antitank ditches protected by mine fields and barbed wire in the immediate vicinity of Haramitog Pass. This center of resistance, which was echeloned to the right rear of the other two, protected the north–south road to Koton and had its right flank anchored in the swamps along the western bank of the Ponorai River to the east. In addition, the Japanese built a company strong point at the village of Muika, just east of the swamp, to protect the road running into Koton from the northeast.

The Japanese erected yet another smaller center of resistance 0.9 miles (1.5 kilometers) east of the Poronai River, This center, which consisted of 24 machine gun and three artillery earth and timber pillboxes, four mortar positions, and 15 bunkers, was designed to protect against any southward Soviet advance east of the river. This center included up to 9,840 feet (3,000 meters) of open combat and communications trenches and was protected by double coiled barbed wire.

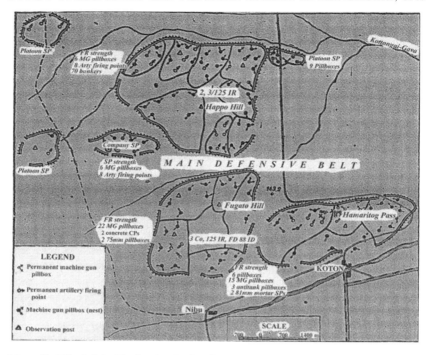

Map 40. The Main Defensive Belt of Japanese Haramitog Fortified Region

All of these centers of resistance and associate strong points were capable of all-round defense and were interconnected by communications trenches, most of which had overhead cover. Heavy forests and brush surrounded all of these defensive positions. While the Japanese had cleared enough of these obstacles to deliver artillery and machine gun fire against an attacking enemy, the remaining trees and brush hindered enemy movement and concentration and obscured enemy observation and fires.

The Japanese constructed their *second defensive belt* at and around Koton and along the southern bank of the Kiton-Gava (River). However, this belt, which extended to a depth of up to 18.6 miles (30 kilometers), contained few if any prepared positions and trenches and posed no obstacle to attacking forces.

Overall, the Haramitog (Koton) Fortified Region contained 17 ferro-concrete pillboxes, 31 artillery and 108 machine gun earth and timber pillboxes, 28 artillery and 18 mortar or grenadier positions, and up to 150 bunkers.[3] All of these were located in heavily forested and brush-covered terrain astride or near the main north–south road. In short, any force attacking south had to do so through the very center of this formidable fortified region.

Even though the Japanese knew that any attacking Soviet force would have to traverse this region and prepare accordingly, they also overestimated the obstacle value of the terrain, particularly the Poronai River, which they believed impassible for any large military force. Therefore, the Japanese 125th Infantry Regiment garrisoned the Haramitog center of resistance with its 1st Battalion (less one company), the Happo Hill center of resistance with its 2d and 3d Battalions, and the Fugato Hill center of resistance with its reconnaissance detachment and one infantry company.

In total, the garrison of the Haramitog Fortified Region numbered 5,400 men, equipped with 42 heavy machine guns, 94 light machine guns, 28 guns and mortars, and 27 grenade launchers. The tactical density of the Japanese defense amounted to 724 (450) men, 5.6 (3.5) heavy machine guns, 12.6 (7.8) light machine guns, 3.7 (2.3) guns and mortars, 12.9 (8) grenade launchers, and 24 (15) pillboxes per 1 mile (1 kilometer) of front.[4] In addition, single infantry companies manned small defensive positions at Ampetsu and the port of Esutoru on the coast of the Tatar Strait.

Other Japanese forces on the island manned light defenses around key ports but no major defensive positions. Nor did the Japanese plan to mine any of the key harbors in the region.

THE SOVIET 16TH ARMY'S OFFENSIVE PLAN

In early August 1945, the 2d Far Eastern Front's 16th Army, the Kamchatka Defensive Region, and the Pacific Fleet's Northern Pacific Flotilla and Petropavlovsk Naval Base were responsible for the defense of the Soviet coast west of the Tatar Strait and the Sea of Okhotsk, northern Sakhalin Island, and the Kamchatka Peninsular. The 16th Army's 56th Rifle Corps and 2d Separate Rifle Brigade occupied defensive positions on northern Sakhalin, and the army's 113th Separate Rifle Brigade manned defenses in the Sovetskaia Gavan' region on the west coast of the Tatar Strait. The 255th Mixed Aviation Division provided air support for the 16th Army. The Kamchatka Defensive Region, supported by the 128th Mixed Aviation Division was responsible for protecting against an enemy amphibious assault in the Avachinsk Bay near Petropavlovsk.[5]

On the evening of 8 August, the forces of the 16th Army and Kamchatka Defensive Region occupied defenses to protect against any amphibious assault, and the Northern Pacific Flotilla and the Petropavlovsk Naval Base began laying mines in the Tatar Strait, the Gulf of Sakhalin, and the approaches to Petropavlovsk. Supporting aviation conducted reconnaissance and air strikes against Japanese ground installations.

After the Far East Command's forces began their invasion of Manchuria proper, late on 10 August, Vasilevsky decided to begin operations against southern Sakhalin and the Kuril Islands and issued appropriate orders to his subordinate commands. He assigned the mission of reducing Japanese defenses on southern Sakhalin Island to Major General A. A. D'iakonov's 56th Rifle Corps of Lieutenant General L. G. Cheremisov's 16th Army, which was subordinate to Purkaev's 2d Far Eastern Front, and the Pacific Fleet's Northern Pacific Flotilla, commanded by Vice Admiral V. A. Andreev (see Map 41).

The order that Vasilevsky sent to Cheremisov through Purkaev at 2200 hours on 10 August required the troops of D'iakonov's 56th Rifle Corps to attack across the state border on Sakhalin Island at 1000 hours the following morning and, in conjunction with the Pacific Fleet, capture the southern half of the island by day's end on 22 August.[6] Cheremisov's operational plan required D'iakonov's 56th Rifle Corps to conduct the army's main attack on Sakhalin Island directly through the Koton (Haramitog) Fortified Region to split the Japanese defensive front in two by reaching Kiton village. Specifically, Cheremisov ordered D'iakonov's rifle corps 'to penetrate the Koton Fortified Region's defenses' and 'advance decisively along the eastern coast of the island in the general direction of Toyohara to destroy the enemy Sakhalin grouping in cooperation with amphibious assaults on the ports of Esutoru and Maoka'.[7]

Cheremisov ordered D'iakonov's 56th Rifle Corp to carry out the operation in three distinct stages. During the first stage, which was to last from 11 through 15 August, the rifle corps was to penetrate the Japanese security belt and prepare to penetrate the Koton Fortified Region's main defensive belt. This required D'iakonov's forces to advance to a depth of 9.3 miles (15 kilometers) at an advance rate of 1.9 miles (3 kilometers) per day, a relatively

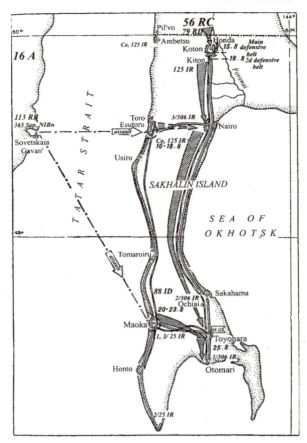

Map 41. Soviet 16th Army's Plan for Conquest of Sakhalin Island

251

slow rate due to the difficult terrain and the absence of detailed intelligence information concerning the Japanese defenses.

During the second and most critical stage of the operation, which was to last from 16 through 18 August, D'iakonov's forces were to penetrate the Japanese main defensive belt and, in the event the Japanese reinforced their positions, conduct an amphibious assault on Esutoru to cut off the road leading northward on the island's western coast. If necessary, the Northern Pacific Flotilla was to conduct the amphibious assault and also cross the island to destroy enemy reserves south of Shikuka on the eastern coast.

During the operation's third stage, which was to last from 19 through 22 August, the rifle corps was to penetrate the Japanese second defensive belt from the march and capture the southern portion of Sakhalin Island in coordination with an amphibious assault on the port of Maoka. This required an advance of 60 miles (96 kilometers) per day, which, as it turned out, was well beyond the force's capabilities. Cheremisov counted on this rapid advance by virtue of the amphibious assault at Maoka, which was located only 44 miles (70 kilometers) from the administrative capital of Sakhalin at Toyohara and 62 miles (100 kilometers) from the port and naval base at Odomari.[8]

In addition to D'iakonov's 56th Rifle Corps, Cheremisov had at his disposal an amphibious assault group made up of the Colonel S. E. Zakharov's 113th Rifle Brigade and 365th Naval Infantry Battalion, supported by ships of the Northern Pacific Flotilla, which were to conduct on-order amphibious assaults against the ports of Toro and Maoka. This force was to sail from the port of Sovetskaia Gavan' on the western coast of the Tatar Strait.

THE 56TH RIFLE CORPS' OFFENSIVE PLAN

On 8 August 1945, D'iakonov's 56th Rifle Corps consisted of the 79th Rifle Division, the 2d and 5th Separate Rifle Brigades, the 214th Tank Brigade, the 678th and 178th Separate Tank Battalions, the Separate Sakhalin Machine gun Regiment, and a variety of supporting artillery, machine gun, and engineer units (see Table 20).[9]

So organized, D'iakonov's entire force numbered about 20,000 men, supported by 95 tanks, 282 guns and mortars, 634 machine guns, and 333 antitank rifles. The 255th Mixed Aviation Division with 106 aircraft and the 100th Reconnaissance Aviation Squadron were to provide air support for the ground forces. This accorded D'iakonov's force superiorities over the opposing Japanese 125th Regiment of 3.7 to 1 in infantry, 10.7 to 1 in artillery, and an absolute superiority in armor and aircraft (see Table 21).[10]

D'iakonov decided to launch his rifle corps' main attack along the Khanda–Koton axis, the road leading southward through the center of Sakhalin Island, where he could best bring his tanks and artillery to bear. Simultaneously,

TABLE 20: COMPOSITION OF SOVIET 56TH RIFLE CORPS, 9 AUGUST 1945

56th Rifle Corps
79th Rifle Division: Major General I. P. Baturov
2d Separate Rifle Brigade
5th Separate Rifle Brigade
214th Tank Brigade: Lieutenant Colonel A. T. Timirgaleev
678th Separate Tank Battalion
178th Separate Tank Battalion
Separate Sakhalin Machine gun Regiment (field fortified region)
274th Artillery Regiment
487th Howitzer Artillery Regiment
433d Gun Artillery Regiment
82d Separate Machine gun-Rifle Company
1 sapper company

TABLE 21: CORRELATION OF FORCES DURING 56TH RIFLE CORPS
PENETRATION OF KOTON FORTIFIED REGION

Forces and Weaponry	Soviet	Japanese	Correlation
Personnel	20,000	5,400	3.7 : 1
Rifle and automatic weapons companies	37	10	3.7 : 1
Machine guns	634	136	4.7 : 1
Antitank rifles	333	–	absolute
Guns and mortars	282	28	10.1 : 1
Grenade launchers	–	97	–
Tanks	95	–	absolute
Aircraft	100	–	absolute

Source: 'Proryv Kotonskogo (Kharamitogskogo) ukreplennogo raiona iapontsev na o. Sakhalin' [The Penetration of the Japanese Koton (Kharamitog) fortified region on Sakhalin island], *Sbornik takticheskikh materialov po opytu Otechestvennoi voiny*, No. 21 (iiul'–avgust 1946 g.) [Collection of tactical examples based on the experience of the Patriotic War, No. 21 (July–August 1946)] (Moscow: Voenizdat, 1947), 75.

he planned to conduct a supporting attack through Muika, 6.2 miles (10 kilometers) to the northeast of Koton, to envelop the fortified region from the east.

Based on this decision, D'iakonov organized his attacking forces into two echelons and a small reserve. The first echelon consisted of the 157th, 165th, and 179th Rifle Regiments of Baturov's 79th Rifle Division reinforced by T-26 tanks from Timirgaleev's 214th Tank Brigade and artillery from the corps' reserve, and the 2d Separate Rifle Brigade was in the corps' second echelon. The 178th and 678th Separate Tank Battalions formed the rifle corps' reserve. The first attack echelon's mission was to penetrate the Japanese first defensive belt, and the second echelon's to capture the Japanese second defensive belt from the march.

Finally, D'iakonov ordered the 5th Separate Rifle Brigade to defend the Okha and Aleksandrovsk oil refineries and the 82d Separate Machine gun-Rifle Company to man defenses at Pil'vo, just north of the state border along the eastern coast of the Tatar Strait.[11]

79TH RIFLE DIVISION PLANNING

Baturov also organized his 79th Rifle Division into two attack echelons, with his 165th and 179th Rifle Regiments in first echelon and the 157th in second, positioned to follow behind and support the 165th Rifle Regiment. His combat order read:

> The forces of the 165th and 179th Rifle Regiments will penetrate the defense and destroy the opposing enemy. The 165th Rifle Regiment will launch the main attack from positions on the northern bank of the Handasa-Gava River in a southerly direction along the Honda (Khanka)–Koton road.
>
> • The 165th Rifle Regiment will destroy the enemy's forward detachments in the security belt and, while attacking in a southern direction, will penetrate the defenses of the Koton (Haramitog) Fortified Region, encircle and destroy the enemy, and prevent his withdrawal to the south;
> • The 179th Rifle Regiment will deliver a secondary attack from positions 1.5 kilometers south of Grudekovo in the direction of Muika, and, while protecting the division's left flank, will cooperate with the 165th Rifle Regiment in the seizure of the Koton Fortified Region, with the immediate mission of capturing the Muika strong point;
> • The 157th Rifle Regiment will attack in second echelon, advancing after the 165th Rifle Regiment, and will be prepared to exploit success in the direction of Koton and Kiton.
>
> After capturing the Koton Fortified Region, the division will continue the attack in a southern direction and capture the Japanese second defensive line in the Kiton region.[12]

Thus, the 165th Rifle Regiment was to attack southward along the Honda–Koton road followed by the 157th Rifle Regiment in second echelon, and the 179th Rifle Regiment was to attack from Muika to envelop the Koton Fortified Region from the east.[13]

Given the paucity of sound intelligence of the exact configuration of the Japanese defenses, Baturov planned to dispatch four reconnaissance detachments or groups into the Japanese rear area two days before the actual attack to obtain intelligence information. Detachments No. 1 and No. 2, each comprising one rifle company, were to penetrate into the Khanda and Muika regions, respectively, and two platoon-size detachments were to reconnoiter toward Hill 274.0 and Muika. Their mission was to confirm the exact location of the forward edge of the Japanese defenses and the Japanese system of fires and capture prisoners and documents revealing Japanese force dispositions and intentions.

When the division's regiments reached the forward edge of the Koton Fortified Region, Baturov planned to conduct a reconnaissance-in-force in the direction of Happo Hill and along the road to Hill 143.2 with two rifle battalions of the 165th Rifle Regiment supported by two artillery battalions. During the attack itself, a reconnaissance detachment made up of a rifle company, a squad of cavalry scouts, and a sapper squad were to advance along the main force's right flank toward the village of Nibu, 1.9 miles (3 kilometers) west of Koton in an attempt to unhinge Japanese defenses from the west.

Given the limited amount of trafficable terrain west of the Poronai River, Baturov's forces were to advance along only two narrow axes of advance, including a main axis only 2.5 miles (4 kilometers) wide out of the corps' entire front of 13.6 miles (22 kilometers). This meant that most of his division was concentrated on a single axis, creating tactical densities of 113 (70) guns and mortars and 39 (24) tanks per mile (kilometer) of front.[14] Cheremisov, D'iakonov, and Baturov counted on the Japanese weaknesses in artillery and tanks to guarantee the subsequent rapid advance southward after the penetration was complete.

To insure that the division advanced rapidly enough, Baturov ordered that all of the regimental and about 50 per cent of the divisional artillery be employed in direct fire to smash enemy defenses before and during the assault. To facilitate close coordination between the artillery and advancing infantry, he ordered the commanders of attached artillery batteries to remain with the company commanders they were supporting. In addition, he established artillery observation posts in close proximity to all forward rifle battalions and used aircraft spotters to observe, correct, and adjust all artillery fires. The remainder of the division's artillery organized into regimental (RAG) and divisional (DAG) artillery groups, which included:

197th Rifle Division Artillery Group (DAG-79)
• 433d Artillery Regiment (minus 1 battalion)
165th Rifle Regiment Artillery Group (RAG-165)
• 487th Howitzer Artillery Regiment
• 2d Battalion, 284th Artillery Regiment
179th Rifle Regiment Artillery Group (RAG-179)
• 284th Artillery Regiment (minus 1 battalion)
Antitank Reserve
• 163d Antitank (Tank Destroyer) Battalion.[15]

Instead of firing a prolonged artillery preparation prior to the infantry assault, Baturov planned on withholding these fires until his forces had overcome the Japanese security belt. All 82 mm mortar units and subunits assigned to the division operated within the combat formations of the advancing rifle forces. Their mission was to smash enemy pillboxes, bunkers, and other obstacles hindering the infantry advance. The division's 45 mm and 76 mm antitank guns accompanied and protected the advancing tank brigades and battalions.

The heavily forested and swampy terrain made it impossible to employ the attached tank brigade and battalions *en masse*, Instead, Baturov assigned them in small groups to operate with and provide direct support to the advancing infantry. Most of the tanks operated along or close to the Khanka–Koton road, and one battalion was assigned to support the secondary attack. Given the heavily wooded and marshy terrain, significant engineer support was necessary to create advance routes and repair and maintain the few roads and bridges in the region, especially for the movement of tanks and artillery.

The supporting 255th Mixed Aviation Division and 100th Reconnaissance Aviation Squadron performed three basic missions: reconnoitering Japanese dispositions and defensive positions, providing direct support for the rifle division's forces during their assault, and destroying Japanese defensive installations within the Koton Fortified Region. The rifle corps planned all air sorties day by day and concentrated the bulk of air support to engage Japanese forces and defenses on the fortified region.

The 79th Rifle Division had been deployed in the immediate vicinity of the border since 1944, and the majority of its officers, non-commissioned officers, and soldiers had served for between four and six years. Consequently, most were quite familiar with the terrain and the general nature of the Japanese defenses. Baturov's troops regularly trained for combat in mountains, forests, and swamps and received high grades for their combat readiness and effectiveness. Throughout 1944 and 1945, the division headquarters and command cadre conducted numerous staff exercises and war-games, many of which replicated attacks on specific objectives within the Japanese Koton (Haramitog) Fortified Region. Since it had practiced many times, the division was able to occupy its jumping-off positions for the attack in only 36 hours.[16]

To support the 79th Rifle Division's assault logistically, the 16th Army created a forward section of an army base in the Onor region north of the border. By 9 August this section maintained logistical reserves amounting to two combat loads of ammunition, three days' rations of foodstuffs and forage, and four refills of fuel for tanks and vehicles. In addition, the division itself carried one combat load of ammunition, two–three days' rations, and one refill of fuel.[17]

PLANNING FOR THE AMPHIBIOUS ASSAULTS ON WESTERN SAKHALIN ISLAND

The Assault on Esutoru

The Northern Pacific Flotilla planned the amphibious landing at Esutoru after the 56th Rifle Corps began its offensive against the Koton Fortified Region (see Map 41). According to the 2d Far Eastern Front's directive, the flotilla was to conduct the assault during the period from 16 through 18 August in close coordination with the 56th Rifle Corps' penetration of the Koton Fortified Region's main defensive belt. The problem was that the flotilla lacked sufficient communications to the 56th Rifle Corps, since 'ignoring the positive experience gained in the war with Fascist Germany, the cooperating headquarters did not exchange their representatives'.[18] Thus, the flotilla did not know precisely what was going on at Koton and, therefore, had difficulty selecting the most suitable moment to conduct its amphibious landing.

The Northern Pacific Flotilla also lacked accurate substantive intelligence regarding Japanese strength and dispositions in the region, in part because of reconnaissance prohibitions prior to 11 August and in part because bad weather prevented aerial and sea reconnaissance thereafter. Therefore, on 14 August the Flotilla commander, Vice Admiral V. A. Andreev, decided to land a reconnaissance force at the small port of Toro (Shakhtersk), several miles north of Esutoru, on the morning of 16 August. The force consisted of the 365th Separate Naval Infantry Battalion and the 2d Battalion of the 16th Army's 113th Rifle Brigade. Andreev hoped that this surprise amphibious assault would distract Japanese attention from Esutoru and create favorable conditions for its subsequent capture by a larger amphibious force.

To conduct the assault at Toro, Andreev organized his assault force into four amphibious assault detachments and a security group, as follows:

- first amphibious assault detachment (artillery support) – the escort ship *Zarnitsa* [Summer Lightning], the minelayer *Okean* [Ocean], and four escort cutters (*MO-29*, *MO-27*, *MO-33*, and *MO-34*);
- second amphibious assault detachment – 14 torpedo cutters;
- third amphibious assault detachment – four trawlers (*T-522*, *T-524*, *T-590*, and *T-591*);
- fourth amphibious assault detachment – two transports (*Krabolov No. 2* and *Krabolov No. 3*) and two escort cutters (*BO-310* and *BO-314*); and
- the security group – five torpedo cutters.[19]

The assault force itself was subdivided into several subgroups, each of which would land in succession. These included:

257

- the first wave, consisting of a 320-man reconnaissance detachment;
- the first echelon, consisting of the 365th Naval Infantry Battalion;
- the second echelon, made up of the 113th Rifle Brigade's 2d Rifle Battalion; and
- the third echelon, consisting of artillery and rear service subunits.

During the first stage of the assault, the preparatory stage, the amphibious force was to concentrate on board ships in the harbor of Sovetskaia Gavan', while ships and aircraft reconnoitered the designated landing area. Flotilla aviation was to strike Japanese targets at port Esutoru for 12–14 hours before the beginning of the landing to divert Japanese attention from the real target of the assault. During the second stage, the assault force was to load its men and equipment on the ships according to a detailed loading plan, while aircraft and naval vessels protected the port.

The third stage involved transporting the amphibious force to its objective in time-phased sequence, with the first wave in the lead. Flotilla aircraft were to pound Japanese defenses at Toro for two to six hours before the lead elements of the landing force reached their landing site. Follow-on echelons were to sail only after the commander of the first wave gave the signal that his landing had been successful.

The first wave of the amphibious assault was to land precisely at 0415 hours on 16 August directly into the wharfs and moorings in the port of Toro. Its immediate mission was to capture the road center and railroad in the town and reconnoiter Japanese defenses in and around Toro and the neighboring hamlet of Nissi-Onura. Once it landed, the first echelon was to capture all of Toro and the villages of Taihai and Neiu-Haku. Together with the forces already landed, the third echelon was to capture in succession, the village of Iama-Sigai and the port and town of Esutoru.

Andreev himself directed the operation, Captain 1st Rank A. I. Leonov commanded the landing force, and Lieutenant Colonel K. P. Tavkhutdinov, the commander of the 113th Rifle Brigade's 2d Battalion, commanded the assault force.[20]

The Assault on Maoka

Planning for the amphibious assault on Maoka began only after the Far East Command was certain that its principal operations against the Kwantung Army were successful (see Map 41). Once they were, on 15 August Purkaev, the 2d Far Eastern Front commander, ordered Cheremisov's 16th Army and the Northern Pacific Flotilla to prepare and conduct an amphibious assault on the major port of Maoka with Colonel S. E. Zakharov's 113th Rifle Brigade and a mixed battalion of naval infantry.

With planning for the assault on Esutoru complete, Andreev decided to plan the Maoka assault while the assault on Toro and Esutoru was in progress. When the ongoing landing at Toro was successful and after Esutoru fell on 17 August, Andreev decided to conduct the Maoka amphibious landing on the morning of 20 August. As was the case at Toro, the landing force was to land in the immediate dock area of Maoka and capture a bridgehead encompassing the town and the nearby railroad stations at Tomamai and Atakai, along the Toyohara axis by day's end on 20 August.[21]

Andreev's Maoka assault force consisted of 17 combat ships and five transports, the 113th Rifle Brigade, a mixed battalion of naval infantry, and 80 aircraft from the Northern Pacific Naval Flotilla. The naval ships formed into three amphibious assault detachments, an artillery support detachment, and a security detachment organized as follows:

- first amphibious assault detachment – seven escort cutters (*BO-302, BO-314, MO-31, MO-25, MO-32, MO-35,* and *MO-63*);
- second amphibious assault detachment – four trawlers (*T-588, T-583, T-522,* and *T-591*);
- third amphibious assault detachment – transports *Vsevolod Sibirtsev, Krabolov No. 3,* and *Izmail,* the rescue ship *Tel'man,* and the tug boat *Bagration*;
- the artillery support detachment – the escort ship *Zarnitsa* [Summer Lightning] and the minelayer *Okean* [Ocean];
- the security detachment – four torpedo cutters (*TKA-631, TKA-641, TKA-645,* and *TKA-646*).[22]

The first wave of the amphibious assault consisted of submachine gunners, the first echelon, the mixed battalion of naval infantry, and the third echelon, Zakharov's 113th Rifle Brigade.

As had been the case at Esutoru, the landing was to occur in stages; a preparatory stage, the sea movement, and the actual landing itself. During the preparatory stage, the 16th Army formed the mixed naval infantry battalion and concentrated the 113th Rifle Brigade, which had been involved in coastal defense, at Sovetskaia Gavan' and assigned all forces their missions. At the same time, naval aircraft reconnoitered and conducted photo–reconnaissance over the Maoka region. The loading of men and equipment on the ships took place in accordance with a detailed loading plan. Because weather forecasts predicted light winds and fog, the plans called for loading 40–50 men on each of the escort cutters and 185–200 men on each trawler. The remaining men and equipment loaded on the transports, with 943 men on board the *Krabolov No. 3,* 639 on the *Izmail,* and 752 on the *Vsevolod Sibirtsev.*[23]

The sea transport of the landing force was to take place from 0700 hours on 19 August to 0450 hours on 20 August under the protective cover of flotilla aircraft. The four trawlers and nine hunter cutters organized anti-submarine and antimine defenses around the convoy. Once at the landing site, one group of ships carrying the first amphibious assault detachment was to penetrate directly into the center of Maoka's harbor, and a second group was to approach and land at the southern side of Maoka's harbor. Both groups were to land their forces directly onto the docks and wharfs at 0450 hours under the protective fires and smokescreens of the cutters and trawlers that had landed each group.

The second echelon of the amphibious assault detachment was to land when the first echelon gave the all-clear signal. The remaining ships would then dock at or deploy to specific points in the port according to the prearranged plan. The transports *Krabolov No. 3* and *Izmail* were to dock in the port's center sector and the *Vsevolod Sibirtsev* in the southern dock area, while the fire support ships were to take up firing positions in the harbor and the security ships were to deploy to areas within the harbor where they could maneuver All the while, aircraft were to engage on-call Japanese targets.[24]

All stages of the amphibious operation were supposed to occur continuously without pause. The first wave, which consisted of 297 submachine gunners, was to capture the port's docks and wharfs and secure a bridgehead to protect the main force's landing. The mixed naval infantry battalion was to follow and seize the central and eastern portions of Maoka, and the 113th Rifle Brigade was to capture the northern and southern parts of the town. By day's end, the amphibious assault force was to capture the railroad stations at Tomamai and Otakai. Subsequently, the 113th Rifle Brigade was to attack eastward along the Maoka–Toyohara railroad and road, and the mixed naval infantry battalion southward along the coastal road toward Honto.

Once again, Andreev directed the operation, Captain 1st Rank A. I. Leonov commanded the landing force, and Colonel Zakharov, the commander of the 113th Rifle Brigade, commanded the assault force.[25]

THE 56TH RIFLE CORPS' ASSAULT ON THE KOTON (HARAMITOG) FORTIFIED REGION

The Battle for the Security Belt, 11–13 August

D'iakonov's forces began their assault at 0745 hours on 11 August (see Map 42).[26] The forward detachment of the 79th Rifle Division's 165th Rifle Regiment, which consisted of the regiment's 2d Battalion, one battalion of the 284th Artillery Regiment, and one battalion of the 214th Tank Brigade, crossed the state border and advanced toward the Japanese police outpost and strong point at Honda (Khanda). Two hours after liquidating Japanese observation posts north of Honda, the forward detachment attacked the strong point, but it was halted by heavy Japanese fire from the southern bank of the Kottonhai-Gava River. Heavy fighting broke out, forcing the entire

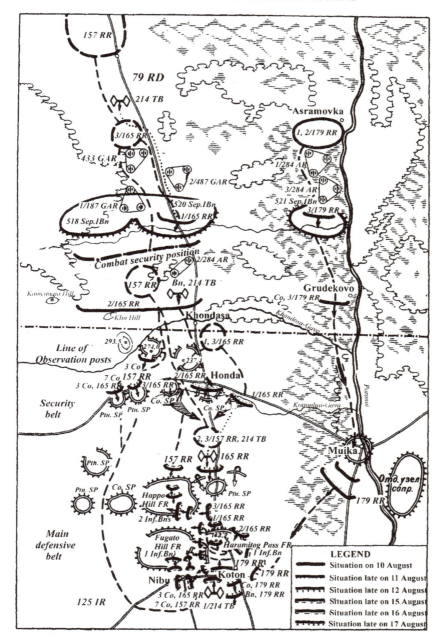

Map 42. Soviet 79th Rifle Division's Penetration of the Haramitog (Koton) Fortified Region, 10–17 August 1945

261

regiment to deploy for combat. However, the regiment's subsequent attack failed when it encountered a hail of withering Japanese fire. It soon became clear that frontal attacks could not succeed since the Japanese defenses were strong and covered by interlocking small arms, machine gun, and artillery fire. The only recourse was to attack the defenses by enveloping its flanks.

Consequently, the commander of the 165th Rifle Regiment left small covering forces along his front and ordered one of his battalions to envelop the Honda strong point from the east and another from the west. At the same time, the reinforced 3d Rifle Company was to attack and capture a small Japanese strong point situated on an un-named hill 1.8 miles (3 kilometers) southwest of Honda. Soon after, the regiment's 1st and 3d Battalions maneuvered 1.8 miles (3 kilometers) forward around the strong point's western and eastern flanks, by day's end encircling Honda and cutting the defending Japanese forces' lines of withdrawal. By this time, the 3d Rifle Company had also captured Hill 274, just west of Honda but had failed to reach its objective to the south. By day's end on 11 August, the 165th Rifle Regiment's forward detachment had captured the northern outskirts of the Honda strong point and dug in along the northern bank of the Kottonkai-Gava River.

At the same time, the advanced battalion of the 179th Rifle Regiment crossed the state border and advanced southward along the swampy banks of the Poronai River, enveloping Japanese defenses at Honda from the east. Encountering little or no resistance, the regiment emerged from the swamps and captured the village of Muika with its police post and associated strong point at 1400 hours, as well as the railroad bridge over the Poronai River by a surprise assault. The regiment then dug in along a line 328 yards (300 meters) south of the village

Thus, Baturov's two first echelon rifle regiments advanced between 3.1 and 6.2 miles (5 and 10 kilometers) on the first day of the offensive, but failed to capture Honda. The advance was relatively slow because of the lack of favorable routes southward from the state border and the presence of Japanese strong points imbedded in rough terrain that made them immune to direct fire. Nor could the heavy artillery engage the strong points since the poor road conditions prevented the artillery's movement forward. While Baturov's first echelon was advancing, his second echelon 157th Rifle Regiment followed, by nightfall reaching the region northwest and west of Honda.

Overnight on 11–12 August, D'iakonov's artillery and mortars deployed forward into new firing positions in the Honda region and at 0730 hours commenced a blistering 30-minute artillery preparation against the defenses in and around the Honda strong point. As the artillery preparation lifted, the 165th Rifle Regiment's battalions attacked the strong point simultaneously from the north and south. The classified Soviet after-action report described the scene:

Firing from ferro-concrete and earth and timber pillboxes, the Japanese resisted fiercely. The tanks accompanying our infantry approached the enemy's permanent fortifications and suppressed them by fire into the embrasures, while supporting the advance of the rifle subunits. The regiment's battalions captured the Honda strong point after a fierce battle. Refusing to be taken prisoner, the Japanese garrison was completely destroyed.[27]

Despite their loss of strong point Honda, the Japanese conducted a fighting withdrawal using small groups and even individuals to man ambushes along the road and in the forests and laying mines and booby traps to slow the Soviet advance. The tactics worked and significantly impeded the forward movement of D'iakonov's force, ultimately preventing him from fulfilling his assigned missions within the designated period of time.

To prevent the Japanese conducting a counterattack against Honda from the strong point located on the un-named hill 1.9 miles (3 kilometers) to the southwest, Baturov ordered the 157th Rifle Regiment to form a detachment consisting of a reinforced rifle company to attack and destroy Japanese defenses on the hill. It was to do so in close coordination with the 165th Rifle Regiment's 3d Rifle Company, which had previously failed to capture the hilltop strong point. Accordingly, the 157th Regiment's 7th Rifle Company marched slowly through the mountainous forests, reached the base of the hill by day's end, and, with the 165th Regiment's 3d Company, assaulted the heights southwest of Honda. However, once again the assault faltered in the face of heavy Japanese fire.

After capturing Muika late on 11 August, early the next morning, the 179th Rifle Regiment left the relative sanctuary of its defenses just south-west of Muika and advanced slowly southwest through the swamps toward the eastern approaches to the Koton Fortified Region in an attempt to envelop the fortified region from the east. However, it too then encountered blistering fire from Japanese strong points located along the road southeast of Koton village, which brought the advance to an abrupt halt. Without artillery support, it was abundantly clear that further assaults would be suicidal. Nevertheless, a Soviet critique noted the beneficial effects of the maneuver:

> One should note that the skillful maneuver, which was in complete accord with the conditions existing on the field of battle, proved completely unexpected for the enemy and, subsequently, created favorable conditions for the capture of the Koton center of resistance.[28]

Late on 12 August, Baturov completed the day's action by reinforcing the positions his 157th and 165th Rifle Regiments had seized west of Honda with machine gun companies from the Sakhalin Regiment.

On D'iakonov's orders, overnight on 12–13 August, Baturov directed his 165th Rifle Regiment to attack along two parallel axes and capture the defensive positions at Koton the following morning. To speed up his forward movement, Baturov reinforced the regiment with most of the tanks from Timirgaleev's 214th Tank Brigade. Supported by the tanks, the 165th Regiment assaulted Japanese defenses in the morning after a 60-minute artillery preparation. Once again, however, the attack faltered against heavy resistance from a strong point north of Koton village:

> Exploiting the mountainous, heavily wooded, and swampy terrain, which was favorable for defense, and relying on a system of permanent fortifications and trenches (especially along the Honda–Koton road), the Japanese launched counterattacks and stubborn resistance to our attacking battalions.[29]

The 179th Rifle Regiment also launched heavy attacks on the morning of 13 August against Japanese defenses southeast of Koton, but its assaults too failed in the face of heavy Japanese resistance. By day's end, the 179th Regiment's lead elements had fought their way into the outskirts of Koton but could advance no further.

Given the 179th Regiment's difficulties, the regimental commander decided to blockade the strong point with two rifle companies while the remainder of his regiment enveloped the Japanese position from the south by marching through the adjacent swamp. After marching all night through waist deep swamp water, early on 15 August the regiment's main body deployed, assaulted, and captured Koton Station, which the surprised Japanese abandoned after a short fight. However, later in the day, the Japanese regrouped and launched several strong counterattacks, which pressed the 179th Rifle Regiment's solders back into defensive positions around the station. Realizing the precarious situation, D'iakonov reinforced the beleaguered defenders of Koton with a tank battalion and artillery regiment, with whose fires the regimental commander decimated the attacking Japanese forces.

Meanwhile, to the west, the 165th Regiment's 3d Rifle Company and the 157th Regiment's 7th Rifle Company fought hard to overcome the strong Japanese resistance on the troublesome hilltop 1.9 miles (3 kilometers) southwest of Honda. After heavy fighting, the two companies managed to wedge their way into the enemy's first line of trenches and foxholes and began a struggle for the center of the strong point.

By day's end on 13 August, Baturov's troops had completely overcome the Japanese security belt and, in a few sectors, had dented the Japanese first defensive belt. However, the forward progress had been agonizingly slow, and the division had utterly failed in its mission to overcome the Japanese security belt from the march. A Soviet critique of the operation explained why:

The principal reason why this was so was the inadequate support that the tanks and aviation provided to the rifle subunits, which resulted from the difficult terrain conditions and the poor flying weather. When the tank subunits were assigned their missions, [the command] failed to take into account sufficiently the movement capabilities of various tank systems when being employed in forested, swampy, and roadless terrain. To a considerable degree, this situation reduced the effectiveness of employing tanks. In addition, shortcomings existed in the organization of cooperation between the infantry and the tanks and their employment on the battlefield. However, the mission assigned to the division to capture the enemy security belt in the first stage of the battle was fulfilled. The division's units set about preparing to penetrate the Koton Fortified Region.[30]

Preparations to Penetrate the Main Defensive Belt, 14–15 August

Baturov's 79th Rifle Division spent all day on both 14 and 15 August preparing to penetrate the Koton Fortified Region's main defensive belt. The only exception was the 179th Rifle Regiment, which launched its successful raid on Koton Station on 15 August. Intensified reconnaissance and interrogation of a Japanese prisoner-of-war on 14 August finally provided the division's staff with a sufficient understanding of the Japanese defenses upon which to base a new attack plan. Given the 179th Rifle Regiment's successful advance into the Japanese rear area, Baturov formulated a plan that altered the axis of his main attack from the north to the west. His new mission to the division required it to, 'conduct the main attack from north to south against the center of resistance on Hill 143.2 and the Haramitog Pass, to capture it, and to conduct a secondary attack against the center of resistance on Mount Happo. Subsequently, encircle and destroy the enemy on Mounts Happo and Fugato.'[31]

Baturov assigned the following mission to his subordinate units:

- The 179th Rifle Regiment, with the 1st and 2d Battalions of the 284th Artillery Regiment and one battalion of the 214th Tank Brigade, will deliver its main attack from the south against the enemy center of resistance at Haramitog Pass and, in cooperation with two battalions of the 165th Rifle Regiment attacking from the north, will capture this center of resistance. Cover the Koton–Kiton road and railroad with one reinforced rifle company to prevent enemy reserves from advancing from the south.
- The 165th Rifle Regiment will launch its main attack with its 1st and 2d Battalions against the center of resistance on Hill 143.2 and, in cooperation with the 179th Rifle Regiment, will capture it. While attacking westward, close off the withdrawal of the enemy on Fugato Hill to the south and, in

cooperation with the 157th Regiment's subunits, encircle and destroy the Japanese garrisons in the centers of resistance on Fugato and Happo Hills.

- The 165th Regiment's 3d Rifle Company and the 157th Rifle Regiment's 7th Rifle Company, which are operating in the region of the strong point 3 kilometers [1.9 miles] southwest of Honda, will capture this strong point and, by attacking to the south, will envelop the Koton Fortified Region from the west, seize Nibu, close off enemy withdrawal routes from the center of resistance on Fugato Hill, and assist the regiment's main force in encircling and destroying the garrison of that center of resistance.
- The 157th Rifle Regiment will attack from the north with its 1st Rifle Battalion against the enemy center of resistance on Happo Hill and, in coordination with the 165th Rifle Regiment's 3d Battalion, will encircle and destroy the enemy on Happo Hill. The 2d and 3d Battalions (less the 7th Rifle Company) will remain in the division commander's reserve.[32]

In accordance with Baturov's order, his subordinate regimental commanders formed their regiments in a single echelon of battalions. The infantry was to 'advance in files in front of the tanks, and, covered from Japanese observation by the high grass, they were to clear the terrain of tank destroyers, cut lanes through the antitank obstacles, and support the movement of the tanks and artillery across the difficult terrain'.[33]

Baturov also directed that assault groups be formed to lead the advancing files of riflemen and destroy any fortified positions encountered in the forward edge of the Japanese defenses and also reserve assault groups to isolate and destroy heavier Japanese strong points. Each assault group consisted of a rifle platoon, a sapper squad, an antitank gun platoon, and two tanks.

The supporting tanks were to advance in line following the infantry and engage any pillboxes they encountered by firing into their embrasures or simply crushing them with their tracks. The division's chief of artillery controlled and coordinated the fires of all artillery operating along the main attack axis. The rifle division formed an artillery group (DAG) consisting of the 284th Artillery and 487th Howitzer Artillery Regiments, and each rifle regiment its own artillery group (RAG) from one battalion of the division's artillery regiment.

Counting 45 mm guns and 82 mm mortars, Baturov was able to concentrate 213 artillery pieces and mortars in the division's main attack sector along the Koton–Kiton road.[34] Much of this artillery was employed in a direct fire role and deployed forward immediately after the advancing infantry. Since few suitable artillery firing positions existed on either side of the road, the artillery fired primarily from positions echeloned in depth along the road itself.

Late on 15 August, the 79th Rifle Division's regiments deployed into their jumping-off positions in the following locations:

- the 1st Battalion, 157th Rifle Regiment – on the northeastern slopes of Happo Hill, 5 miles (8 kilometers) southwest of Honda;
- the 3d Battalion, 165th Rifle Regiment – on the eastern slopes of Happo Hill;
- the 1st and 2d Battalions, 165th Rifle Regiment – north of Haramitog Pass;
- the 179th Rifle Regiment – northeast, north, and west of Koton with one rifle company south of Koton;
- the 2d and 3d Battalions, 157th Rifle Regiment – the division commander's reserve, concentrated on the road 5 miles (8 kilometers) south of Honda; and
- the 214th Tank Brigade (minus 1 battalion) – in jumping-off positions behind the 1st and 2d Battalions, 165th Rifle Regiment with one tank battalion deployed behind the 179th Regiment's combat formation west of Koton.[35]

While Baturov's division was deploying for the assault, on the evening of 15 August, the 165th Rifle Regiment's 3d Rifle Company and the 157th Regiment's 7th Rifle company, which had been fighting a prolonged struggle to envelop the Koton Fortified Region from the west, succeeded in reaching the village of Nibu and captured it in a surprise attack, threatening to unhinge the entire Japanese defense.

The Penetration of the Main Defensive Belt, 15–18 August

Early on the morning of 16 August and before Baturov was able to begin his planned artillery preparations, Japanese forces launched a counterattack in battalion strength in an apparent attempt to thwart the Soviet assault. Attacking in human waves of infantry companies formed in ranks of platoons, the assault faltered with heavy losses in the face of withering fire from concentrated Soviet artillery and machine guns. The 79th Rifle Division answered with a massive one-hour artillery preparation of its own. After the fire lifted, Baturov's forces launched a coordinated assault on all of the Japanese positions to their front.

Within minutes, however, heavy Japanese fire, poor visibility, and the dense forest brought Baturov's assault to a halt. Because of the poor visibility, the artillery fire failed to neutralize enough of the Japanese artillery and machine gun firing positions. Nor was the fire support from the tanks and artillery accompanying the infantry effective:

> The artillery could not conduct fire against the enemy's firing points and soldiers that were situated 50–75 meters in front of our subunits, and the firing points that were located in the depth of the defenses could not be observed. The firing against the artillery positions did not produce the desired effect. As a result, the whole weight of penetrating the fortified region lay on the infantry, the tanks, and, chiefly, on the assault groups.[36]

Attacking along the road, the 1st and 2d Battalions of the 165th Rifle Regiment, supported by the 214th Tank Brigade, smashed the Japanese defenses in the main defensive belt and, slowly advancing forward, captured the strong fortified point on the northeastern slope of Haramitog Pass. The 179th Rifle Regiment, which was attacking northward and northwestward from the railroad station near Koton supported by a battalion of tanks, finally captured Koton after a fierce street battle. After repelling several Japanese counterattacks from the military settlement 547 yards (500 meters) west of Koton, two of the regiment's battalions dug in on the northern outskirts of Koton, and the third battalion occupied defensive positions south of Koton to block the approach of any Japanese reinforcements.

Meanwhile, the 157th Rifle Regiment's 1st Battalion and the 165th Rifle Regiment's 3d Battalion assaulted the Japanese center of resistance on Happo Hill but were able to advance only slightly more than one-half mile (1 kilometer) in the face of fanatical resistance. A Soviet critique captured the ferocity of the fighting:

> The Japanese fought stubbornly on the defense throughout the day, holding back our attacking forces. Exploiting the ferro-concrete fortifications and the favorable mountainous and forested terrain conditions, the enemy launched repeated counterattacks trying to hold on to every meter.[37]

While Baturov's main force was forcing its way into the Japanese main defensive belt, the 3d and 7th Rifle Companies from the 157th and 165th Rifle Regiments, which had captured Nibu the day before, drove further into the Japanese rear area west of Koton, threatening the entire Japanese defense at Koton with encirclement.

By nightfall on 16 August, Baturov's rifle division had smashed its way into the midst of the Japanese main defensive belt of the Koton Fortified Region, ostensibly successfully completing its assigned mission. However, Japanese forces still clung desperately to numerous strong points to his front, and the 79th Rifle Division's rear area was littered with bypassed but still resisting Japanese strong points that had to be eliminated before his division could advance southward. Both D'iakonov and Baturov were heartened when they learned late on 16 August that the 113th Rifle Brigade had seized Esutoru by an amphibious assault and had cut Japanese withdrawal routes southward along the island's main road.

On 17 August Baturov's division continued its operations to clear Japanese forces from the remainder of the fortified region. Advancing slowly forward through the heavy forests, the 157th Rifle Regiment's 1st Battalion and the 165th Rifle Regiment's 3d Battalion fought their way into Japanese defenses on Happo Hill, while the 1st and 2d Battalions of the 165th Rifle Regiment and the 179th Rifle Regiment struggled to liquidate Japanese forces defending the Haramitog Pass center of resistance. By day's end, elements of the two regiments had captured Haramitog and were fighting along the eastern slopes of Fugato Hill. To the south, the 157th and 165th Rifle Regiments' 7th and 3d Rifle Companies attacked northward, penetrated Japanese defenses, and advanced into the center of the defenses on Fugato Hill.

Having already lost the Haramitog center of resistance, the remnants of the Japanese 125th Infantry Regiment defending Happo and Fugato Hills were under assault from all sides and being pounded unmercifully by Soviet artillery and air strikes. Facing this hopeless situation, on the evening of 17 August, the Japanese commander requested permission to surrender his command. The next morning, Colonel Kobayasi, the commander of the Japanese regiment accepted Soviet terms and surrendered his remaining 3,000 men.[38]

Immediately after capturing the Koton Fortified Region, on D'iakonov's orders, Baturov formed a mobile forward detachment and ordered it to advance southward to clear Japanese forces from the remainder of the island. The rest of the rifle division soon followed and captured its ultimate objective, the city of Toyohara, on 25 August, assisted by two small forces that had been air landed north of the city the day before. While D'iakonov had accomplished his assigned mission, he had done so three days later than planned, with serious implications for the planned Soviet assault on Hokkaido.

THE AMPHIBIOUS ASSAULTS ON THE PORT OF TORO, 16–17 AUGUST 1945

On 16 August, the same day that D'iakonov's 56th Rifle Corps began its assault against the Koton Fortified Region's main defensive belt, the Northern Pacific Flotilla landed its amphibious force at the port of Toro, on the western coast of Sakhalin Island (see Map 43). Initially, from 9 through 13 August, flotilla aircraft conducted more than 100 bombing sorties against Japanese forces and facilities on the southern half of Sakhalin Island, including the ports of Toro and Esutoru and Japanese airfields. The actual amphibious landings began early on 16 August in the time-phased sequence called for by the operational plan. Vice Admiral Andreev, the commander of the Northern Pacific Flotilla, directed and coordinated the operation. The amphibious assault force consisted of 1,500 men from the 365th Naval Infantry Battalion and the 113th Rifle Brigade's 2d Battalion.

The first assault detachment, which was transported on the escort ship *Zarnitsa* [Summer Lightning] and four escort cutters, sailed from Sovetskaia Gava' at 2120 hours on 15 August, hindered initially by heavy fog, which limited visibility to from 150 to 607 feet (46 to 185 meters).

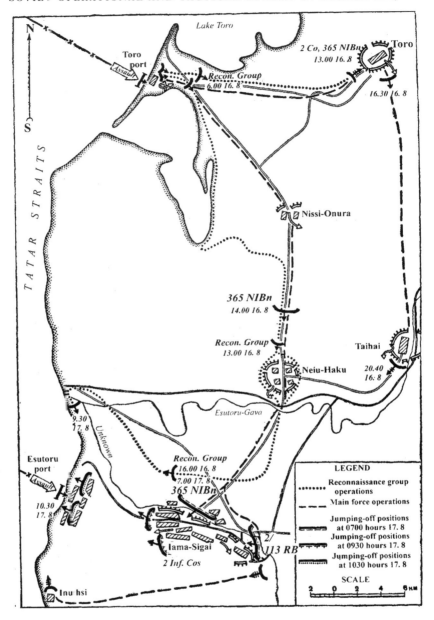

Map 43. The Amphibious Assault on Toro and Esutoru, 16–17 August 1945

However, conditions improved at 0400 hours the next morning, and the convoy approached Toro at 0500 hours, about one hour behind schedule.[39]

Within ten minutes of the ships arriving in Toro harbor, the 140-man reconnaissance detachment landed in the wharf area and captured the port facilities against little or no resistance from the Japanese reservists patrolling the city. After receiving the signal that the reconnaissance detachment had successfully landed, the second amphibious assault detachment departed Sovetskaia Gavan' at 0600 hours, escorted by three torpedo cutters. After experiencing periods of foggy weather during its trip, at 1010 hours on 16 August, the 365th Naval Infantry Battalion landed and consolidated its hold on Toro's port facilities.

Once notified of the second detachment's success, the third amphibious assault detachment, the 113th Rifle Brigade, sailed from Sovetskaia Gavan' on board trawlers. At 1000 hours four trawlers carrying the 2d Battalion, 113th Rifle Brigade, came under fire of Japanese batteries at Esutoru but managed to reach Toro safely and landed its rifle battalion at 1850 hours. The fourth echelon, consisting of the transport *Petropavlovsk*, two large hunter cutters, and other ships, left Sovetskaia Gavan' at 2310 hours and completed unloading its troops and cargo at 1600 hours on 17 August.

Once landed in the port, the 365th Naval Infantry Battalion began advancing along two axes. The 2d Naval Rifle Company moved eastward toward the village of Toro with orders to capture the village and turn south to capture Taihai, and the remainder of the battalion advanced southward toward the villages of Nissi-Onura, Neiu-Haku, and Iama-Sigai on the coastal road to Esutoru to cut Japanese withdrawal routes to the west. The reconnaissance detachment that had initiated the landing at Toro port led both columns. After it landed, the 2d Battalion of the 113th Rifle Brigade was to follow the naval infantry's southward march through Nissi-Onura and assist in the capture of Esutoru.

Against increasing resistance, on 16 August the naval infantry battalion captured Toro and the villages of Nissi-Onura and Neiu-Haku, but its detached company was held up by Japanese defenses at Taihai for a full day. Further south, two companies of Japanese infantry dug in at Iama-Sigai brought the naval infantrymen's advance to an abrupt halt at 1600 hours and forced them to go over to the defense at 2000 hours. With one of its companies engaged at Taihai and another blockading Japanese forces at Neiu-Haku, the remaining two companies lacked the strength necessary to overcome Japanese defenses at Iama-Sigai.

However, at 2200 hours on 16 August, the 113th Rifle Brigade's 2d Battalion and the naval infantry battalion's 3d Company from Taihai reached Iama-Sigai, permitting the commander of the 365th Naval Infantry Battalion, who controlled the entire force, to plan a concerted assault against Japanese defenses the next day. After a 30-minute air and artillery preparation, the combined force attacked at 0700 hours on 17 August and captured the village at 0930 hours after killing an estimated 136 Japanese troops. However, since the rifle battalion's automatic weapons' company failed to cut the Japanese withdrawal routes as ordered, the remnants of the small garrison escaped to the south.[40]

After the short engagement at Iama-Sigai, the reinforced detachment advanced westward toward Esutoru, where it linked up with the 22d Separate Machine gun Company, which had landed from the sea. The combined force cleared all Japanese forces from the port by 1030 hours on 17 August.[41]

The capture of Toro and Esutoru cut Japanese lines of communications along the western coast of Sakhalin Island and compounded the problems faced by the Japanese garrison at Koton by threatening to sever its withdrawal routes to the south.

THE AMPHIBIOUS ASSAULT ON THE PORT OF MAOKA AND THE 87TH RIFLE CORPS OPERATIONS ON SOUTHERN SAKHALIN ISLAND, 19–25 AUGUST

The 56th Rifle Corps' successful penetration operation against Japanese defenses at the Koton Fortified Region in central Sakhalin created fresh opportunities to defeat Japanese forces on southern Sakhalin by means of the amphibious landing at Maoka on 19 August. The Japanese surrender announcement on the same day made the amphibious operation even more important. As a result, the 16th Army assigned the amphibious force the mission 'to occupy the southern region of the island as rapidly as possible and to prevent the enemy from evacuating his forces and valuable materials from Sakhalin to the Japanese home islands'.[42] More important still, rapid occupation of southern Sakhalin Island was absolutely essential if Soviet forces were to gain a lodgment on Hokkaido Island before full Japanese surrender.

The amphibious landing force, consisting of the 365th Naval Infantry Battalion and Zakharov's 113th Rifle Brigade, both of which had conducted the assault on Toro, began leaving the port of Sovetskaia Gavan' at 0650 hours on 19 August in good weather but soon encountered stormy weather that delayed its passage to Maoka and forced the convoy to regroup frequently at sea. The escort ship *Zarnitsa* finally reached the central harbor at Maoka at 0733 hours, almost three hours behind schedule, and immediately began landing its forces in the sequence called for by Cheremisov's plan.

Most of the first wave of the assault landed within four to five minutes, even though one of the cutters (the *MO-35*) lost its way in the fog, was taken under fire by Japanese gunners, and had to land its troops on the northern shore of the harbor. Despite this misfortune, the force was able to link up with its parent 113th Rifle Brigade. Meanwhile, the first wave of submachine gunners successfully seized the dock area and, within 40 minutes, the central port area. The second and third assault echelons then followed them ashore in rapid fashion.

By 1200 hours on 19 August, the mixed naval infantry battalion had cleared all Japanese forces from the central section of the city and was fighting in its southern section. Once it landed, the 113th Rifle Brigade fought its way into the northern and southern sections of the city. Soviet accounts stress the ferocity of the fighting:

> The struggle for the port and city of Maoka was fierce. The enemy, who numbered up to two battalions supported by artillery and machine gun fire, strongly resisted. The poor flying weather deprived the amphibious force of air support, and the artillery fire from our ships was often interrupted since the visibility in the fog at times did not exceed 50–60 meters.
>
> The troops of the assault force and ships operated skillfully in these complex conditions, displaying great fortitude ...
>
> Before Soviet forces approached Maoka, Japanese propaganda successfully intimidated the city's inhabitants with the 'brutality of the Russians', and, as a result, a considerable portion of the population fled into the forests, and part were evacuated to Hokkaido Island. The Japanese propaganda had special influence on women, who were instilled with fear that, without fail, the arrival of the Russians would be accompanied by violence and that the women would be shot and their children strangled.[43]

Despite the resistance, the amphibious assault force captured Maoka within a matter of hours, by Soviet accounts killing more than 300 Japanese soldiers and capturing another 600. The remnants of the garrison fled westward along the railroad and road into the island's interior.

After capturing the port, on 20 August Zakharov's 113th Rifle Brigade advanced eastward along the railroad line to Odomari, capturing the towns of Tomamai and Otakai and approaching the town of Futomata at 1630 hours, where a Japanese force estimated at two battalions occupied hasty defenses. The fight for the two towns lasted for two days, while Soviet ships and aircraft bombarded the Japanese positions. Finally, on the night of 22–23 August, a small force air-assaulted onto the nearby airfield at Konotoro, unhinging the Japanese defenses at Futomata. The same night, Zakharov's rifle brigade captured Futomata and began advancing toward Rudaka and Odomari on Sakhalin's southern coast.

With Zakharov's ground forces pressing on toward Odomari, Andreev, the commander of the Northern Pacific Flotilla, quickly assembled a small force of three naval infantry battalions numbering 1,600 men at Maoka early on 22 August. He planned to land these forces, which formed a provisional brigade and included the experienced 365th Battalion, at Odomari early on 23 August.

With Cheremisov's and Purkaev's approval, Andreev's small amphibious force left Maoka at 0530 hours on 23 August but was caught in a storm at sea and was forced to seek refuge in the port of Honto on the morning of 24 August The small Japanese garrison at Honto immediately surrendered. After the storm subsided in the evening, Andreev left a naval infantry company to garrison the port and put to sea once again at 2000 hours. Andreev's amphibious assault force reached Odomari at 0625 hours on 24 August just as the lead elements of Zakharov's rifle brigade were reaching the city's eastern outskirts. Threatened from land and sea, the Japanese garrison commander surrendered his 3,600 men at 1000 hours.[44]

The capture of Odomari coincided with the advance of D'iakonov's 56th Rifle Corps' forward forces to the northern outskirts of Toyohara, the administrative capital of Japanese southern Sakhalin. The city fell to D'iakonov's forces on 25 August, ending the 16th Army's operations to secure Sakhalin Island.

While Andreev's and D'iakonov's forces were advancing on Odomari and Toyohara, from 22 through 26 August, the three divisions of Major General F. Z. Borisov's 87th Rifle Corps arrived in Maoka after being transported by ship from Vladivostok. The combined force completed clearing the remnants of Japanese forces from southern Sakhalin on 25 and 26 August, capturing 18,320 Japanese soldiers.[45] Thus, the 16th Army succeeded in clearing Japanese forces from Sakhalin Island by 25 and 26 August rather than the 22 August date required by Cheremisov's original plan. The three to four-day delay may have had a decisive influence on Stalin's ensuing decision to cancel the amphibious assault of northern Hokkaido.

CONCLUSIONS

Even though D'iakonov's 56th Rifle Corps and Baturov's 79th Rifle Division played the most significant role in the Sakhalin offensive operation, Soviet operations against Japanese defenses on the island were joint in nature since they involved the close coordination of ground, naval, and air forces. The most compelling and instructive feature of the operation, as well as the most decisive in terms of the operation's ultimate outcome, was the assault on the Koton (Haramitog) Fortified Region.

The penetration of the Koton Fortified Region involved conducting complex maneuvers in extremely restrictive mountainous, heavily wooded, and swampy terrain. The employment of carefully tailored assault groups and maneuver by battalion- and company-size forces played a critical role in the reduction of the heavily fortified defenses. All the while, the amphibious assaults deprived the Japanese of the opportunity to maneuver their forces elsewhere on the island, paralyzed Japanese ability to command and control their forces effectively, and paved the way for complete Japanese defeat.

A formerly classified Soviet study summed up the operations achievements and shortcomings:

> The successful penetration of the Japanese strongly fortified region in the conditions of the Far Eastern theater of military operations depended on:
>
> 1. The maneuver nature of the operations conducted by the division's [79th Rifle Division] units and subunits, which exploited the extensive undefended and, from the enemy's point of view, impassible spaces in the mountainous, heavily wooded, and swampy terrain conditions. The organization and completion of envelopment and turning movements to reach the enemy's flanks and rear was fully justified. [These include], for example, the envelopment and encirclement of the Honda (Khanka) strong point, the enveloping maneuver of the 179th Rifle Regiment against the flank and rear of the Japanese main defensive belt in the Koton region, and the advance of the two rifle companies into the Nibu region.
>
> 2. The correct selection of the main attack axis, which corresponded to the mountainous, heavily forested, and swampy terrain conditions.
>
> 3. The fortunate selection of the axis of the secondary attack by the 179th Rifle Regiment through the Muika region to Koton, which reinvigorated the main axis of advance and had a favorable influence on the success of the penetration.
>
> 4. The organization and operations by the assault groups, which secured the destruction of the enemy's individual firing points impeding the rifle subunits' advance.
>
> 5. The protection of the flanks, intervals between units, and the rear, which was achieved by the constant conduct of reconnaissance and the organization of all-round defense. These measures were accomplished by specially assigned subunits.
>
> 6. Well-organized cooperation between the infantry, artillery, and tanks and uninterrupted command and control of units and subunits during combat.
>
> 7. The correct organization of artillery observation by the dispatch of observers to the forward rifle subunits and the locating of battery commanders with the company commanders.[46]

Yet, after all was said and done, the 56th Rifle Corps took three days longer than planned to reduce the Japanese Koton Fortified Region. This, plus the ensuing delays in the south, resulted in the capture of the island on 26 August, four days after Vasilevsky had ordered. While some Russian sources now claim that this delay was the principal reason why Stalin called off his planned invasion of Hokkaido, given the relative ease with which Soviet amphibious forces captured the ports on southern Sakhalin, however, plus the apparent willingness of Japanese garrisons to surrender without a fight after 22 August, this argument loses much of its credibility.

NOTES

1. Zakharov *et al.*, *Krasnoznamennyi*, 220.
2. Vnotchenko, *Pobeda*, 290. The most detailed account of these and the ensuing battle are found in 'Proryv Kotonskogo (Kharamitogskogo) ukreplennogo raiona iapontsev na o. Sakhalin' [The Penetration of the Japanese Koton (Kharamitog) fortified region on Sakhalin island], *Sbornik takticheskikh materialov po opytu Otechestvennoi voiny*, No. 21 (iiul'–avgust 1946 g.) [Collection of tactical examples based on the experience of the Patriotic War, No. 21 (July–August 1946)] (Moscow: Voenizdat, 1947), 71–84. Prepared by the Directorate for the Study of War Experience of the General Staff and classified secret.
3. V. N. Bagrov, *Iuzhno-sakhalinskaia i Kuril'skaia operatsii (avgust 1954 goda)* [The southern Sakhalin and Kuril operations (August 1945)] (Moscow: Voenizdat, 1959), 17.
4. 'Proryv Kotonskogo', 74.
5. Bagrov, *Iuzhno-sakhalinskaia*, 13.
6. Zakharov *et al.*, *Krasnoznamennyi*, 219, and Bagrov, *Iuzhno-sakhalinskaia*, 24, state that the operation was to be completed by 25 August. V. A. Zolotarev, ed., *Velikaia Otechestvenaia voina 1941–1945 v chetyrekh knigakh*, K. 3 [The Great Patriotic War 1941–1945 in four volumes, Book 3] (Moscow: 'Nauka', 1999), 397 admits that the operation was to be completed by 22 August. For further details on the planning and conduct of the operation, see also Bagrov, *Iuzhno-sakhalinskaia*.
7. Bagrov, *Iuzhno-sakhalinskaia*, 24.
8. Ibid. These calculations are based on D'iakonov's mission to reach Toyohara by 22 rather than 25 August.
9. Vnotchenko, *Pobeda*, 290.
10. 'Proryv Kotonskogo', 75.
11. Vnotchenko, *Pobeda*, 290–1, and Bagrov, *Iuzhno-sakhalinskaia*, 28.
12. 'Proryv Kotonskogo', 75.
13. Henceforth, this chapter will use the Russian designation 'Koton' in lieu of the Japanese name Haramitog.
14. Ibid., 76.
15. Bagrov, *Iuzhno-sakhalinskaia*, 29.
16. 'Proryv Kotonskogo', 77.
17. Ibid.
18. Bagrov, *Iuzhno-sakhalinskaia*, 30.
19. Ibid., 31.
20. Zakharov *et al.*, *Krasnoznamennyi*, 222.
21. Bagrov, *Iuzhno-sakhalinskaia*, 34.
22. Ibid.
23. Ibid., 35.
24. Ibid.
25. Zakharov *et al.*, *Krasnoznamennyi*, 222.
26. Some confusion exists concerning the timing of the 56th Rifle Corps' assault. Vnotchenko, *Pobeda*, 293, stated that it began at 0730 hours, Bagrov, *Iuzhno-sakhalinskaia*, 60, gives the time as 0935 hours, but the classified account 'Proryv

Kotonskogo', 78, puts the time at 0745 hours. Some of this confusion results from confusing preliminary assaults with the main assault and the citation of timing according to differing time zones. The classified study provides the most accurate times.

27. 'Proryv Kotonskogo', 78.
28. Ibid., 79.
29. Ibid.
30. Ibid., 80.
31. Ibid.
32. Ibid., 80–1.
33. Ibid., 81.
34. Ibid.
35. Ibid., 82.
36. Ibid.
37. Ibid.
38. Vnotchenko, *Pobeda*, 293–4.
39. The most detailed description of this landing is found in Bagrov, *Iuzhno-sakhalinskaia*, 70–1.
40. Ibid., 74.
41. For additional details on the Toro and Esutoru assault, see Zakharov *et al.*, *Krasnoznamennyi*, 222–6, and V. Sologub, 'Severnaia Tikhookeanskaia Flotiliia v Iuzhno-Sakhalinskoi operatsii' [The Northern Pacific Flotilla in the southern Sakhalin operation], *VIZh*, No. 2 (February 1980), 46–8.
42. Bagrov, *Iuzhno-sakhalinskaia*, 75.
43. Ibid., 78.
44. Ibid., 81.
45. Ibid.
46. 'Proryv Kotonskogo', 84.

10

The Amphibious Assault on the Kuril Islands

CONTEXT AND TERRAIN

No less s gnificant from a strategic standpoint were the Far East Command's offensive operations against the Kuril Islands (Chishima in Japanese). As far as the geography and terrain are concerned, the Kuril Islands consist of a chain of 30 mid-size and more than 20 smaller islands and rocky shoals that stretch for a distance of 621 miles (1,000 kilometers) from the southern tip of Kamchatka to the northern cost of Hokkaido (see Map 44). As a whole, the islands er compass about 6,023 square miles (15,600 square kilometers) of terrain. The islands are volcanic in origin, including more than 100 volcanoes, 38 of which are still active.

The largest islands in the northern portion of the Kuril Island chain are Paramoshiri (in Russian Paramushir), Onnekotan (Onekotan), and Shumshir (Shumshu). To the south, lie other islands, some even larger, including from north to south, Shinshiri (Simushir), Urup, Etorofu (Iturup), and Kunashiri (Kunashir). The most suitable landing site for military forces in the island chain are located at Kataoka Bay on Shumshir Island and near Kasivabara Bay on Paramoshiri, where the Japanese maintained two small naval bases.[1] Few suitable landing sites exist elsewhere on the islands, other then a few locations suitable for the landing of small diversionary or raiding parties. The climate in the Kuril Islands is severe with low average temperatures, heavy winds, frequent periods of heavy rain, and low visibility and fog. which is densest in July and August during the late summer monsoons.

In August 1945 the Japanese maintained nine airfields and airstrips in the Kurils, six of which were situated on Shumshir and Paramoshiri within range of Kamchatka. The capacity of these airfields was roughly 600 aircraft, although few aircraft were based on the islands in August 1945. The Japanese also maintained naval bases at Kataoka and Kasivabara on Shumshir, adjacent to the Second Kuril Strait. What few roads existed on the Kuril Islands were

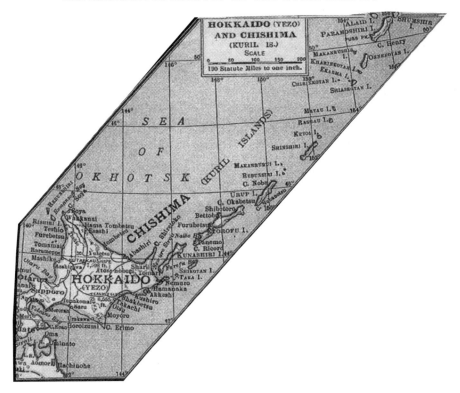

Map 44. The Kuril Islands

primarily dirt and simple cart tracks, most of which served to connect various garrisons and defensive positions. Therefore, the main means of communications were small *Kawasaki* fishing boats, which the Japanese also used to transport and land small amphibious forces.

The northernmost island, Shumshir (in Russian Shumshu), which is located less than 12.4 miles (20 kilometers) from the southern tip of Kamchatka and 180 miles (290 kilometers) by sea from the port of Petropavlovsk, measures 18.6 miles (30 kilometers) from northeast to southwest and a maximum of 6.2 miles (20 kilometers) wide, for an area of 193 square miles (500 square kilometers). Shumshir is separated from the southern tip of Kamchatka by the First Kuril Strait, which is 6.5 miles (10.5 kilometers) wide and from 82 to 131 feet (25 to 40 meters) deep. Shumshir is separated from the neighboring island of Paramoshiri to the south by the Second Kuril Strait, which is more than 1 6 kilometers (1 mile) wide and from 33 to 164 feet (10 to 50 meters deep)

Shumshir Island is the lowest island in the Kuril chain, with heights ranging from sea level in the northeast to Height Marker 189.9 (meters [623 feet]) in the southwest. The central and northern portions of the island are flat and treeless but cut by numerous hollows and ravines carved by small streams. The coast of the island is hilly and rocky, with cliffs often reaching heights of from 590 to 623 feet (180 to 190 meters), and the northern and northwestern part is steep and abrupt, now and then edged with fields of loose rocks and scree. The vegetation on the island is sparse; there are no woods or forests and only small, scattered thickets of creeping alder and pine.

On the northwestern coast of Shumshir Island, Capes Iman-Saki and Kokutan-Saki jut out deeply into the Sea of Okhotsk, forming a shallow bay with a sandy shore behind which low sand dunes stretch out to the cliffs. On the island's southwestern coast adjacent to the Second Kuril Strait the Japanese had constructed a naval base at Kataoka and, three miles away on Paramoshiri Island, another naval base at Kasivabara. The bases, which had only a few ships docked at their ferro-concrete piers, had strong fortifications protecting them from land and sea, and thus, amphibious assaults near them were nadvisable.

The principal road on the island connected the port of Kataoka with Cape Kokutan-Saki, and a number of surfaced and improved dirt roads radiated outward from the main north–south road to the southern, southwestern, western, and northwestern coasts of the island. This road network, whose total length was about 75 miles (120 kilometers), was generally unsuited for vehicular or wheeled transport, and during rainy periods the roads were utterly impassable.

There were two ground airfields on the island, the first with one runway in the island's center and the second with two runways near the naval base at Kataoka. The airfields were suited for operations by all types of aircraft, and they had enough hangers to house two aviation regiments. Lake Bettobu in the northwestern part of the island, which was 0.6 miles (1 kilometer) wide and roughly 10 feet (3 meters) deep, could accommodate landings by amphibious aircraft.

The principal means of communications on Shumshir other than radio was by land line (wire). The main cable line ran from Kataoka to Cape Kokutan-Saki, and it had seven wires, while smaller branch lines extended to all fortifications, defensive positions, and installations.

Paramoshiri Island is larger than Shumshir, encompassing 1,003 square miles (2,600 square kilometers), but Onnekotan Island is also quite large, encompassing 193 square miles (500 square kilometers). The highest points on Paramoshiri and Onnekotan Islands are 5,956 and 4,343 feet (1,816 and 1,324 meters) respectively. While larger than most of the central and northern islands, the islands of Shinshiri, Urup, Etorofu, and Kunashiri to the south are more rugged than their neighbors to the north and average greater heights.

JAPANESE DEFENSES

Lieutenant General Higuchi Kiichiro's Fifth Area Army, which was formed from the Northern Army early in 1944 with its headquarters at Sapporo on Hokkaido, defended Hokkaido and the Kuril Islands, as well as southern Sakhalin. After the Japanese had abandoned Attu and Kiska Islands in the Aleutian Island chain in 1943, the Kurils became the first line of Japanese defenses north of the Home Islands. Japanese ground force strength in the northern Kuril Islands rose from 5,000 men in early 1943 to 60,000 in the summer of 1944, 80 per cent of which were based on Shumshu and Paramoshiri Islands.[2]

Beginning in the summer of 1944, however, the Japanese Imperial Headquarters began deploying troops away from the Kurils to counter the growing US threat in the central and southern Pacific. Consequently, by August 1945 a force of less than 25,000 men defended the northern Kurils. In August 1945, Higuchi's area army defended the Kuril Islands with two infantry divisions, one separate independent mixed brigade, one separate mixed regiment, one tank regiment, and several support units and subunits (see Table 22).

The strength of Japanese forces defending the Kuril Islands in early August was just over 80,000 men, 23,000 of whom were defending the islands of Shumshir and Paramoshiri. However, the Japanese had no ships or aircraft in the region apart from dive-bombers stationed at Kataoka and Kasivabara airfields, which were to be flown by Kamikaze pilots.[3]

TABLE 22: COMPOSITION AND DISPOSITIONS OF JAPANESE FIFTH AREA ARMY, 15 AUGUST 1945

Force	*Location*
The Kurils	
91st Infantry Division	Shumshir, Paramoshiri, Onnekotan, Shiaskotan
Headquarters	Paramoshiri
73d Infantry Brigade	Shumshir
74th Infantry Brigade	Paramoshiri
11th Tank Regiment	Shumshir
129th Independent Mixed Brigade	Urup
41st Separate Mixed Regiment	Matau
Kuril Fortress Artillery Regiment	All islands
31st Antiaircraft Regiment	Shumshir
89th Infantry Division	Etorofu, Kunashiri, and the lesser Kurils
Headquarters	Tennei
43d Infantry Brigade	
69th Infantry Brigade	
Strength	
80,000 men	
60 tanks	
Hokkaido	
Headquarters, Fifth Area Army	Sapporo
42d Infantry Division	Wakkanai
7th Infantry Division	Kushiro
101st Independent Mixed Regiment	Tomakomai
Strength	
115,000 men	
Southern Sakhalin	
88th Infantry Division	
Strength	
19,000 men and 10,000 reservists	

Source: 'File of Messages Exchanged with U. S. Military Mission to Moscow', *SRH-198, Record Group 457* (Washington, DC: Military Branch, MIS, 25 October 1945), 011, 026. Classified Top Secret Ultra.

The Japanese 91st Infantry Division, under the command of Major General Tsutsumi Fusaka, was responsible for the defense of Shumshir, Paramoshiri, Onnekotan, and Shiaskotan Islands but had most of its forces deployed on Shumshir and Paramoshiri (see Table 23).

The Japanese garrison on Shumshir Island consisted of the 91st Infantry Division's 73d Infantry Brigade, one battalion of the 31st Antiaircraft Regiment, one detachment of the Kuril Fortress Artillery Regiment, one engineer regiment, and portions of the 11th Tank Regiment with 60 light tanks. These forces, which totaled six infantry battalions, fielded 60 tanks, 98 guns and mortars, and 200 light and 75 heavy machine guns, supported by only seven aircraft. The bulk of these forces was concentrated at or around Kataoka airfield, and only two infantry battalions with supporting

TABLE 23: COMPOSITION AND DISPOSITIONS OF JAPANESE 91ST INFANTRY DIVISION AND SUPPORTING UNITS, 15 AUGUST 1945

91st Infantry Division	Shumshir, Paramoshiri, Onnekotan, Shiaskotan
Headquarters	Paramoshiri
73d Infantry Brigade	Shumshir
74th Infantry Brigade	Paramoshiri
11th Tank Regiment	Shumshir
129th Independent Mixed Brigade	Urup
41st Separate Mixed Regiment	Matau
Two detachments, Kuril Fortress	
Artillery Regiment	Shumshir and Paramoshiri
18th and 19th Mortar Battalions	Paramoshiri
31st Antiaircraft Regiment	Shumshir and Paramoshiri
Engineer Regiment	
Strength	
12 infantry battalions	
336 light machine guns	
144 heavy machine guns	
160 guns and mortars	
77 light tanks	
24 aircraft	
23,000 men	

Sources: 'Kuril'skaia desantnaia operatsiia (po materialam Kamchatckogo oboronite'nogo raiona)' [The Kuril amphibious operation (based on the materials of the Kamchatke defensive region)] in Sbornik takticheskikh materialov po opytu Otechestvennoi voiny, No. 22 [Collection of tactical materials based on the experience of the Patriotic War, No. 22] (Moscow: Voenizdat, 1947), 67–8; V. N. Bagrov, Iuzhno-sakhalinskaia i Kuril'skaia operatsii (avgust 1945 goda) [The Southern Sakhalin and Kuril operations (August 1945)] (Moscow: Voenizdat, 1959), 12–13; and V. Akshinsky, Kuril'skii desant [The Kuril amphibious assault] (Petropavlovsk, Kamchatka: Dal'nevostochnoe knizhnoe izdatel'stvo, 1984), 12.

weapons were deployed in the northern and northeastern portion of the island.[4]

The garrison on Paramoshiri consisted of the 92d Infantry Division's 74th Infantry Brigade (less two battalions), one battalion of the 11th Tank Regiment with 17 tanks, one detachment of the Kuril Fortress Artillery Regiment, the 18th and 19th Mortar Battalions, and two battalions of the 31st Antiaircraft Regiment, for a total of four infantry battalions, 17 tanks, 70 guns and mortars, and 112 light and 40 heavy machine guns. The majority of these forces were stationed at or near the Kasivabara Naval Base and on Cape Bandzio-Saki. The remaining two battalions of the 74th Infantry Regiment were stationed on Onnekotan, and the 129th Infantry Brigade was headquartered on Urup.[5]

The Japanese force on Shumshir numbered 8,480 men. Another 14,500 troops were available as reinforcements from other islands, in particular, Paramoshiri Island.[6] In addition, Shumshir's 75 miles (120 kilometers) of decent roads made it possible for the Japanese defenders to deploy and maneuver reserves and reinforcements rapidly.

By 1945 the Japanese had erected strong fortifications on both Shumshir and Paramoshiri Islands, but particularly on the former. All sectors of the coast considered suitable for the conduct of amphibious landings were protected by centers of resistance consisting of mutually supporting strong points. The strong points themselves were made up of numerous ferro-concrete and earth and timber pillboxes interconnected by underground communications trenches and full-profile trenches. Antitank ditches and escarpments covered every likely axis of advance by tank forces, and additional strong points, consisting of pillboxes, bunkers, and trench lines, sat atop every hill. Soviet intelligence detected a total of 34 ferro-concrete pillboxes, 24 earth and timber pillboxes and up to 25 miles (40 kilometers) of antitank ditches on Shumshir and 13 ferro-concrete pillboxes, 44 earth and timber pillboxes, and 6.2 miles (10 kilometers) of antitank ditches on Paramoshiri.[7]

The majority of the defenses and firing points on Shumshir Island were located in the southwestern part of the island in the vicinity of the Kataoka Naval Base. In addition, naval batteries on the northern shore of Paramoshiri Island also helped defend the Second Kuril Strait.

In addition to the coastal defenses, the Japanese also erected an important defense line just inland from the coast across the northeastern part of the island from Hill 170.7 (171) to Hill 165. This defense line, which consisted of numerous pillboxes, trenches, and field works forming separate strong points, formed a second line of defense should an amphibious assault succeed.

The Japanese carefully camouflaged all of these defensive works and created a network of false positions and mock-up equipment and weaponry to confuse Soviet military planners. However, since they feared Soviet air strikes, the Japanese deliberately did not store ammunition, fuel, foodstuffs, and other supplies in large warehouse complexes. Instead, they relied on an extensive network of small storage facilities scattered about the island.

Although, as subsequent combat indicated, the Japanese maintained large stocks of explosives on the island, they failed to lay mines on the approaches to the islands and also neglected to install minefields in front of their ground defensive positions. Soviet sources claim, 'It turned out that the Japanese did not manage to emplace the obstacles since they did not expect our amphibious assault landing.'[8]

While the Japanese defending the Kurils were indeed surprised, the surprise resulted as much from who attacked as it did from the fact that the attack was taking place:

Japanese troops on the north Kurils suffered from isolation, uncertainty, and a sinking feeling of having been forgotten by the rest of the country.

Only Tsutsumi and a handful of his staff knew that Stalin had branded Japan an aggressor in a speech commemorating the revolution in November 1944 or that Molotov had notified the Japanese ambassador the following April that Moscow did not intend to renew the neutrality pact. Even Tsutsumi had only a general notion about the Soviet build-up in the Far East ...

The Soviet declaration of war alerted the Kuril garrisons in their new predicament, but more than a week passed without any indications of a Russian assault ...

On the night of 14 August, Tsutsumi received a wire from Fifth Area Army headquarters in Sapporo, ordering him to tune in to an important short wave broadcast from the Emperor next day at noon but not to include men outside his immediate staff. After hearing the Emperor's announcement of the war's end on the fifteenth, Tsutsumi concluded that the Kurils faced imminent occupation by American forces.[9]

THE FAR EASTERN COMMAND'S PLAN

By the second week of August 1945, the successes that Vasilevsky's three *fronts* had recorded in Manchuria and the 56th Rifle Corps' apparent victory on Sakhalin Island had created favorable conditions for operations against the Kuril Islands. Consequently, early on 15 August, Vasilevsky directed Admiral Iumashev, the commander of the Pacific Fleet, and General Purkaev, the commander of the 2d Far Eastern Front, to prepare and conduct an operation to liberate the northern portion of the Kuril Islands.

At the same time, Vasilevsky ordered Cheremisov's 16th Army to land its amphibious assault forces at Maoka on Sakhalin Island, The Pacific Fleet's Military Council, which was responsible for the overall conduct of the Kuril operation, assigned the task of preparing and conducting the amphibious operation against Shumshir Island to the Kamchatka Defensive Region, commanded by Major General A. R. Gnechko, and the Petropavlovsk Naval Base, commanded by Captain 1st Rank D. G. Ponomarev. Gnechko was to command the amphibious operation and Ponomarev the naval landing operation, while Major General P. I. D'aikov, the commander of the 101st Rifle Division, was to command the actual amphibious assault force.

Purkaev issued his directive ordering the amphibious operation's conduct to Gnechko at 0740 hours on 15 August:

> The capitulation of Japan is expected. Exploiting the favorable situation, it is necessary to occupy the islands of Shumshir (Shumshu), Paramoshiri (Paramushir), and Onnekotan (Onekotan). The forces are two regiments of the 101st Rifle Division, all of the ships and naval means of the base,

available ships of the cargo fleet, border guard forces, and the 128th Aviation Division. Have two–three companies of naval infantry of the Petropavlovsk Naval Base ready to employ as a forward detachment. Immediately set about preparing shipping [floating means] and the rifle forces for loading and forming the naval infantry detachment after reinforcing the sailors with an automatic weapons battalion ... The immediate mission is to capture the islands of Shumshir, Paramoshiri, and subsequently, Onnekotan. The base commander, Captain 1st Rank Ponomarev, will determine the landing points. Based on these points, you are responsible for determining the objectives to be seized on each island and the sequence of their seizure ... The forces will be ready to embark on the ships with their weapons and equipment at 1800 hours on 15 August 1945. Submit your operational decision [plan] and associated orders on sea movement to Purkaev, Leonov, and Shevchenko by 1600 hours 15 August 1945.[10]

Thus, the *front's* directive to Gnechko established the composition, the overall aim, and the specific missions to be accomplished in the amphibious operation.

THE KAMCHATKA DEFENSIVE REGION'S OFFENSIVE CONCEPT

Forces from the Kamchatka Defensive Region and ships and units of the Petropavlovsk Naval Base were to conduct the amphibious operation under Gnechko's direction, Ponomarev was to direct the transport and landing of the amphibious landing forces, and D'iakov was to command the actual landing force. D'iakov's force consisted of his 101st Rifle Division (less its 302d Rifle Regiment), one battalion of naval infantry, a company of border guard troops, one battalion of the 428th Howitzer Artillery Regiment, and ships from the Petropavlovsk Naval Base. The 42 aircraft of the 128th Mixed Aviation Division provided air support. Gnechko's reserve, which remained at the naval base in readiness to reinforce the assault, consisted of the 198th Separate Rifle Regiment, the 7th Separate Rifle Battalion, and two artillery battalions (see Table 24)

So configured, D'iakov's assault force numbered seven infantry battalions with 8,824 men supported by 126 guns and 79 mortars (45 mm or greater caliber), 120 heavy and 370 light machine guns, but no tanks.[11]

Gnechko issued orders to D'iakov concerning the amphibious operation at 1500 hours on 15 August (see Map 45). His plan called for a surprise amphibious landing on the northeastern coast of Shumshir Island followed by a main attack southward toward the naval base at Kataoka to capture the

TABLE 24: COMPOSITION OF THE SOVIET KURIL ISLAND AMPHIBIOUS ASSAULT FORCE, 15 AUGUST 1945

101st Rifle Division: Major General D. G. D'iakov
138th Rifle Regiment: Lieutenant Colonel K. D. Merkur'ev
302d Rifle Regiment: (not involved in the assault)
373d Rifle Regiment: Lieutenant Colonel V. G. Gubaidullin
279th Artillery Regiment: Lieutenant Colonel A. K. Tarasov
169th Antitank (Tank Destroyer) Battalion
119th Separate Sapper Battalion
38th Separate Chemical Defense Company
Attached
One Naval Infantry Battalion: Major T. A. Pochtarev
One Border Guard Company, 60th Naval Border Detachment
1st Battalion, 428th Howitzer Artillery Regiment
Reserve
198th Separate Rifle Regiment
7th Separate Rifle Battalion
2d and 3d Battalions, 428th Howitzer Artillery Regiment
Air Support
128th Mixed Aviation Division: Lieutenant Colonel M. A. Eremin
2d Separate Naval Bomber Aviation Regiment: Lieutenant Colonel V. A. Baliasnikov

island. Shumshir would then become a bridgehead for subsequent assaults on Paramoshiri and Onnekotan islands. If conditions were favorable, the subsequent assaults against Paramoshiri and Onnekotan were to be conducted simultaneously.

The assault on Shumshir Island was to begin at 2300 hours on 17 August so that D'iakov's forces could complete clearing Japanese forces from the island by day's end on 18 August. Ponomarev was to transport the assault forces to Shumshir in two amphibious waves. The initial assault on the island was to take place 2.5 miles (4 kilometers) south of Cape Kotomari-Saki on the island's northeastern coast between Cape Kokutan-Saki and the Kokon-Gava River. Gnechko selected this landing site because it offered the landing boats easy access to the beaches, and the coastal artillery on Cape Lopatka, the southernmost tip of Kamchatka, could fire in support of the landing.

Gnechko's order required D'iakov to organize his amphibious assault force into four segments: a forward detachment, two main force echelons, and a demonstrative assault (feint). The forward detachment, commanded by Major P. I. Shutov, the deputy commander of the 138th Rifle Regiment, consisted of the naval infantry battalion (less one company), a company from the 60th Naval Border Guards Detachment, automatic weapons and mortar companies, the reconnaissance and chemical defense platoons from the 302d Rifle Regiment, and a sapper company from the 119th Separate Sapper Battalion. The forward detachment's mission was to land on the coast of Shumshir four kilometers south of Cape Kotomari-Saki at 2300 hours on

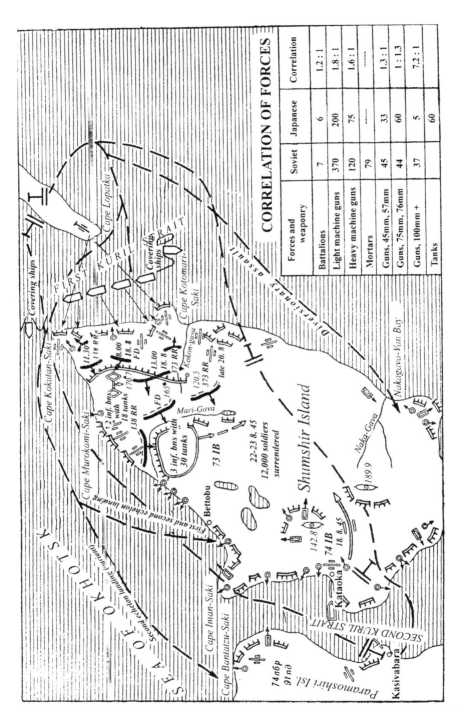

CORRELATION OF FORCES

Forces and weaponry	Soviet	Japanese	Correlation
Battalions	7	6	1.2 : 1
Light machine guns	370	200	1.8 : 1
Heavy machine guns	120	75	1.6 : 1
Mortars	79	——	——
Guns, 45mm, 57mm	45	33	1.3 : 1
Guns, 75mm, 76mm	44	60	1 : 1.3
Guns, 100mm +	37	5	7.2 : 1
Tanks		60	

Map 45. The Assault on Shumshir Island, 18–19 August 1945

17 August, seize a bridgehead between Cape Kokutan-Saki and the mouth of the Kokon-Gava River, and protect the landing of the main amphibious force's first echelon.[12]

The amphibious assault force's first echelon consisted of the 138th Rifle Regiment (less two companies), the 1st Battalion of the 428th Howitzer Artillery Regiment, the 2d Battalion, 279th Artillery Regiment, and the 169th Separate Antitank Artillery Battalion (less one company of antitank rifles), commanded by D'iakov. This force was to follow three hours behind the forward detachment, land at the same location, attack toward Cape Kokutan-Saki and Cape Murokami-Saki, capture Kataoka, and capture all of Shumshir Island by day's end on 18 August.

Thereafter, the first echelon was to prepare to conduct a follow-on amphibious assault on Paramoshiri Island. In a second variant, if Japanese resistance proved weak, the first echelon was to land on the island's west coast near Lake Bettobu and attack southward toward Kataoka. The ships carrying the forward detachment and first echelon were to be set to sea at 2000 hours on 16 August.[13]

The second echelon consisted of the main assault force and its first wave. The first wave was made up of the 2d Battalion and machine gun company from the 373d Rifle Regiment, a company of naval infantry, and a mortar platoon. The main force included the remainder of the 373d Rifle Regiment and the 1st and 3d Battalions of the 279th Artillery Regiment.

Gnechko's plan required the second echelon to conduct its operations according to one of three variants. If the first echelon landed in the same location as the forward detachment, the second echelon was to land at Lake Bettobu and attack toward Kataoka. If the first echelon landed at Lake Bettobu and encountered heavy opposition, the second echelon was to reinforce it. Finally, if Japanese resistance on Shumshir proved to be light, the second echelon was to land on the northeastern coast of Paramoshiri and capture the naval base at Kasivabara. The deputy commander of the 101st Rifle Division, Colonel P. A. Artiushin, commanded the second echelon, which was to set sail at 2100 hours on 16 August.

To deceive the Japanese regarding his actual objectives, Gnechko also planned a demonstrative amphibious assault with two rifle companies from the 138th Rifle Regiment, an automatic weapons company, an 82 mm mortar company, an antitank rifle company, and a naval infantry company from his second echelon. The demonstrative landing was to take place at 0200 hours on 18 August on the southeastern shore of the island near the Naka-Gava River. After landing, the diversionary force was to operate in the Japanese rear area to conceal the actual landing sites.

Under Ponomarev's direction, the Petropavlovsk Naval Base assembled a naval force of 64 ships to transport and support D'iakov's amphibious force (see Table 25).[14]

TABLE 25: COMPOSITION OF SOVIET NAVAL FORCES DESIGNATED TO TRANSPORT AND SUPPORT THE AMPHIBIOUS ASSAULT ON SHUMSHIR ISLAND

Escort ships *Kirov* and *Dzerzhinsky*
Minelayer *Okhotsk*
Floating base *Sever* [North]
Hydrographic ships *Poliarnyi* [Polar] and *Lebed'*
2 self-propelled assault barges
8 *MO-4* escort cutters
4 *Kawasaki* cutters
1 submarine
14 transports *Pugachev, Chapaev, Kokkinaki, Uritskii, Menzhinsky, Turkmen, Burevestnik, Dal'nevostochnik, Krasnoe Znamia* [Red Banner], and *Moskal'vo, Refrigerator ship No. 2, General Panfilov, Maksin Gorky,* and *Volkhov.*
4 trawlers (*Bekha,* Nos. 525, 155, and 156)
2 cutter trawlers (*Nos. 151* and *154*)
16 assault boats (*Nos. 1, 2, 3, 4, 5, 6, 7, 8, 9, 10, 43, 46, 47, 49,* and *50*)
8 smaller craft

Source: 'Kuril'skaia desantnaia operatsiia' [The Kuril amphibious operation] in *Sbornik takticheskikh materialov po opytu Otechestvennoi voiny,* No. 22 [Collection of tactical materials based on the experience of the Patriotic War, No. 22] (Moscow: Voenizdat, 1947), 70.

Ponomarev organized these ships into separate fire support, minesweeping, assault boat, landing boat, security, and covering detachments. Seventy-eight aircraft from the 128th Mixed Aviation Division and a naval aviation regiment were to provide air cover and support for the amphibious landing, which was to commence overnight on 18 August.[15]

The 128th Mixed Aviation Division was to protect the amphibious force's sea movement and pound Japanese defenses in the landing area for one hour prior to the landing. Thereafter, it was to provide on-call support to the landing force commander.

Thus, Gnechko's plan called for successive operations, including:

- the capture of Shumshir Island by day's end on 18 August by the forward detachment and the main force's first echelon and, in the event of strong resistance, the landing of the second echelon on the island;
- if the battle for Shumshir developed favorably, the capture of Paramoshiri Island on the same day by the second echelon, and, if the reverse, to begin the battle for Paramoshiri on the morning of 19 August; and
- the initiation of operations to capture Onnekotan after the seizure of Paramoshiri.[16]

Unfortunately, while the Kamchatka Defensive Region's intelligence organs assessed that the Japanese forces defending Shumshir manned at least 34 pillboxes and 24 bunkers and dugouts protected by up to 25 miles

(40 kilometers) of antitank ditches, it woefully underestimated the strength, scope, and dispositions of Japanese defenses on the island.

Given this underestimation of Japanese strength on Shumshir Island, D'iakov's force was only slightly superior to the defending Japanese forces (see Table 26).

TABLE 26: CORRELATION OF FORCES IN SOVIET ASSAULT ON SHUMSHIR ISLAND

Forces and Weapons	Strength		
	Soviet	Japanese	Correlation
Infantry battalions	7	6	1.2 : 1
Guns 100 mm or larger	37	5	7.2 : 1
Guns 76 mm or 75 mm	44	60	1 : 1.3
Guns 45 mm or 47 mm	45	33	1.3 : 1
120 mm mortars	79	–	Absolute
82 mm mortars	36	–	Absolute
Grenade launchers	–	180	Absolute
Heavy machine guns	120	75	1.6 : 1
Light machine guns	372	237	1.6 : 1
Antitank rifles	215	–	Absolute
Tanks	–	60	Absolute
Aircraft	42	7	6 : 1
Total			
Personnel	8,842	8,480	1 : 1
Guns and 120 mm mortars	205	98	2.1 : 1
Tanks	–	60	Absolute
Aircraft	42	7	6 : 1

Sources: 'Kuril'skaia desantnaia operatsiia' [The Kuril amphibious operation], *Sbornik takticheskikh materialov po opytu Otechestvennoi voiny*, No. 22 [Collection of tactical materials on the experience of the Patriotic War, No. 22] (Moscow: Voenizdat, 1947), 74, and V. N. Bagrov, *Iuzhno-sakhalinskaia i Kuril'skaia operatsii (avgust 1945 g)* [The Southern Sakhalin and Kuril operations (August 1945)] (Moscow: Voenizdat, 1959), 43.

While Soviet forces had a crushing superiority in aircraft and a significant superiority in artillery, the bulk of the supporting Soviet artillery was sea-bound on light ships and was unable to maneuver to support operations inland. Furthermore, the weather, which, for the most part was bad throughout the duration of the operation, also severely limited the effectiveness of Soviet air support. On the other hand, the Japanese were superior in armor, albeit light, and occupied well-prepared defenses. Even though the Japanese tanks were only light models and were susceptible to relatively easy destruction by anti-tank rifle and artillery fire, they accorded the defenders a marked advantage.

All things considered, the landing force's main advantage rested in the element of surprise. If they could land quickly enough to gain a sizeable foothold on the island before the Japanese had time to move forces northward, there was a good chance of success, particularly in light of the potential reinforcements the Kamchatka Defensive Region had available.

THE AMPHIBIOUS ASSAULT FORCE'S PLAN

Gnechko and D'iakov planned to prepare the amphibious operation in three stages, and conduct it in echelon formation by committing their forces into combat in timed-phased sequence. The preparatory stages included assembling, organizing, and training the assault force; loading the force with its equipment and supplies on board ships according to a carefully orchestrated loading plan; and finally, transporting the force by sea to its landing area. The first two stages were to last from 1500 hours on 15 August to 2000 hours on 16 August, an incredibly short period of only 29 hours. The transport stage, which was to begin on 2000 hours on 16 August and last until 2300 hours on 17 August, was an equally short period of 27 hours. The forward detachment was to leave port at 2000 hours on 16 August, and the main force's two echelons one hour later.[17]

In the variant of the operation as it was actually conducted, the ships with the first wave of the assault were to assemble off the coast of Shumshir promptly at 2300 hours on 17 August and begin landing operations at 2400 hours to capture the designated beachhead. The ships carrying the main force's first echelon were to be prepared to land their troops at 2400 hours, hard on the heels of the forward detachment. The demonstrative assault was to land at 0200 hours 18 August in Nana-Gava Bay.

D'iakov, the 101st Rifle Division and assault force commander, ordered his force, 'to conduct the main attack from Cape Kotomari-Saki toward Hill 150.7 [in the island's center] and a secondary attack from the Nakagava-Van Bay toward Hills 189.9 and 140.4 [across the southern part of the island] to penetrate the Japanese coastal defenses, split his combat formation, and destroy the opposing forces'.[18] Subsequently, his force was to capture Kataoka and the entire island. He then assigned the following missions to the three combat elements of his force:

- the *forward detachment* will capture positions from Hill 170.7 through the northeastern slope of Hill 125.9, that is, seize a beachhead 6 kilometers (3.7 miles) wide and 4–5 kilometers (2.5–3.1 miles) deep and dig in to support the landing of the first echelon of the amphibious assault's main force; employ mobile groups to prevent the approach of Japanese reserves from Kataoka;
- after the forward detachment captures the beachhead, the *first echelon* (the 138th Rifle Regiment less two automatic weapons companies and an antitank rifle company) will land in the narrow sector from Cape Kotomari-Saki to

292

the mouth of the Kokan-Gava River, 4 kilometers (2.5 miles) south of Kotomari-Saki and, by attacking toward Hill 142.1, capture the eastern slope of Hill 150.7; subsequently, attack toward Kataoka; a battalion of the 428th Howitzer Artillery Regiment, a battalion of the 279th Artillery Regiment, and the 169th Separate Antitank Battalion will support the regiment's attack;

• the *left [diversionary] detachment* (two automatic weapons companies with an antitank rifle platoon and a sapper squad) will land in Nakagava-Van Bay and destroy the enemy in the vicinity of Hill 86.0; subsequently, by attacking along the road to Kataoka, destroy the enemy's rear services and communications; conduct the landing at 0200 hours 18 August;

• the *second echelon* (the 373d Rifle Regiment) will land following the first echelon and attack on its left flank to exploit success in the direction of Hill 150; if the left detachment's operations are successful, be prepared to land in Nakagava-Van Bay for an attack in the direction of Hill 189.9 and Kataoka; in the event the 138th Rifle Regiment's operations are successful, revert immediately to the immediate control of the commander of the Kamchatka Defensive Region.[19]

D'iakov retained the division's training battalion with automatic weapons, antitank rifle, and sapper companies in his reserve, and ordered them to be prepared to follow the second echelon and attack behind its right flank.

THE TRANSPORT PHASE

The amphibious assault force lifted anchor and left Avchinsk Bay at 0400 hours on 17 August, four hours later than planned. Throughout the entire passage to Shumshir the visibility ranged from 0.6 to 5 miles (1 to 8 kilometers), but the fog made it somewhat difficult to navigate and keep the convoy together. Since the speed of each ship differed, the convoy spread out over time. 'For example, the ferry *Uritskii* had a maximum speed of 5–6 knots. Therefore, it had to leave the column overall and was given an order to follow to the designated location independently under escort of one *MO* cutter for protection.'[20] All day on 17 August, fighter aircraft from the 128th Aviation Division flew protective cover over the convoy.

All radio transmissions were strictly forbidden from the time the convoy left port until it made contact with the enemy. D'iakov and his staff sailed on *Trawler No. 149* and used only light signals (semaphores) to pass instructions to other ships and control the convoy's movement.

The assault force entered the First Kuril Strait at 0215 hours on 18 August. However, the diversionary assault force that was supposed to land in Nakagava-Van Bay could not reach the area due to dense fog, and, fearing they would strike the numerous rocky shoals in the region, the detachment cancelled its diversionary assault and instead reinforced the first echelon. At 0235 hours the coastal batteries of Cape Lopatka opened fire on the Japanese artillery positions on the coast of Shumshir in the assault-landing sector.

The assault boats wheeled toward their designated landing areas between Capes Kokutan-Saki and Kotomari-Saki on the northeastern coast of Shumshir at 0410 hours on 18 August, still undetected by the Japanese because of the dense fog. The assault boats approached the coast without firing a single shot. With the dense fog, the visibility between the boats was still no more than 164–229 feet (50–70 meters), and the Japanese also did not open fire. Since the Soviet batteries on Cape Lopatka were continuing to shell Shumshir at 0400 hours, Soviet critiques assumed, 'the Japanese did not attach importance to the shelling and remained in their deep underground camps'.[21]

The same critiques credit the uneventful passage and successful landing a product of:

- the strict radio silence maintained during the movement;
- the dense fog during the approach to the island's coast;
- the preciseness of command and control during the sea passage; and
- the timely preparation of navigational support in the Cape Lopatka region as well as the assignment of experienced pilots, who had superb knowledge of the peculiarities of boats in the First Kuril Strait, to the assault boats.
- in addition, the periodic day and night raids by our aircraft and the fire raids of the coastal artillery from Cape Lopatka against Shumshir over the course of four days before the amphibious landing lowered the enemy's vigilance.[22]

THE ASSAULT

The Forward Detachment's and First Echelon's Assault Landing

In heavy fog and the light of the approaching dawn, at 0422 hours on 18 August, the first four landing boats of the amphibious assault force's forward detachment, commanded by Shutov, approached the shore and began landing in the precise location intended (see Map 45).[23] By 0500 hours the detachment's main force had completed the landing without firing a single shot or losing a single soldier. The bulk of Shutov's small force headed inland, while one company of naval infantry headed toward Cape Kotomari-Saki to silence the Japanese batteries. After advancing 1.2 miles (2 kilometers) inland from the beaches, the detachment's forward subunits encountered disorganized fire from small groups of Japanese soldiers.[24]

At 0530 hours the Japanese coastal batteries located between Capes Kokutan-Saki and Kotomari-Saki finally opened fire on the assault boats and other craft located in the immediate offshore region. In addition, the Japanese fired on the landing forces from the hulk of the tanker *Mariupol'*, which had sunk in 1943, and on which the Japanese had emplaced 20 75mm guns.[25] While many Japanese subunits near the coast fled in panic, some of the soldiers occupied pillboxes and bunkers in the rear area of the forward detachment's leading subunits as they advanced deeper into the island and opened fire on the coast and beaches.

By 0630 hours the forward detachment had completed landing all of its forces, and its main body was continuing its advance decisively toward Hills 170.7 and 165.[26] One Soviet source noted, 'This was a tactical error by the forward detachment. Only a single company of its naval infantry was directed toward Cape Kotomari-Saki, but it was unable to capture this region and was forced to go over to the defense.'[27]

Thirty minutes later Shutov's forward detachment began an organized assault to capture Hills 170.7 and 125.9, which were located 1.9 miles (3 kilometers) inland. More than a reinforced battalion of Japanese infantry, which had recovered from its initial panic, manned the prepared defensive positions on the two hills opposite the forward detachment's front, and, in the detachment's rear, the Japanese still held firmly to several strong points located on Capes Kokutan-Saki and Kotomari-Saki and delivered heavy machine gun, mortar, and artillery fire into the forward detachment's flanks and rear. Lacking any artillery support, Shutov's forward detachment halted in its tracks in front of the Japanese defenses.[28]

Soon after, the Japanese reinforced their defenses and launched a counterattack supported by 20 tanks. At a cost, the Japanese pressed the forward detachment back 328 yards (300 meters) but lost about 15 tanks and 100 men in the process, and were forced to go on the defense. The fighting ebbed and flowed for about an hour as both sides attacked and counterattacked in rapid succession without substantially altering the situation.[29]

Meanwhile, at 0630 hours the assault force's first echelon began landing in the same landing area employed by the forward detachment. This time, the Japanese began delivering flanking direct fire against the assault boats and other support ships from the batteries located on Capes Kokutan-Saki and Kotomari-Saki, causing the first echelon to suffer heavy personnel and equipment losses. A Japanese account recorded the action:

A boatload of scouts [the forward detachment] managed to slip ashore in the fog at about 5.00 a.m., but no sooner had they signaled the first wave to follow at 5.30 when entrenched Japanese on Capes Kokutan and Kotomari caught the advancing launches in a withering crossfire. Having picked up the noise of motors, the Japanese waited until they could discern the dim outlines of approaching landing-craft before unleashing a hail of lead. Some defenders had turned the hull of a wrecked Soviet tanker into a battery and raked the invaders from close quarters. Gnechko's first wave wilted. Thirteen landing-craft full of troops sank or exploded. Others burst into flames, illuminating the flailing occupants, many of whom leapt into the strait's treacherous currents and disappeared.[30]

The direct fire set fire to two assault boats, and three boats suffered from five to nine direct hits, one of them being wrecked on the coast. According to an after-action report, 'The ammunition on the stricken assault boats began exploding. The personnel began throwing themselves into the water and swimming to reach the shore.'[31] Despite the chaos and carnage, the assault force managed to land with considerable losses, although the engines of some of the assault boats were damaged.

In response to the new threat, the support detachment ships *Kirov*, *Dzerzhinsky*, and *Okhotsk* opened fire on the Japanese shore batteries, but one Japanese battery suppressed and silenced the *Kirov's* fire. The responding fire of the Soviet ships proved ineffective because the Japanese batteries were fortified and well camouflaged.[32]

Compounding the landing difficulties, a loss of communications disrupted command and control of the landing force since, during the landing operation, 21 of the 22 radios assigned to the forward detachment and the accompanying artillery correction posts were dropped into the seawater and would not operate. The headquarters of the Kamchatka Defensive Region, 101st Rifle Division, and 138th Rifle Regiment were still on board the ships and lacked any communications with their subunits that had already landed.

Because it lacked any communications with its units that had already landed, at 0900 hours the Kamchatka Defensive Region headquarters dispatched a forward officer observation point to the coast to determine the situation and receive reports from its subordinate subunits. However, since the officers had no radios, they could not fulfill their assigned mission. The Kamchatka Defensive Region's headquarters finally re-established radio communications with the forward detachment at 1100 hours but only after the detachment was able to use captured Japanese radios to communicate.[33] Consequently Gnechko received the first radio messages relating to the forward detachment's operations five to six hours after it landed, at a time when the detachment was already heavily engaged in heavy fighting for possession of Hill 170.7 and nearby Hill 165.

At 1020 hours Gnechko ordered D'iakov to organize his own observation post over the coast by 1100 hours so that he could exercise more effective command and control over the landed forces. However, 'Later it was determined, that, for unknown reasons, the division commander did not do so until the morning of 19 August. The commander of the Kamchatka Defensive Region organized command and control over his landed units personally and directly through his own staff.'[34]

The main force's first echelon finally completed its landing operation at 0900 hours. However, while it was able to bring its light infantry weapons ashore, it was unable to land much of its supporting artillery because it lacked sufficient means to move the artillery from the ships to the shore, and the landing was still being subjected to heavy fire from the Japanese shore batteries. A Japanese source criticized the forward detachment's decision to move inland, leaving the first echelon to its own devices:

> Those who reached the shore unwisely pushed inland instead of dealing with the Japanese shore positions. Their mistake enabled the undamaged Kokutan and Kotomari batteries bracketing the beachhead to continue firing on reinforcements. Moving inland, attackers found the road to Kataoka blocked by two fortified heights (Hills 165 and 170). Undeterred by pillboxes along the slopes, the Japanese hurled themselves forward.[35]

Although it had suffered considerable losses during its landing, and the 138th Rifle Regiment commander lacked any command and control over his forces since he was still at sea on board a damaged ship, nevertheless the first echelon's forces began advancing against Japanese defenses on Hill 170.7. By 1130 hours the first echelon finally reached the forward detachment's positions, although its units were in a disorganized combat formation. Once forward, the force regrouped its subunits and prepared to assault Japanese defenses on Hill 170.7 together with the forward detachment.

The Second Echelon's Assault Landing and the Struggle for the Center of the Island

At 0930 hours Gnechko ordered the second assault echelon to begin landing in the sector between Capes Kokutan-Saki and Kotomari-Saki. He selected this variant rather than landing the second echelon on Paramoshiri Island so as not to lose time and to prevent the Japanese from driving the forward detachment and first echelon into the sea, which was appearing ever more likely.

As it landed, the second echelon also came under heavy fire from the Japanese batteries on Capes Kokutan-Saki and Kotomari-Saki. The return fire from the naval fire support detachment had little effect on the Japanese batteries because the latter were well camouflaged, visibility was poor, and there were heavy waves on the surface of the First Kuril Strait. Worse still, the persistent fog prevented Soviet aircraft from striking the batteries effectively. Instead, the assault and bomber aircraft pounded Japanese positions at Kataoka and Kasivabara to prevent the Japanese from transferring the 74th Infantry Brigade to reinforce the defenses on Shumshir Island.

As was the case with previous echelons, the second echelon also had to land without its supporting artillery. To overcome the problem of transporting the artillery and supporting tanks, the sailors constructed special berths out of excess logs and rafts while under heavy enemy fire. The second echelon's forces finally completed their landing operations at 1300 hours.[36] By this time, the forward elements of the second echelon were beginning to reach the southeastern slope of Hill 170.7, also in disorganized combat formation, where they halted to regroup and prepare their own assault on the heights. Colonel Artiushin, the commander of the second echelon, immediately assumed command over all forces operating in the region.

While the fighting was going on for Hill 170.7, at 1100 hours the Japanese began deploying their reserves forward, covered by effective machine gun, mortar, and artillery fire, which pinned down the advancing Soviet forces:

> As soon as he received word of the landings, Tsutsumi mobilized all available forces at Kashiwabara (Kasivabara) and Kataoka and sent twenty light tanks to stop the enemy's advance. But anti-tank guns blunted two Japanese armoured attacks, knocking out most of the machines. Shumshu's three fighter planes fared better. Taking off from Kataoka they strafed offshore vessels. In the last kamikaze dive of the war, one of the pilots flung his machine into a Soviet destroyer escort.[37]

All the while, the Japanese coastal batteries on the two flanking capes hindered the unloading of Soviet artillery on the coast. According to the attack plan, the first echelon was to have liquidated the Japanese coastal batteries on the two capes, but it failed to blockade them. Ultimately, it would take until 19 August for the assault force's artillery to suppress these batteries and the division's sappers to first blockade and then destroy these strong points. Meanwhile, the fierce fight raged on for possession of Hill 170.7.

At 1400 hours two battalions of Japanese infantry from the 73d Infantry Brigade, supported by 18 light tanks, launched a heavy counterattack from the region along the southwestern slope of Hill 170.7, trying to force the Soviet assault forces back into the sea. However, with the help of naval gunfire, Artiushin's forces repelled the Japanese assault, destroying 17 of the 18 tanks by concentrated fire from his 100 antitank rifles and four 45 mm antitank guns.[38]

By 1800 hours the Soviet amphibious assault force had regrouped and occupied jumping-off positions for a fresh attack, with Merkur'ev's 138th Rifle Regiment deployed on the hill's northern and northwestern slopes and Gubaidulin's 373d Rifle Regiment on its southeastern slope. The naval artillery, which by this time had finally established an observation post on the shore, prepared fires to block the approach of any Japanese reserves.

At precisely 1800 hours, the assault forces attacked Hill 170.7 supported by the naval artillery and, after heavy resistance, captured its western slope in a fierce two-hour fight. According to classified Soviet reports, during the day the assault force killed 234 Japanese soldiers, wounded another 140, destroyed 17 tanks, and captured 10 guns, and five warehouses.[39] By day's end the assault force had reached the western slopes of Hills 170.7 and 165 and had carved a beachhead 2.5-miles (4-kilometer) wide and 3.1–3.7 miles (5–6 kilometers) deep in the Japanese defenses on northeastern Shumshir Island.[40]

A Soviet after-action report summed up the day's actions, providing the reasons why the assault was ultimately successful:

- In spite of considerable losses in personnel and weapons it suffered during the landing, the disorganized reconnaissance of the Japanese defenses on Capes Kokutan-Saki and Kotomari-Saki, and the measures that were not taken to destroy the enemy there, which caused unjustifiably high casualties on the second echelon and hindered the unloading of the artillery, the first echelon, without direction from the regimental commander, unloaded in heavy fog and, while under fire, independently concentrated in the region of Hill 170.7.
- The second echelon, which landed following the first echelon without communications with the units operating to its front, also strove to widen the beachhead while under the flanking fire of the undestroyed enemy batteries.
- The commander's lack of communications with the landed units from the moment of their arrival in the region of Hill 170.7 had an adverse effect on the exploitation of the forward detachment's success.
- Owing to the heavy fire from the unsuppressed enemy batteries, the landing of the first and second echelons did not occur according to plan, which led to the disorganization of the echelons' combat formations and the disruption of command and control of the forces.
- The fire from the unsuppressed enemy strong points (on Capes Kokutan-Saki and Kotomari-Saki) and the absence of unloading means prevented the timely unloading of artillery; its unloading proceeded so slowly that it deprived the forces of artillery support to the morning of the following day (only 11 guns were unloaded by 0600 hours on 19 August).
- The artillery fire from the ships on Japanese firing positions was of little effect due to the difficulty of correction in the dense fog and the cover of the Japanese batteries in deep firing positions (grottos).

However, despite a series of existing shortcomings, the combat operations on the first day nevertheless had great significance for the development of subsequent phases of the operation. The amphibious assault force's units seized a beachhead that supported preparations for the subsequent attack and the fulfillment of the subsequent missions.[41]

The Battle for the Kataoka and Kasivabara Naval Bases

Thereafter, the battle tilted decisively in the Soviet's favor. After studying the situation, at 2000 hours on 18 August, Gnechko issued an order, stating: 'The mission of the Kamchatka Defensive Region's forces remains the capture of the Islands of Shumshir and Paramoshiri.'[42] He assigned his subordinate forces the following specific missions:

- The reinforced 101st Rifle Division will dig in along its existing line. By operating with strong assault groups, beginning at 2230 hours, destroy the enemy's garrisons on Capes Kokutan-Saki and Kotomari-Saki. After capturing Capes Kokutan-Saki and Kotomari-Saki, beginning at 2400 hours on 18 August, fully complete the unloading of the artillery, in the first instance, the light guns.
- The commander of the Petropavlovsk Naval Base will assemble his ships in a region you designate and, during the night, organize an all-round defense in preparation to repel enemy light naval forces. Support the unloading of the artillery and ammunition for the assault forces operating on the coast with your existing ships and boats.
- The batteries located on Cape Lopatka will suppress the enemy batteries on Capes Kokutan-Saki and Kotomari-Saki by coordinating the firing from correction posts against targets that are threatening the ground forces.
- During the night the 128th Aviation Division will conduct bombing strikes against Kataoka and Bettobu with the mission of neutralizing the artillery located there and preventing the concentration of Japanese forces in these regions.
- The 7th Separate Rifle Battalion (less one company) will be prepared by 1500 hours on 19 August for loading on board ships and transport to Shumshir Island to develop the success of the first echelon along the Hill 170.7 and Bettobu axis.[43]

Overnight on 18–19 August, D'iakov's rifle division regrouped and reorganized, unloaded its artillery, and formed assault groups to destroy the enemy batteries on Capes Kokutan-Saki and Kotomari-Saki. These special assault groups attacked and seized the Japanese coastal artillery batteries on Cape Kokutan-Saki and Kotomari-Saki, and, by 0600 hours the following morning, the landing ships were able to deliver 11 more Soviet artillery pieces on shore. This artillery reached the assault force's forward positions by 1100 hours, providing it with enough firepower to resume its attack. A Japanese account noted the Soviets' success:

> The second day of fighting in the Kurils saw less bloodshed and notable progress for the Russians. Just before dawn on 19 August, sappers crept up to the Kokutan and Kotomari batteries and blew up the bunkers together with their occupants.[44]

Throughout 19 August, while the battle was raging to clear Japanese forces from Capes Kokutan-Saki and Kotomari-Saki, D'iakov's forces fortified their positions and prepared to assault toward Kataoka. By midday about half of the division's artillery and ammunition had reached the forward area.

Even though the Japanese Fifth Area Army had radioed its declaration of surrender to its subordinate troops on 18 August, Japanese forces continued their fanatical resistance on Shumshir Island, opening fire on Soviet ships that were attempting to traverse the Kuril Straits to bring naval gunfire to bear on Japanese port facilities at Kataoka and coastal batteries at Kasivabara. In addition, overnight on 18–19 August, the Japanese brought reserves forward from the southern portion of the island and, at the same time, began transferring forces from the 74th Infantry Brigade across the Second Kuril Strait from the northern part of Paramoshiri Island to Shumshir. By the morning of 19 August, the Japanese had concentrated more than five infantry battalions, supported by up to 60 tanks and 70 guns, opposite the 101st Rifle Division's front.

At 0830 hours on 19 August, Gnechko received a new order from Purkaev's 2d Far Eastern Front, demanding that he accelerate his advance:

The forces of the reinforced 101st Rifle Division (minus one rifle regiment) and the ships of the Petropavlovsk Naval Base will complete the occupation of Shumshir, Paramoshiri, and Onnekotan Islands and destroy and capture the Japanese force no later than 2000 hours on 20 August 1945.[45]

Gnechko responded, 'The enemy is offering stubborn resistance, 17 tanks have been destroyed, but I am arranging to fulfill your mission in combat.'[46] Gnechko then transmitted his own order to D'iakov's division at 0900 hours:

In cooperation with the 128th Aviation Division, the reinforced division's forces will capture the Kataoka Naval Base and the island of Shumshir by 2000 hours 19 August 1945. Be prepared to capture the Naval Base of Kasivabara (on Paramoshiri Island) by day's end on 20 August 1945.[47]

However, Gnechko's forces 'did not begin fulfilling this mission in light of the Japanese command's announcement concerning their readiness to cease military operations'.[48] At 0900 hours on 19 August, a delegation from the Japanese command arrived at Gnechko's headquarters. The delegation's head, a Captain Yamato, presented Gnechko with a declaration prepared by General Tsutsumi, the commander of the Japanese 91st Infantry Division, which read:

Our forces have received the following order:
1. The forces will cease combat operations today, 19 August at 1600 hours
Note: The defensive operations that we are forced to undertake in connection with the active enemy invasion are not combat operations.
2. On the basis of this order, our forces will cease all combat operations today, 19 August at 1600 hours ...
Note: If our forces are attacked after this time, I will resume defensive operations on the basis of this order.

3. Therefore, I request your forces cease combat operations at 1600 hours.[49]

THE DISARMAMENT OF JAPANESE FORCES ON SHUMSHIR ISLAND

At 1700 hours on 19 August, Gnechko met with Major General Suzino Ivao, the commander of the 73d Infantry Brigade, and Lieutenant Colonel Ianaoka Takedsi, the 91st Infantry Division chief of staff, and presented them with demands regarding the immediate and unconditional surrender of Japanese forces. These demands, which the Japanese delegation immediately accepted, stated that combat operations would cease only if and when the entire garrison ceased resistance and surrendered immediately. However, according to classified Soviet accounts, 'the higher Japanese command was slow in fulfilling this demand and still continued to transfer his reserves from Paramoshiri Island'.[50]

At 1000 hours on 20 August, four Japanese coastal batteries opened fire on Soviet ships, which were attempting to enter the Second Kuril Strait to disarm the Japanese coastal defenses. According to Soviet accounts, 'The shelling of the Petropavlovsk Naval Base's ships in the Second Kuril Strait demonstrated that the Japanese were not ceasing resistance and that they were not fulfilling the conditions of their capitulation'.[51]

Japanese sources offer a somewhat different perspective as to why the agreement did not endure:

At 8.00 a.m., Japanese envoys bearing white flags met with Soviet representatives at Takedahama to discuss a ceasefire. Negotiations continued throughout the morning and early afternoon. The Japanese finally agreed to a complete cessation of hostilities at 4.00 p.m. [Tokyo time], and promised to gather unarmed at designated spots on the morrow.

The agreement quickly broke down, seemingly as a result of bad communications rather than bad faith. Japanese sources complain that the Russians made provocative probes in violation of the truce. Soviet accounts affirm that when Gnechko attempted to sail into Kataoka Bay on the morning of 20 August, he was shelled by shore batteries and straffed by aircraft.[52]

Regardless of where the truth lay, at 1200 hours on 20 August, Gnechko ordered the 128th Aviation Division to conduct a heavy bombing raid on Kataoka and Kasivabara. In groups of 12 to 17 aircraft, the division's bombers and fighters struck Kataoka and Kasivabara from 1300 to 1900 hours. To save time, because of the cloud cover, the bombing was conducted at altitudes of from 6,650 to 8,200 feet (2,000 to 2,500 meters).

During the day on 20 August, D'iakov's 101st Rifle Division advanced 3.1–3.7 miles (5–6 kilometers) against heavy Japanese resistance, by day's end reaching positions from the mouth of the Mori-Gava River to the lake 2.5 miles (4 kilometers) west of Hill 125.9, where it ran into prepared and occupied Japanese defenses. While advancing, D'iakov paid particular attention to his left flank, opposite which the Japanese were concentrating reserves, while he prepared to assault Japanese defenses at Kataoka.

At 0700 hours on 21 August, a representative of Gnechko's headquarters personally handed Tsutsumi another set of demands that he and his forces surrender immediately, noting, 'My conditions concerning the capitulation of your forces, which were accepted and signed from your side by Colonel Ianaoka Takedzi, are not being carried out.'[53] At 2140 hours on 21 August, Tsutsumi finally accepted Gnechko's proposal, agreeing to cease combat operations, lay down their weapons, and surrender.[54] Japanese-based accounts confirm the details of Tsutsumi's surrender:

By 21 August the Japanese had little choice but to capitulate unconditionally. Sapporo directed Tsutsumi that morning in no uncertain terms to put himself at the invader's mercy. Accordingly, the commander of the Ninety-first Division signed a final ceasefire agreement in the afternoon and instructed his troops to disarm themselves and await internment. The two remaining aircraft, however, escaped to Hokkaido, where their pilots brought Japan news of the north Kurils' fate.[55]

On 22 and 23 August, Gnechko's forces disarmed a total of 14,800 Japanese soldiers on Shumshir Island, capturing more than 6,000 weapons of various types.[56]

THE CAPTURE OF THE CENTRAL AND SOUTHERN PORTION OF THE KURIL ISLANDS

Between 22 and 28 August, a forward detachment of the Kamchatka Defensive Region landed on and occupied all of the islands in the northern and central portions of the Kuril Island chain southward to Urup Island. Transported by sea, the Kamchatka Defensive Region's forward detachment captured and accepted the surrender of Japanese forces on Onnekotan Island at 1200 hours on 25 August, Matau Island on 26 August, and Urup Island on 29 August. With the landing at Urup Island on 29 August, Soviet forces occupied the entire north half of the Kuril Island chain.

Over a week before, on 23 August, the Pacific Fleet ordered Andreev's Northern Flotilla and Zakharov's 113th Rifle Brigade to seize the southern half of the Kuril Island chain, in particular, the islands of Etorofu (Iturup) and Kunashiri (Kunashir). At that time conditions for the seizure of the islands seemed favorable since the Japanese had lost almost all of southern Sakhalin and the northern Kurils. Furthermore, the Japanese fleet was decimated and inactive in the entire region, and bad weather prevented the few Japanese aircraft in the region from operating.

Andreev assigned the mission of capturing the southern Kurils to a naval infantry detachment commanded by Captain 1st Rank A. I. Leonov. At the time Leonov's detachment, which consisted of three naval infantry battalions, numbering 1,600 men, was *en route* to Odomari from Maoka. After arriving at Odomari on 24 August and participating in its capture, Leonov's detachment regrouped and set sail for the southern Kurils with two naval infantry companies transported by two trawlers.[57]

At 0515 hours on 28 August, Leonov's small task force approached Rubetsu Bay on the western coast of Etorofu (Iturup) Island and halted in the roadstead 749 feet (228 meters) from the shore. The first wave of naval infantry and a small number of sailors landed on small boats with the mission of locating other boats with which to conduct the landing. Five minutes later the sailors commandeered five Japanese self-propelled barges, which the task force used to accelerate the amphibious landing. When the Japanese offered no resistance, a small party consisting of one company of naval infantry landed, met Japanese officials, but asked for assistance when they learned that the Japanese garrison, which wished to surrender, numbered 13,500 men. Leonov then landed the entire detachment and accepted the surrender, while the ships provided security from the sea.[58]

One of Leonov's two naval infantry companies boarded trawler *T-590* on 31 August with orders to sail to Kunashiri Island to accept the surrender of its garrison. Leonov's small force arrived at Furefu (Furukammappa) Bay at 0600 hours on 1 September, landed 30 minutes later, and immediately accepted the surrender of the Japanese garrison on Kunashiri. On the same day, another small task force of the Northern Pacific Flotilla landed subunits of Zakharov's 113th Rifle Brigade on the islands of Kunashiri and Shukotan, just to the east. Within days, the 355th Rifle Division of the 1st Far Eastern Front's 87th Rifle Corps also landed troops on Etorofu and Urup Islands, two rifle regiments and its artillery regiment on the former and one rifle regiment and one artillery battalion on the latter.[59]

Early on 2 September, the Pacific Fleet ordered Andreev's flotilla to occupy the islands of the Lesser Kuril chain, which lay off the northern shore of the Japanese Home Island of Hokkaido. Andreev assigned the task to Captain 3d Rank Chicherin, who formed two groups of ships, each with one trawler and one assault boat, with elements of the 113th Rifle Brigade, to fulfill the mission. The first group was to seize the islands of Suisio-Shima, Iuri-Shima, and Akiiuri-Shima, and the second, Taraku-Shima, Sibetsu-Shima, and Harakura-Shima.

Zakharov detailed one platoon each of submachine gunners to occupy

Taraku-Shima and Suisio-Shima, one rifle platoon each to garrison Sibetsu-Shima and Iuri-Shima, and a reinforced rifle company to occupy Akiiuri-Shima. He decided to simply comb the rest of the islands and take prisoners. Zakharov's brigade occupied all of the islands in the Lesser Kurils between 3 and 5 September.

During the operations to clear Japanese forces from the northern Kuril Islands, Gnechko's amphibious forces captured 30,442 Japanese soldiers, 20,108 rifles, 932 machine guns, 303 guns and mortars, and 60 tanks. During the ensuing five days, Soviet forces captured another 24,000 Japanese.[60] The 2d Far Eastern Front's official report that Purkaev dispatched to Vasilevsky announcing the completion of the Kuril operation stated that his forces had captured 89,831 soldiers, 1,702 officers, 16 generals, and one vice admiral for a total of 91,550 men.[61]

Soviet losses during the Kuril Island operation remain in dispute. The Pacific Fleet's official report on the Battle for Shumshir indicates that Gnechko's force suffered 674 casualties out of over 8,800 men engaged. This figure included 290 irrecoverable losses, including 167 killed or mortally wounded and 123 missing in action and 384 wounded.[62] Given the ferocity of the fighting, this number seems far too low.

Japanese sources indicate that Soviet losses were far higher:

As 18 August ended, both sides were nursing their wounds. Some 8,000 Russians held a precarious foothold on Shumshu but had neither reduced the surrounding batteries nor breached the twin heights before them. Furthermore, they seemed to have incurred heavy casualties. (Soviet sources are silent on this, but Japanese sources estimate that 2,000 died coming ashore.) On the Japanese side, Tsutsumi had lost nearly all of his tanks and a third of his modest air force.[63]

Japanese sources claim that overall Soviet losses amounted to between 2,500 and 3,000 killed and a like number wounded. While this is excessive given the limited size of the Soviet amphibious force, it is quite likely that the Japanese count is closer to the truth than the Pacific Fleet's report. The same Japanese sources indicate that 614 of Tsutsumi's men perished in the fighting.[64] Whichever account is more correct, although brief, the fight for Shumshir was one of the bloodiest engagements during the Soviets' Far Eastern campaign.

CONCLUSIONS

The amphibious operations against the Kuril Islands involved transporting a force of more than 8,000 men more than 497 miles (800 kilometers) by sea with only an extremely limited number of ships. This required stringent security measures to ensure the secrecy of the preparations and subsequent sea movement. The force designated to conduct the landing had performed only defensive missions during the war and was ill prepared to launch a complex amphibious operation. This necessitated extensive training before the operation could be conducted. Furthermore, the designated landing site lacked any port facilities, therefore making it difficult to land heavy weaponry and tanks. Finally, the vital naval base at Kataoka had to be captured by a ground assault from inland rather than by a direct assault from the sea.

Although the amphibious force ultimately fulfilled its mission, it experienced considerable difficulty doing so. During the assault landing itself, these difficulties included poor or non-existent reconnaissance of Japanese defenses, inadequate fire support for the forward detachment and main force's first echelon, and serious disruption of command and control due to a lack of radio communications. After landing, the main force failed to form and employ assault groups with which to attack the Japanese fortified positions on Hill 170.7, permitting the Japanese to reinforce the positions and inflict heavier than expected casualties on Soviet forces. Throughout the operation logistical support was poor, particularly regarding ammunition, because of poor prior planning and the absence of the required number of ships and boats.[65]

The classified Soviet critique provides the most candid assessment of the operation's achievements and shortcomings:

The success of the combat operations of Shumshir Island was achieved as the result of:
- the correct selection of the axes for the joint efforts of the ground forces and naval forces. The successful operations on Shumshir Island pre-determined the destruction of the Japanese main grouping and led directly to the capture of this island – the main position of the entire defense on the Kuril Islands;
- the correct selection of the form of the operation and the most appropriate conditions: surprise and a massive blow along one axis while observing all means of secrecy;
- coordinated operations by ground, naval, and air forces during the period of landing;
- the surprise landing of the forward detachment, which in no little way contributed to the selection of the time to begin the operation (at right) and the selection of the landing region that only light forces were defending, all contributed to the rapid development of success until the enemy's main forces approached from Kataoka;
- the decisive actions of the forward detachment, whose penetration into the depth of the enemy defense and seizure of the beachhead was necessary for the landing of the first echelon; and

306

- the excellent political-morale state of our troops and, by virtue of this, the heroic actions of the subunits and individual soldiers and officers.

Together with this, it is necessary to note that a series of important mistakes were committed during the conduct of the amphibious assault operation.

1. During the time of landing, the 101st Rifle Division's command and control was not near his forces and was improperly organized. Experience persistently requires that the regimental commander and his staff land right after the regiment's lead battalion (immediately following the first echelon regiment). The division commander should have landed immediately after the division's first echelon or simultaneously with it. The regiment and division commanders' means of command and control must be landed earlier so that the observation posts of these commanders can be deployed ahead of time.

2. Our radio stations were not protected by appropriate packing (waterproof bags), and, as a result, the greater portion of them were damaged by water and were out of order for a long time during the moment of crisis in the battle. Furthermore, experience indicates the necessity for specially outfitted radio stations for amphibious assault operations in whatever theater they are conducted.

3. The placing of a great number of radio stations on one ship (the headquarters of the Kamchatka Defensive Region) hindered their work and made command and control difficult. Experience repeatedly confirmed the necessity for the dispersed distribution of radio stations when commanding and controlling operations with ships.

4. The amphibious assault was not provided with a sufficient quantity of unloading equipment (especially for heavy guns and tractors) and floating landing equipment when the landing from the transports was taking place in the conditions of an open roadstead, and, as a result, the landing of personnel and the unloading of equipment was conducted with great delays. As a consequence, the artillery could not participate in combat on the first day of battle (the decisive day of the operation). The absence of the artillery and the clearly inadequate reconnaissance information about the enemy was the main cause of our forces' excessive losses during the landing on the coast. Experience confirms that the provision of floating landing and unloading equipment must be carefully thought out when organizing an amphibious assault operation.[66]

Despite these problems, the combined ground forces of Gnechko's Kamchatka Defensive Region and the ships and naval infantry of Ponomarev's Petropavlovsk Naval Base were able to overcome Japanese defenses and capture the entire northern section of the Kuril Island chain. They did so by taking a strategic gamble that was based in part of the expectation that Japanese capitulation was imminent. Their expectation was correct. As a result, the Soviet Union took possession of the largely barren but strategically vital Kuril Islands.

NOTES

1. This description of the terrain incorporates material from, 'Kuril'skaia desantnaia operatsiia' [The Kuril amphibious operation] in *Sbornik takticheskikh materialov po opytu Otechestvennoi voiny*, No. 22 [Collection of tactical materials on the experience of the Patriotic War, No. 22] (Moscow: Voenizdat, 1947), 67–8. Prepared by the Directorate for the study of war experience of the General Staff of the Soviet Union's Armed Forces and classified secret. See also Bagrov, *Iuzhno-sakhalinskaia i kuril'skaia*, 17–20.
2. John Stephan, *The Kuril Islands* (Oxford: Oxford University Press, 1976), 140–1.
3. Bagrov, *Iuzhno-sakhalinskaia*, 12.
4. 'Kuril'skaia desantnaia operatsiia', 66–7.
5. Ibid., 67.
6. Zakharov *et al.*, *Krasnoznamennyi*, 233.
7. 'Kuril'skaia desantnaia operatsiia', 66.
8. Bagrov, *Iuzhno-sakhalinskaia*, 38.
9. Stephan, *The Kuril Islands*, 162.
10. Vnotchenko, *Pobeda*, 297.
11. Bagrov, *Iuzhno-sakhalinskaia*, 43.
12. 'Kuril'skaia desantnaia operatsiia', 70, and Vnotchenko, *Pobeda*, 297.
13. 'Kuril'skaia desantnaia operatsiia', 70.
14. Vnotchenko, *Pobeda*, 298, and Zakharov *et al.*, *Krasnoznamennyi*, 234, claim that the naval force numbered 64 ships, including 14 transport ships, 16 assault boats, two self-propelled barges, four *Kawasaki* cutters, eight coastal cutters, four trawlers, two cutter-trawlers, the minelayer *Okhotsk*, and the coastal ships *Dzerzhinsky* and *Kirov* to transport, land, and support the amphibious force. This figure probably includes ships added after the first landings.
15. Vnotchenko, *Pobeda*, 298.
16. 'Kuril'skaia desantnaia operatsiia', 71.
17. Ibid., 45.
18. 'Kuril'skaia desantnaia operatsiia', 75.
19. Ibid.
20. Ibid. This classified account is the most candid version of all phases of the operation.
21. Ibid., 76.
22. Ibid.
23. Bagrov, *Iuzhno-sakhalinskaia*, 86. The first four boats were the amphibious boats Nos. 1, 3, 8, and 9.
24. 'Kuril'skaia desantnaia operatsiia', 76.
25. Bagrov, *Iuzhno-sakhalinskaia*, 90.
26. The official classified account, 'Kuril'skaia desantnaia operatsiia', refers to the forward detachment's initial objective as Hill 170.7. Vnotchenko, *Pobeda*, and other unclassified accounts refer to this hill as 171 and associate it with Hill 165, which was located one kilometer to the south. To complicate matters, the Pacific Fleet's official after-action-report refers to Hill 170.7 as Hill 171.2. This study refers to the Hill as 170.7, which includes Hill 165 as well.

27. Bagrov, *Iuzhno-sakhalinskaia*, 96.
28. Vnotchenko, *Pobeda*, 299, claims that the Japanese employed tanks in the defenses, stating: 'Worse still for the attackers, the Japanese began counterattacking with tanks and infantry, but were driven back after losing 15 tanks to Soviet naval gunfire.' The classified after-action reports, however, do not substantiate this claim.
29. Bagrov, *Iuzhno-sakhalinskaia*, 97.
30. Stephan, *The Kuril Islands*, 153.
31. 'Kuril'skaia desantnaia operatsiia', 77.
32. Vnotchenko, *Pobeda*, 299.
33. 'Kuril'skaia desantnaia operatsiia', 77.
34. Ibid.
35. Stephan, *The Kuril Islands*, 163.
36. Vnotchenko, *Pobeda*, 300.
37. Stephan, *The Kuril Islands*, 164.
38. 'Kuril'skaia desantnaia operatsiia', 78, and Bagrov, *Iuzhno-sakhalinskaia*, 98.
39. A. V. Zolotarev, *Russkii arkhiv: Velikaia Otechestvennaia. Sovetsko–iaponskaia voina 1945 goda: Istoriia voenno-politicheskogo protivoborstva dvukh derzhav v 30-40-e gody: Dokumenty i materially v 2 t.*, T. 18 (7–2) [The Russian archives. The Great Patriotic: The Soviet–Japanese War of 1945: A military-political history of the struggle between two powers in the 30s and 40s: Documents and materials in two volumes, Vol. 18 (7–2)] (Moscow: 'Terra', 2000), 30. Note that Vnotchenko and the Far Eastern Military District's 1947 report on the action refer to Hill 170.7 as Hill 171.2. However, the General Staff study entitled 'Kuril'skaia desantnaia operatsiia', is the more recent and hence more accurate account.
40. Bagrov, *Iuzhno-sakhalinskaia*, 99.
41. 'Kuril'skaia desantnaia operatsiia', 79.
42. Ibid.
43. Ibid., 80.
44. Stephan, *The Kuril Islands*, 164.
45. 'Kuril'skaia desantnaia operatsiia', 80.
46. Ibid., 81.
47. Ibid.
48. Ibid.
49. Ibid. For full text, see Zolotarev, *Russkii arkhiv*, T-2, 31.
50. 'Kuril'skaia desantnaia operatsiia', 81.
51. Ibid.
52. Stephan, *The Kuril Islands*, 164–5.
53. Zolotarev, *Russkii arkhiv*, T-2, 31.
54. 'Kuril'skaia desantnaia operatsiia', 82.
55. Stephan, *The Kuril Islands*, 164.
56. Zolotarev, *Russkii arkhiv*, T-2, 32.
57. Ibid.
58. Ibid., 33.
59. Zolotarev, *Russkii arkhiv*, T-2, 46. Earlier, the Far Eastern Command had ordered the 1st Far Eastern Front's 87th Rifle Corps to cooperate with the Northern Pacific Flotilla in mounting an operation to seize Hokkaido Island. However, due in part to the delay in deploying the 87th Rifle Corps to southern Sakhalin and the time it took for the rifle corps to complete the occupation of southern Sakhalin as well as political considerations, Stalin called off the Hokkaido operation. Thereafter, the 87th Rifle Corps assisted in occupying the Kuril Islands.
60. Vnotchenko, *Pobeda*, 301.

61. Zolotarev, *Russkii arkhiv*, T-2, 48.
62. Ibic., 34.
63. Stephan, *The Kuril Islands*, 164.
64. Ibid, 165.
65. For details, see 'Kuril'skaia desantnaia operatsiia', 83.
66. Ibid , 62–3.

11

Conclusions

GENERAL

The Soviet Far East Command's strategic offensive in Manchuria was nothing less than a full-fledged post-graduate exercise for the Red Army. As such, it represented the culmination of a prolonged, arduous, and devastatingly costly education that began on a tragic Sunday morning on 22 June 1941 and ended in the rubble of Berlin in May 1945. An imposing colossus on the eve of war, within days after German Operation Barbarossa began, the world realized the Red Army was a paper colossus with feet of clay. Only after 18 months of a grueling education in deadly combat was the Red Army capable of coping with the *Wehrmacht* in battle; it would take another six months to establish its superiority, and almost two years more before the Red Army vanquished Hitler's legions in their lair, ending Hitler's prospective 1,000-year *Reich*.

In short, it took four years of war and over 10 million dead for the Red Army to develop the strategy and associated operational and tactical techniques that it displayed so effectively and in such deadly fashion in Manchuria. The way that it fought at the strategic, operational, and tactical levels in Manchuria vividly indicated how far the Red Army had come since 1941. These ten case studies demonstrate that careful and detailed planning and imaginative and flexible execution of those plans were the keys to rapid Soviet victory in the campaign.

Soviet planners and commanders had to meet three challenges to achieve victory in Manchuria as Stalin defined it: first, defeat the Kwantung Army in record time, second, surmount formidable terrain obstacles, and third, preempt or overcome Japanese resistance. By meeting the first two challenges successfully, they fulfilled the prerequisites for accomplishing the third. Fortunately, Japanese defensive plans and force dispositions played into Soviet hands. Essentially, the Far East Command achieved absolute victory by 16 August, an astonishingly brief period of seven days. By doing so, Soviet planners exceeded their offensive timetable by three weeks, suffered light casualties, and overwhelmed the Kwantung Army.

Why the Soviet victory? In reality, ultimate Soviet victory was inevitable. The preponderance of Soviet forces, the Red Army's superior weaponry, training, and extensive combat experience, the crumbling Japanese strategic defenses in the Pacific theater, the United States' devastating bombing offensive against Japan (in particular, the use of the atomic bomb), and the weakened state of the Kwantung Army all spelled doom for Japan. The question then becomes, 'Why did the Soviet victory come so quickly?' While it is rather easy to attribute Soviet victory in Manchuria to Japanese weakness and lack of fighting will, these are oversimplifications that mask other more cogent reasons for the quick Japanese defeat. In fact, the Far East Command's strategy and the Red Army's operational and tactical techniques were the most important reasons why the Kwantung Army collapsed so rapidly.

Soviet military planners expected a difficult campaign in Manchuria and prepared accordingly by formulating a bold strategic plan designed to avoid or overcome many of those difficulties. These planners knew and respected the Kwantung Army because the Red Army had fought it in 1938 and 1939, and they also understood the personal courage, skill, and bravery of the Japanese soldier. Even their knowledge that the Kwantung Army was a shell of its former self did not materially lessen that respect. Even though Soviet planners were quite familiar with Japanese defensive plans, they both overassessed Japanese military strength in some of the border regions and feared a tenacious final Japanese 'last stand' in the fabled redoubt area of southern Manchuria.

Based on these assumptions, and perhaps misperceptions as well, the Far East Command's offensive plan required Red Army forces to penetrate quickly into the central Manchurian plain, preempt Japanese defenses, chop up Japanese forces, and defeat them in piecemeal fashion before they could consolidate in the redoubt region. To do so required a conscious Soviet decision to launch its offensive along multiple axes, across seemingly impassable terrain, in as rapid a fashion as possible. When they did so, even Soviet commanders were astonished at their own success.

EXPLOITATION OF TERRAIN

When planning the Manchurian offensive, the Red Army General Staff and the Far East Command well understood that mastering Manchuria's difficult terrain was vital for the achievement of victory in the region. Therefore, they formulated their plans and configured their forces to take maximum advantage of this terrain. Assuming that they could gain as much advantage by operating across seemingly impassable terrain that the Japanese chose not to defend as they could by attacking across defended, so-called high-speed avenues of approach, they deployed their forces so as to exploit virtually every axis of advance into Manchuria, whether good or bad. The Soviets were correct in this assumption.

By carefully tailoring each and every one of their combat forces with the support necessary to overcome specific terrain problems, the Far East Command's three operating *fronts* were able to operate successfully along virtually every axis of advance into Manchuria. At one extreme of the spectrum, in the 1st Far Eastern Front's sector, the 5th Army's heavy compliment of artillery, armor, and engineers enabled Krylov's forces to overcome strong Japanese fortifications constructed in heavily wooded terrain astride the best axes of advance into eastern Manchuria. Krylov's employment of carefully tailored assault groups and mobile forward detachments allowed his forces to smash, isolate, and bypass the formidable Japanese fortifications in record time and then dash rapidly into the Japanese depths and preempt an effective subsequent Japanese defense.

In the same *front*, Beloborodov's 1st Red Banner Army employed skillfully tailored march–column formations to penetrate 12.4 miles (20 kilometers) of mountainous and heavily forested but lightly defended terrain. Building roads as they advanced, Beloborodov's forces easily brushed aside token Japanese resistance and emerged in the Japanese operational rear area after advancing only 18 hours. While doing so, Beloborodov proved the utility of armor forces even in such challenging terrain.

In the 1st Far Eastern Front's sector north of Lake Khanka, Zakhvataev's small 35th Army launched its assault with two rifle divisions across a major river and through miles of seemingly impenetrable marshland. Even though his armor faltered in the swamps, Zakhvataev's imaginative employment of engineers enabled the two rifle divisions to cross the marshes and emerge intact astride the important Japanese communications route from Mishan to Hutou, deep in the Japanese rear area.

In the Trans-Baikal Front's sector in western Manchuria, Liudnikov's 39th Army confounded Japanese military planners by thrusting two full rifle corps, led by a tank division and two tank brigades, through the supposedly roadless and impassable Grand Khingan Mountains. While the bulk of Liudnikov's army burst into the rear of the surprised Japanese force, a single rifle division isolated and neutralized the only formidable fortified Japanese defenses in western Manchuria.

Along the Sungari River in the 2d Far Eastern Front's sector, Mamonov's 15th Army conducted joint operations with the Amur River Naval Flotilla, in the process traversing more than 124 miles (200 kilometers) of swamp and marshland by conducting a series of amphibious assaults coordinated with the simultaneous advance of a ground force.

On Sakhalin Island, Cheremisov's 16th Army and Andreev's Northern Pacific Naval Flotilla resorted to joint operations to overcome Japanese defenses. Even in the 56th Rifle Corps' sector on Sakhalin Island, where terrain was exceedingly restrictive, D'iakonov's forces were able to employ tactical maneuver extensively to defeat the Japanese defenders of the Koton Fortified Region. The skillfully orchestrated multiple amphibious assaults at Toro and Maoka also succeeded, even though stubborn Japanese resistance and logistical difficulties delayed the progress of Soviet forces.

In the Kuril Islands, too, the scratch Soviet forces deployed by Gnechko's Kamchatka Defensive Region and Ponomarev's Petropavlovsk Naval Base were able to overcome the strong Japanese fortress on rocky and barren Shumshir Island and capture the remainder of the northern Kuril Islands by exploiting the element of surprise, even though Japanese resistance proved more effective than anticipated.

While dramatic successes in their own right, the Sakhalin and Kuril offensives contributed to the only major Soviet failure during its Far Eastern campaign; namely, the unsuccessful attempt to seize a foothold on the Japanese Home Island of Hokkaido. However, while the stout Japanese defense of Sakhalin and the Kuril Islands clearly disrupted the Soviet timetable for capturing Hokkaido, political rather than military reasons probably prompted Stalin's decision to abort the Hokkaido amphibious landing.

In all of these cases, Soviet planners tailored their forces in accordance with the terrain and the nature of defending Japanese forces. While some armies were heavy and consisted of multiple rifle corps and massive quantities of artillery and armor, others were small and contained only a few rifle divisions and rifle brigades. In all instances, however, each force was assigned the requisite quantity of artillery, armor, and engineer support necessary to fulfill its mission successfully. In each and every case, opposing Japanese commanders were astonished at the Soviets' flexibility and, most important, their ability to advance over terrain the Japanese considered impassable for major military forces.

SURPRISE

One of the most important reasons why the Red Army was able to achieve victory in Manchuria so quickly was its ability to achieve surprise. While the Far East Command achieved strategic surprise over the Japanese by employing an elaborate deception plan, it also achieved operational and tactical surprise. By definition, a force can achieve surprise by choosing unexpected attack axes, employing unique attack forms and formations, and by exploiting darkness and bad weather to conceal the form and intent of an attack. The Soviets exploited all of these opportunities in Manchuria.

First, the Red Army deliberately and systematically operated across terrain the Japanese believed was unsuited for the conduct of large- or even small-scale military operations. Strategically, the Far East Command committed

Malinovsky's Trans-Baikal Front to combat in a region over which the Japanese believed an army, to say nothing of a full *front*, could not operate. Operationally, all of the Far East Command's *fronts* employed full armies in regions where the Japanese thought only light forces could operate. The passage of Liudnikov's 39th Army across the Grand Khingans, the advance by Beloborodov's 1st Red Banner Army through the Pogranichnaia Mountains in eastern Manchuria, and the advance, albeit slow, of Zakhvataev's 35th Army through the swamps and marshes north of Lake Khanka all capitalized on Japanese misconceptions concerning the Red Army's capability to exploit unfavorable terrain.

On numerous occasions, Soviet forces also surprised the defending Japanese forces at the tactical level. For example, the rifle corps and rifle divisions of Krylov's 5th Army rendered the strong Japanese fortified defenses at and around Suifenho utterly superfluous by maneuvering through the dense forests and rugged hills on their flanks. The rifle divisions of Beloborodov's 1st Red Banner Army advanced surreptitiously through a sector the Japanese left virtually undefended except for scattered security outposts. The divisions of Zakhvataev's 35th Army did the same when they negotiated the swamps north of Lake Khanka, and, with significant naval support, the rifle divisions of Mamonov's 15th Army steamed and marched up the Sungari River to Chiamussu. In all of these cases, the Japanese were simply unprepared to deal with such unexpected large-scale attacks. The attacks deprived the Japanese of any initiative and prevented them from regaining it throughout the remainder of the offensive.

The Far East Command also surprised the Japanese by the form of its offensive. Since they were expecting Soviet forces to penetrate and reduce their defenses by frontal assaults, the Japanese were utterly unprepared to cope with the Soviets' extensive employment of enveloping maneuvers and deep exploitation operations. The tactical envelopment of Japanese fortified defenses at Suifenho by Krylov's 5th Army and the armor-led deep thrusts toward Mutanchiang that followed, the flanking maneuver to bypass the Hutou fortress by Zakhvataev's 35th Army, and the amphibious envelopment of Japanese forces forward of Chiamussu by Mamonov's 15th Army completely confounded the respective Japanese commands. In western Manchuria, the operational envelopment of the few Japanese fortified regions by Liudnikov's 39th Army preempted and collapsed Japanese defenses in the west in record time.

The Far East Command also surprised the Japanese by violating Japanese stereotypes regarding how the Red Army structured and echeloned its forces for combat. Rather than adhering rigidly to two-echelon operational and tactical formations, the Soviets flexibly tailored their armies, rifle corps, and rifle divisions to match the strength and configuration of Japanese forces, the nature of the terrain, and their forces' assigned missions and objectives.

While Krylov formed his 5th Army into two echelons of rifle corps, rifle divisions, and rifle regiments, Beloborodov organized his 1st Red Banner Army into a single echelon of rifle corps. Zakhvataev's 35th Army attacked in a single echelon with three rifle divisions abreast, as did Mamonov's 15th Army along the Amur River. Both Luchinsky and Liudnikov deployed their 36th and 39th Armies in a single echelon of rifle corps. Compounding the confusion generated by these varied echelonment patterns among the Japanese defenders, many of the attacking Soviet armies entered combat from the march in pre-combat march-column formation (for example, the 39th Army, 6th Guards Tank Army, and Soviet–Mongolian Cavalry-Mechanized group).

All other factors aside, the Soviets' timing of the offensive most surprised the Kwantung Army. As early as May 1945, the *Stavka* had selected mid-August as the most propitious time to begin the campaign. It did so in part because of the amount of time necessary to regroup the requisite forces to Manchuria and, in part, because August was the final month of the rainy season when frequent heavy thunderstorms and rains inundated Manchuria and caused extensive heavy flooding. While the monsoon weather would produce difficult conditions in which to launch the offensive, it would also help conceal attack preparations and reinforce existing Japanese complacency. When the *Stavka* accelerated its offensive timetable by setting 9 August as the attack date, it only increased the degree of surprise.

The deliberate Soviet exploitation of inclement weather and darkness had a devastating effect on the Japanese. Surprise was total, and many Japanese defensive positions fell to the Soviet troops without any struggle. The forward and intermediate Japanese defensive lines crumbled, and the defenders were never able to recover from the surprise sufficiently to regroup and establish new defenses. Soviet critiques consider the achievement and exploitation of surprise as one of the most important lessons of the Manchurian campaign.

MANEUVER

In all aspects of their strategic, operational, and tactical planning, the Far East Command and its three subordinate *fronts* strove to employ combat techniques suited to the successful conduct of deep operations, which it believed were essential to the achievement of quick victory. The most important of these techniques were the conduct of extensive maneuver at all levels of command, the task-organization (or tailoring) of forces to suit them to perform their assigned missions, and what Soviet theorists call 'strengthening the blow' [*narashchivanie sil*], meaning steadily increasing the application of military power by means of time-phased commitment of forces to battle. Collectively, these techniques sought not only to defeat the Japanese but also to overcome terrain obstacles and beat the clock. In retrospect, the terrain and time requirements proved to be even more formidable and vexing problems for the Soviets to master than Japanese armed resistance.

Throughout the operation, but particularly during its initial stages, Soviet commanders maneuvered their forces on a large scale and at every level of command, seeking to envelop, isolate, and bypass Japanese forces. To do so more effectively, tank forces spearheaded the advance in most operational sectors. At the highest level, the forces of Malinovsky's Trans-Baikal and Meretskov's 1st Far Eastern Fronts conducted a broad strategic envelopment of the entire Kwantung Army. Armies, rifle corps, and even rifle divisions also relied on envelopment maneuvers. For example, in regions that the Japanese only lightly defended, Soviet forces enveloped those defensive positions with tank-heavy forward detachments, which then led the pursuit deep into the Japanese rear area.

Liudnikov employed this technique when his 39th Army enveloped and bypassed the Halung-Arshaan Fortified Region, as did Luchinsky's 36th Army when its advance swept eastward past Hailar. In those instances where Soviet forces faced more difficult terrain, such as in the sectors of Beloborodov's 1st Red Banner and Zakhvataev's 35th Army, they conducted the same enveloping maneuvers, only at a slower pace. Even where Japanese resistance was the heaviest, such as in the sector of Krylov's 5th Army, assault groups and advanced battalions relied on maneuver to envelop Japanese strong points and fortified regions to more limited depths into the Japanese defenses. In some cases, such as along the Sungari River, on southern Sakhalin, and in the Kurils, amphibious assault forces performed the same envelopment function, this time by river and sea.

After successfully enveloping Japanese forces, Soviet forces wasted little time in reducing isolated or bypassed enemy strong points. Instead, they simply continued their pursuit deep into the Japanese rear areas, usually relying on tank-heavy forward detachments to spearhead their pursuit. These determined pursuits generated high offensive momentum and prevented the Japanese from erecting new lines to the rear. The Kwantung Army's usually disjointed and always ineffective efforts to stem the Soviet juggernaut also produced total paralysis in the Japanese command and control system.

FLEXIBLE TASK ORGANIZATION FOR COMBAT

To a considerable extent, the Soviet commands were able to maneuver effectively because they carefully task-organized their forces at every level of command so that each force could better accomplish its assigned mission. For example, at the lowest level, the Soviets formed small platoon- to company-size assault groups consisting of infantry, sappers, artillery, and armor to engage and destroy specific Japanese strong points. These small combined-arms tactical groups dealt effectively with Japanese strong points and fortified positions during the initial stage of the campaign (the 5th Army for example) and during its later stages, when the Soviets reduced bypassed fortified regions such as Hutou and Hailar (the 35th and 36th Armies).

Once the assault groups had accomplished their work, the Soviets employed advanced battalions, which were also task-organized with sapper, armor, and artillery support, to lead the advance of Soviet main force divisions and corps. So organized, these advance battalions were better able to cope with enemy resistance and terrain challenges in their specific sectors. For example, the advanced battalions in the 5th Army differed significantly from those operating in the 1st Red Banner, 35th, or 15th Armies' sectors primarily due to terrain considerations and the strength of Japanese defenses. Finally, main force divisions and their parent rifle corps also contained those combined-arms elements, primarily armor, artillery, and engineers, necessary for them to perform their missions.

Above and beyond these line forces, Soviet commands formed and employed numerous forward detachments at every command level either to initiate the attack or to lead the subsequent pursuit. As a rule, tank battalions or tank brigades formed the nucleus for forward detachments. Around this armored core, Soviet commanders added truck-mounted motorized infantry, sappers, antiaircraft, antitank, and artillery subunits to form unique mini task forces, each of which was capable of conducting semi-independent or, for a brief time, even independent operations.

In general, the parent force's mission and the nature of the terrain through which it had to operate dictated the size and composition of each forward detachment. For example, because the 39th Army's objectives were so deep and the enemy's defenses in its sector were so fragmented, Liudnikov allocated a full tank division to serve as the army's forward detachment. At lower levels in his army, the rifle corps led their advance with tank brigades, and the rifle divisions with reinforced self-propelled artillery battalions. Some divisions, such as those in Beloborodov's 1st Red Banner Army, employed rifle battalions reinforced by tanks and sappers as forward detachments.

Elsewhere Luchinsky's 36th Army used a forward detachment formed around the nucleus of the 205th Tank Brigade to lead its advance to Hailar, and Beloborodov's 1st Red Banner Army employed the 257th Tank Brigade to spearhead his drive to Pamientung. In general, the use of carefully task-organized shock groups, advanced battalions, and forward detachments permitted Red Army forces to reduce Japanese defenses by a combination of fire and maneuver, rather than by massed and costly infantry assault.

TIME-PHASED COMMITMENT OF FORCES TO COMBAT

Soviet forces achieved much of their combat success, particularly during the initial stages of the offensive, by committing their task-organized forces into combat in carefully time-phased fashion to strengthen the attack as they were delivering it. For example, Krylov's 5th Army began its attack with small reconnaissance units, and followed by committing to combat tailored assault groups from the first echelon rifle divisions' advanced battalions. After the advanced battalions had exploited the assault groups' success, the lead rifle divisions' first echelon rifle regiments joined battle. Zakhvataev's 35th Army led its attack with reconnaissance detachments and border guards units, followed by the rifle divisions' advanced battalions and main force regiments. The troops of Beloborodov's 1st Red Banner Army inched forward through the dense forests led by small, road-building forward detachments at the head of each advancing regimental column. Follow-on regimental columns widened the roads as they advanced, adding momentum to the army's advance. The rifle division of Liudnikov's 39th Army advanced in pre-combat march formation with an army forward detachment (a tank division) in front, followed successively by the rifle corps' forward detachments (tank brigades), the rifle divisions' forward detachments (self-propelled artillery regiments), and the divisions' main forces also marching in columns.

This time-phased commitment of forces permitted Soviet army and *front* commanders to build up combat power along each axis steadily and project that power inexorably forward into the depths of the Japanese defenses. Rather than smashing the Japanese defenses by wave after wave of assaulting troops, the Soviets shattered and broke up the defenses by projecting forces forward along hundreds of separate axes. The unrelenting pressure on the entire Japanese front, coupled with forces knifing into, between, around, and through Japanese forces, collapsed the entire Japanese defensive structure. In many respects, these assaults resembled infiltration tactics conducted on a massive scale. The resultant intermingling of forces and Soviet forces operating deep in the Japanese rear area along so many axes produced wholesale confusion among the Japanese defenders.

As illustrated by these ten case studies, the operational and tactical techniques the Red Army employed in August 1945 illustrate how much the Red Army had learned in four years of intense war. Contrary to stereotypical Western views of the Red Army, they also reveal an imaginative and flexible Soviet approach to the conduct of war. Like their Soviet predecessors, Russian military analysts still study the Manchurian campaign in great detail. So did the United States Army officer corps, so much so that they honored the memory of 'August Storm' by naming their lightning 1991 war against Iraq 'Operation Desert Storm'.

319

Appendix 1: Soviet Documents on the Sakhalin Operation Combat

Order of the 2d Far Eastern Commander to the 16th Army Commander on An Offensive with the Mission of Capturing the Southern Part of Sakhalin Island

0030 hours 10 August 1945

I ORDER:

1. On the morning of 11 August 1945, the 56th Rifle Corps will launch an offensive with the overall mission of clearing the Japanese from Southern Sakhalin; the 56th Rifle Corps immediate mission is to capture the towns of Sikiga, Sikuka, and Nairo with mobile (tank) units no later than 12 August.

2. I am allowing you to transfer two separate tank battalions from the Aleksancrovsk region to the Anorsk axis.

3. Present to me copies of all orders given.

Purkaev
Leonov
Shevchenko

Source: A. V. Zolotarev, *Russkii arkhiv: Velikaia Otechestvennaia. Sovetsko-iaponskaia voina 1945 goda: Istoriia voenno-politicheskogo protivoborstva dvukh derzhav v 30-40-e gody: Dokumenty i materially v 2 t.,* T. 18 (7-2) [The Russian archives. The Great Patriotic: The Soviet–Japanese War of 1945: A military-political history of the struggle between two powers in the 30s and 40s: Documents and materials in two volumes, Vol. 18 (7-2)] (Moscow: 'Terra', 2000), 7.

Combat Report of the 56th Rifle Corps Commander to the 16th Army Commander Concerning the Capture of Koton

1816 hours 16 August 1945

Having launched an offensive in difficult mountainous, forested, and swampy conditions on 11 August, after overcoming the security belt and destroying three strongly fortified company strong points in it by an enveloping maneuver in the flanks and rear, on 16 August the 56th Rifle Corps, in cooperation with aviation, penetrated the strongly fortified enemy position north of Koton (the Haramitog Fortified Region), and, having destroyed the enemy's broken-up strong point in piecemeal fashion, captured the town of station of Koton. As a result of the heavy fighting in the roadless, almost impassible, mountainous, forested, and swampy region, the corps' forces smashed the enemy 125th Infantry Regiment, captured and destroyed 66 permanent ferro–concrete fortifications, and several warehouses. Prisoners and trophies were captured, which I am determining more precisely. I am continuing the attack in the direction of Kiton.

I present to you for government award: Major General V. A. Baturov, Lieutenant Colonel Timirgaleeva, Lieutenant Colonel Kudriavtsev, Lieutenant Colonel Kurmanov, Captain Zaitsev, and Major Tregubenko. I request you permit me to present the remaining list.

D'iakonov

Source: A. V. Zolotarev, *Russkii arkhiv: Velikaia Otechestvennaia. Sovetsko-iaponskaia voina 1945 goda: Istoriia voenno-politicheskogo protivoborstva dvukh derzhav v 30-40-e gody: Dokumenty i materially v 2 t.,* T. 18 (7-2) [The Russian archives. The Great Patriotic: The Soviet–Japanese War of 1945: A military-political history of the struggle between two powers in the 30s and 40s: Documents and materials in two volumes, Vol. 18 (7-2)] (Moscow: 'Terra', 2000), 7–8.

Report by the Chief of Staff of the High Commander of Forces in the Far East to the Chief of the Red Army General Staff Concerning the Cessation of Combat Operations on Sakhalin Island

25 August 1945

In connection with the fact that, in broadcasts on 25 August, Japanese radio (Tokyo) reported that, in spite of the absence of resistance, Soviet aviation and forces are continuing combat operations on Sakhalin Island, the High Command ordered us to report to you about the actual situation on Sakhalin.

Contrary to the assurances of General Hata, the chief of staff of the

Kwantung Army, to all intents and purposes Japanese resistance on Sakhalin Island just ceased at day's end on 23 August.

The attempts by the 113th Rifle Brigade's units to advance from Maoka to Futomata were being repelled by enemy fire until late evening on 22 August, where 19 men were killed and 65 wounded.

Twice, the brigade was forced by the enemy to withdraw, after losing 219 men killed and 680 wounded just on 22 and 23 August.

There were no combat operations beginning on 24 August 1945.

Ivanov

Source: A V. Zolotarev, *Russkii arkhiv: Velikaia Otechestvennaia. Sovetsko-iaponskaia voina 1945 goda: Istoriia voenno-politicheskogo protivoborstva dvukh derzhav v 30-40-e gody: Dokumenty i materially v 2 t.,* T. 18 (7-2) [The Russian archives. The Great Patriotic: The Soviet–Japanese War of 1945: A military-political history of the struggle between two powers in the 30s and 40s: Documents and materials in two volumes, Vol. 18 (7-2)] (Moscow: 'Terra', 2000), 19.

Combat Report of the 2d Far Eastern Front Commander to the High Commander of Soviet Forces in the Far East Concerning the Completion of the Liberation of the Southern Part of Sakhalin Island

0500 hours 25 August 1945

I am reporting that the 113th Rifle Brigade occupied the port of Otomari [Odomari] on the night of 24–25 August. The naval amphibious assault from the Sovetskaia Gavan' Naval Base landed in Otomari at 0600 hours on 25 August.

Air assaults seized Toyohara and Otiai at 1740 hours on 24 August.

The army commander and his operational group will transfer to Toyohara by 1500 hours on 25 August.

The mission, which You assigned, regarding the occupation of Southern Sakhalin has been carried out ahead of time.

Purkaev
Lukashin
Shevchenko

Source: A. V. Zolotarev, *Russkii arkhiv: Velikaia Otechestvennaia. Sovetsko-iaponskaia voina 1945 goda: Istoriia voenno-politicheskogo protivoborstva dvukh derzhav v 30-40-e gody: Dokumenty i materially v 2 t.,* T. 18 (7-2) [The Russian archives. The Great Patriotic: The Soviet–Japanese War of 1945: A military-political history of the struggle between two powers in the 30s and 40s: Documents and materials in two volumes, Vol. 18 (7-2)] (Moscow: 'Terra', 2000), 22.

Political Report of the Chief of the 16th Army's Political Department to the Member of the Military Council of the High Command of Soviet Forces in the Far East Concerning the Course of Capitulation of Japanese Forces on Sakhalin Island

26 August 1945

I am reporting that, during 23 August, the army's units and formations operating on Sakhalin are continuing their movement to the south. The forward detachments have pushed forward and occupied Monguntoma and Mongui.

The Japanese are blowing up roads and bridges and setting fire to towns and villages as they retreat. As a rule, the local population in all population points are being taken away or fleeing into the mountains. In some towns, in particular Nairo, population remains, but only male. A part of the soldiers and officers have disguised themselves, thrown away their weapons, torn off their rank insignia, and are posing as civilian population.

During interrogations, the soldiers and officers state that they have been ordered to cease all military operations and offer no resistance.

On 23 August the army commander received a representative and the chief of staff of the 88th Infantry Division, Colonel Suzuki, who stated the demands of the Japanese command on Sakhalin.

1. All officers of the surrendering units of the Japanese Army on Sakhalin are to keep their side arms.

2. Do not use the term 'prisoner' for the surrendering Japanese forces.

3. Allow the Japanese officers to live together with their families.

4. Isolate the Korean population [living on southern Sakhalin] from the Japanese.

Major General Cheremisov, the 16th Army commander, gave no such promises, but instead proposed they lay down their weapons and turn over all personnel, arms, and other military equipment according to the document by 1500 hours on 25 August.

Colonel Suzuki agreed to report to the command and requested to extend the period to 27 August so that the Japanese Army command could surrender all of his force's units and subunits in timely fashion.

I am reporting that the political and morale state of our forces is completely healthy. The personnel are burning with one desire – to occupy all of Southern Sakhalin as fast as possible.

The Party-political apparatus and the formations' political organs are guaranteeing the fulfillment of the orders of the 2d Far Eastern Front commander by their work. They are conducting their work in the safeguarding of high combat readiness and Bolshevik vigilance and the correct treatment of the civilian population, and are permitting no instances of improper behavior.

The chief of the 16th Army's Political Department, Shmelev

Source: L. V. Zolotarev, Russkii arkhiv: Velikaia Otechestvennaia. Sovetsko-iaponskaia voina 1945 goda: Istoriia voenno-politicheskogo protivoborstva dvukh derzhav v 30-40-e gody: Dokumenty i materially v 2 t., T. 18 (7-2) [The Russian archives. The Great Patriotic: The Soviet–Japanese War of 1945: A military-political history of the struggle between two powers in the 30s and 40s: Documents and materials in two volumes, Vol. 18 (7-2)] Moscow: 'Terra', 2000), 20.

Political Report of the Chief of the 16th Army's Political Department to the Member of the Military Council of the High Command of Soviet Forces in the Far East Concerning the Completion of the Capture of the Southern Part of Sakhalin Island

26 August 1945

The army's forward units completed the occupation of Southern Sakhalin on 25 August. The remnants of the 88th Infantry Division's units are continuing to lay down their weapons and be taken prisoner. The 79th Rifle Division's 157th Rifle Regimen is at Toyohara, and the division's remaining units are moving. Part of the 214th Tank Brigade's force is in Otoma-i, and the remainder is moving.

The 2d Separate Rifle Brigade is at Nairo and Sikuka. The 113th Rifle Brigade's 14th Separate Rifle Battalion is at Osaka, the 2d Separate Rifle Battalion at Toyohara, the 1st Separate Rifle Battalion is moving from Rudaka to Otomari [Odomari], and the 3d Separate Rifle Battalion is at Rudaka. The army's headquarters command post is at Toyohara.

Today we received an order from the 2d Far Eastern Front commander, which pointed out that units of the 1st Far Eastern Front's 87th Rifle Corps are replacing the southern units along the Nedo–Saka–Ehama line. The ma n administrative-economic command and control organ (direction of the railroad, post, telegraph, bank, etc.) is located in Toyohara. Therefore, one *oblast'* [region] has been divided into two parts with forces subordinate to two *fronts*, and this can produce difficulties and confusion in command and con rol and the establishing of a firm occupation regime.

A train carrying the 79th Rifle Division derailed at 1530 hours on 25 August: two were killed and ten wounded, and, on the night of 25 August, a captured cutter sank. I cleared up the derailment and also established movement along the railroad greater than 15 kilometers [per hour] only with the compulsory [use of] a controlling locomotive. I demanded increased vigilance and suspiciousness on the part of party organizations and demanded they explain to all personnel that, in spite of the erection of red and white flags that indicate the present desires of the Japanese to fulfill our demands, they are capable of the most insidious tricks of sabotage. The mood of the personnel is completely healthy and cheerful despite the difficult conditions of the march, since in some sectors the road is completely impassible for a distance of 5–10 kilometers [3.1–6.2 miles], and the personnel have to carry all of their equipment by hand.

Shmelev

Source: A. V. Zolotarev, *Russkii arkhiv: Velikaia Otechestvennaia. Sovetsko-iaponskaia voina 1945 goda: Istoriia voenno-politicheskogo protivoborstva dvukh derzhav v 30-40-e gody: Dokumenty i materially v 2 t.*, T. 18 (7-2) [The Russian archives. The Great Patriotic: The Soviet–Japanese War of 1945: A military-political history of the struggle between two powers in the 30s and 40s: Documents and materials in two volumes, Vol. 18 (7-2)] (Moscow: 'Terra', 2000), 21.

Report by the Pacific Fleet Headquarters to the Headquarters of the High Commander of Soviet Forces in the Far East Concerning the Completion of the Transfer of the 87th Rifle Corps to Sakhalin Island

12 September 1945

The unloading of the 264th Rifle Division's last regiment on Sakhalin Island was completed at 1900 hours on 1 September 1945. Thus, the transfer of the 87th Rifle Corps to Sakhalin Island is fully completed.

Frolov

Source: A. V. Zolotarev, *Russkii arkhiv: Velikaia Otechestvennaia. Sovetsko-iaponskaia voina 1945 goda: Istoriia voenno-politicheskogo protivoborstva dvukh derzhav v 30-40-e gody: Dokumenty i materially v 2 t.*, T. 18 (7-2) [The Russian archives. The Great Patriotic: The Soviet–Japanese War of 1945: A military-political history of the struggle between two powers in the 30s and 40s: Documents and materials in two volumes, Vol. 18 (7-2)] (Moscow: 'Terra', 2000), 23.

Appendix 2: Soviet Documents on the Kuril Amphibious Assault Operation

Warning Order from the 2d Far Eastern Front Commander to the Commander of the Kamchatka Defensive Region on the Conduct of an Operation to Capture the Islands in the Kuril Chain – Shumshu, Paramushir, and Onekotan

0430 hours 15 August 1945

The capitulation of Japan is expected. Exploiting the favorable situation, it is necessary to occupy the islands of Shumshir (Shumshu), Paramoshiri (Paramushir), and Onnekotan (Onekotan).

I am entrusting the operation to you personally. Your deputy is Captain 1st Rank Ponomarev, the commander of the Petropavlovsk Naval Base. The forces are two regiments of the 101st Rifle Division, all of the base's ships and naval equipment, available ships from the cargo fleet, border guard forces, and the 128th Aviation Division. Have two–three companies of naval infantry from the Petropavlovsk Naval Base ready to employ as a forward detachment. Immediately begin preparing shipping [floating means] and the rifle forces for loading and creating the naval infantry detachment after reinforcing the sailors with an automatic weapons battalion. Prepare radio equipment and establish reliable communications with me and with the Petropavlovsk Base during the passage and while conducting the operation.

Confirm receipt.

Purkaev
Leonov
Shevchenko

Source: A. V. Zolotarev, *Russkii arkhiv: Velikaia Otechestvennaia. Sovetsko-iaponskaia voina 1945 goda: Istoriia voenno-politicheskogo protivoborstva dvukh derzhav v 30-40-e gody: Dokumenty i materially v 2 t.*, T. 18 (7-2) [The Russian archives. The Great

Patriotic: The Soviet–Japanese War of 1945: A military–political history of the struggle between two powers in the 30s and 40s: Documents and materials in two volumes, Vol. 18 (7-2)] (Moscow: 'Terra', 2000), 24.

Order of the 2d Far Eastern Front Commander to the Commander of the Kamchatka Defensive Region Concerning the Completion of the Occupation of the Islands of Shumshu, Paramushir, and Onekotan

20 August 1945

I ORDER:

Complete the occupation [of Shumshu], and disarm and capture Japanese forces on Shumshu, Paramushir, and Onekotan Islands no later than 2000 hours on 20 August 1945 with the 101st Rifle Division (less one rifle regiment).

Establish the headquarters of the 101st Rifle Division at Kataoka.

Feed the prisoners in accordance with Japanese ration norms at the expense of local Japanese resources.

Confirm receipt.

Purkaev
Leonov
Shevchenko

Source: A. V. Zolotarev, *Russkii arkhiv: Velikaia Otechestvennaia. Sovetsko-iaponskaia voina 1945 goda: Istoriia voenno-politicheskogo protivoborstva dvukh derzhav v 30-40-e gody: Dokumenty i materially v 2 t.*, T. 18 (7-2) [The Russian archives. The Great Patriotic: The Soviet–Japanese War of 1945: A military–political history of the struggle between two powers in the 30s and 40s: Documents and materials in two volumes, Vol. 18 (7-2)] (Moscow: 'Terra', 2000), 40–1.

Directive Order of the 2d Far Eastern Front to the Commander of the Kamchatka Defensive Region Concerning the Occupation of the Northern Islands in the Kuril Chain

20 August 1945

Your immediate mission is to occupy the islands of Shumshir and Paramushir completely and, subsequently, occupy all islands to Simushir (Simusiru-To) inclusively, while occupying with garrisons all islands on which Japanese garrisons are located. Complete the occupation by 25 August 1945.

Purkaev
Leonov
Shevchenko

Source: A. V. Zolotarev, *Russkii arkhiv: Velikaia Otechestvennaia. Sovetsko-iaponskaia voina 1945 goda: Istoriia voenno-politicheskogo protivoborstva dvukh derzhav v 30-40-e gody: D•kumenty i materially v 2 t.*, T. 18 (7-2) [The Russian archives. The Great Patriotic⌐ The Soviet–Japanese War of 1945: A military-political history of the struggle between two powers in the 30s and 40s: Documents and materials in two volumes, Vol. 18 (7-2)⌐ (Moscow: 'Terra', 2000), 41.

Report of the Pacific Fleet Commander to the High Commander of Soviet Forces in the Far East Concerning the Capitulation of Japanese Forces on Shumshu Island

20 August 1945

According to a report from the commander of the Petropavlovsk Naval Base and the commander of the Kamchatka Defensive Region, the Japanese forces on Shumshu Island began laying down their weapons at 1900 hours on 19 August 1945. At 0800 hours on 20 August 1945, General Suchimo Ivava, the commander of the 73d Infantry Brigade, and the chief of staf of the group of forces on the Kuril chain signed the conditions of capitulation.

Amphibious assaults are being prepared for landing on the other islands.

The amphibious assault forces fought for Shumshu Island, which was exceptionally fortified, with exceptional heroism.

The unloading of artillery and combat equipment is continuing.

The Commander of the Pacific Fleet, Iumashev
The Member of the Pacific Fleet's Military Council, Zakharov

Source: A. V. Zolotarev, *Russkii arkhiv: Velikaia Otechestvennaia. Sovetsko-iaponskaia voina 1945 goda: Istoriia voenno-politicheskogo protivoborstva dvukh derzhav v 30-40-e gody: Dokumenty i materially v 2 t.*, T. 18 (7-2) [The Russian archives. The Great Patriotic: The Soviet–Japanese War of 1945: A military-political history of the struggle between two powers in the 30s and 40s: Documents and materials in two volumes, Vol. 18 (7-2)] (Moscow: 'Terra', 2000), 41.

Combat Report of the 2d Far Eastern Front Commander to the High Commander of Soviet Forces in the Far East Concerning the Course of the Capitulation on Shumshu Island

2154 hours 22 August 1945

I am reporting that the Japanese on Shumshu Island began to lay down their weapons at 1400 hours on 22 August 1945.

To this end, I have assigned representatives of the Kamchatka

Defensive Region headed by Lieutenant Colonel Voronov, the Kamchatka Defensive Region's chief of staff.
I will report results additionally.

Purkaev

Leonov

Shevchenko

Source: A. V. Zolotarev, *Russkii arkhiv: Velikaia Otechestvennaia. Sovetsko-iaponskaia voina 1945 goda: Istoriia voenno-politicheskogo protivoborstva dvukh derzhav v 30-40-e gody: Dokumenty i materially v 2 t.,* T. 18 (7-2) [The Russian archives. The Great Patriotic: The Soviet–Japanese War of 1945: A military-political history of the struggle between two powers in the 30s and 40s: Documents and materials in two volumes, Vol. 18 (7-2)] (Moscow: 'Terra', 2000), 43.

Combat Report of the 2d Far Eastern Front Commander to the High Commander of Soviet Forces in the Far East Concerning the Course of the Amphibious Assault on the Kuril Islands

2220 hours 23 August 1945

The forces of the Kamchatka Defensive Region, under the command of Major General Comrade Gnechko, occupied the ports of Kataoka and Kasivabara and cleared the island of Shumshu and the northeastern part of the island of Paramushir at 1700 hours on 23 August 1945.

Purkaev

Leonov

Shevchenko

Source: A. V. Zolotarev, *Russkii arkhiv: Velikaia Otechestvennaia. Sovetsko-iaponskaia voina 1945 goda: Istoriia voenno-politicheskogo protivoborstva dvukh derzhav v 30-40-e gody: Dokumenty i materially v 2 t.,* T. 18 (7-2) [The Russian archives. The Great Patriotic: The Soviet–Japanese War of 1945: A military-political history of the struggle between two powers in the 30s and 40s: Documents and materials in two volumes, Vol. 18 (7-2)] (Moscow: 'Terra', 2000), 44.

Report by the High Commander of Soviet Forces in the Far East to the *Stavka* of the Supreme High Command Concerning the Situation in the Zone of the Kuril Islands and on Sakhalin Island

23 August 1945

I am reporting on the situation at 1200 hours on 23 August 1945 (Far Eastern time) in the zone of the Kuril Islands and Sakhalin Island.

In accordance with my demands announced through General Hata, by order of the Japanese Main Headquarters, the massive capitulation of Japanese forces on the northern half of the Kuril Islands has begun on the morning of 23 August. Japanese Lieutenant General Tsutsumi Fusaki, the commander of the defense of this part of the islands, is directing the capitulation. Upon the confirmation of our plan, the island of Shumshir and the northern half of Paramushir Island must be occupied fully during 24 August, the southern half of Paramushir on 24 August, and the group of small islands located immediately south of Paramushir Island on 25 August.

According to General Tsutsumi, all of the up to 16,000 Japanese soldiers and officers will be transferred to us here.

Today, during a meeting at 1500 hours between our General Gnechko and Japanese General Tsutsumi, I clarified the intentions of the commander of the Japanese defenses in the southern part of the Kuril Islands, and I presented him with a demand for immediate capitulation. According to General Hata, the Japanese forces here have also received orders to capitulate.

Simultaneously, this morning the Pacific Fleet's aircraft, together with those of the 1st Far Eastern Front, are conducting reconnaissance of the southern part of the Kuril Islands with the mission of establishing communications with the commander of the defense and discussing with him the capitulation.

Beginning on the morning 23 August, trawlers of the Pacific Fleet are investigating the sea approaches to these islands. On the night of 24 August, the Pacific Fleet command will send a group of combat ships with an assault force to the islands. When the first two rifle divisions of the 87th Rifle Corps approach Sakhalin Island, one of them will be sent to fortify the southern islands for us. In addition, the preparations for the operation to occupy these islands by force are continuing by all possible means.

On Sakhalin Island the main force of the Japanese 88th Infantry Division in the southern part of the island is capitulating today. I assigned Purkaev the categorical mission to complete clearing all of the islands by the morning of 25 August.

After the final occupation of Sakhalin Island and when the 1st Far Eastern Front's 87th Rifle Corps approaches its southern part, the demarcation line between the 1st and 2d Far Eastern Fronts will pass several kilometers north of the port Maoka–Toyohara line so that Meretskov's forces can prepare for subsequent operations on the southern part of Sakhalin or, relying on it, firmly consolidate the southern part of the Kuril Island chain.

I will begin the operation against Hokkaido only in accordance with Your additional order, and before that time, not a single vessel will sail.

In accordance with Your orders concerning the necessity for firmly consolidating our positions in the Kuril Islands and having appropriate forces in the immediate vicinity of the La Perouse Strait on the southern part of Sakhalin Island, I consider it expedient to conduct the following regrouping of the ground forces, aviation, and ships of the Pacific Fleet in the nearest future.

1. On the Kuril Islands, after their final capture, have the 101st Rifle Division, two separate rifle regiments, and two artillery regiments in the northern part from Shumshu Island to Simushir inclusive. Subsequently, my intent is to send one additional antiaircraft artillery battalion to this area. At first, all of these forces will be subordinate to the commander of the 2d Far Eastern Front's Kamchatka Defensive Region.

One rifle division from the 1st Far Eastern Front's 87th Rifle Corps and one rifle brigade with appropriate ground and antiaircraft artillery will occupy the southern part of the Kuril Islands from Simushir Island (exclusive) to Kunashir Island (inclusive). These forces will be subordinated through the 87th Rifle Corps commander to the commander of the 35th Army, whose headquarters I have in mind to transfer to the southern part of Sakhalin.

At first, the ground forces indicated above will cooperate with aircraft based on Kamchatka and Sakhalin Island until such time as the opportunity appears to re-base them in part on the Kuril Islands.

2. At present, I am beginning the transfer of the 255th Rifle Division and the 145th Gun Artillery Regiment from the 2d Far Eastern Front through Komsomol'sk and Sovetskaia Gavan' and further by sea to reinforce the Kamchatka peninsula.

I will reinforce the existing aircraft on the Kamchatka peninsula, which consists of the 128th Mixed Aviation Division (two fighter regiments of 70 'King Cobra' aircraft and one bomber regiment with 30 'Bastion' ['Flying Fortress'] aircraft), by transferring the 53d Bomber Aviation Division with 80 Il-4 aircraft from the 1st Far Eastern Front. To control this aviation, I consider it expedient to transfer the headquarters of the 18th Aviation Corps to Kamchatka. In addition, after an inspection of the airfield on Paramushir Island, we will transfer the mixed aviation division ('Air Cobras', 'Flying Fortresses', and 'Catalinas') from the Pacific Fleet.

Additionally, we have directed ships of the Pacific Fleet's line to Kamchatka in order to have a division of torpedo cutters (12), a brigade of escort ships (15 ships, counting 6 arriving from America), and a brigade of submarines (12 boats) there by 1 September 1945.

3. We believe it necessary to have [the following] on Sakhalin: in its northern half one rifle division, one rifle brigade, one separate rifle regiment, one separate rifle battalion, one separate tank brigade, one separate tank battalion, and one RGK artillery regiment from the 2d Far Eastern Front; and on the southern half, two rifle divisions with the 87th Rifle

Corps' headquarters, one rifle brigade, two GGK artillery regiments, and the 35th Army's headquarters from the 1st Far Eastern Front.

Additionally, from aviation forces, we will send the 6th [Aviation] Corps of Tu-2s (the 334th and 326th Aviation Divisions) and the 190th Fighter Division, all from the Trans-Baikal Front, to the 255th Mixed Aviation Division, which is already there. At first, we will entrust the commander of the 6th Aviation Corps with the control the air force units indicated.

4. The 3d Mechanized Corps of Comrade Obukhov and the 126th Mountain Rifle Corps, which are arriving in the Far East [Command], are being sent to the Coastal Region of the 1st Far Eastern Front, the former to the Voroshilov region and the latter to the Chuguevka region.

5. We request you approve these measures.

Vasilevsky

Shikin

Ivanov

Source: A. V. Zolotarev, *Russkii arkhiv: Velikaia Otechestvennaia. Sovetsko-iaponskaia voina 1945 goda: Istoriia voenno-politicheskogo protivoborstva dvukh derzhav v 30-40-e gody: Dokumenty i materially v 2 t.,* T. 18 (7-2) [The Russian archives. The Great Patriotic: The Soviet–Japanese War of 1945: A military-political history of the struggle between two powers in the 30s and 40s: Documents and materials in two volumes, Vol. 18 (7-2)] (Moscow: 'Terra', 2000), 44–5.

Telegram from the 1st Far Eastern Front Commander to the Pacific Fleet Commander Concerning Joint Operations for the Transfer of the 87th Rifle Corps' 355th Rifle Division to the Southern Kuril Islands

28 August 1945

1. Since you consider it impossible at present to transfer the 264th Rifle Division from Ol'ga Bay through the La Perouse Strait to the region of the southern Kuril chain, I request you send transport to the Otomari region by the morning of 3 September 1945 for the loading and transfer of the 87th Rifle Corps' 355th Rifle Division to the Kuril Islands. The division will move from the Maoka region to the Otomari region on foot.

2. During the transfer of the 355th Rifle Division to the region of the Kuril Islands, I request you have in mind sending two regiments of the 355th Rifle Division to Iturup (Etoforu) Island and one regiment to Kunashir Island.

3. I request you report on your decision, the beginning of the transfer, and the landing of the 355th Rifle Division on the islands of Iturup and Kunashir.

Meretskov

Shtykov

Krutikov

Source: A. V. Zolotarev, *Russkii arkhiv: Velikaia Otechestvennaia. Sovetsko-iaponskaia voina 1945 goda: Istoriia voenno-politicheskogo protivoborstva dvukh derzhav v 30-40-e gody: Dokumenty i materially v 2 t.*, T. 18 (7-2) [The Russian archives. The Great Patriotic: The Soviet–Japanese War of 1945: A military-political history of the struggle between two powers in the 30s and 40s: Documents and materials in two volumes, Vol. 18 (7-2)] (Moscow: 'Terra', 2000), 46.

Order of the 1st Far Eastern Front Commander to the 87th Rifle Corps Commander Concerning the Transfer of his Forces to the Kuril Islands

2230 hours 29 August 1945

I ORDER you to accelerate the loading of the 113th Rifle Brigade and the 355th Rifle Division on transports and their transfer to the Kuril Islands in every way possible.

To that end:

1. Assemble the 113th Rifle Brigade in the Otomari [Odomari] region during the first half of 30 August and load it on transports during the second half of 30 August and dispatch it for the occupation of Kunashir Island and Shikotan Island.

The 113th Rifle Brigade will occupy and firmly consolidate on these islands.

2. Bring the 355th Rifle Division to the Otomari region on 1 September by forced march, load it on transports on the night of 2 September, and dispatch it to occupy Iturup and Urup Islands.

Land two regiments, the artillery regiment (less one battalion), and the headquarters on Iturup Island and one rifle regiment and an artillery battalion on Urup Island.

The 355th Rifle Division will occupy and consolidate on these islands.

Report receipt and fulfillment.

Meretskov
Shtykov
Krutikov

Source: A. V. Zolotarev, *Russkii arkhiv: Velikaia Otechestvennaia. Sovetsko-iaponskaia voina 1945 goda: Istoriia voenno-politicheskogo protivoborstva dvukh derzhav v 30-40-e gody: Dokumenty i materially v 2 t.*, T. 18 (7-2) [The Russian archives. The Great Patriotic: The Soviet–Japanese War of 1945: A military-political history of the struggle between two powers in the 30s and 40s: Documents and materials in two volumes, Vol. 18 (7-2)] (Moscow: 'Terra', 2000), 46.

Report of the 2d Far Eastern Front Commander to the High Commander of Soviet Forces in the Far East Concerning the Occupation of the Northern and Central Islands of the Kuril Chain

30 August 1945

Your order concerning the occupation of the Kuril Islands by the forces of the 2d Far Eastern Front from Simushir to Urup (inclusive) by 1200 hours on 30 August 1945 has been carried out.

The landing of separate units with supplies on the islands of Urup has been completed.

Purkaev
Leonov
Shevchenko

Source: A. V. Zolotarev, *Russkii arkhiv: Velikaia Otechestvennaia. Sovetsko–iaponskaia voina 1945 goda: Istoriia voenno-politicheskogo protivoborstva dvukh derzhav v 30-40-e gody: Dokumenty i materially v 2 t.,* T. 18 (7-2) [The Russian archives. The Great Patriotic: The Soviet–Japanese War of 1945: A military-political history of the struggle between two powers in the 30s and 40s: Documents and materials in two volumes, Vol. 18 (7-2)] (Moscow: 'Terra', 2000), 47.

Report of the Pacific Fleet Commander to the High Commander of Soviet Forces in the Far East about the Capitulation of Enemy Forces on Iturup Island

30 August 1945

I am reporting that, according to a report by Captain 1st Rank Leonov, who landed on Iturup Island, the island's garrison's of more than 10,000 men under the command of a lieutenant-general laid down its weapons at 1430 hours on 30 August 1945.

Iumashev

Source: A. V. Zolotarev, *Russkii arkhiv: Velikaia Otechestvennaia. Sovetsko–iaponskaia voina 1945 goda: Istoriia voenno-politicheskogo protivoborstva dvukh derzhav v 30-40-e gody: Dokumenty i materially v 2 t.,* T. 18 (7-2) [The Russian archives. The Great Patriotic: The Soviet–Japanese War of 1945: A military-political history of the struggle between two powers in the 30s and 40s: Documents and materials in two volumes, Vol. 18 (7-2)] (Moscow: 'Terra', 2000), 47.

Combat Report of the 2d Far Eastern Front's Military Council to the High Commander of Soviet Forces in the Far East Concerning the Completion of the Operation to Capture the Kuril Islands

30 August 1945

1. The *front's* forces completed the amphibious assault landings on the islands of Uruppu (Urup), Simushir, and Ketoi with the amphibious assault units of the Kamchatka Defensive Region on 30 August 1945.

In Manchuria, the *front's* forces are continuing to prepare units to withdraw to the territory of the USSR and withdraw RGK artillery units to the state border. The forces on Sakhalin Island are dispersing to the points where they will be permanently stationed.

2. The *Kamchatka Defensive Region* – During the day, the reinforced assault detachment of the 302d Rifle Regiment (less one rifle battalion) landed an assault force of one reinforced rifle battalion on the northeastern part of Uruppu (Urup) and one reinforced rifle battalion in Simusiri-Van Bay (Sinsiru Bay in the southeastern part of Simushir). An assault by border guards in the strength of one border detachment landed on Ketoi Island. With the landing of amphibious assaults on these islands, the Kamchatka Defensive Region's operation to occupy the Kuril Islands – and the islands of the Kuril chain – has been completed. Two regiments of the 255th Rifle Division began loading on transports in the port of Sovetskaia Gavan' on the morning of 30 August, and the remaining units are following by rail between Komsomol'sk and Sovetskaia Gavan'.

3. The *Northern Pacific Flotilla (NPF)* – The amphibious assault detachment of the NPF, which landed on Etorofu (Iturup) Island (Kuril Island), is continuing to disarm the enemy. According to NPF data, the 3,600-man garrison on the island has surrendered. The weapons concealed by the Japanese and the shells, bullets, and different equipment have been handed over and destroyed. A detachment of sailors has landed on Cape Nisi-Iotoro-Misaki (at the La Perouse Strait) on Sakhalin Island with the mission of organizing observation posts and communications. There was no resistance.

Information about losses, prisoners, and trophies as of 29 August 1945.

While securing *front's* rear area, NKVD forces lost one killed and four wounded in combat with separate groups of concealed Japanese.

During the course of 29 August 1945, 592 soldiers, 15 officers, one rear-admiral (the representative of the Naval Fleet for Supplying Southern Sakhalin, Rear Admiral Kuraki Goiti – Japanese) were disarmed and taken prisoner.

All told, from 9 through 29 August inclusively, 89,831 soldiers, 1,702 officers, 16 generals, and one rear admiral have been captured. Trophies through 29 August include 117 horses, 13 grenade launchers, five guns, 68 machine guns, 2,766 rifles, 61,000 bullets, 128 bicycles, 22 vehicles, one tractor, one cutter, 5 locomotives, 11 food warehouses, 6 quartermaster warehouses, and 1 artillery warehouse. Overall, trophies seized from 9 through 29 August include 646 horses and 2,000 seized earlier (see Report No. 15) for a total of 2,646, 239 grenade launchers, 196 guns, 48,124 rifles, 1,923 machine guns, 364,000 bullets, 130 bicycles, 182 vehicles, 4 tractors, 25 cutters, 38 locomotives, 43 food warehouses, 10 quartermaster warehouses, and 10 artillery warehouses. Information on remaining types of trophies has not changed. We are continuing to calculate prisoners and trophies.

Conclusions:

1. The operations by the *front's* forces to capture the Kuril Islands has been completed.

2. The *front's* forces are continuing to prepare units to return to the USSR.

Purkaev
Leonov
Shevchenko

Source: A. V. Zolotarev, *Russkii arkhiv: Velikaia Otechestvennaia. Sovetsko-iaponskaia voina 1945 goda: Istoriia voenno-politicheskogo protivoborstva dvukh derzhav v 30-40-e gody: Dokumenty i materially v 2 t.*, T. 18 (7-2) [The Russian archives. The Great Patriotic: The Soviet–Japanese War of 1945: A military-political history of the struggle between two powers in the 30s and 40s: Documents and materials in two volumes, Vol. 18 (7-2)] (Moscow: 'Terra', 2000), 48.

Report by the Pacific Fleet's Chief of Staff to the Chief of Staff of the High Command of Soviet Forces in the Far East Concerning the Landing of an Amphibious Assault on Kunashir Island

1 September 1945

At 0600 hours on 1 September 1945, a group of sailors landed in the Furukama and Seseki regions on Kunashir Island. There was no resistance.

We are landing a reinforced automatic weapons battalion of the 113th Rifle Brigade.

Frolov

Source: A. V. Zolotarev, *Russkii arkhiv: Velikaia Otechestvennaia. Sovetsko-iaponskaia voina 1945 goda: Istoriia voenno-politicheskogo protivoborstva dvukh derzhav v 30-40-e gody: Dokumenty i materially v 2 t.*, T. 18 (7-2) [The Russian archives. The Great Patriotic: The Soviet–Japanese War of 1945: A military-political history of the struggle between two powers in the 30s and 40s: Documents and materials in two volumes, Vol. 18 (7-2)] (Moscow: 'Terra', 2000), 48.

Instructions of the 2d Far Eastern Front Commander to the Commander of the Kamchatka Defensive Region Concerning the Dispositions of Soviet Forces on the Kuril Islands

5 September 1945

1. I approve the disposition of the Kamchatka Defensive Region's forces on the Kuril Islands, as presented to me in No. 391.NShCh dated 3 September 1945:

(a) 302d Rifle Regiment (minus 2d Rifle Battalion) with the 2d Battalion, 279th Artillery Regiment – Matsuva (Matau) Island.

(b) One rifle company, 2d Battalion, 302d Rifle Regiment – Siasikotan (Shiaskotan) Island.

(c) One rifle platoon, 302d Rifle Regiment – Kharumukotan (Kharinkotan) Island.

(d) 2d Battalion, 302d Rifle Regiment (minus the 2d Battalion) with one battery, 279th Artillery Regiment – Onekotan Island.

(e) 373d Rifle Regiment and 279th Artillery Regiment (less the 2d Battalion) – southwestern part of Paramushir Island.

(f) 968th Rifle Regiment, 367th Separate Artillery Battalion, and 183d Separate Antiaircraft Artillery Battalion – northeastern part of Paramushir Island (Kasivabara and Bandzio-Saki).

(g) 101st Rifle Division headquarters, training battalion and specialized units – Kasivabara.

(h) 133d Rifle Regiment, 32d Tank Brigade, 428th Howitzer Artillery Regiment, 169th Antitank Regiment, 123d Separate Artillery Battalion, and 1589th Antiaircraft Artillery Division – Siumusio (Shumshir).

(i) 7th Separate Rifle Battalion – Cape Lopatka.

(j) 5th Separate Rifle Battalion and 362d Separate Artillery Battalion – Ust'-Kamchatka.

(k) 198th Separate Rifle Regiment – Ust'-Bol'sheretsk (my directive No. 496/NShCh dated 5 September 1945).

2. Submit your decision on the disposition of forces in the Petropavlovsk-on-Kamchatka region by 10 September 1945.

Purkaev

Leonov

Shevchenko

Source: A. V. Zolotarev, *Russkii arkhiv: Velikaia Otechestvennaia. Sovetsko-iaponskaia voina 1945 goda: Istoriia voenno-politicheskogo protivoborstva dvukh derzhav v 30-40-e gody: Dokumenty i materially v 2 t.*, T. 18 (7-2) [The Russian archives. The Great

Patriotic: The Soviet–Japanese War of 1945: A military-political history of the struggle between two powers in the 30s and 40s: Documents and materials in two volumes, Vol. 18 (7-2)] (Moscow: 'Terra', 2000), 48–9.

Bibliography

Note: In bibliographical entries, *VIZh* is used to denote articles from *Voenno-istoricheskii zhurnal* [Military-historical journal].

PRIMARY SOURCES

Antonov, N. A. *Nastuplenie 6-i gvardeiskoi armii v Man'chzhurskoi operatsii (avgust 1945g.)* [The 6th Guards Tank Army's offensive in the Manchurian operation (August 1945)]. Moscow: Voroshilov Academy of the General Staff, 1978.

—— *Sovetskoe voennoe iskusstvo v kampanii na Dal'nem vostoke (9 avgusta–2 sentiabria 1945 g.)* [Soviet military art in the Far East campaign (9 August–2 September 1945)]. Moscow: Voroshilov Academy of the General Staff, 1981.

Boevoi sostav Sovetskoi armii, chast' 5 (ianvar'–sentiabr' 1945 g.) [The combat composition of the Soviet Army, Part 5 (January–September 1945). Moscow: Voenizdat, 1990.

Eronin, N. V. *Strategicheskaia peregruppirovka Sovetskikh vooruzhennykh sil (pri podgotovka Dal'nevostochnoi kampanii 1945 goda* [The strategic regrouping of the Soviet armed forces (during the preparations for the 1945 Far Eastern campaign of 1945]. Moscow: Voroshilov General Staff Academy, 1980. Classified secret.

Khrenov, A. F. *Inzhenernoe obespechenie nastupatel'nykh operatsii (po opytu Volkhovskogo, Karel'skogo, 1-go i 2-go Dal'nevostochnykh i Zabaikal'skogo frontov)* [Engineer support of offensive operations (based on the experiences of the Volkhov, Karelian, 1st and 2d Far Eastern, and Trans-Baikal Fronts)]. Moscow: Voenizdat, 1952. Classified secret.

Komandovanie korpusnogo i divizionnogo zvena Sovetskikh vooruzhennykh sil perioda Velikoi Otechestvennoi voiny 1941–1945 gg. [The commanders of the Soviet Armed Forces at the corps and division level during the Great Patriotic War 1941–1945]. Moscow: Frunze Academy, 1964. Classified secret.

'Kuril'skaia desantnaia operatsiia (po materialam Kamchatskogo oboronitel'nogo raiona)' [The Kuril amphibious operation (based on materials of the Kamchatka defensive region)] in *Sbornik takticheskikh primerov po opytu Otechestvennoi voiny*, No. 22 [Collection of tactical materials based on the experiences of the Patriotic War, No. 22]. Moscow: Voenizdat, 1947. Prepared by the Directorate for the Study of War Experience of the General Staff and classified secret.

Nastavlenie po proryvu pozitsionnoi oborony (proekt) [Instructions on the penetration of a positional defense (draft)]. Moscow: Voenizdat, 1944. Trans. Directorate of Military Intelligence, Army Headquarters, Ottawa, Canada.

Polevoi ustav Krasnoi armii 1944 [Field regulations of the Red Army 1944]. Moscow: Voenizdat, 1944. Trans. Office, Assistant Chief of Staff, G-2, General Staff, US Army, 1951.

'Proryv Kotonskogo (Kharamitogskogo) ukreplennogo raiona iapontsev na o. Sakhalin (po materialam shtaba Dal'nevostochnogo voennogo okruga)' [The penetration of the Japanese Koton (Haramitog) fortified region on Sakhalin Island (based on materials of the Far Eastern Military District)] in *Sbornik takticheskikh primerov po opytu Otechestvennoi voiny*, No. 21 *(iiul –avgust 1946 g.)* [Collection of tactical examples based on the experiences of the Patriotic War, No. 21 (July–August 1946)]. Moscow: Voenizdat, 1947. Prepared by the Directorate for the Study of War Experience of the General Staff and classified secret.

'Proryv Volynskogo ukreplennogo raiona 72-m strelkovym korpusom (po materialam 1-go Dal'nevostochnogo fronta)' [The penetration of the Volynsk fortified region by the 72d Rifle Corps (based on materials from the 1st Far Eastern Front)] in *Sbornik takticheskikh primerov po opytu Otechestvennoi voiny*, No. 21 *(iiul'–avgust 1946 g.)* [Collection of tactical examples based on the experiences of the Patriotic War, No. 21 (July–August 1946)]. Moscow: Voenizdat, 1947. Prepared by Directorate for the Study of War Experience of the General Staff and classified secret.

Shevchenko, V. N. *Problema podgotovki i vedeniia nastupatel'noi operatsii na Dal'nevostochnom TVD po opytu Man'chzhurskoi operatsii* [The problems of regrouping and the conduct of offensive operations in the Far Eastern theater of military operations based on the experiences of the Manchurian operation]. Moscow: Voroshilov Academy of the General Staff, 1988.

Tsygankov, P. Ia. *Osobennosti voennogo iskusstva Sovetskikh voisk v voine protiv militaristskoi iaponii* [The features of the military art of Soviet forces in the war against militaristic Japan]. Moscow: Frunze Academy, 1980.

Zolotarev, V. A., ed. *Russkii arkhiv: Velikaia Otechestvennaia: General'nyi shtab v gody Velikoi Otechestvennoi voiny: Dokumenty i materially, 1944–1945 gg.*, T. 23 (12-4) [The Russian archives: The Great Patriotic: The General Staff in the Great Patriotic War: Documents and materials, 1944–1945),

Vol. 23 (12–14)]. Moscow: 'Terra', 2001.

——*Russkii arkhiv: Velikaia Otechestvennaia: Prikazy Narodnogo komissara oborony SSSR (1943–1945 gg,),* T. 13 (2-3) [The Russian archives: The Great Patriotic: Orders of the USSR People's Commissariat of Defense (1943–1945), Vol. 13 (2–3)]. Moscow: 'Terra', 1997.

——*Russkii arkhiv: Sovetsko–iaponskaia voina 1945 goda: Istoriia voenno-politicheskogo protivoborstva dvukh derzhav v 30-40-e gody: Dokumenty i materialy v 2 t.,* T. 18 (7–1) [The Russian archives: The Soviet–Japanese War of 1945: A military-political history of the struggle between two powers in the 30s and 40s: Documents and materials in two volumes, Vol. 18 (7–1)]. Moscow: 'Terra', 1997.

——*Russkii arkhiv: Velikaia Otechestvennaia. Sovetsko–iaponskaia voina 1945 goda: Istoriia voenno-politicheskogo protivoborstva dvukh derzhav v 30–40-e gody: Dokumenty i materially v 2 t.,* T. 18 (7–2) [The Russian archives. The Great Patriotic: The Soviet–Japanese War of 1945: A military-political history of the struggle between two powers in the 30s and 40s: Documents and materials in two volumes, Vol. 18 (7-2)]. Moscow: 'Terra', 2000.

—— *Russkii arkhiv: Velikaia Otechestvennaia: Stavka VKG: Dokumenty i materially 1944–1945,* T. 16 (4–5) [The Russian archives: The Great Patriotic: The Stavka VKG: Documents and materials 1944–1945, Vol. 16 (4-5)]. Moscow: 'Terra', 1999.

BOOKS

Akshinsky, V. *Kuril'skii desant* [The Kuril amphibious assault]. Petropavlovsk, Kamchatka: Dal'nevostochnoe knizhnoe izdat'elstvo, 1984.

Bagramian, I. Kh., ed. *Istoriia voin i voennogo iskusstva* [History of war and military art]. Moscow: Voenizdat, 1970.

—— *Voennaia istoriia* [Military history]. Moscow: Voenizdat, 1971.

Bagrov, V. N. *Iuzhno-sakhalinskaia i Kuril'skaia operatsii (avgust 1945 goda)* [The southern Sakhalin and Kuril operations (August 1945)]. Moscow: Voenizdat, 1959.

Bagrov, V. N., and N. F. Sungorkin. *Krasnoznamennaia amurskaia flotiliia* [The Red Banner Amur Flotilla]. Moscow: Voenizdat, 1976.

Beloborodov, A. *Skvoz ogon i taigu* [Through the fire and taiga]. Moscow: Voenizdat, 1969.

'Boeicho Bo-ei Kenshujo Senshishitsu' [Japan Self-defense Forces, National Defense College Military History Department]. *Senshi sosho: Kantogun (2)* [Military history series: The Kwantung Army, Vol. 2]. Tokyo: Asagumo Shinbunsha, 1974.

341

Boiko, V. R. *Bol'shoi Khingan–Port Artur* [The Grand Khingans–Port Arthur]. Moscow: Voenizdat, 1990.

Chistiakov, I. M. *Sluzhim otchizne* [In the service of the fatherland]. Moscow: Voenizdat, 1975.

Coox, A. D. *Soviet Armor in Action Against the Japanese Kwantung Army.* Baltimore, MD: Operations Research Office, Johns Hopkins University Press, 1952.

Despres, J., L. Dzirkals, and B. Whaley. *Timely Lessons of History: The Manchurian Model for Soviet Strategy.* Santa Monica, CA: Rand, 1976.

D'iakonov, A. A. *General Purkaev.* Saransk, USSR: Mordovskoe Knizhnoe Izdatel'stvo, 1971.

Feis, Herbert. *The Atomic Bomb and the End of World War II.* Princeton, NJ: Princeton University Press, 1966.

Gel'fond, G. M. *Sovetskii flot v voine s iaponiei* [The Soviet fleet in the war with Japan]. Moscow: Voenizdat, 1958.

Griaznov, B. *Marshal Zakharov.* Moscow: Voenizdat, 1979.

Grishin, I. P., *et al. Voennye sviazisty v dni voiny i mira* [Military signalmen in wartime and peacetime]. Moscow: Voenizdat, 1968.

Gusarevich, S. D., and V.B. Seoev. *Na strazhe Dal'nevostochnykh rubezhei* [At the limits of the Far Eastern borders]. Moscow: Voenizdat, 1982.

Handbook of Foreign Military Forces, Vol. 2, USSR, Pt. 1: The Soviet Army (FATM-11-10). Fort Monroe, VA: US Army Office, Chief of Army Field Forces, 1952. Restricted but re-graded to unclassified.

Hayash , Saburo, and Alvin Coox. *Kogun: The Japanese Army in the Pacific War.* Quantico, VA: Marine Corps Association, 1959.

Istoriia Ural'skogo voennogo okruga [A history of the Ural Military District]. Moscow: Voenizdat, 1970.

Istoriia vtoroi mirovoi voiny 1939–1945 [A history of the Second World War 1939–1945]. Moscow: Voenizdat, 1980.

Ivanov, S. P., ed. *Nachal'nyi period voiny* [The initial period of war]. Moscow: Voenizdat, 1974.

'Japanese Preparations for Operations in Manchuria, January 1943–August 1945', *Japanese Monograph No. 138.* Tokyo: Military History Section, US Army Forces Far East, 1953.

Kabanov, S. I. *Pole boia-bereg* [The field of battle, the coast]. Moscow: Voenizdat, 1977.

Kamalov, Kh. *Morskaia pekhota v boiakh za rodinu (1941–1946 gg.)* [Naval infantry in combat for the Homeland, 1941–1945]. Moscow: Voenizdat, 1966.

Kazakov, K. P. *Vsegda s pekhotoi, vsegda s tankami* [Always with the infantry, always with the tanks]. Moscow: Voenizdat, 1973. Trans. Leo Kanner Associates for the US Army Foreign Science and Technology Center, 6 February 1975.

Khetagurov, G. I. *Ispolnenie dolga* [Performance of duty]. Moscow: Voenizdat, 1977.

Khrenov, A. F. *Mosty k pobede* [Bridges to victory]. Moscow: Voenizdat, 1982.

Kir'ian, M. M., ed. *Fronty nastupali: Po opytu Velikoi Otechestvennoi voiny* [The *fronts* are attacking: Based on the experiences of the Great Patriotic War]. Moscow: 'Nauka', 1987.

Kovalev, I. V. *Transport v Velikoi Otechestvennoi voine (1941–1945 gg.)* [Transport in the Great Patriotic War, 1941–1945]. Moscow: 'Nauka', 1981.

Kozhevnikov, M. N. *Komandovanie i shtab VVS Sovetskoi Armii v Velikoi Otechestvennoi voine 1941–1945 gg* [The command and staff of the air force of the Soviet Army in the Great Patriotic War 1941–1945]. Moscow: 'Nauka', 1977.

Krivel', A. M. *Eto bylo na Khingane* [It was in the Khingans]. Moscow: Politizdat, 1985.

Krivosheev, G. F., ed. *Rossiia i SSSR v voinakh XX veka: Statisticheskoe issledovanie* [Russia and the USSR in Twentieth Century Wars: A statistical survey]. Moscow: 'Olma-press', 2001.

Krupchenko, I. E., ed. *Sovetskie tankovie voiska 1941–45* [Soviet tank forces, 1941–45]. Moscow: Voenizdat, 1973.

Krylov, N. I., N. I. Alekseev, and I. G. Dragan. *Navstrechu pobede: Boevoi put 5-i armii, oktiabr 1941g–avgust 1945g* [Toward victory: The combat path of the 5th Army, October 1941–August 1945]. Moscow: 'Nauka', 1970.

Kumanev, G. A. *Na sluzhbe fronta i tyla: Zheleznodorozhnyi transport SSSP nakanune i v gody Velikoi Otechestvennoi voiny 1938–1945* [In the service of front and rear: The rail transport of the USSR on the eve of and during the Great Patriotic War]. Moscow: 'Nauka', 1976.

Kurochkin, P. A., ed. *Obshchevoiskovaia armiia v nastuplenii* [The combined-arms army in the offensive]. Moscow: Voenizdat, 1966.

Kusachi Teigo. *Sonohi, Kantogun wa* [That day, the Kwantung Army]. Tokyo: Miyakawa shobo, 1967.

Lisov, I. I. *Desantniki: Vozdushnye desanty* [Airlanded troops: Airlandings] Moscow: Voenizdat, 1968.

Liudnikov, I. I. *Cherez Bol'shoi Khingan* [Across the Grand Khingans]. Moscow: Voenizdat, 1967.

—— *Doroga dlinoiu v zhizn* [The long road in life]. Moscow: Voenizdat, 1969.

Losik, O. A. *Stroitel'stvo i boevoe primenenie sovetskikh tankovykh voisk v gody Velikoi Otechestvennoi voiny* [The formation and combat use of Soviet tank forces in the Great Patriotic War]. Moscow: Voenizdat, 1979.

Manosov, V. F., ed. *Razgrom Kvantungskoi armii iaponi* [The destruction of the Japanese Kwantung Army]. Moscow: Voenizdat, 1958.

Mee, Charles L. *Meeting at Potsdam*. New York: M. Evans, 1975.

Meretskov, K. A. *Serving the People*. Moscow: Progress Publishers, 1971.

Milovsky, M. P., ed. *Tyl Sovetskoi armii* [The rear services of the Soviet Army]. Moscow: Voenizdat, 1968.

Nedosekin, R. *Bol'shoi Khingan* [The Grand Khingans]. Moscow: Izdatel'stvo DOSAAF, 1973.

'New Soviet Wartime Divisional TO&E', *Intelligence Research Project No. 9520*. Washington, DC: Office, Assistant Chief of Staff, Intelligence, US Department of the Army, 15 February 1956. Secret but regraded to unclassified in 1981.

Nikulin, Lev. *Tukhachevsky: Biograficheskii ocherk* [Tukhachevsky: A biographical essay]. Moscow: Voenizdat, 1964.

Organization of a Combat Command for Operations in Manchuria. Fort Knox, KY: The Armor School US Army, May 1952. Regraded as unclassified on 12 April 1974.

Osvobozhdenie Korei [The liberation of Korea]. Moscow: 'Nauka', 1976.

Ota Hisao. *Dai 107 shidan shi: Saigo made tatakatta Kantogun* [A history of the 107th Division: The Kwantung Army that resisted to the last]. Tokyo: Taiseido Shoten Shuppanbu, 1979.

Ovechkin, K. *Cherez Khingan* [Across the Khingans]. Moscow: DOSAAF, 1982.

Pitersky, N. A. *Boevoi put' Sovetskogo Voenno-morskogo Flota* [The combat path of the Soviet fleet]. Moscow: Voenizdat, 1967.

Platonov, S. P., ed. *Vtoraia mirovaia voina 1939–1945 gg.* [The Second World War 1939–1945]. Moscow: Voenizdat, 1958.

Pliev, I. A. *Cherez Gobi i Khingan* [Across the Gobi and Khingans]. Moscow: Voenizdat, 1965.

——— *Konets Kvantunskoi armii* [The end of the Kwantung Army]. Ordzhonikidze: Izdatel'stvo 'IN' Ordzhonikidze, 1969.

Pospelov, P. N., ed. *Istoriia Velikoi Otechestvennoi voiny Sovetskogo Soiuza 1941–45 v shesti tomakh, T 5* [A history of the Great Patriotic War of the Soviet Union 1941–45 in six volumes, Vol. 5]. Moscow: Voenizdat, 1963.

Radzievsky, A. I. *Tankovyi udar* [Tank blow]. Moscow: Voenizdat, 1977.

——— ed. *Armeiskie operatsii: primery iz opyta Velikoi Otechestvennoi voiny* [Army operations: examples from the experience of the Great Patriotic War]. Moscow: Voenizdat, 1977.

——— ed. *Proryv (Po opytu Velikoi Otechestvennoi voiny 1941–1945 gg.)* [Penetration (Based on the experiences of the Great Patriotic War 1941–1945)]. Moscow: Voenizdat, 1979.

——— ed. *Taktika v boevykh primerakh (diviziia)* [Tactics by combat example (the division)]. Moscow: Voenizdat, 1976.

——— ed. *Taktika v boevykh primerakh (polk)* [Tactics by combat example (the regiment)]. Moscow: Voenizdat, 1974.

Ranseikai, ed. *Manshukokugunshi* [History of the Manchukuoan Army] Tokyo: Manshukokugun kankokai, 1970.

'Record of Operations Against Soviet Army on Eastern Front (August 1945)', *Japanese Monograph No. 154.* Tokyo: Military History Section, US Army Forces Far East, 1954.

'Record of Operations Against Soviet Russia on Northern and Western Fronts of Manchuria and in Northern Korea (August 1945)', *Japanese Monograph No. 155.* Tokyo: Military History Section, US Army Forces Far East, 1954.

Rudenko, S. N., ed. *Sovetskie voenno-vozduzhnye sily v Velikoi Otechestvennoi voine 1941–1945 gg.* [The Soviet air force in the Great Patriotic War 1941–1945]. Moscow: Voenizdat, 1968.

Salmanov, G. I., ed. *Ordena Lenina Zabaikal'skii* [The order of Lenin Trans-Baikal]. Moscow: Voenizdat, 1980.

Samsonov, A. M., ed. *Sovetskii soiuz v gody Velikoi Otechestvennoi voiny 1941–1945* [The Soviet Union in the Great Patriotic War 1941–1945]. Moscow: 'Nauka', 1976.

Seaton, Albert. *Stalin as Military Commander.* New York: Praeger, 1976.

Sergeev, I. D., ed. *Voennaia entsiklopediia v vos'mi tomakh,* T. 4 [Military encyclopedia in eight volumes, Vol. 4]. Moscow: Voenizdat, 1999.

Shashlo, T. *Dorozhe zhizni* [The paths of life]. Moscow: Voenizdat, 1960.

Shchen'kov, Iu. M. 'Man'chzhuro–Chzhalainorskaiia operatsiia 1929' [Manchurian–Chalainor Operation of 1929]. *Sovetskaia voennaia entsiklopediia* [Soviet military encyclopedia]. Moscow: Voenizdatel'stvo, 1978. 5:127–8.

Shikin, I. V., and B. G. Sapozhnikov. *Podvig na Dal'nem-vostochnykh rubezhakh* [Victory on the far eastern borders]. Moscow: Voenizdat, 1975.

Shtemenko, S. M. *The Soviet General Staff at War, 1941–1945.* Moscow: Progress Publishers, 1974.

'Small Wars and Border Problems', *Japanese Studies on Manchuria*, Vol. 11, Pt. 2. Tokyo, Military History Section, US Army Forces Far East, 1956.

Sovetskaia voennaia entsiklopediia [The Soviet military encyclopedia]. 9 Vols. Moscow: Voenizdat, 1976–80.

Stephan, John. *The Kuril Islands.* New York: Oxford University Press, 1976.

'Strategic Study of Manchuria Military Topography and Geography: Regional Terrain Analysis', *Japanese Studies on Manchuria*, Vol. 3, Pts. 1–4. Tokyo: Military History Section, US Army Forces Far East, 1956.

Strokov, A. A., ed. *Istoriia voennogo iskusstva* [A history of military art]. Moscow: Voenizdat, 1966.

'Study of Strategical and Tactical Peculiarities of Far Eastern Russia and Soviet Far East Forces', *Japanese Studies on Manchuria*, Vol. 13. Tokyo: Military History Section, US Army Forces Far East, 1955.

Sukhorukov, D. S., ed. *Sovetskie vozdushno-desantnye* [Soviet air landing forces]. Moscow: Voenizdat, 1980.

Tsirlin, A. D., P. I. Buriukov, V. P. Istomin and E. N. Fedoseev. *Inzhenernye voiska v boiakh za Sovetskuiu rodiny* [Engineer forces in combat for the Soviet fatherland]. Moscow: Voenizdat, 1970.

Ustinov D. F., ed. *Istoriia vtoroi mirovoi voiny 1939–1945 v dvenadtsati tomakh*, T. 11 [A history of the Second World War 1939–45 in 12 vols, Vol. 11]. Moscow: Voenizdat, 1980.

Vasilevsky, A. M. *Delo vsei zhizni* [Life's work]. Moscow: Politizdat, 1975.

Vnotchenko, L. N. *Pobeda na dal'nem vostoke: Voenno-istoricheskii ocherk o boevykh deistviiakh Sovetskikh voisk v avguste–sentiabre 1945 g.* [Victory in the Far East: A military-historical survey about the operations of Soviet forces in August–September 1945]. Moscow: Voenizdat, 1966 and 1971.

Vorob'ev, F. D., and V. M. Kravtsov. *Pobedy Sovetskikh vooruzhennykh sil v Velikoi Otechestvennoi voine 1941–1945: Kratkii ocherk* [The victory of the Soviet armed forces in the Great Patriotic War 1941–45: A short survey]. Moscow: Voenizdat, 1953.

Werth, Alexander. *Russia at War 1941–1945*. New York: Dutton, 1964.

Zabaikal'skii voennyi okrug [The Trans-Baikal Military District]. Irkutsk: Vostochno-Sibirskoe Knizhnoe Izdatel'stvo, 1972.

Zakharov, M. V., ed. *Final: istoriko-memuarny ocherk o razgrome imperialis-ticheskoi iapony v 1945 godu* [Finale: A historical memoir-survey about the rout of imperialistic Japan in 1945]. Moscow: 'Nauka', 1969.

—— et al., ed., *50 let Vooruzhennykh sil SSSP* [50 years of the Soviet armed forces] Moscow: Voenizdat, 1968.

—— et al., ed. *Final: istoriko-memuarny ocherk o razgrome imperialisticheskoy iapony v 1945 godu* [Finale: A historical memoir-survey about the rout of imperialistic Japan in 1945]. Moscow: Progress Publishers, 1972.

Zakharov, S. E., V. N. Bagrov, S. S. Bevz, M. N. Zakharov, and M. P. Kotukhov, *Krasnoznamennyi tikhookeanskii flot* [The Red Banner Pacific Fleet]. Moscow: Voenizdat, 1973.

Zavizion, G. T., and P. A. Kornyushin. *I na Tikhom Okeane* [And to the Pacific Ocean]. Moscow: Voenizdat, 1967.

Zenkoku Kotokai [National Hutou Society], ed. *So Man kokkyo: Koto yosai no senki* [The Soviet Manchurian border: The battle record of the Hutou Fortress]. Tokyo: Zenkoku Kotokai jimukyo-ku, 1977.

Zolotarev, V. A. *Velikaia Otechestvennaia voina 1941–1945: Voenno-istoricheskie ocherki v chetyrekh knigakh*, K. 3, *Osvobozhdvenie* [The Great Patriotic War 1941–1945: A military-historical survey in four books, Book 3, Liberation]. Moscow: 'Nauka', 1999.

ARTICLES

Anan'ev, I. 'Sozdanie tankovykh armii i sovershenstvovanie ikh organizatsionnoi struktury' [The creation of tank armies and the perfecting of their organizational structure]. *VIZh*, No. 10 (October 1972), 38–47.

Bagramian, I. and I. Vyrodov. 'Rol' predstavitelei Stavki VGK v gody voiny: Organizatsiia i metody ikh raboty' [The role of the *Stavka* of the Supreme High Command representatives in the war years: The organization and method of their work]. *VIZh*, No. 8 (August 1980), 25–33.

Beloborodov, A. 'Besslavnyi konets Kvantunskoi armii' [The inglorious end of the Kwantung Army'. *Voennii vestnik* [Military herald], No. 9 (September 1970), 97–101.

—— 'Na sopkakh Man'chzhurii' [In the hills of Manchuria]. Pts. 1, 2. *VIZh*, No. 12 (December 1980), 30–6, and No. 1 (January 1981), 45–51.

Bichik, V. S. 'Nekotorye osobennosti tylovogo obespecheniia voisk 1-go Dal'nevostochnogo fronta v Man'chzhurskoi operatsii' [Some peculiarities of the 1st Far Eastern Front's rear service support in the Manchurian operation], *VIZh*, No. 8 (August 1985), 38–41.

Butkov, P. P., and V. V. Shmidt. 'Osobennosti tylovogo obespecheniia v gorno-pustynnoi mestnosti' [The peculiarities of rear service support in swampy desert terrain]. *VIZh*, No. 9 (September 1988), 38–45.

Dragon, I. G. 'Cherez sopki, taigu i bolota Man'chzhurii' [Across the hills, taiga, and swamps of Manchuria]. *VIZh*, No. 8 (August 1988), 62–86.

Dunnin, A. 'Razvitie sukhoputnykh voisk v poslevoennym periode' [The development of ground forces in the postwar period]. *VIZh*, No. 5 (May 1978), 33–40.

Ezhakov, V. 'Boevoe primenenie tankov v gorno-taezhnoi mestnosti po opytu 1-go Dal'nevostochnogo fronta' [The combat use of tanks in mountainous-taiga regions based on the experience of the 1st Far Eastern Front]. *VIZh*, No. 1 (January 1974), 77–81.

Frantsev, O. K. 'Primenenie aviatsii v Man'chzhurskoi operatsii' [The employment of aviation in the Manchurian operation]. *VIZh*, No. 8 (August 1985), 20–4.

Galitsky, V. P., and V. P. Zimonin. 'Desant na Khokkaido Otmenit'! (Razmyshleniia po povodu odnoi nesostoiasheisia operatsii)' [Cancel the amphibious assault against Hokkaido! (Reflections concerning one operation that did not take place)]. *VIZh*, No. 3 (March 1994), 5–10.

Galitson, A. 'Podvig na dal'nevostochnykh rubezhakh' [Victory on the far eastern borders]. *VIZh*, No. 1 (January 1976), 110–13.

Garkusha, I. 'Osobennosti boevykh deistvii bronetankovykh i mekhanizirovannykh voisk' [The characteristics of combat operations of armored and mechanized forces]. *VIZh*, No. 9 (September 1975), 22–9.

Garthoff, Raymond L. 'Soviet Operations in the War with Japan, August 1945'. *US Naval Institute Proceedings*, No. 92 (May 1966), 50–63.

—— 'The Soviet Manchurian Campaign, August 1945'. *Military Affairs*, No. 33 (October 1969), 31–6.

Germanov, G. P. 'Rabota zheleznodorozhnogo transporta pri podgotovke i provedenii Man'chzhurskoi operatsii [The work of railroad transport during the preparation and conduct of the Manchurian operation]. *VIZh*, No. 8 (August 1985), 42–6.

Ivanov, 5. P. 'Victory in the Far East'. *Voennyi vestnik* [Military herald], No. 8 (August 1975), 17–22, trans. Office, Assistant Chief of Staff, Intelligence, US Department of the Army.

—— 'Sokrushitel'ny udar [A shattering blow]. *Voennyi vestnik*, No. 8 (August 1980), 15–17.

Ivanov, S. P., and N. Shekhavtsov. 'Opyt raboty glavnykh komandovanii na teatrakh voennykh deistvii' [The experience of the work of high commands in theaters of military action]. *VIZh*, No. 9 (September 1981), 18.

Kalashnikov, K. 'Na dal'nevostochnykh rubezhakh' [On the far eastern borders]. *VIZh*, No. 8 (August 1980), 55–61.

'Kampaniia sovetskikh vooruzhennikh sil na dal'nem vostoke v 1945g (facti i tsifry)' [The campaign of the Soviet armed forces in the Far East in 1945: Facts and figures]. *VIZh*, No. 8 (August 1965), 64–74.

Khrenov, A. F. 'Wartime Operations: Engineer Operations in the Far East'. *USSR Report: Military Affairs No. 1545* (20 November 1980), 81–97. In JPRS 76847. Trans. Foreign Broadcast Information Service from the Russian article in *Znamia* [Banner], August 1980.

—— 'Inzhernernoe obespechenie nastupleniia v Man'chzhurskoi operatsii' [Engineer support of the offensive in the Manchurian operation]. *VIZh*, No. 8 (August 1985), 29–32.

Kireev, N , and A. Syropiatov. 'Tekhnicheskoe obespechenie 6-i gvardeiskoi tankovoi armii v Khingano-Mukdenskoi operatsii' [Technical support of the 6th Guards Tank Army in the Khingan–Mukden operation]. *VIZh*, No. 3 (March 1977), 36–40.

Kireev, N , and P. Tsigankov. 'Osobennosti podgorovka v gorno-pustynnoi mestnosti po opytu Zabaikal'skogo fronta v 1945 godu' [The peculiarities of preparing and conducting operations in mountainous-desert terrain based on the experiences of the Trans-Baikal Front in 1945]. *VIZh*, No. 8 (August 1978), 13–20.

Kovtun-Stankevich, A. 'Zapiski voennogo komendanta Mukdena' [The notes of the military commandant of Mukden], *VIZh*, No. 1 (January 1960), 51–71.

Krupchenko, I. E. 'Nekotorye osobennosti Sovetskogo voennogo iskusstva' [Some characteristics of Soviet military art]. *VIZh*, No. 8 (August 1975), 17–27.

—— 'Pobeda na dal'nem vostoke' [Victory in the Far East]. *VIZh*, No. 9 (August 1970), 8–10.

—— '6-ia gvardeiskaia tankovaia armiia v Khingano-Mukdenskoi operatsii' [The 6th Guards Tank Army in the Khingan–Mukden Operation]. *VIZh*, No. 12 (December 1962), 15–30.

Kumin, L. G. 'Partiino-politicheskaia rabota v Man'chzhurskoi operatsii' [Party-political work in the Manchurian operation]. *VIZh*, No. 8 (August 1985), 47–51.

Kurochkin, P. A. 'V shtabe glavkoma na dal'nem vostoke' [In the staff of the high command in the Far East]. *VIZh*, No. 11 (November 1967), 74–82.

Kurov, M. 'Togda, v avguste 1945-go' [Then, in August 1945]. *Vestnik protivovozdushnoi oborony* [Herald of air defense], No. 8 (August 1990), 89–91.

Larchenkov, V. 'Banzai to the Soviet Union'. *Soviet Soldier*, No. 7 (July 1991), 66–8.

Liudnikov, I. '39-ia armiia v Khingano-Mukdenskoi operatsii' [The 39th Army in the Khingan–Mukden Operation]. *VIZh*, No. 10 (October 1965), 68–78.

Loskutov, Iu. 'Iz opyta peregruppirovki 292-i strelkovoi divizii v period podgotovki Man'chzhurskoi operatsii' [From the experience of 292d Rifle Division's regrouping during the preparatory period for the Manchurian operation]. *VIZh*, No. 2 (February 1980), 22–8.

Luchinsky, A. A. 'Zabaikal'tsy na sopkakh Man'chzhurii' [Trans-Baikal troops in the hills of Manchuria]. *VIZh*, No. 8 (August 1971), 67–74.

Malin'in, K. 'Razvitie organizatsionnykh form sukhoputnykh voisk v Velikoi Otechestvennoi voine' [The development of ground forces' organizational structure in the Great Patriotic War]. *VIZh*, No. 8 (August 1967), 35–8.

Maliugin, N. 'Nekotorye voprosy ispol'zovaniia avtomobil'nogo transporta v voennoi kampanii na dal'nem vostoke' [Some questions on the use of automobile transport in the military campaign in the Far East]. *VIZh*, No. 1 (January 1969), 103–11.

Maslov, V. 'Boevye deistvia tikhookeanskogo flota' [The combat operations of the Pacific Fleet]. *VIZh*, No. 9 (August 1975), 28–37.

Medvedev, N. E. 'Tylovoe obespechenie 5-i armii v Kharbino-Girinskoi operatsii [The rear service support of the 5th Army during the Harbin–Kirin operation]. *VIZh*, No. 8 (August 1987), 32–9.

Meretskov, K. A. 'Dorogami srazhenii' [Along combat roads]. *Voprosy istorii* [Questions of history], No. 2 (February 1965), 101–9.

Mikhalkin, V. M. 'Boevoe primenenie artillerii v Man'chzhurskoi operatsii' [The combat employment of artillery in the Manchurian operation]. *VIZh*, No. 8 (August 1985), 25–8.

Novikov, A. 'Voenno-vozdushnye sily v Man'chzhurskoi operatsii' [The air force in the Manchurian operation]. *VIZh*, No. 9 (August 1975),

66–71.

Pavlov, B. 'In the Hills of Manchuria'. *Voennyi vestnik* [Military herald], No. 8 (August 1975), 30–2. Trans. Office of the Assistant Chief of Staff, Intelligence, US Department of the Army.

Pechenenko, S. 'Armeiskaia nastupatel'naia operatsiia v usloviiakh dal'nevostochnogo teatra voennykh deistvii' [An army offensive operation in the conditions of the Far Eastern theater of military operations]. *VIZh*, No. 8 (August 1978), 42–9.

—— '363-ia strelkovaia diviziia v boiakh na Mishan'skom napravlenii' [The 363d Rifle Division in combat along the Mishan axis]. *VIZh*, No. 7 (July 1975), 39–46.

Platonov V., and A. Bulatov. 'Pogranichnie voiska perekhodiat v nastuplenie' [Border troops go over to the offensive]. *VIZh*, No. 10 (October 1965), 11–16.

Pliev, I. A. 'Across the Gobi Desert'. *Voennyi vestnik* [Military herald], No. 8 (August 1975), 14–17. Trans. Office of the Assistant Chief of Staff, Intelligence, US Department of the Army.

Popov, N. 'Razvitie samokhodnoi artillerii' [The development of self-propelled artillery]. *VIZh*, No. 1 (January 1977), 27–31.

Popov, S. 'Artilleristy v boiakh na Bol'shom Khingane' [Artillerymen in combat in the Grand Khingans]. *VIZh*, No. 8 (August 1985), 88–93.

'Razgrom Kvantunskoi armii: 30-letie pobedy nad militaristskoi iaponiei' [The rout of the Kwantung Army: The 30th anniversary of the victory over militarist Japan]. *VIZh*, No. 8 (August 1975), 3–16.

Savin, A. S. 'Spravedlivyi i gumannyi akt SSSR' [The just and humanitarian act of the USSR]. *VIZh*, No. 8 (August 1985), 56–62.

Sekistiv, V. A. 'Kritika burzhuaznykh fal'sifikatsii roli SSSR v razgrome militaristskoi Iaponii' [Criticism of bourgeois falsifiers of the USSR's role in the defeat of militaristic Japan]. *VIZh*, No. 8 (August 1985), 63–6.

Shelakhov, G. 'S vozdushnym desantam v Kharbin' [With the air landing at Harbin] *VIZh*, No. 8 (August 1970), 67–71.

—— 'Voiny-dal'nevostochniki v Velikoi Otechestvennoi voine' [Far easterners in the Great Patriotic War]. *VIZh*, No. 3 (March 1969), 55–62.

Shtemenko, S. M. 'Iz istorii razgroma Kvantunskoi armii' [From the history of the rout of the Kwantung Army]. Pts. 1, 2. *VIZh*, No. 4 (April 1967), 54–66, and No. 5 (May 1967), 49–61.

Sidorov, A. 'Razgrom iaponskogo militarizma' [The rout of Japanese militarism]. *VIZh*, No. 8 (August 1980), 11–16.

Sidorov, M. 'Boevoe primenenie artillerii' [The combat use of artillery]. *VIZh*, No. 9 (September 1975), 13–21.

Sidorov, V. 'Inzhenernoe obespechenie nastupleniia 36-i armii v Man'chzhurskoi operatsii' [Engineer support of the 36th Army's offensive in the Manchurian operation]. *VIZh*, No. 4 (April 1978), 97–101.

Sokolov, V. I. 'Sviaz' v Man'chzhurskoi operatsii' [Communications in the Manchurian operation]. *VIZh*, No. 8 (August 1985), 33–6.

Sologub, V. 'Partpolitrabota v 12 ShAD VVSTOF v voine s imperialisticheskoi iaponiei' [Political work in the 12th Assault Aviation Division of the Pacific Fleet Air Force in the war with imperialist Japan]. *VIZh*, No. 8 (August 1982), 80–3.

Sukhomlin, I. 'Osobennosti vzaimodeistviia 6-i gvardeiskoi tankovoi armii s aviatsiei v Man'chzhurskoi operatsii' [Characteristics of the cooperation of the 6th Guards Tank Army with aviation in the Manchurian operation]. *VIZh*, No. 4 (April 1972), 85–91.

Timofeev, V. '300-ia strelkovaia diviziia v boyakh na Mudan'tsianskom napravlenii' [The 300th Rifle Division in combat along the Mutanchiang axis]. *VIZh*, No. 8 (August 1978), 50–5.

Tret'iak, I. 'Ob operativnoi obespechenii peregruppirovki voisk v period podgotovki Man'chzhurskoi operatsii' [Concerning the operational security of regrouping forces during the preparatory period of the Manchurian operation]. *VIZh*, No. 11 (November 1979), 10–15.

—— 'Organizatsiia i vedenie nastupatel'nogo boia' [The organization and conduct of offensive battle]. *VIZh*, No. 7 (July 1980), 42–9.

—— 'Razgrom Kvantunskoi armii na Dal'nem vostoke' [The destruction of the Kwantung Army in the Far East]. *VIZh*, No. 8 (August 1985), 9–19.

Tsirlin, A. D. 'Organizatsiia vodosnabzheniia voisk Zabaikal'shogo fronta v Khingano-Mukdenskoi operatsii' [The organization of water supply of the Trans-Baikal Front's forces during the Khingan–Mukden operation]. *VIZh*, No. 5 (May 1963), 36–48.

Tsygankov, P. 'Nekotorye osobennosti boevykh deistvii 5-i armii v Kharbino-Girinskoi operatsii' [Some characteristics of the 5th Army's combat operations during the Harbin–Kirin operation]. *VIZh*, No. 8 (August 1975), 83–9.

Vasilevsky, A. 'Kampaniia na dal'nem vostoke' [The campaign in the Far East]. *VIZh*, No. 10 (October 1980), 60–73.

—— 'Pobeda na Dal'nem vostoke' [Victory in the Far East]. Pts. 1, 2. *VIZh*, No. 8 (August 1970), 3–10, and No. 9 (September 1970), 11–18.

—— 'The Second World War: The Rout of Kwantung Army'. *Soviet Military Review*, No. 8 (August 1980), 2–14.

Vigor, Peter W., and Christopher Donnelly. 'The Manchurian Campaign and Its Relevance to Modern Strategy'. *Comparative Strategy*, No. 2 (February 1980), 159–78.

Yamanishi Sakae. 'ToManshu Koto yosai no gekito' [Eastern Manchuria: The fierce battle of the Hutou Fortress]. *Rekishi to Jinbutsu* (August 1979), 98–107.

Zakharov, M. V. 'Kampaniia Sovetskikh Vooruzhennykh Sil na Dal'nem Vostoke (9 avgusta–2 sentiabria 1945 goda)' [The Soviet Armed Forces' campaign in the Far East, 9 August–2 September 1945]. *VIZh*, No. 9 (September 1960), 3–16.

—— 'Nekotorye voprosy voennogo iskusstva v Sovetsko-iaponskoi voine 1945-goda' [Some questions concerning military art in the Soviet–Japanese War of 1945]. *VIZh*, No. 9 (September 1969), 14–25.

Index

353